THE TREATY OF AMSTERDAM IN PERSPECTIVE

CONSOLIDATED TREATY ON EUROPEAN UNION

The full text of all the changes and additions incorporated into
the **Treaty of Rome**, the **Single European Act** and the **Maastricht Treaty**
by the **Treaty of Amsterdam** together with an analysis of the extra powers of the
European Community Institutions

BRITISH MANAGEMENT DATA FOUNDATION

The Treaty of Amsterdam in Perspective - Consolidated Treaty on European Union

First Published in January 1998 by:

British Management Data Foundation

Highfield

Longridge

Sheepscombe

STROUD

Gloucestershire.   GL6 7QU

Tel: (01452) 812837   Fax: (01452) 812527

ISBN No: 0 9520 366 2 2

CONTENTS

The **British Management Data Foundation** was formed in 1979. It is an independent body supported by a wide range of major British companies and is concerned with matters affecting the global competitiveness of its member companies to whom it gives independent advice and data.

The aim of all BMDF activities is to achieve a better understanding of current core issues so as to enable companies and organisations concerned to make more informed decisions.

Director: Anthony Cowgill MBE BSc CEng FIMechE FIEE Hon FMS

Deputy Director: Andrew Cowgill BSc ACA ATII

* * * * * * *

PREFACE

The Treaty of Amsterdam was signed on 2 October 1997. All the Member States have to ratify the Treaty by their respective legislative procedures for it to become law.

The intentions for the Treaty were ambitious and included the granting of legal personality to the Union, internal and external security, including the introduction of the Schengen agreement into the main Treaty and regulations on visas and immigration, and the development of the role of the European Community institutions in preparation for enlargement.

In the event, the aims were only partially achieved and this leaves the further development of the European Community to be continued at the next Inter-Governmental Conference, which is expected to be in the year 2000.

As such, Amsterdam is not a Treaty in its own right, but is the successor to the Maastricht Treaty in the development of the Treaties establishing the European Union. It follows the format of the previous Treaties (the Single European Act and the Maastricht Treaty) in being a series of amendments and additions to the Treaty of Rome.

The general approach taken in this book is that the new provisions introduced by each successive Treaty should be placed in the context of the preceding Treaties and the differences highlighted in order that the implications can be fully understood and how the fundamental law of the Community has been altered and developed.

The format follows 'The Maastricht Treaty in Perspective – Consolidated Treaty on European Union', first published by the British Management Data Foundation in October 1992. There is a summary of the key issues covered by the Treaty, a discussion on the additional 'competences' of the European institutions and a three-column analysis of the development of competences from the Treaty of Rome to the Treaty of Amsterdam.

The three-columnar approach allows the reader to assess how the Treaties have progressed and developed and shows the details of the changes introduced by Amsterdam to the overall European Treaty. This includes the identification of the Articles and sentences that have been repealed by Amsterdam.

The Treaty of Rome and the Single European Act have been combined into one column for clarity and in order to highlight the amendments and additions introduced by the Treaty of Amsterdam and the Maastricht Treaty. If readers wish to see the changes made to the original Treaty of Rome by the Single European Act, they should refer to 'The Maastricht Treaty in Perspective'.

The changes to the Treaty on European Union introduced by the Treaty of Amsterdam have been integrated into the text of the existing Treaty and **are shown in bold text**. A fuller explanation of the text is shown on page VII.

This book includes the full text of the Treaty on European Union (except the Titles III and IV – see next paragraph), as amended by Amsterdam, as well as all of the associated Protocols, including those introduced by previous Treaties. The remaining Articles of the Treaty of Amsterdam, which do not directly refer to adjustments to the Treaties, and all of the Declarations agreed at Amsterdam are also shown, starting on page 161.

Title III, the European Coal and Steel Community, and Title IV, the European Atomic Energy Community, have not been included, as the amendments introduced by Amsterdam are principally concerned with administrative matters intended to bring these two Treaties in line with the Treaty on European Union and the Treaty establishing the European Community.

The Appendices include additional documents agreed at Amsterdam, in particular a Resolution by the European Council on the new Exchange-Rate Mechanism to be introduced when the Single Currency starts on 1 January 1999.

Sources and References:

The text of the Treaty of Amsterdam and the Treaty on European Union is drawn from the official texts of the Treaties:

*   The Treaty of Amsterdam; Official Journal 97/C 340/01, the Luxembourg official publication, ISSN 0378-6986, dated 10 November 1997 [ISBN 011-916-2938].

*   European Union: Consolidated Treaties; the Luxembourg official publication, FX-08-97-606-EN-C, dated 2 October 1997 [ISBN 92-828-1640-0].

*   Treaties establishing the European Communities, Cm 3151 HMSO January 1996 [ISBN 0-10-1315120].

*   Treaty of Amsterdam, Cm 3780 HMSO October 1997 [ISBN 0-10-1378025].

* * * * * * *

NOTES ON THE TEXT

Structure of the Treaty

The complete Treaty on European Union is essentially formed by four distinct **Treaties**.

1.   Treaty on European Union:
    *   Title I - Common Provisions;
    *   Title V - Common Foreign and Security Policy;
    *   Title VI - Police and Judicial Co-operation in Criminal Matters;
    *   Title VII - Closer Co-operation;
    *   Title VIII - Final Provisions.

2.   Title II - Treaty establishing the European Community.

3.   Title III - Treaty establishing the European Coal and Steel Community.

4.   Title IV - Treaty establishing the European Atomic Energy Community.

The 'Treaty on European Union' was introduced by the Maastricht Treaty by adding the Titles on 'Common Provisions', 'Final Provisions', 'Common Foreign and Security Policy' and 'Police and Judicial Co-operation in Criminal Matters'. These latter two Titles, with Title II, the Treaty establishing the European Community, form the 'Three Pillars' of the European Union.

The Treaty of Amsterdam has added Title VII on 'Closer Co-operation' and renumbered the Articles in Title II and in the Titles making up the Treaty on European Union. As a consequence of the renumbering, and to make sense of the number sequence in the Treaty on European Union, the whole Treaty has now been split into two parts with the Treaty establishing the European Community being separate to the Treaty on European Union.

New Article Numbering System

The Treaty of Amsterdam introduced **a new numbering system** for the Articles of the Treaty on European Union (Titles I, V, VI, VII and VIII) and the Treaty establishing the European Community (Title II). There are now **two** numbering systems, one for the Treaty on European Union and a separate numbering system for the Treaty establishing the European Community.

This can lead to some confusion in trying to identify a particular Article brought forward from the previous Treaties. The new numbering system, in particular, has changed the method of identifying the Articles of the **Treaty on European Union** from letters to **numbers.**

To help in locating a particular Article in this book, the old Article letter or number is shown after the new Article number.

The new numbering system has been used throughout the analyses, the Treaty and the associated documents. **The new Article numbers are highlighted in Bold.**

Other aspects of the new numbering system

The renumbering of the Articles by the Treaty of Amsterdam is technically only valid after the Treaty has been ratified by all of the Member States' governments. However, in this book **the new numbering has been used throughout the Treaty and the associated documents, including the Protocols and the Declarations**, in order to simplify cross-referencing.

Where the references could lead to confusion as regards which Title the Article refers to, the relevant Title has been added [in brackets] to help identification. These references do not form part of the formal treaties and have been added to aid readers of this book.

The renumbering is part of the process to simplify and update the Treaties by removing those Articles and paragraphs which by their nature have lapsed and are no longer relevant (eg Articles relating to the transitional stages of the Internal Market and time limits for implementation of Community measures).

Order of the Titles in the Treaty and in this Book

The Treaties have been laid out in the order of the Treaty on European Union first, followed by the Treaty establishing the European Community. This is to place together the Titles which make up the 'Treaty on European Union', since the new numbering system would cause confusion if the Treaty establishing the European Community was placed in between Titles I and V.

The Treaties establishing the Coal and Steel Community and the Atomic Energy Community **(Titles III and IV) have not been included** as the amendments made by Amsterdam essentially bring these two Treaties in line with the Treaty establishing the European Community in terms of the powers of the Community institutions. In addition, the Coal and Steel Treaty expires on 23 July 2002.

The use of Italics and Bold in the Text

Notes have been added to the text to help in understanding of the changes made by the Treaty of Amsterdam. These are in *italics* and do not form part of the Treaty but are added to aid readers of this book.

A particular example of this is the references after the Articles in Titles V and VI. These have been substantially restructured and expanded by the provisions of Amsterdam and the old Article numbers, showing how the new Articles have been drawn from the previous Treaties, are shown in brackets after each relevant Article.

All the new Articles and changes to the existing Articles are shown **in bold**. This includes those Articles, paragraphs and sentences which have been deleted or repealed as part of the simplification process.

Protocols

All of the Protocols attached to the main Treaties are shown, including the Protocols on the European Investment Bank and the Court of Justice. The Protocols added by Amsterdam are shown **in bold**. The Protocols which are specifically attached to the Treaties establishing the Coal and Steel Communities and the Atomic Energy Communities are not shown.

* * * * * * *

THE TREATY OF AMSTERDAM

NOTES ON SOME KEY ISSUES

Introduction

The aim of the Treaty of Amsterdam is to revise the Treaties to prepare the European Union for the changes facing Europe. This includes the enlargement of the Union by admitting new Member States from Eastern Europe, the effects of globalisation on employment, international crime and the environment.

The approach of the Union is now, in general, to place more importance on the role of the Community institutions in forming guidelines and Community-wide law that would provide the bases for action by the Member States. This is termed the **'Community Method'** and fundamentally changes the approach for several policies, including the foreign and security policy and police and judicial co-operation, from one where the Member States instigate actions to one where the Community acts and the Member States follow the lead given by the Community institutions.

The simplification and **renumbering of the Articles** has led to the Treaty effectively being split into two, with the Treaty on European Union forming one and the Treaty establishing the European Community forming the other.

Main Areas

The main areas that have been introduced by the Treaty or have had major changes to them are:

1. **An area of freedom, security and justice**

(a) **Fundamental Rights**. The Union will be based on the fundamental principles of liberty, democracy, respect for human rights and fundamental freedoms and the rule of law (Article 6, Title I).

The breach of these fundamental rights and principles by a Member State will cause that State to lose certain rights, particularly voting rights (Article 7, Title I).

(b) **Free movement of persons, asylum and immigration**. This is a new title and includes a protocol on incorporating the **Schengen *acquis*** into the Treaty. The United Kingdom and Ireland obtained an opt-out from the terms of the Schengen *acquis* and this is intended to last for five years for Ireland and until such time as the United Kingdom elects to enter the agreement. The previous UK government negotiated this opt-out.

(c) **Non-discrimination**. The Council, acting *unanimously*, will adopt measures to act against discrimination based on sex, racial or ethnic origin, religion, disability, age or sexual orientation (Article 13).

2. **The relationship between the Union and the citizen**

(a) **Social Policy**. The United Kingdom has agreed to the 'Social Chapter' of the Maastricht Treaty and so the Agreement on Social Policy, attached to the Maastricht Treaty as a Protocol, has now been incorporated into the main body of the Treaty.

The Council is now able to effect the provisions on Social Policy under the legislative procedure of the EU Treaty itself regarding the whole Community, rather than the involvement of the individual Member States that had signed the Protocol.

(b) **Employment**. The growing concern over the high levels of unemployment in the Community has led to a broad-based policy being introduced. The general competence will remain with the Member States but the Council will co-ordinate their actions by issuing guidelines, acting by **qualified majority**. The European Council will annually review the state of unemployment and give the political impetus for action.

(c) **Environment**. The policies on the protection of the environment should be incorporated into all relevant Community acts and will be considered by the Council, the Commission and the European Parliament when they consider any proposed harmonisation measure.

(d) **Subsidiarity and Proportionality**. The Treaty attaches a **Protocol** (Protocol no 30, page 153) which is intended to define precisely the criteria for the application of these principles, including the strict observance and consistent implementation, by all the Community institutions. This indicates that where an issue is considered to be one that affects a number of Member States or the harmonisation of laws, the Community would be better to act rather than the individual States.

3.   Common Foreign and Security Policy

The Treaty of Amsterdam has substantially restructured and expanded the policy and has incorporated and rewritten the existing provisions. The object is to make the policy more coherent and consistent as a Community-wide approach, with the Community taking on a more active leadership role in formulating and guiding policy. The Member States will ensure that their national policies conform to the Community's approach.

A Declaration (Declaration no 3, page 175) has been attached to the Treaty describing the increased importance the Western European Union and its possible future integration into the European Union. The Declaration acknowledges the continuing importance of NATO to the defence of Europe and describes how the Union will foster closer relations with the WEU.

4.   Police and Judicial Co-operation in Criminal Matters

The Heading of this Title has been changed from 'Justice and Home Affairs', emphasising the change in approach to emphasis the new leadership and guiding role of the Community and to make the policy more far-reaching.

This will include closer co-operation between the judicial, police forces, and customs authorities of the Member States and harmonising action among the Member States in matters concerning crime, race and xenophobia.

5.   Institutions of the Community

The number of areas where **qualified majority** voting by the Council has been greatly expanded and there is further involvement of the European Parliament in the adoption of European legislation with the extension of **co-decision**.

6.   Closer Co-operation or flexibility

Individual Member States will be able to use the institutional framework of the Community to develop closer bi-lateral links with one another in specific areas without involving all of the Member States. The intention is that as more European states join the Union, more flexibility is required to allow some Member States to move at different speeds on certain areas, eg EMU and closer co-operation in Police and Judicial matters (Article 40, Title VI). The Council will authorise this co-operation acting by **qualified majority**.

* * * * * * *

LEGISLATIVE PROCEDURES

One of the most important aspects of the Treaty of Amsterdam is the extension of the role of **qualified majority voting**, the use of '**co-decision**' (Article 251) and '**co-operation**' (Article 252) between the Council and the European Parliament and the role of the European Parliament in giving its **assent** to proposed acts.

The following summaries show the major areas in which the Council will act by qualified majority voting and the involvement of the European Parliament in the legislative process through the co-decision and assent procedures.

The Article references are to the **new numbering system** used in the Treaty.

The areas marked **in bold** are new provisions introduced by the Treaty of Amsterdam.

THE COUNCIL

QUALIFIED MAJORITY VOTING

The voting by the representatives from each Member State is weighted in accordance with the provisions of Article 205.

New Provisions introduced by the Treaty of Amsterdam

Breach of Community's principles

Article 7, Title I
- Suspension of a Member State's rights.

Closer Co-operation
(*for the European Community (Title II) and Police and Judicial Co-operation – Title VI*)

Article 11, Title II; Article 40, Title VI
- Authorisation of use of Community institutions (*a national veto applies, in which case the matter is referred to the European Council, which will act by unanimity*).

Customs Co-operation

Article 135

Data protection

Article 286
- Establishment of independent advisory authority on data protection.

Employment

Article 123
- guidelines.

Employment

Article 129
- incentive measures to encourage co-operation between Member States.

Fraud

Article 280
- Countering fraud.

THE COUNCIL

QUALIFIED MAJORITY VOTING
(continued)

Internal Borders	**Article 62** - Removal of border controls under the Schengen *acquis*.
Outermost regions	**Article 299(2)**
Public health	**Article 152(4)** - Detailed measures.
Social Policy	**Article 137(2)** - Social exclusion. **Article 139(2)** - Agreements between management and labour (some aspects by unanimity). **Article 141(3)** - Equality of opportunity and treatment of men and women.
Statistics	**Article 285** - Preparation of statistics.
Transparency	**Article 255**
Voting Rights of Member States	**Article 309** - Suspension of voting rights for breach of Community principles.
Foreign and Security Policy	**Article 23, Title V** - Implementing decisions (*a national veto applies in matters of national security, in which case the decision is referred to the European Council, which will vote by unanimity*).

Existing Provisions modified by the Treaty of Amsterdam

Right of Establishment	Article 46(2) - Co-ordination of provisions laid down by law, regulation or administrative action for special treatment for foreign nationals.
Research and Technological Development	Article 166(1) - Adoption of the research framework programme. Article 166(2) - Adapting or supplementing the research framework programme. Article 172 - Setting up of joint undertakings in R&TD.

Existing Provisions modified by the Treaty of Amsterdam
(continued)

Common Agriculture Policy	Article 37
	- implementation
Common Commercial Policy	Article 132
Common Customs Tariff	Article 26
Competition	Article 83
	- Common rules on Competition
Economic and Monetary Policy	Article 99
	- Formulation of guidelines for economic policy of Member States.
	Article 104
	- Assessment of excessive Member States' excessive government deficits.
	Article 121
	- Assessment of which Member States should join the third stage of EMU.

THE EUROPEAN PARLIAMENT

ASSENT PROCEDURE

The European Parliament may endorse proposed acts by the Council and this procedure generally covers international matters. The Treaty of Amsterdam has extended this to cover breaches of the fundamental principles of the Community.

New Provisions introduced by the Treaty of Amsterdam

Breach of fundamental rights	**Article 7, Title I**
	- Sanctions in the event of a serious and persistent breach of fundamental rights by a Member State.

Existing Provisions not amended by the Treaty of Amsterdam

Accession procedure for new States	Article 49, Title VIII
Monetary Policy	Articles 105(6) and 107
	- Powers of the ECB
Structural and cohesion funds	Article 161

Existing Provisions not amended by the Treaty of Amsterdam
(continued)

Uniform electoral procedure

Article 190(4)
- Proposals by the European Parliament for a uniform electoral procedure.

International agreements

Article 300(3), second sub-para.
- Conclusion of certain international agreements.

THE EUROPEAN PARLIAMENT

CONSULTATION PROCEDURE

There are areas where the European Parliament is not directly involved in the legislative procedure and the Council will take into account the opinion of the Parliament before voting on a particular proposal from the Commission.

New Provisions introduced by the Treaty of Amsterdam

Closer Co-operation

Article 11
- Authorisation of the use of Community institutions.

Discrimination

Article 13

Visas, Asylum and Immigration

Article 67
- Adoption of measures on the area, and election to change the voting process to co-decision after five years.

Employment

Article 128(2)
- Guidelines for Member States.
Article 130
- Formation of an Employment Committee.

Common Commercial Policy

Article 133(5)
- Extension to international negotiations.

Social Policy

Article 137(3)
- Action in certain areas of social policy, where the Council acts unanimously (eg social security and dismissal).

Overseas Territories

Article 299
- Application of the Treaty to overseas territories.

New Provisions introduced by the Treaty of Amsterdam
(continued)

Police and Judicial Co-operation

Article 42, Title VI
- Council to decide whether this area should fall under the provisions of Visa, Asylum and Immigration, with the associated voting procedure.

THE EUROPEAN PARLIAMENT

CO-OPERATION PROCEDURE

This procedure, under Article 252, is a modified version of the full co-decision procedure. The procedure allows the Parliament to propose amendments to a proposal by the Commission and the Council must take the Parliament's opinion and the amendments into account before voting on the proposed act. The Treaty of Amsterdam has reduced this procedure mainly to aspects of the Economic and Monetary Policy.

The provisions of the Treaty that used to be covered by Article 252 and are now adopted by the co-decision procedure are listed below under the Co-decision Procedure.

Principal Provisions

Guidelines for Economic Policy

Article 99(5)
- Rules for multilateral surveillance.

Overdraft Facilities for Community Institutions

Article 101
- Prohibition

'No Bail-Out' Clause for liability of other Member States' debts

Article 103
- Definition of the applicability of the prohibition.

Harmonisation of coins for the Euro

Article 106

Agreements between the Community and other states or international organisations

Article 300(3)

CO-DECISION PROCEDURE

The Co-decision procedure is the mechanism whereby the Council and the European Parliament are both involved in the adoption of an Act, under Article 251. The intention is that the European Parliament has equal status as the Council. The process is described more fully in the 'Development of Competences' summary on pages XXX111 - XXXIV.

New Provisions introduced by the Treaty of Amsterdam

Customs Co-operation	**Article 135**
Data Protection	**Article 286** - Establishment of independent advisory authority on data protection.
Employment	**Article 129** - Incentive measures.
Fraud	**Article 280** - Countering fraud affecting the financial interests of the Community.
Public health	**Article 152** (former basis Article 37 - consultation) - minimum requirements regarding quality and safety of organs; - veterinary and phytosanitary measures with the direct objective the protection of public health.
Social policy	**Article 141** - Equal opportunities and treatment.
Statistics	**Article 285** - Production of Statistics.
Transparency	**Article 255** - General principles.

Existing Provisions modified by the Treaty of Amsterdam

Citizenship - Freedom of Movement	Article 18(2) (*The Council will act unanimously*) - Provisions for facilitating the exercise of citizens' right to move and reside freely within the territory of the Member States. (*Before Amsterdam: assent*)
Development co-operation	Article 179 (*Before Amsterdam: co-operation*)

CO-DECISION PROCEDURE

Existing Provisions modified by the Treaty of Amsterdam
(continued)

Discrimination	Article 12 - Rules to prohibit discrimination on grounds of nationality. (*Before Amsterdam: co-operation*)
Environment	Article 175(1) - Action by the Community in order to achieve the objectives of Article 174. (*Before Amsterdam: co-operation*)
European Regional Development Fund	Article 162 - Implementing decisions. (*Before Amsterdam: co-operation*)
European Social Fund	Article 148 - Implementing decisions. (*Before Amsterdam: co-operation*)
Freedom of Movement	Article 42 (*The Council will act unanimously*) Internal market - rules on social security for Community immigrant workers. (*Before Amsterdam: consultation*)
Research and Technological Development	Article 172, 2nd sub-para. - Adoption of measures referred in Articles 167,168 and 169 - framework programme. (*Before Amsterdam: co-operation*)
Right of establishment	Article 46(2) - Co-ordination of provisions laid down by law, regulation or administrative action for special treatment for foreign nationals. (*Before Amsterdam: consultation until end of transitional period*)
Right of establishment - self-employed persons	Article 47(2) (*The Council will act unanimously*) - Co-ordination of the provisions laid down by law, regulation or administrative action in Member States concerning the taking up and pursuit of activities as self-employed persons. - Amendment of existing principles laid down by law governing the professions with respect to training and conditions of access for natural persons. (*Before Amsterdam: consultation*)

CO-DECISION PROCEDURE
(continued)

Social Policy

Article 137
(*The Council will act unanimously in some areas*)
- Directives for minimum requirements for gradual implementation of the Community's Social Policy.
  (*Before Amsterdam: co-operation*)

Trans-European Networks

Article 156
- Guidelines and other measures.
  (*Before Amsterdam: co-operation*)

Transport policy

Article 71(1)
- Common rules applicable to international transport to or from the territory of a Member State or passing across the territory of one or more Member States;
- the conditions under which non-resident carriers may operate transport services within a Member State;
- measures to improve transport safety.
  (*Before Amsterdam: co-operation*)

Transport policy

Article 80
- sea and air transport.
  (*Before Amsterdam: co-operation*)

Vocational training

Article 150(4)
- Measures to contribute to the achievement of the objectives of Article 150.
  (*Before Amsterdam: co-operation*)

* * * * * * *

ECONOMIC AND MONETARY UNION

Introduction

Although the subject of the Single Currency was not discussed in the debates on the Treaty of Amsterdam, this summary is included owing to its importance to the development of the European Union. The conditions for the start of EMU were introduced by the Maastricht Treaty and this Treaty was principally concerned with the development of the Single Currency and the criteria necessary for the start of the 'Third Stage' of Monetary Union. This stage marks the introduction of the Euro.

The Maastricht Treaty completely replaced the terms of the Treaty of Rome and the Single European Act in this area and the changes are shown on pages LXXII - LXXIX, together with a detailed summary of the policy incorporated by the Maastricht Treaty.

Since the Maastricht Treaty was signed in 1992, there have been further developments on the conditions that Member States which join the Single Currency must meet. These have been consolidated into the 'Stability Pact', which essentially requires the joining States to maintain their economies under the same conditions necessary to meet the criteria for entry into the Single Currency. The Stability Pact was discussed by the European Council of Amsterdam in June 1997 and it was agreed that the two Regulations which make up the Pact should be formally adopted by the Council without delay.

In addition to discussing the Stability Pact, the European Council adopted a Resolution on the fundamental principles and elements of the **new Exchange-Rate Mechanism** (ERM II), which would operate for those Member States which did not join the Euro on 1 January 1999. The national currencies would be allowed to fluctuate by 15% from the central rate. The Resolution is shown on page 283.

The purpose of the Economic and Monetary Policy is to provide a legal framework for Economic and Monetary Union, leading to the establishment of a single currency, which will be formed at the start of the Third Stage.

The structure of the policy was formed in 1989 following a report of the committee of European central bankers under the chairmanship of the Commission President Jacques Delors; the report is known as 'The Delors Report'.

The policy identifies three stages, of which the First, begun on 1 July 1990, was already under way before the Maastricht Treaty was ratified. This stage concerned the start of the Exchange Rate Mechanism. The Second Stage started on 1 January 1994, and related to the transfer of monetary and economic policy, including exchange rate policy, to the European institutions. The Treaty does not describe the detailed methodology of how the Single Currency and the irrevocable fixing of parities will take place.

The date for the start of the Third Stage was agreed at the Madrid Summit on 15 - 16 December 1995 where the European Council agreed that the date should be 1 January 1999 In addition, it was agreed that the Single Currency would be called the Euro.

Criteria for the Single Currency

The criteria for entry to the Third Stage forms the central part of the provisions of the Treaty and is causing concern among the Member States on whether they will be able to meet these strict terms.

Member States must fulfil the four necessary conditions for the adoption of the Single Currency. These conditions are:

(1):   The **average rate of inflation** is no more than 1½% greater than the three best performing Member States for one year before the agreement for the start of the Third Stage.

(2):   There is **no excessive budget deficit**. The two criteria used to assess budgetary discipline are:

    (a):   the ratio of the planned or actual government **budget deficit** to GDP at market prices does **not exceed 3%**;

    (b):   the ratio of **government debt** to GDP at market prices does **not exceed 60%**.

These two criteria must either be strictly adhered to or the deficit must be shown to be exceptional and temporary, or it is sufficiently diminishing and approaching the reference values (Article 104.2).

(3):   The currency has stayed within the **normal fluctuation margins of the Exchange Rate Mechanism** over a period of two years before the agreement for the start of the Third Stage, without devaluing against the currency of any other Member State.

(4):   The average nominal **long-term interest rate** does not exceed, by more than 2%, the rates of the three best performing Member States, over a one year period before the agreement for the Start of the Third Stage.

These criteria are shown in two Protocols and are shown on pages 146 - 147. The Protocols modify the strict terms of the Treaty by stating that inflation and interest rates will be measured taking into account any differences in national definitions. In addition, the Council, acting *unanimously*, will be able to adopt appropriate criteria which would then replace the terms of the Protocols.

Selection of Member States for the Single Currency

Until the start of the Third Stage (the formation of the Single Currency), all fifteen Member States, including those which do not initially join the Single Currency, will be involved in the Council's decision-making and in the committees concerned with the formation of the Single Currency.

The committees are the Monetary Committee in the Second Stage and the Economic and Financial Committee in the Third Stage (although the Council, acting by a qualified majority may define the composition of the Committee and therefore could exclude those Member States which do not join the Third Stage) and the European Monetary Institute (Articles 114, 117, 121 and 122).

The Council of Ministers, acting by **qualified majority** and on the advice of the Commission, shall decide whether:

(a): each Member State fulfils the criteria for the adoption of a single currency;

(b): a majority of the Member States fulfil the criteria for the adoption of a single currency.

The Council's recommendations will be passed to the European Council. The European Parliament will be consulted and its opinion passed to the European Council.

The European Council, acting by **qualified majority**, on the basis of the reports from the Council of Ministers, the Commission, the European Parliament and the EMI will decide the following:

(a): whether a majority of the Member States fulfil the necessary conditions for the adoption of a single currency;

(b): whether it is appropriate for the Community to enter the Third Stage.

The European Council, acting by **qualified majority**, before 1 July 1998, will confirm which Member States fulfil the necessary conditions for the adoption of a single currency.

Formation of the Single Currency

The Council, acting with the *unanimity* of the Member States fulfilling the criteria for acceptance to the Third Stage, will adopt the conversion rates at which the currencies will be irrevocably fixed and the Euro will be substituted for these currencies. The Euro will be a currency in its own right (the ECU remains the title of the 'basket of currencies').

Where a Member State wishes to join the Single Currency after it has been formed, the Council, acting *unanimously*, shall agree the rate at which the Euro will be substituted for the national currency of the joining country (Article 123.5).

The ECB will be formed at the start of the Third Stage. The capital of the ECB will initially be ECU 5,000 million, subscribed by the national central banks of the Member States which enter the Third Stage. In addition, the foreign reserves of the Member States will be passed to the ECB, up to an initial amount of ECU 50,000 million (*Protocol of the ESCB and the ECB*: Articles 28 and 30).

The calculation of the amounts which each country would have to pay would be based on the relative size of the national population and GDP (*Protocol of the ESCB and the ECB*: Article 29).

Member States which do not join the Single Currency

Those States which do not meet the criteria will remain in the Second Stage. The United Kingdom and Denmark are not obliged to enter the Third Stage without separate decisions by their respective governments and parliaments and these 'opt-outs' are described in Protocols attached to the Treaty.

The countries which remain in the Second Stage (the "pre-ins") are not involved in the decisions of the Council concerning the ESCB and the ECB once the decision to enter the Third Stage has been made. This also applies when the Third Stage has begun regarding the conversion rates of the national currencies with the Euro, and only those countries which are included in the Single Currency will be eligible to vote (Article 123).

The actions of the ESCB and the ECB will not apply and will not have direct effect on monetary policy of the countries which do not enter Monetary Union. As a result, the national central banks of these countries will be independent of the ECB (Article 122.5 and *Protocol of the ESCB and the ECB*: Article 43).

The national central banks of these countries will not be required to provide the appropriate portion of funds for the European Central Bank. However, the national central banks may have to **contribute to the operational costs** of the ECB by paying a minimal percentage of the costs, if the General Council of the ECB decides that they should (*Protocol of the ESCB and the ECB*: Article 48).

In this situation, the General Council will act by a majority of at least two-thirds majority and half of the shareholders, all of whom will be Member States which have entered the Single Currency (*Protocol of the ESCB and the ECB*: Article 10).

At least once every two years, the Commission and the ECB will report to the Council on the fulfilment of the convergence criteria by the Member States remaining in the Second Stage, other than the UK. The Council, acting by **qualified majority**, will decide which of these Member States may join the Single Currency.

The Economic and Financial Committee will continue to monitor the Member States which remain in the Second Stage as regards their monetary and financial situation and general payments system and report regularly to the Council and the Commission (Article 114.4).

The United Kingdom and the other Member States which do not enter the Third Stage will continue to use and issue their own national bank notes.

Each Member State which remains in the Second Stage will continue to treat its exchange rate policy as a matter of common interest and shall respect the framework of the European Monetary System (Article 124).

The Opt-out of the United Kingdom

The opt-out secured by the United Kingdom means that the country does not have to proceed to the Third Stage without a separate decision by the Government and Parliament. As a result, the United Kingdom will maintain its powers in monetary policy and the provisions of the ESCB and the ECB will not directly apply (*Protocol on certain provisions relating to the United Kingdom*: Articles 4 and 8).

In order for the opt-out to take effect, **the UK must notify the Council of its decision not to proceed to the Third Stage** (*Protocol on certain provisions relating to the United Kingdom*: Article 2).

If the United Kingdom **does decide to join** the Single Currency before the start of the Third Stage (i.e. before the Single Currency has begun), then it must notify the Council within the specified time limits depending on the particular situation:

(1):   If the date for the start of the Single Currency has **not been finalised** before the end of 1997 (and therefore EMU will start on 1 January 1999), the United Kingdom must notify the Council by **1 January 1998**.

(2):   If the date for the start **has been finalised**, the United Kingdom must notify its intention to join the Single Currency before the Council of Ministers makes its assessment on which Member States fulfil the criteria for entry into the Single Currency (*Protocol on certain provisions relating to the United Kingdom*: Article 1).

The terms of the Maastricht Treaty have to a certain extent been over-ridden by the agreement at the Madrid Summit. As a result, the United Kingdom has to inform the Council of its intention to join the Third Stage by 1 January 1998.

If the United Kingdom chooses to enter monetary union **after the start** of the Single Currency, the Council will be notified and, if the conditions are met, the UK will join the Single Currency and the Bank of England will pay its appropriate share of the capital for the ECB (*Protocol on certain provisions relating to the United Kingdom*: Article 10).

As the United Kingdom will be represented in the Council and Committees meetings (described above), it will be involved in the discussions leading up to the formation of the Single Currency and the start of the Third Stage, irrespective of whether or not it decides to join the Single Currency.

However, the UK will not be able to vote in matters relating to the ESCB or the ECB, including the appointment of the officials of the ECB. In addition, it will not be involved in the decisions regarding the agreeing of the conversion rates of the national currencies and the ECU (*Protocol on certain provisions relating to the United Kingdom*: Articles 5 and 7).

Process to introduce the Single Currency

The completion of the transition to EMU is expected to take four years, to July 2002, owing to the complexity of the operation and to allow time for the changes of management and information systems in the participating countries.

The process has been organised into three distinct phases:

Phase A:

Before July 1998, the European Council will decide which Member States fulfil the entry criteria and which should participate in the Single Currency.

During this Phase, the framework for the ESCB and the ECB to operate in Euros will be finally tested, the operational instruments required to conduct monetary and exchange rate policy in the Euro will be introduced and the transfer of funds from the national central banks to the ESCB will take place.

Additional measures would include the preparation of the technical specifications of the notes and coins of the Euro and the preparation of each country's transition plans for the introduction and use of the Euro.

Phase B:

This is the effective start of EMU and corresponds to 'Stage Three' described in the Maastricht Treaty. This Phase, also called the transitional period, consists of the irrevocable fixing of parities of the national currencies and the introduction of the Euro (in a non-cash form).

The ECU, representing the 'basket of currencies', would be replaced by the Euro at an exchange rate of 1:1.

In order to provide momentum to the introduction of the Single Currency, a 'critical mass' of activities in the Euro would be encouraged.

These activities would include the progressive change-over of the banking and financial sector, monetary and exchange rate policy and capital markets to begin operating in the Euro.

During this Phase, private businesses could conduct some of their business in Euros, and consumers would continue to use their national currencies while dual pricing would steadily appear.

Phase C:

The Euro and the national currencies would circulate in parallel in this Phase, which would last the few months necessary to complete the final transition to the Single Currency. This period would include the completion of the change-over of the private non-bank sector and the withdrawal of national banknotes and coins.

Proposed Legal Framework

A proposed Council Regulation will provide the legal framework for the introduction and use of the Euro and would come into force on 1 January 1999. This framework will be based on Articles 123.4 and 308 of the Treaty and will apply to all countries in the European Union.

Article 308 is a general enabling provision of the Treaty and is used where there are no specific powers available to the Community in the area under consideration. Article 308 states that the Council may take appropriate measures to attain the objectives of the Community in the course of the operation of the common market.

Article 123.4 will apply to those countries in EMU after 1 January 1999 and Article 308, introduced by the Treaty of Rome, affects all Member States. The Council will act *unanimously* under both of these Articles, but only those Member States participating in EMU will be eligible to vote under Article 123.4.

Under the terms of the proposed legal framework, the conversion rates of the national currencies to the Euro would be rounded to six significant figures. The framework also proposes that the introduction of the Euro will not disrupt contracts, therefore the terms of any legal instrument will not be altered and debt can be paid in Euros or national currencies.

Proposed Stability Pact

The Stability Pact will operate from 1 January 1999, once the Single Currency has been formed, and is intended to ensure that the Euro would be able to maintain its value. The convergence criteria of the Maastricht Treaty would be incorporated into 'convergence contracts', committing the participating countries to form **stability programmes** to ensure medium-term budgetary discipline.

The stability programmes would be submitted to the Council before 1 January 1999, covering at least the following three years; updated programmes would be submitted on an annual basis. The programmes would contain *inter alia:*

* medium-term objectives for the surplus/deficit as a ratio of GDP;

* summary of measures to achieve the objectives and methods of adjustment to prevent any divergence from the objectives;

* main assumptions about expected economic developments, including real GDP growth, unemployment and inflation.

The structure of the Stability Pact is intended to allow the participating countries room to manoeuvre in adapting to exceptional and cyclical pressures while avoiding excessive deficits. The approach is to be both preventative and dissuasive.

Penalties for Breach of Stability Pact Criteria:

The Stability Pact would be monitored by the Council, acting with the advice of the Commission and the Economic and Financial Committee, and enforced by imposing a series of penalties on a Member State where it exceeded the criteria of government budget deficit of 3% of GDP or government debt of 60%, unless there were temporary and exceptional circumstances (e.g. an economic recession of 'unusual magnitude' or an unusual event outside the Member State's control).

Penalty for Government Deficit:

The penalty would consist of the Member State lodging a compulsory non-interest bearing deposit with the Commission, and would be composed of two parts:

(a): Fixed: 0.2% of the country's GDP;

(b): Variable: 0.1% of GDP for every 0.1% excess over the deficit criteria.

There would be a ceiling for the penalties on each Member State of 0.5% of GDP.

Penalty for Government Debt:

This would be a fixed penalty of 2% of the Country's GDP.

A Member State would have 10 months to finalise and ratify a programme of correcting measures, before the penalties would be applied. If the excessive deficit remains after two years, the deposit would become a definitive fine, paid to the EU budget; at the same time, a new non-interest bearing deposit would be required from the Member State, calculated on the same basis as the first deposit.

The penalty is required to be approved by a two-thirds majority vote by the Member States participating in EMU. The penalty may be cancelled by the Council if the Member State is making significant progress to correct the excess deficit or debt.

Proposed New Exchange Rate Mechanism

A new Exchange Rate Mechanism would be formed on 1 January 1999, based around the Euro, to act as a framework to support the final stages in convergence for the countries which are **not** participating in EMU.

The central rates and fluctuation margins will be set by the Council, the ECB, the national central banks of the non-participating countries and the Commission. Under the terms of the Resolution adopted by the European Council at Amsterdam, the fluctuation margins will be 15%.

Any Member State wishing to join but not participating in the Single Currency would have to be a member of the new ERM and would be required to submit convergence programmes before 1 January 1999. These programmes would have the same structure as the stability programmes for the Countries in EMU and would be monitored by the Community institutions

There would be a system of penalties put in place in order to prevent a Member State, which did not join the Single Currency, from devaluing its currency and gaining a competitive advantage against the Euro.

'Stability' Committee

The Economic and Financial Committee, described in Article 114.2, would be formed at the start of the Third Stage, consisting of representatives of the ECB, the Commission and the countries participating in the Single Currency.

It would act as a 'Stability Council' to monitor the stability and convergence programmes and enforce the Stability Pact. This committee would act as an advisor to the Council and the Commission and attempt to reconcile the Treaty commitments for the fifteen Member States and the commitments of the Single Currency for the fewer countries which would join.

* * * * * * *

DEVELOPMENT OF COMPETENCES OF THE INSTITUTIONS OF THE EUROPEAN UNION

Introduction

The powers of the Community institutions have steadily increased with each successive European Treaty and the relationship between the sovereign Member States and the Community has altered as a consequence.

The role of the Community institutions and the use of qualified majority voting by the Council was extended by the Maastricht Treaty and while the concept of subsidiarity was introduced, the process of harmonisation of laws across the European Union necessitated the involvement of the Community institutions and their domination over national law. Nonetheless, the Member States were still able to determine their course of action in many areas and the Community would support the States' actions, for example, in Foreign Policy and Police and Judicial Co-operation.

The **Treaty of Amsterdam** has extended the areas where the Council may vote by qualified majority and has increased the involvement of the European Parliament in the formation of legislation, by developing the use of **Co-Decision**. In addition, the Treaty has widened the role of the Community in initiating legislation and producing guidelines for Member States to follow. The intention is that the '**Community Method**' will become increasingly important with the relationship with the Member States altering to one where the Community will determine the courses of action. This is particularly important in such areas as Employment, Foreign Policy and Police and Judicial Co-operation.

The Treaty agreed at Amsterdam is not an entity in its own right but is a series of amendments to the Treaty on European Union and the Treaty establishing the European Community as formulated by the Treaty of Rome, with amendments by the Single European Act and the Maastricht Treaty, and to the Treaties establishing the Coal and Steel Community and the Atomic Energy Community.

One area, which was not examined or changed by the Treaty of Amsterdam, was the Economic and Monetary Policy, leading to Monetary Union. The European Parliament has limited involvement in the decision-making process and the Treaty of Amsterdam has not changed this.

Another area that was looked at during the discussions leading up to the Treaty of Amsterdam was the granting of legal personality to the European Union. This was not included in the final act as many of the Member States did not wish to pass too much power to the institutions of the Union.

The European Parliament held a debate the Amsterdam Treaty on 19 November 1997 and passed a Resolution, in which the Parliament acknowledged that the Treaty gives precedence to the 'Community Method' and considered that the Treaty marks a further step towards European political union.

The 'Preamble' or the 'Chapeau'

The introductory Resolutions and Affirmations by the Heads of State (the 'Preamble' or the 'Chapeau') at the beginning of the Treaties on European Union and establishing the European Community were written after the Treaties had been formulated and serve to describe, in general terms, the issues agreed and, like the Declarations attached to the end of the Treaty of Amsterdam, **are not legally binding**. The Preambles are important in that they are intended to express the clear common political will among the contracting parties and to define the intentions of the Community.

The Preamble therefore forms the basis of interpretation of the Treaties and the basis for any further directives and regulations (e.g. on EMU and health and safety of workers).

Amsterdam introduces two specific clauses into the Preambles. The first is in the Preamble to the Treaty on European Union, on fundamental social rights as defined in the Social Charter of 1989. The UK government at the time did not sign the Social Charter and the inclusion of the reference to it in the Treaty (Article 136) implies that the UK now accepts the terms of the Charter. The second clause has been included in the Treaty establishing the European Community and concerns the promotion of education.

Competences in New Areas

The new areas to which the competence of the Council has been extended are :

(1):   **Breach of Fundamental Principles :** Articles 6 and 7, Title I.

A new Article has been introduced describing the Fundamental Principles of the Union as being founded on the principles of liberty, democracy, and respect for human rights and fundamental freedoms.

If the European Council considers that there has serious breach of these principles by a Member State, the Council, acting by **qualified majority** (without taking into account the votes of the Member State involved), may suspend rights from that Member State, including voting rights in the Council. Other obligations under this Treaty will continue to apply to the Member State.

(2):   **Free Movement of Persons, Asylum and Immigration :** Articles 61 – 79

The measures concern the free movement of persons within the Community while maintaining external border controls. The intention is to make the co-operation between the Member States more coherent and consistent, rather than using the provisions of the police and judicial co-operation in Title VI.

Generally, the Council will act *unanimously*, with the option of changing this to **qualified majority voting** after the first five years after the introduction of these provisions. In the case of visas for stays of less than three months, the Council will act by **qualified majority** as soon as Amsterdam comes into effect.

Amsterdam also introduces the terms of the **Schengen *acquis***, agreed by the majority of the Member States in 1985 and 1990, into the Treaty. The Schengen *acquis* concerns the gradual abolition of checks at the common borders of the signatory countries, and is described in detail in a **Protocol** (Protocol no 2 on page 100) attached to the Treaty.

The Council will act with the *unanimity* of the countries that have signed the Schengen *acquis*.

The United Kingdom and Ireland (which did not sign the Schengen *acquis*) and Denmark have arranged exclusions from the Treaty provisions, shown in two Protocols attached to the Treaty. These three countries are able to retain their own border controls. The Treaty provisions and the Schengen *acquis* will not be binding on these countries.

If the UK chooses to 'opt-in' to any of the aspects on open borders, the other countries already in the Schengen *acquis* will vote by *unanimity* on whether this should be allowed (Article 4 of Protocol no 2). The UK's government wanted this to be by qualified majority voting and the actual method of voting is seen as a mistake in the negotiations. As a result, the UK inserted a Declaration in an attempt to rectify this (Declaration 46, on Article 5 of Protocol no 2).

(3): **Employment** : Articles 125 - 130

The growing concern over the high levels of unemployment in the Community has led to an explicit Treaty policy being introduced. The general competence will remain with the Member States but the Community will co-ordinate their actions. The European Council will annually review the state of unemployment and give the political impetus for action.

The Council, acting by **qualified majority**, will issue guidelines for the Member States to follow. These guidelines should be consistent with the Economic Policy of the Union, as described in Articles 98 - 124. The Member States must report annually to the Council on how they have implemented these guidelines. In addition, the Council, acting under the co-decision process, may issue incentive measures to encourage co-operation among the Member States.

An Employment Committee will be formed by the Council and will have advisory status to promote co-ordination between Member States.

(4): **Closer Co-operation or 'Flexibility'** : Articles 43 – 45, Title VII

Individual Member States will be able to use the institutional framework of the Community to develop closer links with one another in specific areas without involving all of the Member States. The intention is that as more European states join the Union, more flexibility is required to allow some Member States to move at different speeds on certain matters, eg EMU and to the closer co-operation in Police and Judicial matters, referred to in Article 40 of Title VI.

Member States that intend to establish closer co-operation with each other may be authorised by the Council, acting by a **qualified majority**. The matter can be referred to the European Council for decision by *unanimity*. The facilities of the Community may be used provided that the aims of the Community are respected.

The Council will authorise this co-operation acting by **qualified majority**. If a Member State opposes the use of qualified majority for authorisation, the Council, acting by **qualified majority**, will refer the matter to the European Council, who will act *unanimously*.

Any Member State that wishes to be involved in the co-operation must notify the Council and the Commission. The Council will decide within four months on the request. The Council may vote by **qualified majority** to delay the decision.

(5): **Environment** : Article 6

The protection of the environment both in each Member State and the Union as a whole is becoming an increasingly important issue, as pollution in one Member State can affect the whole Community. As a consequence of this area effectively becoming a supra-national concern, the policies on the environment will come under the authority of the Community institutions through the harmonisation of laws.

The decision-making process has been amended by the Treaty and is included in the Approximation of Laws (Articles 94 – 97). The intention is that the protection of the environment should be incorporated into all relevant Community acts and will be considered by the Council, the Commission and the European Parliament when they consider any proposed harmonisation measure.

If, as a consequence of a harmonisation measure, a Member State intends to introduce additional policies concerning the protection of the environment in that particular State, the Commission has to be informed and give its approval before the legislation can be implemented (Article 95(3)). This is to allow the Commission to consider if the policy affects the Internal Market.

Other New Areas

(a)	Customs Co-operation	Article 135	Co-decision (QMV)
(b)	Data Protection	Article 286	Co-decision (QMV)
(c)	Expansion of the European Union	Article 49, Title VIII	Unanimity
(d)	Non-Discrimination	Article 13	Unanimity
(e)	Statistics	Article 285	Co-decision (QMV)

Competences extended in existing areas

In addition to extending the involvement to the new areas described above, aspects of the existing Treaty establishing the European Community have been rewritten and extended, to alter and increase the powers of the European Institutions.

These areas are as follows:

(1):   **Citizenship of the Union :** Articles 17 - 22

Citizenship of the Union is intended to complement and not replace national citizenship. The Council will act *unanimously* following the method of co-decision with the European Parliament, described in Article 251.

(2):   **Social Provisions** : Articles 136 - 145

The chapter on Social Provisions has been substantially restructured and expanded by the Treaty of Amsterdam. The principal change has been the repeal of the Protocol on Social Policy and the Agreement on Social Policy (the 'Social Chapter') agreed at Maastricht and their incorporation into the main body of the Treaty. This is due to the UK agreeing to sign the 'Social Chapter' at Amsterdam.

The consequence is that the Council is able to effect the provisions of Social Policy under the legislative procedure of the EU Treaty itself regarding the whole Community, rather than the involvement of the individual Member States that had signed the Protocol. In addition, the terms of the Social Charter of 1989, which the UK Government had not signed, has been implicitly included in Treaty by the Preamble and Article 136.

Parts of the previous Treaty provisions have been retained and partially rewritten and the Articles renumbered. Some additional provisions have been added.

The Council, acting by **qualified majority** following the procedure of **co-decision,** will adopt directives for the minimum requirements for the above, without discriminating against employees in small and medium-sized businesses. Before Amsterdam, the Council acted by qualified majority under the co-operation procedure of Article 252.

There are some new Articles introduced by the Treaty of Amsterdam :

* **Social Exclusion**. The Council, acting by **qualified majority** following the procedure of co-decision, may also adopt measures to encourage co-operation between Member States (Article 137.2).

* **Equal Opportunities.** The Council, acting by **qualified majority** following the procedure of co-decision, will adopt measures to ensure equal opportunities for men and women (Article 141.3). Until now, the Community has had to use more general provisions of the Treaty to introduce directives on equal pay and equal treatment which required unanimity (Articles 94 and 308 respectively).

      *   The Commission will produce an **Annual Report** to the European Parliament, the Council and the Economic and Social Committee on the progress of the implementation of the social policies (Article 143).

(3):   **Fraud :** Article 280

The Article has been altered to emphasise the guiding role of the Community and enables the Council acting by **qualified majority** following the procedure of **co-decision**, to adopt measures to counter fraud to deter and give protection in the Member States. Each year, the Commission will report to the Council on the measures taken against fraud.

Subsidiarity and Proportionality

The concept of **Subsidiarity** is described in Article 5(b) and the Community shall act either within the terms of the Treaty (i.e. within its exclusive competence) or where it can be more successful in achieving a particular objective than an individual Member State.

Proportionality is described in Article 5(b), third paragraph, where any action of the Community will not go beyond what is necessary to achieve the objectives of the Treaty.

Where the Treaty calls for harmonisation measures or for general guidelines in a particular area, the Member States are unlikely to be able to act, since this necessarily involves supra-national action (e.g. Articles 136 and 137 on the harmonisation of workers' health and safety). As a consequence, the Community will tend to retain overall competence in the majority of the Treaty provisions, although the individual Member States are able to decide how to apply particular acts in their own countries.

The implication is that the institutions of the Community will act unless the Community considers that an initiative regarding a particular policy can be left to the Member States alone. **In practice, since the Community has exclusive competence in drawing up measures that concern the development of the Common Market, the application of the principle of subsidiarity is quite restricted.**

The intention is for the two principles to operate in turn, where Subsidiarity will determine whether action should be taken at Community level. Once the decision to act has been taken, Proportionality will operate in limiting the scope and ensuring that the action complies with the terms of the Treaty.

At a Seminar which took place before the Maastricht Treaty agreement, all the jurists present, including the former President of the Court of Justice, affirmed that subsidiarity is 'political in essence' and not legal. As a result, the European Council should be the judge in the last resort.

The Treaty of Amsterdam attaches a **Protocol to the Treaty** (Protocol no 30, page 153) which is intended to define precisely the criteria for the **application of the principles of Subsidiarity and Proportionality**, including the strict observance and consistent implementation, by all the Community institutions. Community legislation must be justified, in terms of Subsidiarity and Proportionality, qualitatively and preferably quantitatively (Protocol, Para 4).

The Protocol reinforced the principle that Subsidiarity does not question the exclusive powers of the Community institutions defined by the Treaty, as interpreted by the Court of Justice, and that **the Subsidiarity criteria will only apply where the Community has shared competence with the Member States** (Protocol, Para. 3).

Member States are required to take all appropriate measures to fulfil their Treaty obligations and not to prevent the attainment of the Treaty objectives (Article 5 and Protocol, Para. 8).

Transparency : Article 207.3

The purpose of this Provision is to ensure that decisions of the Union's institutions should be taken as openly as possible. The Council will determine the conditions in which the public will be able to see documents relating to the institutions, results and explanations of votes, and minutes of meetings.

Common Foreign and Security Policy : Articles 11 to 28, Title V

The Treaty of Amsterdam has substantially restructured and expanded the policy and has incorporated and rewritten the existing provisions from the Maastricht Treaty. The object of the redrafting is to make the policy more coherent and consistent as a Community-wide approach. The consequence of this is that the Community will take on a more active leadership role in formulating and guiding policy, which until Amsterdam had been the responsibility of the individual member States acting together. The Member States will ensure that their national policies conform to the Community's approach.

The common foreign and security policy includes all matters relating to the security of the Union, including the progressive framing of a common defence policy as well as humanitarian and rescue tasks, peacekeeping and combat forces.

The European Council will define the principles and the general guidelines on strategies where the Member States have important interests in common. These strategies will set out the objectives, duration and the means made available for the Community to act.

In the majority of cases, the Council will take decisions acting *unanimously*. Any Member State abstaining will not hinder Union action, but that Member State will not have to implement the decision. In certain cases, such as when the Council will act by qualified majority when making decisions on joint actions. If a member of the Council opposes the adoption of a decision taken by qualified majority, the Council will refer the matter to the European Council, which will decide *unanimously* on the matter.

The Role of the Western European Union

A Declaration (Declaration no 3, page 175) concerning the role of the Western European Union (WEU) has been attached to the Treaty and this describes the increased importance the WEU and its possible future integration into the European Union. The Declaration acknowledges the continuing importance of NATO to the defence of Europe and describes how the Union will foster closer relations with the WEU.

The European Council will give guidance on the activities of the WEU and may decide to integrate the WEU into the Union. The Council, with agreement with the institutions of the WEU, will adopt the necessary arrangements for the Member States to participate in the decisions of the WEU. Member States will be recommended to adopt such decisions.

Police and Judicial Co-operation in Criminal Matters : Articles 29 – 42, Title VI

The Heading of this Title has been changed from 'Justice and Home Affairs', emphasising the change in approach to make the policy clearer and more far-reaching to provide citizens with a high degree of safety within an area of freedom, security and justice.

This will include closer co-operation between the judicial, police forces, and customs authorities of the Member States and harmonising action among the Member States in matters concerning crime (especially drug-related), race and xenophobia.

The policy has been largely rewritten by the provisions of the Treaty of Amsterdam to emphasise and strengthen the new leadership and guiding role of the Community and to reduce the initiative of the Member States.

The role of Europol has been formalised in the Treaty and the Council will promote co-operation through Europol to tackle organised crime by the preparation, co-ordination and completion of specific investigations.

The Council will act *unanimously* to define the approach and the framework of the Community's Policy and to harmonise the laws of the Member States and it will act by **qualified majority** on specific matters arising from the framework which are necessary to operate at Union level. The Council will consult the European Parliament before adopting any measure, but the Parliament will not be directly involved in the legislation.

The Court of Justice has been given increased jurisdiction to give preliminary rulings on the validity and interpretation of framework decisions and to review the legality of actions by the Community and Member States on the grounds of lack of competence, the misuse of powers or disputes over the interpretation of the decisions.

Member States may make a declaration accepting that the Court of Justice has jurisdiction to give preliminary rulings for the national courts to follow (Article 35(2)). Under Declaration No 10 (see page 180), Member States may also pass national legislation so that the final national court of appeal must refer unresolved matters to the Court of Justice. However, the Court of Justice will have **no** jurisdiction to review internal national security in any Member State (Article 35(5)).

A Co-ordinating Committee will be formed and consist of senior officials and will co-ordinate, give opinions and contribute to the Council's discussions.

Closer co-operation, or 'flexibility', between individual Member States within the policy of police and judicial co-operation is specifically mentioned in the Treaty, both in this Title and the new Title VII on Closer Co-operation, discussed above.

Definitions of 'Qualified Majority' and actions under Articles 251 - 252

The Council may act by **qualified majority** in a number of areas of the Treaty. The voting arrangements are shown in Article 205, where the votes of each country are weighted by reference to the relative size of the country.

The total number of votes in the Council is 87 and there have to be 62 votes in favour for an act to be adopted on a proposal from the Commission, and there have to be 62 votes in favour, cast by at least ten members, for an act to be adopted in other cases.

The result of this is that a country could be *unanimously* against a particular ruling, but could be ignored as the votes from the other countries would over-rule and the decision would then be binding on that country. A minority vote of at least 26 votes is needed to block a proposal.

Co-Decision

One of the major changes in the Treaty of Amsterdam has been the extension of the role of the European Parliament in the decision-making process. Under **Article 251**, the Council will act on an equal basis with the Parliament in legislative matters. However, co-decision does not extend to situations where the Council acts in an executive capacity.

The Treaty of Amsterdam has simplified the co-decision process from the terms introduced by the Maastricht Treaty and the method by which the Parliament will be involved will be as follows:
-       The Commission will submit a proposal for a new piece of legislation;

- The European Parliament, acting by an absolute majority, will give its opinion on the proposal to the Council;
- If the Parliament does not suggest any amendments, the Council will act by **qualified majority** to vote on the proposal;
- If the Parliament **rejects** the proposal, then it will not become law;
- If the Parliament suggests any amendments, the Council and the Commission must consider these;
- If the Commission accepts the amendments, the Council will act by **qualified majority** to accept the amended proposal as law;
- If the Commission rejects the amendments of the Parliament, the Council will act *unanimously* to decide whether to adopt the amended act;
- If the Council does not agree to accept the amended text, the matter is passed to the Conciliation Committee. The Conciliation Committee consists of equal members of the Council and the Parliament and will debate and vote on the act. If the Conciliation Committee rejects the amended text, the act will not be adopted.

Powers of the Institutions

The powers of the institutions, as well as their formation and structure, are summarised as follows:

* **European Parliament :** Articles 189 - 201.

 The European Parliament is composed of representatives of the Member States and is involved in the legislative process by giving an opinion on proposals from the Commission.

 The Treaty of Amsterdam extended the powers and the involvement of the Parliament in the legislative process; the method of co-decision is described above and the areas where the involvement of Parliament has changed are summarised on pages XI – XVIII, in the analysis of the Legislative Procedures.

 The intention is that the Parliament will have essentially three methods of being involved in the legislative process: co-decision, assent and consultation. A fourth method, co-operation under Article 252, is now restricted to Economic and Monetary Policy.

 The number of MEPs representing each Member State is 626 and the composition of the Parliament is shown in Article 190. The number of MEPs, which each country has, is weighted in accordance with relative size. Amsterdam has set an upper limit on the number of MEPs as 700. This has been introduced in anticipation of the enlargement of the Union and it is felt that the numbers must be restricted.

 The Parliament shall act by an absolute majority of the votes cast (Article 198). If five countries agree to a proposal from the Commission (e.g. Belgium, Germany, France, Italy and Spain), the other countries of the EC will not have any influence over the proposal.

* **The Council of Ministers :** Articles 202 - 210.

 The role of the Council is to co-ordinate the general economic policies of the Member States and to create European law by adopting the proposals made by the Commission. The Council is composed of representatives from each of the 15 Member States, who are usually government ministers authorised to commit the government of their respective Member States to the Council's decisions.

 The intention is that qualified majority voting will become the normal method of voting for Council business, since this will prevent one country from holding up Community legislation by the use of a veto for matters which have previously required *unanimity*. This is particularly relevant in the future enlargement of the European Union.

The Presidency was last held by the United Kingdom from 1 July 1992 to 31 December 1992 and will next be held from 1 January 1998 to 30 June 1998 (Article 203).

Article 203 was altered by the Treaty of Accession of Austria, Finland and Sweden, so that the order in which each Member State holds the presidency will now be determined by the Council, acting *unanimously*.

* **The Commission** : Articles 211 - 219.

The Commission acts as the executive and the 'guardian' of the Treaty, and it instigates all proposals affecting European law and the term of office is five years.

There are now 20 members from the Member States (with Austria, Finland and Sweden); the larger Member States (Germany, France, Italy, Spain and the UK) have two members, while the other countries provide one commissioner each.

Amsterdam has introduced a provision that the European Parliament will approve the appointment of the President of the Commission (Article 214).

During the discussions at Amsterdam relating to the enlargement of the Union, the future number of members of the Commission was reviewed, particularly the difficulty of providing useful roles for all of the members. No final conclusions were reached to amend the Treaty but this is a consideration for future treaties.

The involvement of national parliaments in the legislative process is incorporated into the Treaty by a Protocol (Protocol no 9, page 109) so that the Commission will provide all consultation documents and proposals for legislation.

* **The Court of Justice** : Articles 220 - 245.

The Court is the final arbiter in disputes over interpretation of the Treaties. There are two courts: the Court of First Instance (created by the Single European Act) and the Court of Justice.

The Court of First Instance has been formed to hear cases from individuals, such as employment and competitiveness issues and so release the Court of Justice to concentrate on the interpretation of Community law, acts by the Community Institutions and on cases brought by Member States.

There are 15 judges appointed to each court for a renewable six-year term. Each of the Member States provides one judge for each court.

Amsterdam has extended the Court's jurisdiction in Police and Judicial Co-operation (Title VI) so that it may give preliminary rulings on the framework decisions promoting co-operation and harmonisation of criminal law in the Community.

* **The European Council** : Article 4.

The European Council consists of the Heads of State or Government with their respective foreign ministers and senior Commission officials and is referred to in the Treaty as either the European Council or 'the Council, meeting in the composition of [the] Heads of State or of Government'.

It provides the general political impetus for the development of the Union, defines the approaches and guidelines in important areas (e.g. Economic and Monetary Union), expresses the common position in questions of external relations and initiates co-operation in new areas of activity. Its role has widened to act as an unofficial final court of appeal where differences of opinion between the Council of Ministers and the Commission can be discussed and agreements reached. In general, its powers and role have not been defined by the Treaty to the same manner as for the other institutions, but when it acts in matters within the scope of the Treaty, it does so following the provisions relating to the Council of Ministers.

Amsterdam has extended the powers of the European Council, specifically in the areas of the breach of the Community's fundamental principles by a Member State, closer co-operation (the flexibility provisions), employment, foreign and security policy and police and judicial co-operation.

The European Council is also involved in the agreement of the broad guidelines of economic policies of the Member States and the Community (Article 99.2) and the decision-making on the transition to the Third Stage of Economic and Monetary Union, including which Member States meet the criteria for the Single Currency. The European Council will act by **qualified majority**.

* **The Court of Auditors** : Articles 246 - 248.

The Court consists of 15 members, one from each Member State, and acts as the auditors to the Community, examining the accounts of all revenue and expenditure of the Community. It reports annually to the European Parliament and the Council. In addition, it is also able to report on specific subjects either on its own initiative or at the request of the Community.

* **The Economic and Social Committee** : Articles 257 - 262.

This is an advisory body formed by the Treaty of Rome, consisting of 222 members (after the accession of Austria, Finland and Sweden) drawn from the Member States, and is composed of representatives of employers, employees, the professions and the general public. It is intended to advise the Council and the Commission on such matters as the social chapter, taxation, agriculture and transport.

The composition of the Committee is shown in Article 258.

* **The Committee of the Regions** : Articles 263 - 265.

This Committee was formed under the Maastricht Treaty to be an advisory body to the Commission and the Council on regional matters (e.g. education, public health and economic and social cohesion). It consists of 222 members, appointed for a renewable term of four years, representing regional and local bodies (e.g. County Councils) and the composition is shown in Article 263.

Methods of Enforcement of the Treaty

The European Community can enforce the Treaty by different methods. These are described in Articles 249 and 253, 254 and 256 and comprise regulations, directives and decisions (which are binding) and recommendations and opinions (which are not binding but are for guidance).

Approximation of Laws

In Articles 94 - 97, the Council has powers to issue directives to harmonise the laws in each Member State to enable the establishment and functioning of the Common Market. Under the terms of the Treaty, the Council will generally act by *unanimity* but it will act by **qualified majority** voting, following the procedure of **co-decision** where the directives concern the Internal Market.

* * * * * * *

ANALYSIS OF THE
DEVELOPMENT OF THE POWERS ('COMPETENCES')
OF THE INSTITUTIONS OF THE EUROPEAN UNION

Introduction

The analysis in the tables on the following pages is intended to show how the authority (or 'competence') of the Institutions of the European Union has developed and expanded since the original Treaty of Rome and how the Community has become more highly structured.

This analysis also acts as a summary of the Treaties, highlighting the major changes and complements the description of the 'Competences agreed at Amsterdam', given on the preceding pages.

Interpretation of the Tables

The Tables are laid out to compare the four Treaties: the **Treaty of Rome**, at the time of the accession of Great Britain in 1973 combined with the **Single European Act**, which made major modifications for the Single Market, the adjustments made by the provisions of the **Maastricht Treaty** and the additions and amendments of the **Treaty of Amsterdam**.

Owing to the limitation of space, the Treaty of Rome and the Single European Act have been combined in the first column and the changes to the voting structure arising from the accession of Austria, Finland and Sweden have been included in this column.

* The changes and additions, which the Maastricht Treaty and the **Treaty of Amsterdam** incorporate into the Treaty of Rome, are shown next to the relevant provisions. Where there has been no change to the existing law, there is either a blank space or an indication that there are no changes.

* Where there is a new area introduced by either Maastricht or Amsterdam, the policies are shown in the order of the Articles as modified by the Treaty of Amsterdam and where there is a space in the earlier Treaties this shows that this is a new 'competence'.

* Notes on the amendments are shown in the text of the table *in italics* and these are intended to help to clarify the changes. This is particularly relevant for the new areas introduced by Amsterdam, including Visas, Asylum and Immigration, Employment, and Customs Co-operation. In addition, the changes to the Social Provisions have been shown as a separate summary.

* Owing to its importance, the provisions of the Maastricht Treaty affecting Economic and Monetary Policy have been shown separately.

* In order that the development of the competences can be understood more readily, the order of the Articles has been reorganised within the text of the table and within the particular policy. In some areas, the impact of the Protocols is included. As a result, the Article numbers are shown underneath the heading of each policy and not necessarily after each paragraph.

* The Council may adopt laws by either voting unanimously or by a majority of its members. The circumstances under which these methods apply vary depending on the context. This is indicated in the table, with *unanimity shown in italics* and **majority voting shown in bold.** Voting by majority can either be by a simple majority or by a qualified majority.

A **qualified majority** is calculated on the respective number of votes that each Member State holds, described in Article 205. In the Treaty of Amsterdam, the arrangements for this form of voting, and the process of consultation between the Council and the European Parliament, are defined in Articles 251 and 252.

In particular, the development of **Co-Decision** between the Council and the European Parliament is shown under Article 251.

These Articles prescribe different procedures. Where majority voting is designated for a particular policy area, the Article number is shown in the text of the table to indicate which procedure applies.

The tables examine the expansion of the provisions of Titles I, II, V, VI, the new Title VII and VIII.

New Numbering System

The **new numbering system** introduced by the Treaty of Amsterdam is used throughout the analysis, except where the old Articles have been repealed by either the Maastricht Treaty or the Treaty of Amsterdam.

This system has been used in order to avoid confusion where references are made to different Articles. This may lead to some difficulties, with the numbering system being used for both the Treaty on European Union (effectively Titles I, V, VI, VII and VIII) and the Treaty establishing the European Community (Title II). Where there appears to be an ambiguous reference, the name or number of the Title or Treaty is shown.

* * * * * * *

DEVELOPMENT OF 'COMPETENCES'
The Treaty of Rome to the Treaty of Amsterdam

CONSOLIDATED TREATY ON EUROPEAN UNION

Treaty of Rome and Single European Act	Maastricht Treaty	Treaty of Amsterdam
Title I : **Common Provisions :** (Articles **1 – 7**)		
	This Title was introduced by the Maastricht Treaty and acts as an introduction and a general summary of the objectives of the European Union and of the institutions of the Community, including the European Council. It is legally binding.	*The Treaty of Amsterdam revises the Common Provisions and adds new provisions on the treatment of Member States which breach the principles of the Union.* *The Treaty also introduces **a new numbering system** for both the overall Treaty and Title II, the Treaty establishing the European Community.*
	The Member States establish among themselves a European Union, marking a new stage in the process of creating an ever-closer union among the peoples of Europe, where decisions are taken as closely as possible to the citizen. (Article **1**).	*In addition :* Decisions are taken as openly as possible.
	The Union shall have the following objectives (*inter alia*): (a) To promote balanced and sustainable economic and social progress, through the creation of an area without internal borders, economic and social cohesion and the establishment of EMU, leading to the single currency; (b) The formation of a common foreign and security policy; (c) To develop co-operation on justice and home affairs; (d) Ensuring the effectiveness of the mechanisms and the institutions of the Community. (Article **2**).	*Changed to :* (a) To promote economic and social progress and **to achieve** balanced and sustainable development and a **high level of employment** through the creation of an area without internal borders, economic and social cohesion and the estab-lishment of EMU, leading to the single currency; *In addition :* (e) To maintain and develop the Union as an area of freedom, security and justice in which the free movement of persons is assured, in conjunction with measures on external border controls, immigration, asylum and combating crime.
	The Union will be served by a single institutional framework. The Council and the Commission will ensure the consistency and continuity of the activities of the Union (Article **3**).	*In addition :* The Council and the Commission **will co-operate** to ensure the consistency and continuity of the activities of the Union.

Treaty of Rome and Single European Act	Maastricht Treaty	Treaty of Amsterdam
Common Provisions : (Continued)		
		In addition : The Union is founded on the principles of liberty, democracy, respect for human rights and fundamental freedoms. (Article **6**). The European Council, acting *unanimously* on a proposal by ⅓ of the Member States or by the Commission and after obtaining the consent of the European Parliament, may recognise a serious breach of these principles by a Member State (Article **7**.1). Once this has been established, the Council, acting by **qualified majority**, may suspend rights from that Member State, including voting rights in the Council. Other obligations under this Treaty will continue to apply to the Member State (Article **7**.2). The Council, acting by **qualified majority**, may later decide to alter these measures. The Council will act without taking into account the votes of the Member State involved. A **qualified majority** will be weighted as in Article **205**(2). The European Parliament will act by a two-thirds majority of the votes cast.
	Articles **8 – 10** : *These Articles refer to the **amendments** to the Treaties establishing the three European Communities made by the Maastricht Treaty.*	

Treaty of Rome and Single European Act	Maastricht Treaty	Treaty of Amsterdam
Title V : **A Common Foreign and Security Policy :** (Articles **11 - 28**)		
Co-operation in the sphere of Foreign Policy (Title III) : *This Title was introduced by the Single European Act and was subsequently repealed and replaced by new provisions of the Maastricht Treaty.*	**A Common Foreign and Security Policy** (Articles J - J.11 [old numbering])	*The Treaty of Amsterdam has substantially restructured and expanded the provisions to cover Articles 11 to 28, and has incorporated and rewritten the existing provisions from the Maastricht Treaty.* *The overall approach has been to make the Community more responsible for foreign and security policy by taking on a more leading role in the formation of policy.*
The Member States shall endeavour jointly to formulate and implement a European foreign policy. They undertake to inform and consult each other on any foreign policy matters of general interest.	The Union and the Member States shall define and implement a common policy to cover all areas of foreign and security policy (Article **11**).	*Replaced by:* The **Union** will define and implement the policy.
	The objectives of the policy are (*inter alia*): (a) to safeguard the common values, fundamental interests and independence of the Union; (b) to strengthen the security of the Union and the Member States; (c) to promote international co-operation; (d) to develop and consolidate democracy and the rule of law. (Article **11**).	*(a) has additional objective :* (a) To safeguard the **integrity** of the Union; *(b) replaced by:* (b) to strengthen the security of the Union;
	The Union shall pursue these objectives by: (a) establishing systematic co-operation between Member States; (b) by gradually implementing joint action. (Article **12**).	*Replaced by:* The Union shall pursue the objectives by : (a) defining the principles and general guidelines for the policy; (b) deciding on common strategies; (c) adopting joint actions and common positions; (d) strengthening systematic co-operation between Member States (Article **12**).
Member States shall give due consideration to the positions of other Member States before forming their own policies.	The European Council shall define the principles and general guidelines of the policy (Article J.8 [old numbering]).	*Article renumbered 13, in addition :* The European Council shall define the principles **including matters with defence implications.**

Treaty of Rome and Single European Act	Maastricht Treaty	Treaty of Amsterdam
A Common Foreign and Security Policy : (Continued)		
Member States shall ensure that common principles and objectives are gradually developed and defined.	The Council, acting *unanimously*, shall take the decisions necessary for defining and implementing the policy (Article J.8(2) [old numbering]).	*Replaced by :* The Council will take decisions acting *unanimously* (including agreements with individual states or international organisations, Article **24**). Abstentions will not prevent adoption of decisions. Any Member State abstaining will not hinder Union action (Article **23**).
The foreign ministers of each Member State and a representative of the Commission shall meet under the framework of 'European Political Co-operation'. The Presidency of the Council shall be the president of this 'Co-operation' and this Member State shall be responsible for initiating action and co-ordinating the positions of the Member States (Article **18**).	The Council, when adopting a joint action, shall define those matters on which decisions will be taken by **qualified majority** (Article J.3(2) [old numbering]).	The Council will act by **qualified majority** when adopting joint actions. The votes will be weighted under Article **205**(2) of Title II (TEC) and there must be 62 votes cast in favour by at least 10 members. If a member of the Council opposes the adoption of a decision taken by qualified majority, the Council will refer the matter to the European Council, which will decide *unanimously* on the matter. (Article **13**)
	The Council shall ensure the unity, consistency and effectiveness of action by the Union (Article **13**). Member States shall support the Union's policies actively and unreservedly in a spirit of loyalty and mutual solidarity and shall refrain from any action which is contrary to the interests of the Union. The Council shall ensure that these principles are complied with. (Article **11**). Member States shall inform and consult one another on any matter of general interest (Article **16**). Where appropriate, the Council shall define a common position and the Member States shall ensure that they conform to and uphold this policy. The Council shall decide whether a matter should be the subject of joint action.	

Treaty of Rome and Single European Act	Maastricht Treaty	Treaty of Amsterdam
A Common Foreign and Security Policy : (Continued)		
	The Council shall define the scope, general and specific objectives, duration, means, procedures and conditions for the implementation of this policy (Article **14**).	
	Joint actions shall commit Member States to the common position. (Article **15**).	
Member States shall organise discussions with third countries whenever they consider it to be necessary. The Member States and the Commission, through mutual assistance, shall increase their co-operation with third countries and international organisations.	The delegations of the Member States and the Commission in third countries shall co-operate to ensure that the policies of the Union are complied with and implemented. (Articles **19** and **20**).	
	The Union requests that the Western European Union (WEU) shall elaborate and implement the decisions of the Union which relate to defence. The WEU is considered to be an integral part of the Union. The Council, acting *unanimously*, shall adopt the necessary practical arrange- ments for the involvement of the WEU.	
Nothing in this Treaty shall impede the continued close co-operation of certain Member States within NATO.	These provisions will not prevent close co-operation of certain Member States within NATO, as long as this co-operation does not run counter to or impede the co-operation provided for in this Treaty (Article **17**).	
	The Commission shall be fully associated with the work in relation to the foreign and security policy (Article **27**).	
	The Council may determine whether operational expenditure should be charged to the Community or to the Member States (Article **28**).	

Treaty of Rome and Single European Act	Maastricht Treaty	Treaty of Amsterdam
A Common Foreign and Security Policy : (Continued)		*In addition :* The European Council shall decide on common strategies where the Member States have important interests in common. These strategies will set out the objectives, duration and the means made available. The Council shall ensure the unity, consistency and effectiveness of action by the Union (Article **13**). The Council will adopt joint actions and positions. These will define the approach and address specific situations and the action to be taken by the Union. Member States will ensure that their national policies conform to the common position. The Commission may submit proposals to the Council to ensure the implementation of a joint action. (Articles **14** and **15**). The common foreign and security policy includes all matters relating to the security of the Union, including the progressive framing of a common defence policy as well as humanitarian and rescue tasks, peacekeeping and combat forces. The European Council may decide to form a common defence from the common defence policy. The European Council may decide to integrate the WEU into the Union, as the WEU is an integral part of the Union. Therefore the Union will foster closer relations with the WEU. Member States will be recommended to adopt such decisions (Article **17**). The Union will use the WEU and the European Council will be competent to give guidance on the activities of the WEU. The Council, with agreement with the institutions of the WEU, will adopt the necessary arrangements for the Member States to participate in the decisions of the WEU.

Treaty of Rome and Single European Act	Maastricht Treaty	Treaty of Amsterdam
A Common Foreign and Security Policy : (Continued)		The Presidency (of the Council) will be assisted by the Secretary-General of the Council who will act as the High Representative for the common policy. The Secretary-General will be helped by the deputy Secretary-General of the Council, who will be responsible for running the General Secretariat. If need be the Presidency of the Council will be assisted by the next Member State to hold the Presidency. The Commission will be fully involved in the role of the Presidency being responsible for the common policy of the Union (Article **18**). The Council will be assisted by the Secretary-General in preparation of policy decisions (Article **26**). Operational costs will be borne by the Community budget, unless the Council decides otherwise, acting *unanimously*. Expenditure will be charged to the Member States, based on GDP, if not charged to the Community budget, unless the Council, acting *unanimously*, decides otherwise. (Article **28**(3)).

Treaty of Rome and Single European Act	Maastricht Treaty	Treaty of Amsterdam
	Title VI : **Co-operation in the fields of Justice and Home Affairs :** (Articles K - K.9 [old numbering])	*The Heading for this Title has been changed to:* **Police and Judicial Co-operation in Criminal Matters.** *These Articles have been largely rewritten by the provisions of the Treaty of Amsterdam (Articles 29 – 42). In particular, Articles 29, 30, 31 and 35 are new and Articles 34 and 40 are substantial expansions of earlier articles.* *The new and rewritten Articles place more emphasis on the leadership and guiding role and activities of the Community and less on the initiative of the Member States. This is intended to strengthen the powers of the Community in co-operating and developing common action.* *The role of Europol in co-ordinating the co-operation among the Member States has been formalised in the Treaty.*
	Member States shall regard the following as matters of common interest: (1) Asylum policy; (2) Rules governing people crossing external borders of the Member States; (2) Immigration policy; (3) Combating drug addiction; (4) International fraud; (5) Judicial co-operation in civil and criminal matters; (6) Customs co-operation; (7) Police co-operation regarding terrorism, drug trafficking and other forms of serious international crime, in connection with a Union-wide system of exchanging information within a European Police Office. (Article K.1 [old numbering])	*Replaced by:* The Union's objective will be to provide citizens with a high degree of safety within an area of freedom, security and justice. The objective will be achieved by the following (*inter alia*): (1) Developing common action among the Member States in criminal, race and xenophobia matters; (2) Closer co-operation between judicial, police forces, and customs authorities; (3) Member States' criminal laws being made similar to one another (Article **29**).
		Common action in police co-operation will include: (1) Operational co-operation for criminal offences; (2) Collection and exchange of information, including financial data; (3) Training, secondments and forensic research (Article **30**).

Treaty of Rome and Single European Act	Maastricht Treaty	Treaty of Amsterdam
	Co-operation in the fields of Justice and Home Affairs : (Continued)	
		The Council will promote co-operation through Europol and shall, within five years of the date of this Treaty:
		(1) Enable Europol to support the preparation, co-ordination and completion of specific investigations;
		(2) Enable Europol to ask Member States to co-ordinate their investigations;
		(3) Promote co-operation against organised crime;
		(4) Establish a cross-border research network (Article **30**(2)).
		Common action on judicial co-operation in criminal matters will include:
		(1) Aiding co-operation in proceedings and the enforcement of decisions;
		(2) Aiding extradition;
		(3) Ensuring compatibility of rules to improve co-operation;
		(4) Preventing conflicts of jurisdiction;
		(5) Progressively adopt minimum rules on criminal acts (Article **31**).
		The Council will decide on the conditions and limitations under which Member States' authorities may act in other Member States (Article **32**).
	Member States shall co-ordinate their action through the Council. On the initiative of any Member State or the Commission, the Council may:	*Replaced by:* The Council shall take measures and promote co-operation and, acting *unanimously* on the initiative of a Member State or the Commission, may:
	(a) adopt joint positions and promote any co-operation appropriate to the objectives of the Union.;	(a) Define the approach of the Union;
	(b) act where it considers that the objectives of the Community can be better achieved than by the individual Member States acting on their own;	(b) Adopt framework decisions to make the laws of the Member States approximately the same. These decisions will be binding on the Member States;
	(c) draw up conventions.	

Treaty of Rome and Single European Act	Maastricht Treaty	Treaty of Amsterdam
	Co-operation in the fields of Justice and Home Affairs : (Continued)	

Treaty of Rome and Single European Act	Maastricht Treaty	Treaty of Amsterdam
		(c) Adopt decisions on any other matter relevant to this Title; the Council acting by **qualified majority** will adopt measures necessary to implement the decisions at Union level;
(d) Establish conventions which the Member States will be recommended to adopt; there will be a time limit set for this adoption.
	The Council will act *unanimously*, except on procedural matters and where it decides that action is better at Community level.
In these cases, the Council will act by **qualified majority** weighted under the terms of Article **205**(2), with 62 votes in favour by at least 10 members.
Specific measures implementing these joint actions will be adopted by the Council, acting by a majority of two-thirds of its members.
(Article **34**). | *In addition :*
Generally, when adopted by at least half of the Member States, conventions will enter into force in those Member States which have adopted them (Article **34**).

The Court of Justice will have jurisdiction to give preliminary rulings on the validity and interpretation of framework decisions (Article **35**).

Member States may accept, by making a declaration, that the Court of Justice is able to give preliminary rulings for the national courts to follow on matters arising from the framework decisions in this Title.

Member States may, at the time of making the declaration, follow the terms of **Declaration No 10** so that the final national Court of Appeal must refer the matter to the Court of Justice.

Once the declaration has been made:
(a) The courts of the Member State may request the Court of Justice to give a ruling where the national courts have no judicial remedy to a decision made by the national courts;
(b) Any court or tribunal of that Member State may request the Court of Justice to give a preliminary ruling. |

Treaty of Rome and Single European Act	Maastricht Treaty	Treaty of Amsterdam
	Co-operation in the fields of Justice and Home Affairs : (Continued)	
		Any Member State may submit statements to the Court.
		The Court of Justice will have **no** jurisdiction to review national security in any Member State.
		The Court of Justice will have jurisdiction to review the legality of decisions on the grounds of lack of competence, the misuse of powers or disputes over their interpretation (Article **35**).
		A Co-ordinating Committee will be formed and consist of senior officials and will co-ordinate, give opinions and contribute to the Council's discussions.
		The Council will consult the European Parliament before adopting any measure. The European Parliament will have a time limit, not less than three months, to form an opinion (Article **39**).
		Member States intending to establish closer co-operation between themselves may use the facilities of the Community, provided that the aims of the Community are respected.
		The Council will authorise this co-operation acting by **qualified majority**, after having the opinion of the European Parliament and the Commission.
		If a Member State opposes the use of qualified majority for authorisation, the Council, acting by **qualified majority**, will refer the matter to the European Council, who will act *unanimously*.
		The votes of the Council will be weighted following the terms of Article **205**(2) and there will need to be 62 votes in favour by at least 10 members to adopt the measure (Article **40**).

Treaty of Rome and Single European Act	Maastricht Treaty	Treaty of Amsterdam
	Co-operation in the fields of Justice and Home Affairs : (Continued)	
		Any Member State which wishes to involved in the co-operation must notify the Council and the Commission. The Council will decide within four months on the request. The Council may vote by **qualified majority** to delay the decision (Article **40**). [*See also Title **VII** below*].
		Expenditure will be charged to the Community, unless the Council acts *unanimously* to charge the Member States (in the proportion of GNP) (Article **41**).
	A Co-ordinating Committee shall be formed, to give opinions for the attention of the Council and to contribute to the discussions of the Council.	
	The Commission shall be fully associated with the work of the Council and the Committee (Article **36**).	
	The Court of Justice shall interpret the provisions and rule on any dispute (Article **35**).	
	These provisions shall not affect the responsibilities of the Member States to maintain law and order and safeguard their internal security.	
	The Council, acting *unanimously*, may decide whether the expenditure relating to the implementation of these provisions should be charged to the Community or to the Member States. (Article **41**).	
	The Council, acting *unanimously*, may decide to apply the provisions relating to the issue of visas and the procedures for this (Article 100c of the TEC [old numbering]) and may define the voting conditions for this. (Article **42**).	*Changed to:* The Council, acting *unanimously*, after consulting the European Parliament, may decide that closer police and judicial co-operation will fall under Articles **61** – **69** of the TEC (free movement of persons) and will define the method of voting (Article **42**).

Treaty of Rome and Single European Act	Maastricht Treaty	Treaty of Amsterdam
		Title VII : **Closer Co-operation :** (Articles **43 – 45**) *This is a new Title introduced by the Treaty of Amsterdam and allows individual Member States the 'flexibility' to form closer links with other Member States, without involving the whole Community.* *In particular, this relates to the closer co-operation in Police and judicial matters referred to in Article 40 of Title VI, described above.* Member States which intend to establish closer co-operation with each other may be authorised by the Council, acting by a **qualified majority** under the terms of Article **205**(2) on a proposal by the Commission and after consulting the European Parliament. The matter can be referred to the European Council for decision by *unanimity*. The Member States can use the institutions of the Community as long as the co-operation *inter alia*: (a) furthers the aims of the Union and at protecting and serving the Union; (b) respects the principles of the Treaties (c) is only used as a last resort; (d) concerns at least a majority of member States and is open to all Member States; (e) does not affect the competences or rights of non-participating Member States; (f) does not concern areas which fall within the exclusive competence of the Community; (g) does not affect Community policies, actions or programmes (Article **11** of the TEC).

Treaty of Rome and Single European Act	Maastricht Treaty	Treaty of Amsterdam
Title VIII : **Final Provisions :** (Articles **46** - **53**)		

The government of any Member State or the Commission may submit proposals for the amendment of any of the treaties of the European Union. The Council, after consulting the European Parliament and where appropriate, the Commission, may determine the amendments to be made. These amendments will come into force on being ratified by all of the Member States (Article **48**).

A conference will be held in 1996 to discuss and revise the provisions of this Treaty, in order to further the aims of the Treaty in accordance with those objectives listed in Articles **1** and **2**. *(Common Provisions, Title I).*

Any European state may apply to the Council for membership of the Union. The Council may accept the state into the Union by voting *unanimously*, after consulting the Commission and the European Parliament (which shall act by an absolute majority). The conditions for admission will be agreed by each of the Member States with the applicant state and ratified by all of the contracting states (Article **49**).

In addition:
Any European state which respects the principles of liberty, democracy (described in Article **6** of the Common Provisions in Title I) may apply for membership of the EU (Article **49**).

The Treaty will be ratified by the 'High Contracting Parties', following their particular constitutional requirements.

The Treaty will come into force on 1 January 1993, if all of the Member States have ratified the Treaty. Failing that, the Treaty will come into force on the first day of the month after the last Member State has signed.

* * * * * * *

CONSOLIDATED TREATY ESTABLISHING THE EUROPEAN COMMUNITY

Title II : The Treaty establishing the European Community

Treaty of Rome and Single European Act	Maastricht Treaty	Treaty of Amsterdam
Principles : (Articles **1 - 16**)		*The Treaty of Amsterdam introduces a new numbering system for the Articles of this Title and a separate numbering system for Titles I, V, VI, VII and VIII – collectively the Treaty on European Union.*
A European Economic Community will be established.	*The Principles in the Treaty of Rome have been replaced by the following :* A **European Community** will be established.	
The Community, by establishing a Common Market and by progressively approximating the economic policies of the Member States, shall have the task of promoting : (a) a harmonious development of economic activities; (b) a continuous and balanced expansion; (c) an increase in stability; (d) an accelerated raising of the standard of living; (e) closer relations between the states belonging to the Community.	The Community, by establishing : (1) A Common Market; (2) An economic and monetary union; and by implementing the common policies and activities, (*shown below*), shall have the tasks of promoting : (a) a harmonious and balanced development of economic activities; (b) sustainable and non-inflationary growth respecting the environment; (c) a high degree of convergence of economic performance; (d) a high level of employment and of social protection; (e) the raising of the standard of living and quality of life; (f) economic and social cohesion and solidarity among Member States.	*In addition :* (e) a high level of protection and improvement of the quality of the environment; (f) equality between men and women; *Amended to :* (c) A high degree of **competitiveness** and convergence of economic performance;
The activities of the Community shall include : (a) The elimination of customs duties and restrictions on imports and exports between Member States; (b) A common customs tariff and a common commercial policy towards third countries; (c) Abolition of obstacles to the freedom of movement for persons, services and capital; (d) A common policy for agriculture; (e) A common policy for transport; (f) A system to ensure that competition in the Common Market is not distorted;	*The activities of the Community in the Treaty of Rome are expanded:* (1) *Article 3.b in the Treaty of Rome becomes:* 'a common commercial policy'; (2) *The Maastricht Treaty adds the following (lettering from the Treaty):* (j) Strengthening of economic and social cohesion; (k) A policy for the environment; (l) Strengthening of the competitiveness of Community industry; (m) Promotion of research and technological development; (n) Establishment and development of trans-European networks;	*The activities are expanded by one additional factor :* (i) the promotion of co-ordination between employment policies of the Member States with a view to enhancing their effectiveness by developing a co-ordinated strategy for employment.

Treaty of Rome and Single European Act	Maastricht Treaty	Treaty of Amsterdam
Principles : (Continued)		

Treaty of Rome and Single European Act

(g) To co-ordinate the economic policies of Member States and rectify any disequilibria in their balances of payments;
(h) Approximation of the laws of Member States to the extent necessary for the proper functioning of the Common Market;
(i) Creation of the European Social fund;
(j) Establishment of a European Investment Bank;
(k) Association of overseas countries.

Maastricht Treaty

(o) Attainment of a high level of health protection;
(p) Education, training and the development of the cultures of the Member States;
(q) A policy for development co-operation;
(r) Increase trade through the association of the overseas countries;
(s) Strengthening of consumer protection;
(t) Measures in the spheres of energy, civil protection and tourism.

(Articles 8 - 8c become 14 and 15).

In addition :
In accordance with the principle of an open market economy and free competition, the Member States and the Community will adopt the economic policy, based on the close co-ordination of their individual economic policies, to include the irrevocable fixing of exchange rates leading to the introduction of a single currency and the conduct of a single monetary policy and exchange rate policy; the objectives of both is to maintain price stability (Article **4**).

Subsidiarity and Proportionality :
(Article **5**)

The institutions of the Community will act if the Community considers that an initiative cannot be left to the Member States alone.
This is particularly relevant where the Treaty calls for harmonisation, since this necessarily involves supranational action.
***Subsidiarity** will determine whether action should be taken at Community level. **Proportionality** will operate in limiting the scope and ensuring that the action complies with the terms of the Treaty.*

Treaty of Amsterdam

In addition :
The Community shall aim to eliminate inequalities and to promote equality between men and women.

*The Treaty of Amsterdam attaches a Protocol to the Treaty which is intended to define precisely the criteria for the **application of the principles of Subsidiarity and Proportionality**, including the strict observance and consistent implementation, by all the Community institutions.*

The references to paragraphs are to this Protocol.

Community legislation must be justified, in terms of Subsidiarity and Proportionality, qualitatively and preferably quantitatively (Para 4).

Treaty of Rome and Single European Act	Maastricht Treaty	Treaty of Amsterdam
Principles : (Continued)		

The Commission should:

(a) Consult widely before proposing legislation;

(b) Justify the relevance of its proposals;

(c) Ensure that the financial and administrative burden falling on the community is minimised and proportionate to the objective;

(d) Submit an annual report to the European Council, the Council and the European Parliament. (Para 9).

The Council will inform the European Parliament of its position on the application of these principles.

Subsidiarity :

The Community will act either within the powers of the Treaty or where the proposed action can be better achieved by the Community rather than by the Member States.

The principle of Subsidiarity does not question the powers of the Community defined by the Treaty, as interpreted by the Court of Justice.

The Subsidiarity criteria will NOT apply where the Community has exclusive competence (Para. 3).

Subsidiarity is a dynamic concept and should be applied in the context of the Treaty, allowing the powers of the community to be expanded where necessary.

The following guidelines should be used:

(a) The issue has trans-national aspects;

(b) Action by the Member States or lack of action would conflict with the requirements of the Treaty;

(c) Community action would produce clear benefits (Para. 5).

Community action should be as simple as possible, with directives being preferred as the Member States can choose how to enforce them.

Member States are required to take all appropriate measures to fulfil their Treaty obligations and not to prevent the attainment of the Treaty objectives (Article 5 and Protocol, Para. 8).

Treaty of Rome and Single European Act	Maastricht Treaty	Treaty of Amsterdam
Principles : (Continued)		
	Proportionality : Any action by the Community will not go beyond what is necessary to achieve the objectives of the Treaty.	Community measures should leave as much scope for national decision and respect national arrangements.
		Environment : Environmental protection requirements must be included in Community policies and activities. (Article **6**).
	A European System of Central Banks, a European Central Bank and a European Investment Bank shall be established, with their powers limited by the protocols attached to the Treaty.	
Member States shall co-ordinate their respective economic policies to the extent necessary to attain the objectives of this Treaty. **The Institutions of the Community shall take care not to prejudice the internal and external financial stability of the Member States.**	~ *Article repealed.*	
The Council may, by **qualified majority**, adopt rules to prohibit any discrimination on the grounds of nationality (Article **12**).	*In addition:* The method of the qualified majority voting is defined by Article **252**.	*Changed to :* The Council will act by **qualified majority under Article 251.**
		Discrimination: The Council, acting *unanimously* on a proposal form the Commission and after consulting the European Parliament, may take action to prevent discrimination based on sex, race or ethnic origin, religion, disability, age, or sexual orientation (Article **13**).
The Common Market will be established progressively during a transitional period of twelve years.		
The transitional period will not last longer than fifteen years from the date of the Treaty of Rome (i.e. to 1 January 1973). The expiry date shall constitute the latest date by which all the rules laid down must enter into force and all the measures required for establishing the Common Market must be implemented.		

Treaty of Rome and Single European Act	Maastricht Treaty	Treaty of Amsterdam

Principles :
(Continued)

The Stages involved in this may be extended or curtailed by the Council acting *unanimously*.
The Commission will report to the Council before 31 December 1988 and again before 31 December 1990 on the progress to the Internal Market.

The Internal Market will be introduced over a period expiring on 31 December 1992.
The Council, acting by **qualified majority**, will determine the guidelines for progress (Article **14**).

When drawing up its proposals for the Common Market, the Commission shall take into account the differences in development of the economies of the Member States and may propose appropriate provisions.
If there are derogations for certain Member States, they must be of a temporary nature (Article **15**).

Public services provided by the Community and Member States will comply with the principles of the EU and will not be supported by national aid which discriminates against free trade (Article **16**).

Citizenship of the Union :
(Articles **17** - **22**)

Every person who is a national of a Member State shall become a citizen of the Union, subject to the terms of this Treaty.
The Council shall act *unanimously* to adopt provisions to establish the right of every citizen to move and reside freely within the territory of the Member States.
Citizens will have the right to vote and to stand as candidates in municipal and European Parliament elections in the country they are residing.
The detailed arrangements will be adopted by the Council, acting *unanimously*.

In addition :
Citizenship of the Union shall complement and not replace national citizenship.
Changed to :
The Council will act *unanimously* under **Article 251**.

Treaty of Rome and Single European Act	Maastricht Treaty	Treaty of Amsterdam
Principles : (Continued)		
	Citizens have the right to diplomatic cover from any of the Member States in any third country where his own country is not present. Citizens have the right to petition the European Parliament and the Ombudsman.	*In addition :* All Citizens may write to any of the Institutions in any of the official languages and have an answer in the same language.
	Member States shall establish the necessary rules before 31 December 1993. The Council, acting *unanimously*, every 3 years may make provisions to strengthen or to add to the rights of citizenship.	
Free movement of goods : (Articles **23 – 31**) The Community shall be based on a customs union which will prohibit any customs duties being placed on imports and exports of goods between Member States.		
The Commission shall determine the methods of administering co-operation and shall lay down the provisions applicable to trade between Member States.		*~ Article repealed.*
(1) Customs Union : (Articles **25 - 27**) Member States shall refrain from introducing any new customs duties between themselves; customs duties in existence between Member States shall be progressively abolished.		*Changed to :* Customs duties between Member States will be prohibited on imports and exports.
The Commission shall decide by directives the timetable for this abolition. The Council shall act by **qualified majority** to adopt the timetable.		*~ Article repealed.*
The Council, acting by **qualified majority**, shall issue directives to settle any special problems. These provisions may be amended by the Council, acting by **qualified majority**.		*~ Articles repealed.*

Treaty of Rome and Single European Act	Maastricht Treaty	Treaty of Amsterdam

(1) Customs Union :
(Continued)

The Council shall determine the duties in the common customs tariff, acting *unanimously* during the first two Stages and by **qualified majority** thereafter.

Changed to :
The Council, acting by **qualified majority** will fix the common customs tariff.

The Council, acting by **qualified majority**, may grant a Member State a reduced rate of duty where the supply of goods to meet a demand is such that this is necessary.
The Commission may authorise a Member State, which has special diffi-culties, to adjust the tariffs. Such authorisation may only be granted for a limited period.

~ Articles repealed.

Any alterations or suspension of duties shall be decided by the Council, acting by **qualified majority**. The Council may act by **qualified majority** to decide on alterations which shall not exceed 20% of the rate of duty for a period of six months. The Commission will be guided by (inter alia):
(a) The need to promote trade and competition in the Community;
(b) To avoid serious disturbances in the Member States' economies.

~ Article repealed.

(2) Elimination of Quantitative Restrictions between Member States:
(Articles **28 - 31**)

Title changed to:
'Prohibition of quantitative restrictions'

Restrictions on imports and exports (i.e. quotas) shall be prohibited between Member States, unless justified on grounds of public policy or security.

~ Articles repealed.

The quotas in existence shall be progressively reduced during the transitional period. During that period, the quotas shall be progressively abolished in accordance with the detailed pro-visions laid down in the Treaty.

Treaty of Rome and Single European Act	Maastricht Treaty	Treaty of Amsterdam

Treaty of Rome and Single European Act

(2) Elimination of Quantitative Restrictions between Member States:
(Continued)

The Commission shall issue directives to establish the procedure and timetable for Member States to abolish any quotas between themselves.

The Commission shall define the appropriate quotas and the Council, acting by **qualified majority**, may modify these quotas.
The Council, acting *unanimously* for the first two stages and by **qualified majority** thereafter, may amend the procedures for the procedure to abolish the quotas.

Member States will ensure that there is no discrimination on goods between Member States.
Member States will not introduce any restrictions on goods (Article **31**).

Agriculture :
(Articles **32** - **38**)

The Common Market shall apply to agriculture and agricultural products.

The Council, acting by **qualified majority**, shall decide what these products are.

The operation and development of the Common Market for agricultural products must be accompanied by the establishment of a Common Agricultural Policy (CAP) among the Member States.

The Council, acting *unanimously* for the first two Stages and by **qualified majority** thereafter, shall make regulations, issue directives and take decisions to work out and implement the CAP.

The Council may authorise aid to be given if:
(a) Protection of enterprises handicapped by structural or natural conditions;
(b) Economic development programmes (Article **36**).

Treaty of Amsterdam

~ Articles repealed.

~ Article repealed.

~ Article repealed.

Treaty of Rome and Single European Act	Maastricht Treaty	Treaty of Amsterdam
Agriculture : (Continued)		
The Commission will submit proposals for implementing the CAP. The Council, acting by **qualified majority**, may replace the national market organisations by the common organisation (Article **37**.3). The Council, acting *unanimously*, shall determine objective criteria for the establishment of minimum price systems and for the fixing of such prices. The Council, acting by **qualified majority**, may rectify any decisions taken by the Member States which do not conform to the CAP.		*~ Article repealed.*
At the end of the transitional period, the Council, acting by a majority based on the weighting in Article **205**(2), will determine the system of minimum prices to be used.		*~ Article repealed.*
The Council may, acting *unanimously*, allow compensation payments to Member States which import raw materials from third countries (Article 45.3 [old numbering]).		*~ Article repealed.*
Free Movement of Persons, Services and Capital :		
(1) Workers : (Articles **39** - **42**)		
Freedom of movement for workers shall entail the abolition of any discrimination based on nationality between workers of the Member States.		
The Council, acting by **qualified majority**, shall issue directives or make regulations setting out the measures required to bring about the freedom of movement of workers.	The Council shall adopt directives to free the movement of workers, acting by **qualified majority under Article 251**.	
The Council shall act *unanimously* to adopt social security measures for the freedom of movement of Community immigrant workers (Article **42**).		*Method of voting changed :* The Council will act *unanimously* under **the procedures of Article 251**.

Treaty of Rome and Single European Act	Maastricht Treaty	Treaty of Amsterdam

(2) Right of Establishment :
(Articles **43** - **48**)

Restrictions on the right of freedom of establishment of a citizen of the Union in any Member State will be abolished.

Freedom of establishment shall include the right of nationals of a Member State to take up and pursue activities as self-employed persons and to set up and manage businesses, agencies, branches or subsidiaries in any Member State.

The Council, acting *unanimously*, before the end of the First Stage, shall draw up a general programme for the abolition of any existing restrictions.

~ Article repealed.

The Council, acting *unanimously* for the First Stage and by **qualified majority** thereafter, shall issue directives to implement the general programme (Article **44**).

The method of voting is replaced by : The Council shall act by **qualified majority under Article 251**.

The Council, acting *unanimously* shall issue directives for the co-ordination of provisions for special treatment of foreign nationals (Article **46**).

The method of voting is replaced by : The Council shall act by **qualified majority under Article 251**.

The Council, acting *unanimously* during the First Stage and by **qualified majority** thereafter, shall issue directives for the mutual recognition of formal qualifications.
The Council shall issue directives for the co-ordination of the laws in each Member State concerning the activities of self-employed persons. The Council will act *unanimously* for the First Stage and by **qualified majority** thereafter.

The method of voting changed to : The Council will act by **qualified majority under Article 251**.

The Council shall act *unanimously* to issue directives, regarding training and conditions for entry into the professions, where this will require at least one Member State having to change its existing laws.

The method of voting changed to : The council will act *unanimously* under **the procedure of Article 251**.

Treaty of Rome and Single European Act	Maastricht Treaty	Treaty of Amsterdam

(3) Services :
(Articles **49** - **55**)

Restrictions will be abolished regarding the freedom of a national of one Member State to provide services to nationals of any Member State.
Services are defined as including activities in industry, commerce, crafts and the professions.

The Council, acting by **qualified majority**, may extend the provisions to cover nationals of third countries who are living in the Community.

The Council shall act by **qualified majority** on proposals from the Commission in relation to the general programme for the abolition of existing restrictions.

The Council, acting *unanimously* during the First Stage and by **qualified majority** thereafter, shall issue directives for the abolition of the restrictions.
The Council, acting by **qualified majority**, may extend the provisions to nationals of third countries.

(4) Capital and Payments :
(Articles **56** - **60**)

During the Transitional Stage, Member States shall abolish between themselves all restrictions on the movement of capital and current payments relating to the movement of capital belonging to nationals of Member States.

The Council, acting *unanimously* for the first two Stages and by **qualified majority** thereafter, shall issue the necessary directives to implement the freedom of movement of capital and payments.
The Council, acting by **qualified majority**, shall issue directives regarding the progressive co-ordination of exchange policies to endeavour to attain the highest possible of liberalisation.
Unanimity is required to reverse this process.

The Maastricht Treaty replaces the whole of the Chapter on Capital and Payments, with effect from 1 January 1994 as it is assumed that the Transitional Period has finished.

Replaced by :
Restrictions on the movement of capital and capital between Member States and between Member States and third countries shall be prohibited as from 1st January 1994.

The Council, acting by **qualified majority**, may adopt measures on the movement of capital to and from third countries.
Unanimity is required to reverse this process of liberalisation.

Treaty of Rome and Single European Act	Maastricht Treaty	Treaty of Amsterdam
(4) Capital and Payments : (Continued) Member States shall avoid introducing any new exchange restrictions on the movement of capital. If this occurs, the Commission can make recom-mendations to that Member State. If the capital markets of a Member State are disturbed by capital movements, the Commission may authorise that State to take protective measures. The Council may, by **qualified majority**, revoke this.	*In addition :* Member States have the right to apply: (1) the appropriate provisions of their own tax law which has different treatments for tax-payers depending their residence and the location of their capital. (2) take all appropriate measures to prevent tax avoidance, ensure the security of financial instit-utions and to maintain public security. (Article **58**). The Council, acting by **qualified majority**, may take safeguard mea-sures against third countries regarding secure operation of Economic and Monetary Union. A Member State, for serious political reasons, may take unilateral measures against a third country; the Council, acting by **qualified majority**, may decide that the Member State shall amend or abolish such measures. (Article **60**).	

Treaty of Amsterdam

Free Movement of Persons, Asylum and Immigration :
(Articles **61 – 79**)

This is a new Title and the measures concern the free movement of persons within the Community while maintaining external border controls, including the issue of visas. The intention is to make the co-operation between the Member States more coherent and consistent.
*The Title introduces the terms of the **Schengen acquis** into the Treaty on European Union. The Schengen acquis concerns the gradual abolition of checks at the common borders of the signatory countries, and is described in detail in a Protocol attached to the Treaty.*
The United Kingdom and Ireland (which did not sign the Schengen acquis) and Denmark have arranged exclusions from the Treaty provisions, shown in two additional Protocols. These allow the three countries to retain their own border controls. The Treaty provisions and the Schengen acquis will not be binding on these countries.

The Council will adopt measures to progressively establish an area of freedom, security and justice.
These measures will concern *inter alia*:
(a) free movement of persons together with measures with respect to external borders control, asylum and immigration, refugees and displaced persons and crime (to be introduced within a period of five years of the date of this Treaty);
(b) Asylum, immigration and safe-guarding the rights of third country nationals;
(c) Police and judicial co-operation in civil and criminal matters concerning national borders;
(d) Encouraging and strengthening administrative co-operation between the Member States (Article **61**).

The Council will adopt measures, within five years of the date of the Treaty, on the crossing of external borders of the Member States concerning the following (*the method of voting is noted after each item*):
(a) Standards and procedures on checks on persons (*unanimously)*;
(b) Rules on visas for stays of no more than three months:
    (1) Uniform format of visas and the countries which require visas (**qualified majority**);
    (2) Procedures and conditions for issuing visas and rules for a uniform visa (*unanimously* for five years and then by **qualified majority under Article 251**).

Member States will still be able to negotiate or conclude agreements with third countries as long as they respect Community law (*Protocol on External Relations*).

The measures on asylum, refugees and displaced persons and immigration policy will include:
(a) minimum standards for the reception of asylum seekers, their qualification as asylum seekers and the procedures for granting or withdrawing refugee status;
(b) minimum standards on giving temporary protection;
(c) conditions of entry and residence and the issuing of long-term visas (Article **63**).

Member States will not be prevented from introducing national provisions which are compatible with this Treaty (Article **63**.5).

Member States still retain the responsibility of law and order and internal security.

If Member States have an emergency situation due to an inflow of people from third countries, the Council may, acting by **qualified majority**, adopt provisional measures (to last no longer than six months) to help the Member States concerned (Article **64**).

Member States shall be regarded as being safe countries for asylum matters and therefore a national of one Member State will not generally be considered admissible for asylum in another Member State unless *inter alia*:
(a) if there is a serious breach by a Member State of the fundamental principles on which the Community is founded (Article **6** of the Common Provisions, see page 8);
(b) if a Member State should so decide for a particular application.

Judicial co-operation in civil matters will be aimed at:
(a) improving and simplifying the system of co-operation of passing documents, taking evidence, and the recognition and enforcement of decisions;
(b) promoting the compatibility of laws and jurisdiction, including the rules on civil procedure (Article **65**).

Treaty of Amsterdam

Free Movement of Persons, Asylum and Immigration :
(Continued)

The Court of Justice may give preliminary rulings on any matter which a national court of a Member State requests a ruling.

The Court of Justice cannot rule on any matter of Member State's national law and order or internal security (Article **68**).

Method of voting :

The Council will act *unanimously* (after consulting the European Parliament) on a proposal from the Commission or from a Member State for a transitional period of five years from the date of the Treaty.

After this period of five years:
(a) the Council will act on proposals from the Commission, which will examine requests from the Member States;
(b) The Council, acting *unanimously* after consulting the European Parliament, will decide whether to act by **qualified majority** under **Article 189b** for measures under this Title and for adapting the powers of the Court of Justice.

The Schengen *acquis:*

The Council, acting *unanimously*, shall within five years, introduce measures to remove any controls on persons crossing internal borders (Article **62**).

The Schengen *acquis* (*shown in the Protocol integrating the Schengen acquis into the European Union*) is intended to enhance European integration. The Council will act *unanimously* to decide on the legal basis for each of the provisions or decisions adopted under the Schengen *acquis*.

The UK, Ireland and Denmark will continue to maintain their border controls with the other EU Member States as is considered necessary for the purpose of:
(a) verifying the right to enter the UK, Ireland and Denmark of EU and EEA citizens as well as other nationals whose right to enter has been conferred by Community law;
(b) deciding whether to grant other persons permission to enter the UK (*Protocol on the application of certain aspects of Article 14 to the United Kingdom*, Article 1 and *Protocol on the position of Denmark*, Articles 1 & 2).

The UK and Ireland may continue to have special travel arrangements between themselves (*Protocol on the application of certain aspects of Article 14 to the United Kingdom* , Article 2).

The other Member States may exercise controls on persons seeking to enter from the UK or Ireland (*Protocol on the application of certain aspects of Article 14 to the United Kingdom,* Article 3).

The UK, Ireland and Denmark will not bear any financial consequences of measures brought under the Treaty provisions unless either of them agree to adopt the proposed measures (*Protocol on the position of the United Kingdom and Ireland,* Article 5 and *Protocol on the position of Denmark*, Article 3).

Denmark may have up to six months after the Council has decided to act to choose whether to implement a Council proposal or initiative into national law (*Protocol on the position of Denmark, Article 5*).

Ireland and Denmark may inform the Council of their wish to opt back into the terms of the Treaty, in which case the Schengen acquis would apply, (*Protocol on the position of the United Kingdom and Ireland*, Article 3 *and Protocol on the position of Denmark*, Article 1 & 2).

The UK may select which specific Council measures it chooses to follow (*Protocol on the position of the United Kingdom and Ireland*, Article 3).

If Ireland or the United Kingdom wish to take part in the Schengen acquis, the Council will decide on the *unanimity* of the currently participating countries (*Protocol integrating the Schengen acquis*, Article 4).

Treaty of Rome and Single European Act	Maastricht Treaty	Treaty of Amsterdam

Transport :
(Articles **70 – 80**)

The Community shall have a common transport policy, whereby there will be common rules for international transport between and across Member States.

In addition:
The Council shall lay down measures to improve transport safety

The Council will act *unanimously* for the first two Stages and then by **qualified majority** thereafter to achieve the common transport policy. The provisions will concern:
(a) common rules for international transport to or from Member States' territory;
(b) conditions for non-resident carriers to operate.

The Council shall act by **qualified majority** under Article **252**.

Additional provision:
(c) measures to improve transport safety.

Method of voting changed to :
The Council will act by **qualified majority under Article 251** (Article **71**.1).

Where there is a serious effect on the standard of living in a particular region, the Council may act *unanimously*.

The Council will act *unanimously* after consulting the European Parliament and the Economic and Social Committee.

Each Member State must have the *unanimous* approval of the Council to have provisions less favourable to other Member States' carriers as opposed to their own (Article **72**).

The Council, acting by **qualified majority**, within two years of the Treaty being in force, shall lay down rules for the abolition of discrimination of carriers from different Member States charging different rates for the carriage of goods.

The Council will be able to adopt any measures to further the aims of a common transport policy.
The Commission can investigate any case of discrimination, either on its own initiative or on application from a Member State. The Commission can take any decision it considers necessary to resolve the discrimination.

An Advisory Committee, selected by the governments of the Member States, shall be attached to the Commission.

Treaty of Rome and Single European Act	Maastricht Treaty	Treaty of Amsterdam

Transport :
(Continued)

The Commission may consult the committee about transport matters whenever it considers it to be desirable.
(Article **79**).

The Commission shall act by **qualified majority** to decide on what provisions to be decided on sea and air transport.
(Article **80**).

Changed to :
The Council will act by **qualified majority** under Article **252** (Article **80**.2).

Changed to :
The Council will act by **qualified majority under Article 251.**

Common Rules on Competition, Taxation and Approximation of Laws:

(1)   Rules on Competition :
(Articles **81 - 86**)

Any agreement which prevents, restricts or distorts competition within the Common Market shall be prohibited.

The Council shall act *unanimously* to adopt regulations or directives to prohibit any such agreements.

Changed to:
The Council, acting by a **qualified majority**, will adopt appropriate regulations and directives to implement the rules on competition.

If these provisions are not adopted within three years of the date of the treaty, then the Council, acting by **qualified majority**, shall enforce the prohibitions, by **fines and periodic penalties** (Article **83**.2a).

Dumping: The Commission will lay down rules for the prevention of dump-ing of goods within the Common Market.

~ Article repealed.

Aid granted by States: Any aid granted by a Member State which distorts competition shall be incompatible with the Common Market, in so far as it affects trade between Member States.

Aid considered to be compatible with the Common Market includes:
(1)   economic development of poorer areas;
(2)   development of economic activities or areas, which does not affect the common interest.

In addition:
(3)   aid to promote culture and heritage conservation, which does not affect trading conditions.

Treaty of Rome and Single European Act	Maastricht Treaty	Treaty of Amsterdam

(1) Rules on Competition :
(Continued)

The Council, acting by **qualified majority**, may adopt any category of state aid which is compatible with the Treaty and make any appropriate regulations to prohibit aid which distorts competition.

The Commission shall keep all systems of aid under constant review. The Commission can decide that the Member State must abolish any aid which is incompatible with the Treaty.

In addition:
The Council will consult the European Parliament.

(2) Tax Provisions :
(Articles **90 - 95**)

Member States shall not impose any tax on the goods of another Member State which is in excess of that imposed on similar domestic products.

Member States shall repeal any existing laws which conflict with this Treaty.

~ Paragraph deleted.

Where the average rates of tax in a Member State do not conform to the provisions of the Treaty, the Comm- ission will issue directives or decisions to the state concerned.

~ Article repealed.

The Council, acting *unanimously*, after consulting the European Parliament, will adopt proposals for the harmonisation of legislation regarding turnover taxes and indirect taxation (ie VAT), for the purpose of the process of harmonisation for the establishment and functioning of the Internal Market.

In addition:
The Council will consult the Economic and Social Committee.

(3) Approximation of Laws :
(Articles **94 - 97**)

The Council, acting *unanimously*, will issue Directives for the approximation [*or   harmonisation*] of laws, regulations and provisions in the Member States directly affecting the establishment and functioning of the Common Market. (Article **94**).

Treaty of Rome and Single European Act	Maastricht Treaty	Treaty of Amsterdam

(3) Approximation of Laws :
   (Continued)

The European Parliament and the Economic and Social Committee shall be consulted where Directives would mean the amendment of legislation in any of the Member States.

Replaced by :
The Council will consult the European Parliament and the Economic and Social Committee when issuing Directives to promote the Common Market.

The Council, acting by **qualified majority**, shall adopt measures for the approximation of laws which have as their objective the achievement of the Common Market [*as described in Article 14*].

Changed by :
The Council will act by **qualified majority under Article 251**.

These measures will **not** include:
(a)   fiscal provisions;
(b)   free movement of people;
(c)   rights of employed people.

The Commission, in drawing up these measures, will have a high base level of protection on health, safety, environmental and consumer protection.

In addition :
The Commission, the European Parliament and the Council will take into account any new development of scientific knowledge.

If, after a harmonisation measure has been adopted, Member States will inform the Commission of any new national laws based on new scientific evidence.

Within six months of being notified, the Commission may approve, adapt or reject the national provisions if they restrict the functioning of the Internal Market.

If the Commission does not form an opinion in the six months, the provisions will be approved.

The six month period may be extended by a further six months.

When a Member State raises a specific problem on public health, already covered by a harmonisation measure, the Commission shall decide whether to propose measures to the Council. (Article **95**.3-8).

Treaty of Rome and Single European Act	Maastricht Treaty	Treaty of Amsterdam
(3) Approximation of Laws : (Continued)		
The Commission shall draw up a list of laws in Member States which have not been harmonised by 1992.		*~ Article repealed.*
The Council, acting by **qualified majority**, may decide that the provisions in force must be recognised as being equivalent to those applied in other Member States.		
	In addition : The Council, acting *unanimously*, shall determine which third countries require visas. The Council, by **qualified majority**, may introduce visa requirements for up to six months in emergencies of a sudden inflow of nationals from that country into the Community.	*~ Articles repealed.*
	From 1 January 1996, the Council shall act by **qualified majority**. Before that date, the Council, acting by **qualified majority**, shall issue a uniform format of visa. This Article will not affect the responsibilities of the Member States in co-operation in the Co-ordinating Committee in 'Justice and Home Affairs' (Articles 100c and 100d [old numbering]).	*~ Articles repealed.*
Where differences in law distorts the conditions of competition, the Commission will consult the Member State concerned and then make proposals to correct them. The Council, acting *unanimously* for the first stage and by **qualified majority** thereafter, shall issue the necessary directives to eliminate the distortions. The Commission and the Council may take any other appropriate measures they consider necessary.		*Changed to:* The Council will act by **qualified majority** to issue the necessary directives (Article **96**).

Economic Policy :
(Articles **98** - **124**)

The following analysis shows the development of Economic Policy leading to Economic and Monetary Union. Since the Policy has been rewritten in the Maastricht Treaty, the layout takes each Treaty in turn as there is no direct comparison between the three Treaties.

There have been no changes made to this Policy by the Treaty of Amsterdam.

Treaty of Rome and Single European Act

Conjunctural Policy :
(Article **99**)

Member States shall regard their economic policies and the process to combine their economic policies as a matter of common concern. Member States will consult one another and the Commission on any appropriate measures to be taken.
The Council, acting *unanimously*, may decide on the appropriate measures.
The Council, acting by **qualified majority**, may adopt any directives to give effect to the measures decided.

Balance of Payments :
(Articles **101** - **111**)

The Member States shall ensure the equilibrium of its overall balance of payments, maintain confidence in its currency and a stable level of prices.
Member States shall co-ordinate their economic policies.
A Monetary Committee shall be formed to promote the co-ordination of the policies.
The Commission shall make recommendations to the Council on how to achieve this co-operation.

Member States shall declare their readiness to undertake the liberalisation of payments between one another and they undertake not to introduce any new restrictions on transfers relating to invisible trade.
Member States shall treat its policy regarding rates of exchange as a matter of common concern.

If a Member State changes its rate of exchange, the Commission may authorise the other Member States to take the necessary measures to counter the consequences of this.
The authorisation will be for a limited period and the Commission shall determine the details of the measures to be taken.

The following articles refer to the Economic Policy up to the start of the Third Stage. The amendments made by the **Maastricht Treaty** *are noted below in italics.*

Where a Member State is in difficulties regarding its balance of payments, to the extent that it threatens the functioning of the Common Market, the Commission shall investigate the situation.
The Commission shall make recommendations to the state concerned.
The Council, acting by **qualified majority**, shall grant any mutual assistance as is appropriate; it shall adopt directives or decisions which lay down the conditions and details for the assistance.

The Commission shall authorise the state which is in difficulties to take protective measures *if the Council does not grant the assistance*. The Commission shall determine the conditions and the details for these measures. The authorisation for this may be revoked by the Council, acting by **qualified majority.** *This provision shall cease to apply from the Third Stage.*
(Article **119**).

Where there is a sudden crisis in the balance of payments in a Member State, *and the Council and the Commission have not taken a decision on this*, that State may take protective measures. *These measures must cause the least disturbance to the Common Market.*
The Council, acting by **qualified majority**, may decide that the Member State shall amend, suspend or abolish the protective measures taken. *This provision shall cease to apply from the Third Stage.* (Article **120**).

Treaty of Rome and Single European Act

Co-operation in Economic and Monetary Policy (Economic and Monetary Union) :

*Article **98** was added by the **Single European Act** in order to incorporate on a formal basis the aim of establishing a Single Currency.*

Member States shall co-operate to ensure the convergence of economic and monetary policies, necessary for the further development of the Community (*i.e. EMU*), by ensuring the equilibrium of their overall balance of payments, maintaining confidence in their currencies and maintaining a stable level of prices.

They shall respect the existing powers of the European Monetary System and the development of the ECU.

Maastricht Treaty

*In the Maastricht Treaty, the whole of the Title on **Economic Policy** has been replaced and re-titled:*
Economic and Monetary Policy :

The purpose of the Economic and Monetary Policy is to provide a legal framework for economic and monetary union, leading to the establishment of a single currency.
The policy identifies three Stages:
*The **First Stage** started on 1 July 1990, following the acceptance of the 'Delors Report' and the coming into force of a directive on the free movement of capital.*
*The **Second Stage** started on 1 January 1994.*
*The **Third Stage** will start on 1 January 1999, if the date for the beginning of this Stage has not been set by 31 December 1997. This Stage is the formal start of the Single Currency and EMU. The Treaty does not describe the detailed methodology of how the Single Currency will be introduced.*

At the start of the Second Stage, the European Monetary Institute was formed and will prepare for the introduction of the Single Currency. It will be replaced, in the Third Stage, by the European Central Bank.

The Maastricht Treaty is principally concerned with the Second and Third Stages of Economic and Monetary Union. Until the start of the Second Stage, the provisions of the Treaty of Rome, the Single European Act and the associated directives would remain in force.

The name of the Single Currency has been agreed to be the 'Euro', after the date of the signing of the Maastricht Treaty. As the term 'ECU' is used in the Treaty, this has been retained in the following analysis. The Euro will be the unit of the Single Currency while the ECU will continue to be the unit of the 'basket of currencies' in the Second Stage.

Second Stage of Economic and Monetary Union :

Economic Policy :

Member States shall regard their economic policies as a matter of common concern and will co-ordinate their economic policies with the Council, with the intention to achieve the objectives of the Community, *i.e. Economic and Monetary Union, as described in Article 2* (Article **98** and **99**).

The Council, acting by **qualified majority**, may formulate a draft for broad guidelines of the economic policies of the Member States and the Community.
The Council, acting by **qualified majority**, may adopt a recommendation setting out the guidelines, which have been agreed by the European Council.

The Council will monitor the economic developments and the consistency of the economic growth in each Member State and the Community.
For the purposes of this multilateral surveillance, Member States must provide information about the important measures they have taken regarding their economic policies.
The Council, acting by **qualified majority** under Article **252**, may adopt detailed rules for the surveillance procedure.

Where the economic policies of a Member State are not consistent with these guidelines or they risk jeopardising the proper functioning of the Common Market, the Council, acting by **qualified majority**, may make recommendations to that Member State.
The Council, acting *unanimously*, may decide on measures appropriate to the situation, if severe difficulties arise in the supply of certain products.

Maastricht Treaty

Economic and Monetary Policy :
(Continued)

Where a Member State is in severe difficulties, the Council, acting *unanimously*, may grant Community aid to that Member State. If the difficulties are caused by natural disasters, the Council will act by **qualified majority**.

The Community shall not be liable for the commitments of Member States.
A Member State shall not be liable for the commitments of another Member State (Article **103**).
The Council, acting by **qualified majority** under Article **252**, may specify the prohibitions.

Member States shall endeavour to avoid excessive government budget deficits. The Commission will monitor the budgets and budgetary discipline in the Member States, based on two reference values of excessive government budget deficits (Article **104**). *See Criteria for Entry to Third Stage, below.*

Where a Member State does not meet the requirements of the Treaty, or if the Member State has met the criteria requirements and the Commission considers that there is a risk of an excessive deficit, the Commission shall make recommendations to the Council (Article **104**.3).
The Council will make recommendations to the Member State for it to take measures to correct the deficit.

Monetary Policy in the Second Stage:

The **European Monetary Institute** (EMI) would be formed at the start of the Second Stage and is intended to act to co-ordinate the monetary policies of the Member States and make the preparations required for the formation of the ESCB.
It will usually act by a simple majority of its members to form and give recommendations and opinions.

The EMI is composed of the 15 governors of the national central banks of the Member States (*after the accession of Austria, Finland and Sweden*).

It shall have the following principal tasks :
(a)   strengthen co-operation between the national central banks;
(b)   strengthen the co-ordination of the monetary policies of the Member States with the aim of ensuring price stability;
(c)   monitor the functioning of the European Monetary System;
(d)   hold consultations on the stability of financial institutions and markets;
(e)   take over the tasks of the European Monetary Co-operation Fund, which will be dissolved;
(f)   facilitate the use of the ECU and oversee its development and smooth the functioning of the ECU clearing system.

Additional tasks will be:
(a) hold regular consultations concerning monetary policy;
(b) be consulted by the national monetary authorities before they take decisions on monetary policy.

The EMI will be funded by the national central banks of the Member States. The Council of the EMI will determine the size of the capital, acting by a **qualified majority** of two-thirds of the members.

The **share of the capital** which each national central bank will be required to pay will be calculated as the sum of the following:
(a)   50% of the share based on the proportion of the population of the Community in the Member State in the penultimate year before the establishment of the EMI;
(b)   50% of the share based on the proportion of the GDP of the Community produced by the Member State in the last five years before the penultimate year of the formation of the EMI (*Protocol on the EMI, Article 16*).

A **Monetary Committee** shall be set up at the start of the Second Stage. This committee will consist of two representatives from each Member State and from the Commission, including from those countries which remain in the Second Stage and will have the principal tasks of :
(a)   keeping under review the monetary and financial position of the Member States and of the Community;
(b)   to help with the work of the Council and the EMI in the economic and monetary policy;
(c)   to examine the movement of capital and the freedom of payments.

Maastricht Treaty

Transition to the Third Stage :

In order that the Third Stage can take place, there will be a transitional process to prepare the Community (Articles 116 - 124).

All Member States are obliged to respect the will of the Community to enter swiftly into the Third Stage, and will not prevent the Community from entering the Third Stage.
The Community Institutions and the Member States shall expedite all preparatory work in 1998 to ensure that the Community will irrevocably enter the Third Stage on 1 January 1999 and that the ECB and the ESCB will be able to start to fully operate from this date (*Protocol on the transition to the Third Stage of EMU*).

For the preparation of the Third Stage, the EMI shall *(inter alia)* :
(a)   Prepare the instruments and procedures necessary for the single monetary policy and the Single Currency;
(b)   Prepare the rules for the national central banks to operate in the European System of Central Banks (ESCB);
(c)   Promote the efficiency of cross-border payments;
(d)   Supervise the technical preparation of ECU bank notes.

At the latest by 31 December 1996, the EMI shall specify the regulatory, organisational and logistical framework necessary for the ESCB to perform its tasks in the Third Stage, following the principle of an open market economy with free competition (*Protocol on the EMI, Article 4*).

Criteria for entry to the Third Stage :

Member States must fulfil the necessary criteria for the adoption of a single currency. The Commission and the EMI will report to the Council on whether the Member States have met these conditions. The four criteria are :

(1)   The **average rate of inflation** is **no more than 1½%** greater, over a one year period before the report, than the three best performing Member States.

Inflation will be measured taking into account any differences in national definitions.

(2)   There is **no excessive budget deficit**. The deficits of the Member States will be monitored by the Commission. The two criteria used to assess budgetary discipline are defined as:
(a)   The ratio of the planned or actual **government deficit** to GDP at market prices **does not exceed 3%**;
(b)   The ratio of **government debt** to GDP at market prices **does not exceed 60%**.

These criteria must either be strictly adhered to or the deficit must be shown to be exceptional and temporary, or it is sufficiently diminishing and approaching the reference values.

(3)   The currency has stayed within the **normal fluctuation margins of the Exchange Rate Mechanism** over a period of **two years** before the date of the report, without devaluing against the currency of any other Member State;

(4)   The average nominal **long-term interest rate** does **not exceed, by more than 2%** over a one year period before the report, the rates of the three best performing Member States.

Interest rates will be measured taking into account any differences in national definitions.

The Council, acting *unanimously* may alter the details of the convergence criteria for price stability on inflation and interest rates (*Protocol on the Convergence Criteria, Article 6*).

The Council, acting by **qualified majority**, on the basis of the reports from the Commission and the EMI, shall decide whether:
(a)   Each Member State fulfils the criteria for the adoption of a single currency;
(b)   A majority of the Member States fulfil the criteria for the adoption of a single currency.

The Council's recommendations will be passed to the European Council. The European Parliament will be consulted and its opinion passed to the European Council.

Maastricht Treaty

Economic and Monetary Policy :
(Continued)

The European Council, acting by **qualified majority**, on the basis of the reports from the Council, the Commission, the European Parliament and the EMI, and not later than 31 December 1996, will decide the following:
(a)   Whether a majority of the Member States fulfil the necessary conditions for the adoption of a single currency;
(b)   Whether it is appropriate for the Community to enter the Third Stage;
(c)   The date for the start of the Third Stage.

If by 31 December 1997, the date has not been set, the Third Stage shall start on 1 January 1999.

The European Council, acting by **qualified majority**, before 1 July 1998, will confirm which Member States fulfil the necessary conditions for the adoption of a single currency.

Those States which do not meet the criteria will remain in the Second Stage.

At least once every two years, the Commission and the ECB will report to the Council on the fulfilment of the convergence criteria by the Member States remaining in the Second Stage; the Council, acting by **qualified majority**, will decide which of these Member States may join the Single Currency.

During the Second Stage, Member States shall start the process leading to the independence of their central banks, so that by the start of the Third Stage, the national legislation is compatible with the Treaty.

The EMI and the Commission shall report to the European Council on the progress of the Member States in fulfilling the obligations regarding the achievement of Economic and Monetary Union.

Third Stage of Economic and Monetary Union :

The **European Central Bank** (ECB) will be formed and will take over the functions of the EMI. The EMI will then be put into liquidation, and all its assets will be passed to the ECB.

An **Economic and Financial Committee** will be formed and take over the functions of the Monetary Committee (described above), which will then be dissolved. All the Member States will be represented by two members each, unless the Council, acting by **qualified majority**, decides to modify the composition of the Committee.

The Council, acting with the *unanimity* of the Member States fulfilling the criteria for acceptance to the Third Stage, will adopt the conversion rates at which the currencies will be irrevocably fixed and the ECU will be substituted for these currencies. The ECU will become a currency in its own right.

Economic Policy :

*The Economic Policy in the **Third Stage** will include the provisions of the Second Stage and shall have the following additions*:

(1)   Where a Member State is in difficulties caused by exceptional occurrences beyond its control, the Council, acting *unanimously*, may grant Community financial assistance. Where the difficulties are caused by natural events, the Council can act by **qualified majority**.

(2)   Member States shall avoid excessive government budget deficits. *An excessive government budget deficit is defined above in the **Criteria for Entry to the Third Stage**.*
Member States must report planned and actual deficits promptly and regularly to the Commission.

(3)   Where a deficit occurs and a Member State fails to put into practice the recommendations of the Council, the Council can demand that the State concerned shall take the appropriate measures to correct the deficit.

Maastricht Treaty

Economic and Monetary Policy :
(Continued)

Economic Policy :
(Continued)

(4)   If the Member State fails to comply with a decision relating to the deficit, **the Council may impose fines on the Member State** and invite the European Investment Bank to reconsider its lending policy to that State. In addition, the Member State will be required to place **a non-interest bearing deposit** of an appropriate size with the Community until the excessive deficit has been corrected (Article **104**.11).

Monetary Policy :

*Monetary policy in the **Third Stage** will be guided by the ECB and the ESCB.*

The provisions of the Second Stage will continue to apply; there will be some additional provisions for the Third Stage and these will include the following :

The ESCB shall have, as its primary objective, the maintenance of price stability and support the objectives *inter alia* of economic and monetary union, convergence of economic performance, as shown in Article **2**.

The ESCB will act in accordance with the principle of an open market economy with free competition, and in accordance with the aims of price stability, the conduct of a single monetary policy and exchange rate policy, and supporting the general economic policies in the Community.

The basic tasks of the ESCB will be :

(1)   Define and implement the monetary policy of the Community;

(2)   Conduct foreign exchange operations of the ECU consistent with the aims of price stability and to form formal agreements with non-Community currencies;

(3)   Hold and manage the official foreign reserves of the Member States;

(4)   Promote the smooth operation of payment systems.

The ECB will be consulted on any proposal in its area of competence.

The Council, acting *unanimously*, may confer on the ECB specific tasks relating to the prudential supervision of credit institutions.

The ECB will have a Governing Council, which will consist of the Executive Council and the governors of the national central banks of the Member States, and will act usually by a simple majority.

The Executive Council will be composed of six members: the President, the Vice-President and four other members.

The capital of the ECB will be provided by the national central banks of the Member States and will initially be ECU 5,000 million.

This amount may be altered by the Governing Council, acting by **qualified majority** of at least two-thirds majority, with the votes weighted in proportion to the level of the subscribed capital.

The share of the capital which each national central bank will be required to pay will be calculated in the same manner as for the EMI, described above.

The statistical data for these criteria will be provided by the Commission (*Protocol on the ESCB, Article 29*).

The foreign reserve assets of the national central banks will be transferred to the ECB, up to an amount of ECU 50,000 million. This will not include the Member States' own currencies, ECUs, IMF reserves and Special Drawing Rights.

The contributions of each Member State will be based on the level of the subscribed capital (*Protocol on the ESCB, Article 30*).

Maastricht Treaty

Economic and Monetary Policy :
(Continued)

Monetary Policy :
(Continued)

The ECB will have the exclusive right to authorise the issue of bank notes within the Community. Only these bank notes will be legal tender within the Community.

Coins may be issued by Member States; the Council, acting by **qualified majority** under Article **252**, may adopt measures to harmonise the denomination and technical specifications of all coins to be issued.

The ESCB and the ECB will be totally independent of any Community institution or Member State government.

The ESCB and the ECB will be able to make regulations, decisions (binding), recommendations and opinions (not binding) in order to carry out the tasks defined in the Treaty.

The ECB will be exempt from **any** form of taxation.

The ECB will be entitled to **impose fines or periodic penalties** on undertakings for failure to comply with its directives and regulations (Article **110**.3).

The Council, acting *unanimously*, may conduct formal agreements on exchange rate systems for the ECU with non-Community concerns.

The Council, acting by **qualified majority**, may adopt, adjust or abandon the central rates of the ECU within the exchange rate system.

The purpose of these provisions is to ensure that the Community expresses a single position; the Commission shall be fully associated with these negotiations.

Decisions made by the Council will be binding on the ECB and Member States.

The Council, acting by **qualified majority**, will decide on the Community position at international level.

Where a Member State is in difficulties with regards to its balance of payments, to the extent of jeopardising the Common Market, the Commission shall investigate and make recommendations to that State.

The Council, acting by **qualified majority**, may grant any mutual assistance and shall adopt directives or decisions to lay down the conditions for this assistance.

The Court of Justice will have jurisdiction to give judgement on the fulfilment by national central banks and Member States of all obligations under the Treaty, including complying with the acts of the ECB (Articles **228**, **230** and **237**.d).

'Opt-out' of the United Kingdom :

The United Kingdom will not be obliged or committed to move to the Third Stage, unless there is a separate decision to do so by the British Government and Parliament. This is described in the 'Protocol on certain provisions relating to the United Kingdom' attached to the Treaty.

The effect of the 'Opt-out' is that the United Kingdom will be able to retain its powers of monetary policy and will not be influenced directly by the ECB, once this institution has been formed at the start of the Third Stage.

Procedure if the UK decides to join the Single Currency:

The UK will have to fulfil the **four entry criteria**, *described above*.

If the UK wishes to join the Single Currency **before the start** of the Third Stage, it will have to inform the Council before the time when the Council decides which of the Member States fulfil the entry criteria. The rest of the Protocol will not have effect and the UK would be bound by the terms of the main Treaty.

Maastricht Treaty

Economic and Monetary Policy :
(Continued)

'Opt-out' of the United Kingdom :
(Continued)

Procedure if the UK decides to join the Single Currency :
(Continued)

If the date for the start of the Third Stage has **not been set**, the UK must inform the Council of its intention to join the Third Stage by 1 January 1998 (*the Third Stage would begin on 1 January 1999 under the terms of the Treaty*).

If the UK decides to join **after the start of the Third Stage**, it will notify the Council, which will then decide if the UK fulfils the conditions for entry.

The Bank of England will be obliged to send its share of the subscribed capital to the ECB, transfer its foreign reserve assets and contribute to the reserves of the ECB in the same manner as the other Member States which had joined the Single Currency.

Procedure if the UK decides not to join the Single Currency:

The UK **must inform the Council of the decision** not to join the Third Stage in order that the opt-out would apply (*Paragraph 2 of the Protocol*).
Once the Council has been informed, the UK will not have to subscribe its capital or assets to the ECB, as described above, and the following will apply:

(1)   The UK will retain its powers over monetary policy and the fines and penalties, described in Articles **104**.11 and **110**.3, will not apply (*described above*);

(2)   The UK will not be counted as one of the Countries when the Council decides if a majority of Member States fulfil the criteria (*hence the number of Member States comprising a majority will be fewer*).

(3)   The actions, regulations, decisions and opinions of the ESCB and the ECB will not affect the UK, and the UK will not be obliged to follow the rulings of these bodies.

(4)   The UK will not be eligible to receive any of distribution of the net profits of the ECB.

(5)   The UK will continue to have the right to issue and use its own bank notes.

(6)   The UK will not be involved in the election of the officials of the ESCB or the ECB.

(7)   The UK will be obliged to follow the requirements of the Member States which stay in the Second Stage. This will include operating within the framework of the European Monetary System and will have to respect the existing powers of the Community (Article **124**).

(8)   The UK will not be involved in the decision for the adoption of the conversion rates of the national currencies, where they will be fixed to form the ECU.
Likewise the UK will not be involved in the decision of the conversion rate of a national currency of a Member State which subsequently decides to join the Single Currency.

(9)   The UK may have to contribute a minimal percentage of the operational costs of the ECB, if the General Council of the ECB decides (*Protocol of the ESCB and the ECB, Article 48*).

Involvement of the UK in the decisions leading to the formation of the Single Currency:

Irrespective of the decision on whether to join the Single Currency, the UK will be involved in the Council decisions up to the start of the Third Stage and in the Committees which have been formed in the Second Stage to prepare the Single Currency (i.e. the Monetary Committee, the European Monetary Institute and the Economic and Financial Institute).

Treaty of Rome and Single European Act	Maastricht Treaty	Treaty of Amsterdam

Employment :
(Articles **125** – **130**)

This a new area introduced by the Treaty of Amsterdam and is intended to improve the level of employment in the Community, in particular by providing incentives to reduce unemployment.

Member States and the Community shall work towards developing and promoting a co-ordinated strategy for employment.

The European Council will assess the employment situation each year and make conclusions based on a joint annual report by the Council and the Commission.
The annual report will be based on an examination of how each Member State has implemented the employment policies of the Community.

The Council, acting by **qualified majority** on a proposal from the Commission, will **give guidelines on the employment policies for the Member States**.
The Council's guidelines will be based on the conclusions of the European Council and the opinions of the European Parliament, the Economic and Social Committee, the Committee of the Regions and the Employ-ment Committee.
(Article **128**).

The **Employment Committee** will be formed by the Council, after consulting the European Parliament.
The Committee will have advisory status to promote co-ordination between Member States.

Its tasks will include:

(a) Monitoring employment policies in the Member States and the Community;
(b) Formulating opinions at the request of the Council or the Commission or on its own initiative.

There will be two members appointed by each of the Member States and the Commission (Article **130**).

Treaty of Rome and Single European Act	Maastricht Treaty	Treaty of Amsterdam

Employment :
(Continued)

Each Member State will provide an annual report to the Council and the Commission showing how the policies have been implemented.

The Council will carry out an annual examination of the Member States' implementation and, acting by a **qualified majority** on a proposal from the Commission, make recommendations to the Member States.

The Council, acting by **qualified majority under Article 251** after consulting the Economic and Social Committee and the Committee of the Regions, may **issue incentive measures to encourage co-operation between Member States**.
These measures will not include harmonisation of the Member States' laws (Article **129**).

Common Commercial Policy :
(Articles **131** - **134**)

By creating a customs union, the Member States aim to contribute to the harmonious development of world trade (Article **131**).

The Maastricht Treaty changes the title of this section from the 'Commercial Policy' to the 'Common Commercial Policy'.

The Council shall act *unanimously* for the first two Stages and then by **qualified majority** thereafter to issue Directives for Member States to harmonise their commercial policies and to co-ordinate their policies to give aid for exports to third countries in order to prepare the conditions necessary for a common policy (Article **132**).

*The Maastricht Treaty assumes that the Transitionary Stages are complete; as a result, the Council shall now act by **qualified majority** in the areas where it had to act unanimously under the terms of the Treaty of Rome.*

Where agreements with third countries are being negotiated, the Council shall authorise the Commission to negotiate with these third countries, within the framework of such directives as the Council may issue to it. The Council will act by **qualified majority** (Article **133**.4).

In addition :
The Council will act *unanimously* when agreeing reciprocal rights and by **qualified majority** for other agreements.
The Commission will conduct these negotiations and the Council will conclude them. *The European Parliament is specifically not to be consulted.* (Article **133**.3 and Article **300**.3).

In Addition :
The Council, acting *unanimously* and after consulting the European Parliament, may apply the terms of the Common Commercial Policy to international negotiations on services and intellectual property (Article **133**.5).

Treaty of Rome and Single European Act	Maastricht Treaty	Treaty of Amsterdam

Common Commercial Policy :
(Continued)

The Council, the Commission or a Member State may obtain the opinion of the Court of Justice on whether an agreement is compatible with the provisions of the Treaty (Article **300**).

During the Transitional Period, the Member States shall consult one another to harmonise the action they take.

~ Article repealed.

Once the Transitional Period has finished, the Commission will conduct all negotiations and the Council, acting by **qualified majority**, may issue any directives for this purpose.

Where the pursuit of this policy could lead to a Member State having trading difficulties, the Commission shall authorise that state to take the necessary protective measures.

If a Member State decides to take protective measures on its own initiative, the Commission may decide to instruct that state to amend or abolish those measures Article **134**).

Customs co-operation :
(Article **135**)

The Council, acting in accordance with **Article 251**, shall take measures to strengthen customs co-operation between Member States and with the Commission.

Treaty of Rome and Single European Act	Maastricht Treaty	Treaty of Amsterdam

Social Policy, Education, Vocational Training and Youth :

(1) Social Provisions :
(Articles **136** - **145**)

	A small number of changes were made to the text of the Treaty by Maastricht. However, the addition of the **Protocol on Social Policy** *and the* **Agreement between the Member States (with the exception of the UK)** *meant that substantial changes were made to the Social provisions in the form of the 'Social Chapter', attached to the Maastricht Treaty which did not form part of the main Treaty.*	*The chapter on* **Social Provisions** *has been substantially restructured and expanded by the Treaty of Amsterdam. The principal change has been the repeal of the* **Protocol on Social Policy** *and the* **Agreement on Social Policy** *(the 'Social Chapter') agreed at Maastricht.*
		With the UK agreeing to sign the 'Social Chapter', the Protocols have now been incorporated into the main body of the Treaty and this forms the majority of the changes.
		Parts of the previous Treaties have been retained and partially rewritten and the Articles renumbered.
		Owing to these changes, the summary of the new Treaty provisions are shown separately below.
		The Social Charter of 1989 is specifically referred to in Article 136. The principal points of the charter are:
		1. *Promotion of employment;*
Member States agree on the need to promote improved working conditions and an improved standard of living for workers.		2. *Improvement of living and working conditions, including health and safety of workers;*
Member States believe that this will develop from the Common Market and from laws and regulations, which will support the harmonisation of social systems.		3. *Dialogue between management and labour.*
		All of these are included in the provisions of the Social Chapter and the new Articles introduced by the Treaty of Amsterdam.
The Council shall promote close co-operation between Member States in the social field, especially in relation to (*inter alia*):		
(a) Employment;		*As a consequence of the provisions being brought into the Treaty, the Council is now able to use the legislative process of the Treaty regarding the whole Community, not just the States which had signed the Charter.*
(b) labour law and working conditions;		
(c) social security;		
(d) the right of association and collective bargaining between employers and workers (Article **137**).		
To this end, the Commission shall make studies and have consultations at international level and then make recommendations to the Member States, after consulting the Economic and Social Committee.		*The Council can use* **qualified majority voting** *in areas such as equal treatment and equal opportunities, which had to have been passed by unanimity before.*
		The legislative method of passing law has changed to **Co-decision** *(under Article 251) from Co-operation (under Article 252).*

Treaty of Rome and Single European Act	Maastricht Treaty	Treaty of Amsterdam

Social Policy, Education, Vocational Training and Youth :

(1) Social Provisions :
(Continued)

The Member States shall pay particular attention to encouraging improvements in the working environment with regards the health and safety of workers and shall have the aim of harmonising conditions in this area.

The Council, acting by **qualified majority**, after consulting the Economic and Social Committee, shall adopt directives for the minimum requirements for the policy implementation. (Article **137**.2).	The Council, acting by **qualified majority**, under Article **252** (ie co-operation), shall adopt the directives for the minimum requirements.	The Council shall act by **qualified majority under Article 251** (ie co-decision).

The Commission shall develop dialogue between management and labour at European level, which could lead to relations based on agreement. (Article **139**).

Each Member State shall ensure and maintain the principle of equal pay for equal work for men and women. (Article **141**).

Member States shall endeavour to maintain the existing equivalence between paid holiday schemes. (Article **142**).

The Council, acting *unanimously,* shall assign to the Commission tasks in connection with the implementation of common measures, including social security for migrant workers. (Article **144**).

The European Parliament may invite the Commission to draw up reports on particular problems concerning social conditions (Article **145**).

Treaty of Amsterdam

Social Policy, Education, Vocational Training and Youth :

Social Provisions :
(Articles **136 – 145**)

*This is a summary of the complete Treaty provisions, incorporating the **Protocol on Social Policy** and the **Agreement on Social Policy** from the Maastricht Treaty into the Treaty. The majority of the text has not actually been altered by the Treaty of Amsterdam, as this Treaty has principally consolidated the Protocol into the main text.*

New Articles introduced by the Treaty of Amsterdam are indicated by a note in italics.

The Member States shall bear in mind the 'Social Charter' of 1989 and shall implement measures which will have, *inter alia*, the following objectives:

(a)   Promotion of employment;
(b)   Improved living and working conditions;
(c)   Proper social protection;
(d)   Dialogue between management and labour. (Article **136**)

Member States believe that this will develop from the Common Market and from laws and regulations, which will support the harmonisation of social systems.

The Community shall support and complement the activities of the Member States in the following:

(a)   Improvement of the working environment to protect workers' health and safety;
(b)   Working conditions;
(c)   Information and consultation of workers;
(d)   Integration of persons excluded from the labour market;
(e)   Equality between men and women for opportunities and treatment at work. (Article **137**.1)

The Council, acting by **qualified majority under Article 251** after consulting the Economic and social Committee, will adopt directives for the minimum requirements for the above, without discriminating against employees in small and medium-sized businesses.
The Council, acting by **qualified majority under Article 251** after consulting the Economic and social Committee, may also adopt measures to encourage co-operation between Member States to deal with social exclusion (Article **137**.2) *New provision in the Treaty of Amsterdam.*

In the following areas, the Council will act *unanimously*, after consulting the European Parliament and the Economic and Social Committee:

(a)   Social security and social protection of workers;
(b)   Protection of workers on termination of employment;
(c)   Representation and collective defence of workers and employers;
(d)   Conditions of employment for third country nationals in the Community;
(e)   Financial contributions for promotion of employment and job-creation. (Article **137**.3)

A Member State may entrust the implementation of directives to management and labour; however, the measures must have been implemented by the date on which the Directive would become effective and the Member State must be able to guarantee that the directive will be implemented (Article **137**.4).

The provisions above will **not** apply to:

(a)   Pay;
(b)   The right of association;
(c)   The right to strike or the right to impose lock-outs. (Article **137**.6)

Treaty of Amsterdam

Social Policy, Education, Vocational Training and Youth :

Social Provisions :
(Continued)

The Commission will promote the consultation of management and labour at Community level and seek advice on any proposed directives. The Commission will help to promote dialogue between management and labour (Article **138**).

If appropriate, the dialogue may lead to contractual relations between management and labour at Community level.

Any agreements at Community level will be implemented by collective bargaining either in accordance with national practice or by Council decisions.
The Council will act by **qualified majority**, except where the agreements refer to matters in Article **137**.3 where it will act *unanimously* (*described above*).

The Council shall promote close co-operation between Member States in all social policy fields, especially in relation to:
(a)   Employment;
(b)   labour law and working conditions;
(c)   basic and advanced vocational training;
(d)   social security;
(e)   occupational hygiene;
(f)   the right of association and collective bargaining between employers and workers (Article **140**).

To this end, the Commission shall make studies and have consultations at international level and then make recommendations to the Member States, after consulting the Economic and Social Committee.

Equal pay for men and women must be applied in the Member States.

'Pay' is defined as the ordinary or basic minimum wage or salary plus additional consideration.
Equal pay without sexual discrimination means:
(a)   Pay for the same work will be calculated on the same basis;
(b)   Pay for the same work will be the same for the same job calculated at the same time rates (Article **141**.1-2).

The Council, acting by **qualified majority under Article 251** and after consulting the Economic and Social Committee, will adopt measures to ensure equal opportunities (Article **141**.3) *New Article in the Treaty of Amsterdam.*

The Commission will write an annual report to the European Parliament, the Council and the Economic and Social Committee on the progress of the implementation of the social policies (Article **143**) *New Article in the Treaty of Amsterdam.*

The Council, acting *unanimously,* shall assign to the Commission tasks in connection with the implementation of common measures, including social security for migrant workers (Article **141**).

The European Parliament may invite the Commission to draw up reports on particular problems concerning social conditions (Article **145**).

Treaty of Rome and Single European Act	**Maastricht Treaty**	**Treaty of Amsterdam**
(2) European Social Fund : (Articles **146** - **148**)		
The Fund shall be set up to improve opportunities for employment of workers. It shall have the task of making the employment of workers easier and of increasing their geographical and occupational mobility within the Community.	*In addition :* The Fund will act through vocational training and re-training for workers in the Internal Market to facilitate their adaptation to industrial and production systems changes.	
The Fund shall be administered by the Commission, aided by a committee; this will have governments, trade unions and employers' organisations on it.	The Council, acting by **qualified majority** under Article **252**, shall adopt implementing decisions on the Fund.	*Changed to :* The Council will act by **qualified majority under Article 251**. (Article **148**).
The Fund will provide up to 50% of the necessary expenditure (the Member States concerned shall provide the balance).	*The remainder of the provisions relating to the European Social Fund are included in the Articles for **Economic and Social Cohesion**, shown in Articles 158 - 162.*	
The Fund will grant aid for the benefit of workers made unemployed. The money will only be granted if the workers have to change their occupation. The Council, acting by **qualified majority**, may rule that all or part of the assistance shall be stopped, or, acting *unanimously*, determine what new tasks may be given to the Fund. The Council, acting by **qualified majority**, shall lay down the details of the conditions under which the Fund shall operate.		
The Council, acting by a **majority of its members** shall lay down the general principles for implementing a common vocational training policy.		
	(3) Education, Vocational Training and Youth : (Articles **149** - **150**)	
	The Community shall contribute to the development of quality education by encouraging co-operation between Member States.	
	Community action will be aimed at (*inter alia*): (a) Developing the European dimension in education; (b) Encouraging mobility of students and teachers.	

Treaty of Rome and Single European Act	Maastricht Treaty	Treaty of Amsterdam
	(3) Education, Vocational Training and Youth : (Continued)	
	The Council, acting by **qualified majority under Article 251**, shall adopt incentive measures and recommendations (excluding any harmonisation of national laws) to help in the achievement of these objectives.	
	The Community shall implement a vocational training policy with the aim of (*inter alia*): (a) Facilitating adaptation to industrial changes; (b) Improving initial and continuing vocational training (Article **150**).	
	The Community and the Member States shall foster co-operation with third countries.	
	The Council, acting by **qualified majority** under Article **252**, shall adopt measures to help achieve these objectives, excluding any harmonisation of national laws.	*Changed to :* The Council will act by **qualified majority under Article 251**.
	Culture : (Article **151**)	
	The Community shall contribute to the flowering of the cultures of the Member States.	
	Action by the Community shall be aimed at encouraging co-operation between Member States, including (*inter alia*): (a) The improvement of knowledge and dissemination of the culture and history of the European peoples; (b) The conservation and safeguarding of cultural heritage of European significance.	
	The Community shall take cultural aspects into account in its action under other provisions in this Treaty.	*In addition :* In particular, in order to respect and to promote the diversity of cultures (Article **151**.4).

Treaty of Rome and Single European Act	Maastricht Treaty	Treaty of Amsterdam
	Culture : (Continued) The Council, acting *unanimously*, shall adopt incentive measures and recommendations, excluding any harmonisation of national laws, to achieve these objectives.	
	Public Health : (Article **152**)	
	The Community shall contribute towards ensuring a high level of human health protection.	*Article rewritten and expanded :* A high level of human health protection shall be ensured in the definition and implementation of all Community policies and activities. *In addition :*
	Community action shall be directed towards the prevention of diseases (particularly major health scourges eg drugs) by promoting research into the causes and by health education. (Article **152**.1).	Community action, complementing national policies, shall be directed towards improving public health and obviating sources of danger to human health.
	Health protection requirements shall form a constituent part of the Community's other policies.	*No changes but incorporated into the above.*
	Member States shall co-ordinate among themselves their policies and programmes. The Commission shall make any useful initiative to promote such co-ordination.	*In addition :* The Community shall encourage co-operation between the Member States and lend support where necessary.
	The Community and the Member States shall foster co-operation with third countries.	
	The Council, acting by **qualified majority under Article 251** after consulting the Economic and Social Committee and the Committee of the Regions, shall adopt incentive measures, excluding any harmonisation of national laws, to help to achieve these objectives. The Council, acting by a **qualified majority**, shall adopt recommendations. (Article **152**.4).	*Article rewritten and enlarged.* *The method of voting will remain the same :* The Council will contribute to the achievement of the objectives *noted above* by: (a) Measures setting high standards of quality and safety of human organs and blood; (b) Measures regarding animal and plant hygiene affecting human health; (c) Incentive measures to protect and improve human health, excluding any harmonisation of laws.

Treaty of Rome and Single European Act	Maastricht Treaty	Treaty of Amsterdam
	Public Health : (Continued)	
		In addition : Community action shall respect the responsibilities of the Member States regarding health services, medical care and blood and organ donations (Article **152**.5).
	Consumer Protection : (Article **153**) The Community shall contribute to the attainment of a high level of consumer protection through the completion of the Internal Market and measures to support the health and safety of consumers.	*Article expanded and reordered.* *In addition* : The Community shall promote the interests of consumers and their right to information, education and to organise themselves to safeguard their interests. *In addition* : Consumer protection requirements will be taken into account in Community policies and activities.
	The Council, acting by **qualified majority under Article 251** after consulting the Economic and Social Committee, shall adopt specific action, supporting the policies of the Member States, to protect the health, safety and economic interests of consumers.	
	Trans-European Networks : (Articles **154 – 156**) In order to promote the harmonious development of the Community and the Internal Market, the Community shall contribute to the establishment and development of trans-European net-works for transport, telecommunications and energy infra-structures. In order to achieve these objectives, the Community shall establish a series of guidelines covering the objectives, priorities and broad lines of measures for the networks.	

Treaty of Rome and Single European Act	Maastricht Treaty	Treaty of Amsterdam
	Trans-European Networks : (Continued)	
	In addition, it shall implement any measure that may prove necessary, in particular the field of technical standardisation and it may support the financial efforts of the Member States through feasibility studies, loan guarantees or interest rate subsidies (Article **155**.1).	*Article **155**.1, third indent, rephrased:* The Community may support common interest projects supported by the Member States.
	The Community may also contribute through the Cohesion Fund. *This is described in Article **161**.*	
	The Commission may take any initiative to promote co-ordination between the Member States.	
	The Council, acting by **qualified majority under Articles 251** and **252**, shall adopt guidelines to promote the inter-connection and inter-operability of the national networks.	The Council will act by **qualified majority under Article 251** for all guidelines and detailed measures.
	Industry : (Article **157**)	
	The Community and the Member States shall ensure that the conditions necessary for the competitiveness of the Community's industry exist. Their action shall include the speeding up of the adjustment of industry to structural changes and encouraging a favourable environment. The Commission shall take any initiative to promote the co-ordination of the action of the Member States and the Community.	
	The Community shall contribute to the achievement of these objectives through its actions in the policies of other provisions of this Treaty.	
	The Council, acting *unanimously*, shall decide on specific measures to support the action of the Member States.	

Treaty of Rome and Single European Act	Maastricht Treaty	Treaty of Amsterdam

Economic and Social Cohesion :
(Articles **158** - **162**)

In order to promote its harmonious development, the Community shall take actions to lead to the strengthening of economic and social cohesion.
This will include the aim of reducing disparities between the various regions and the backwardness of the least-favoured regions.

In addition :
The least-favoured regions or islands.

Member States shall co-ordinate their economic policies to achieve these objectives.

The Community shall support this by use of **Structural Funds**.
The Structural Funds are :
(1)   European Agricultural Guidance and Guarantee Fund, Guidance Section;
(2)   European Social Fund;
(3)   European Regional Development Fund.

In addition :
The Commission shall submit a report to the European Parliament and the Council every three years on the progress made, (the report shall include appropriate proposals).

If specific actions are required outside of the Funds, these can be adopted by the Council acting *unanimously*.
The Council, acting *unanimously*, shall define the tasks, primary objectives and organisation of the **Structural Funds**.
The Council shall define the general rules applicable to the Funds and the provisions to ensure their effectiveness.

The Council, acting *unanimously*, shall set up a **Cohesion Fund**, which must be formed before 31 December 1993.
This fund shall provide a financial contribution to projects in the fields of 'environment' and 'trans-European networks' in Member States which have a per capita GNP of less than 90% of the Community average.
The intention is that these Member States will be able to fulfil the conditions for EMU, under Article **104**.

The European Regional Development Fund is intended to help redress the principal regional imbalances in the Community, in regions where development is lagging behind and in declining industrial regions.

Treaty of Rome and Single European Act	Maastricht Treaty	Treaty of Amsterdam

Economic and Social Cohesion :
(Continued)

The Commission shall submit comprehensive proposals to the Council on amendments to the structure and operational rules of the funds to classify and rationalise their tasks in order to increase their efficiency and to co-ordinate their activities.

There will be a greater flexibility in allocating the funds to needs not specified in the current regulations.

Community involvement will be adjusted to achieve economic and social cohesion.

The Community will reassess the ability of individual Member States to contribute to the system of own resources (*Protocol on Economic and Social Cohesion*).

The Council shall act *unanimously* on these proposals and shall act by **qualified majority** to implement decisions on the Funds.

The Council, acting by **qualified majority** under Article **252**, shall decide on how the European Regional Development Fund shall be implemented (Article **162**).

The Council will act by **qualified majority under Article 251**.

Research and Technological Development :
(Articles **163 – 173**)

The Community shall aim to strengthen the scientific and technological basis of European industry and to encourage it to become more competitive at international level.

The Community shall support organisations in their research with the aim of exploiting the Internal Market, especially by the opening up of national public contracts, definition of common standards and the removal of legal and fiscal barriers.

The Community will carry out the following activities:
(a) implementation of programmes, by promoting co-operation and demonstration with third countries;
(b) dissemination of the results of the research;
(c) stimulation of training and mobility of researchers.

Treaty of Rome and Single European Act	Maastricht Treaty	Treaty of Amsterdam
Research and Technological Development : (Continued)		
The Commission shall take any useful initiative to co-ordinate the R&TD activities between the Community and Member States.		
The Council, acting *unanimously* after consulting the European Parliament and the Economic and Social Committee, shall adopt a research framework programme and any joint undertakings. The framework programme will be adapted or supplemented as necessary.	*Changed to :* The Council will act *unanimously* following the procedures of Article **251**.	*Changed to :* The Council will act by **qualified majority under Article 251.**
The framework programme will: (a) establish the objectives and fix the respective priorities; (b) the main lines of research envisaged; (c) the financial involvement of the Community.		
The Council will, acting by **qualified majority** after consulting the Economic and Social Committee, will adopt specific programmes developed in each research area and define the detailed arrangements for the dissemination of the results from the programmes.	*Changed to :* The Council will act by **qualified majority** after consulting the European Parliament (Article **166**.3).	
The rules on supplementary research programmes, participation and co-operation involving individual Member States will be adopted by the Council.	The Council will act by **qualified majority** under Article **252**.	The Council will act by **qualified majority under Article 251**.
The Council will make provision for the participation of other Member States in the research of individual Member States. In these cases the Council will act by **qualified majority**.	*In addition :* The Council, acting *unanimously* after consulting the European Parliament, shall set up joint undertakings for Community R &TD. (Articles **171 - 172**).	*Changed to :* The Council will act by **qualified majority under Article 251** to set up the joint undertakings.

Treaty of Rome and Single European Act	Maastricht Treaty	Treaty of Amsterdam

Environment :
(Articles **174** - **176**)

The action of the Community shall have the following objectives : (1) preserve, protect and improve the quality of the environment; (2) protect human health; (3) prudent and rational utilisation of natural resources. The action shall be based on the principles that preventive action should be taken, damage should be rectified at source and the polluter should pay.	*In addition :* Community policy shall aim at a high level of protection. *There is an additional objective for the action of the Community, which is:* (4) to promote measures at international level to deal with regional and world-wide environmental issues.	*The concerns regarding the environment were highlighted at Amsterdam, but the main alterations to the Treaty were made in the general Articles, so that environmental protection will be integrated into all relevant Community legislation (principally Article 6).*
Environmental protection requirements shall be a component of other policies of the Community. The Community shall take action where this can be better attained at community level than at national level.	*Changed to :* Environmental protection requirements must be integrated into the definition and implementation of other Community policies. Harmonisation measures will be adopted; these will allow Member States to take provisional measures of a non-economic nature, subject to Community inspection.	~ *Sentence repealed.*
The Council, acting *unanimously*, will decide on what action is to be taken by the Community and shall define those matters where the decisions shall be by qualified majority.	The Council, acting by **qualified majority** under Article **252**, shall decide on what action the Community shall take (*See also **Cohesion Fund**, Article **161***). Where the Commission has submitted a proposal, the Council, acting *unanimously*, shall adopt policies on the following : (1) provisions primarily of a fiscal nature; (2) measures concerning town and country planning; (3) measures which significantly affect a Member State's choice between different energy sources.	The Council will act by **qualified majority under Article 251**.
	General action programmes setting out objectives shall be adopted by the Council, acting by **qualified majority** under **Article 251**, after consulting the Economic and Social Committee.	*In addition:* The Council will consult the committee of the Regions.

Treaty of Rome and Single European Act	Maastricht Treaty	Treaty of Amsterdam

Environment :
(Continued)

Member States shall finance and implement the policy. Where the costs to a Member State appear to be too great, the Council shall provide funds from the Cohesion Fund.

Development Co-operation :
(Articles **177** - **181**)

Community policy will contribute to the objective of developing and consol-idating democracy and the rule of law; it shall foster, in the developing countries :
(1) sustainable economic and social development;
(2) smooth and gradual integration into the world economy;
(3) the campaign against poverty.
The Council, acting by **qualified majority** under Article **252**, shall adopt measures to further these objectives.
The European Investment Bank shall contribute to the implementation of these measures.
Member States and the Community shall co-ordinate their policies and the Commission shall take any useful initiative to promote this co-ordination.

Within their respective levels of competence, the Member States and the Community will co-operate with third countries and international organisations.

The Council will act by **qualified majority under Article 251**.

Association of the Overseas Countries and Territories :
(Articles **182** - **188**)

Non-European Countries which have a special relationship with one or more of the Member States will be able to continue this association with the Community.

Treaty of Rome and Single European Act	Maastricht Treaty	Treaty of Amsterdam

Association of the Overseas Countries and Territories :
(Continued)

The aim of the Association will be to promote the economic and social development of the Countries and will have the following objectives:
(1) Member States will trade with the Countries in the same way as with other Member States.
(2) Each country will trade with the other Countries and Member States in the same way as with the Member States with which it has a special relationship.
(3) Member States will contribute to the investments needed for the development of the Countries.
(4) All tenders will be open to all nationals of the Member States.
(5) Nationals of Member States will have the same rights to settle in the Countries as they do in other Member States, following the laws of this Treaty.

Customs duties on imports between Member States and the Countries will be abolished following the same procedures as the Stages in abolition of trade between the Member States under the terms of this Treaty.

The Countries may impose levies to aid their development. These levies must be progressively reduced to the same level as those between the Country and the Member State with which it has a special relationship.

If the level of duties on imports from a third country into one of the Countries is such that it affects the trade of any Member State, then that Member State may apply to the Commission to propose measures to correct the situation.

The Council will act *unanimously* to define the detailed rules and procedures for the association of the overseas countries and territories with the Community.

Treaty of Rome and Single European Act	Maastricht Treaty	Treaty of Amsterdam

The Institutions :
(Articles **189 - 267**)

(1) The European Parliament :
    (Articles **189 - 201**)

The Parliament shall consist of 198 delegates, selected from the Member States.
This has been progressively increased to 626 by the accession of Greece, Spain, Portugal, Austria, Finland and Sweden.

In addition :
There will not be more than 700 members of the European Parliament (Article **189**).

In the event of amendments to the number of representatives from each Member State, the numbers elected must ensure appropriate represent-ation of the peoples of the States in the Community (Article **190**.2).

The Council, acting *unanimously*, shall lay down the provisions for the elections to the Parliament.

In addition :
The Council shall obtain the assent of the Parliament (which shall act by a majority of its component members) before laying down the appropriate provisions for the elections.

In addition :
The European Parliament, with the opinion of the Commission and the approval of the Council (acting *unanimously)*, shall lay down the regul-ations and conditions concerning the conduct of its members.
(Article **190**.4).

The Parliament shall vote by an absolute majority of the votes cast.
Where the Parliament co-operates with the Council in the adoption of laws, the procedure, described in Article 149 (old numbering – since repealed by Maastricht) is as follows:

In the Maastricht Treaty, these provisions have been repealed and replaced by Articles 251 – 252, described below under the heading 'Provisions common to several Institutions'.

The Treaty of Amsterdam further amends the method of voting with the intention of simplifying the process and developing the concept of Co-decision between the Council and the European Parliament.
This process is described in Article 251.

The Council shall act by **qualified majority** on a proposal from the Commission, after obtaining the opinion of the European Parliament. The Parliament will be fully informed of the reasons for the acceptance of the proposal by the Council.

Replaced by :
The European Parliament shall parti-cipate in the process of legislation, by giving its opinion to the Council, following the procedures of Articles **251** and **252**.
Where the European Parliament con-siders that Community action is required, it may request the Commission to propose legislation.
(Article **192**).

If the Parliament approves the act, it shall be adopted.

The Parliament, within three months and by an absolute majority, may propose amendments or reject the proposed act.

Treaty of Rome and Single European Act	Maastricht Treaty	Treaty of Amsterdam

(1)   The European Parliament :
    (Continued)

If the Parliament has rejected the proposed act, the Council must act *unanimously* to adopt the law.

Where the Parliament has suggested amendments, the Commission shall re-examine the proposal, taking into account these proposed amendments.

The Council, acting *unanimously*, may adopt these amendments which the Commission has not accepted.

The Council, acting by **qualified majority**, shall adopt the re-examined proposal and, acting *unanimously*, may amend the proposal.

A motion against the Commission may be brought in front of the Parliament.
If the motion is carried by a majority of two-thirds, then the Commission shall resign as a body (Article **201**).

In addition :
The Parliament may, at the request of ¼ of its members, set up a temporary Committee of Inquiry to investigate alleged contravention or maladministration in the implementation of Community law (Article **193**).

The Parliament shall appoint an Ombudsman to investigate complaints from any citizen of the Union concerning instances of maladministration in the activities of the Community institutions, with the exception of the Court of Justice (Article **195**.1).

(1)   The Council :
    (Articles **202 - 210**)

The Council shall ensure the co-ordination of the general economic policies of the Member States and has the power to take decisions.
The Council may confer powers on the Commission for the implementation of the rules the Council lays down. The Council reserves the right to exercise directly implementing powers itself.

C

Treaty of Rome and Single European Act	Maastricht Treaty	Treaty of Amsterdam

(2) The Council :
(Continued)

The Council shall consist of one representative from the government of each Member State.

In addition :
The representative must be at ministerial level and be authorised to commit the government of that Member State.
(Article **203**).

Changed to :
The office of president shall be held in turn by each Member State for 6 months in the order decided by the Council, acting *unanimously* (Article **203**).

The presidency will be held in turn by each Member State in the Council for a six month period. The order is laid down in the Treaty.
On the Accession of Austria, Finland and Sweden, this has changed to 'the order decided by the Council, acting unanimously'.

The Council will vote by a majority of its members, except where otherwise stated (Article **205**).

Under **qualified majority** voting, the Council will weigh the votes according to the allocation given to the Member States (Article **205**):
(a) For proposals from the Commission, at least 54 votes in favour to pass the act.
On the accession of Austria, Finland and Sweden, the number of votes required has been increased to 62.
(b) In other cases, at least 54 votes to be cast by at least 8 members.
The number of votes has been increased by the accession of the new countries to 62 votes cast by at least 10 members.

Changed to :
(a) For proposals from the Commission, at least 62 votes in favour;
(b) In other cases, at least 62 votes in favour cast by at lest 10 members.

Unanimity will be required for any amendments to the proposals.
Where the Council acts in co-operation with the European Parliament, the Council shall act by **qualified majority**.

These *Articles have been repealed and replaced by Articles 251 and 252 and are described below, under the heading of Provisions common to several Institutions, described below.*

The procedures are described above under Article 149 [old numbering].

The Council may request the Commission to undertake any studies or to submit any appropriate proposals.

Treaty of Rome and Single European Act	Maastricht Treaty	Treaty of Amsterdam

(2) The Council :
   (Continued)

A Committee of Permanent representatives will be responsible for preparing the work of the Council.

In addition:
The Committee may adopt procedural decisions under the terms of the Council's Rules of Procedure (Article **207**.1).

In addition :
The Council will be assisted by a General Secretariat, under the direction of Secretary-General.

Replaced by :
The General Secretariat will be under the responsibility of a Secretary-General seconded by a Deputy Secretary-General.

The Secretary General will be appointed by the Council, acting *unanimously* (Article **207**.2).

In addition :
The Deputy Secretary-General will be appointed by the Council, acting *unanimously.*

In addition:
Transparency:
The Council will determine the conditions in which the public will be able to see Council documents, results of votes and explanations of votes, and minutes of meetings (Article **207**.3).

(2) The Commission :
   (Articles **211 - 219**)

The Commission shall ensure that the provisions of this Treaty and the measures taken by the institutions are applied, formulate recommendations and have its own power of decisions.
The Commission shall consist of **20** members (*after the accession of Austria, Finland and Sweden*) appointed for a term of 4 years, which is renewable. They will be appointed by the common accord of the Governments of the Member States; there must be at least one member from each Member State, but no more than two.

In addition and replaced by :
The President and other members of the Commission, whose term begins on 7 January 1993, shall end their term on 6 January 1995.
From 7 January 1995, the term of office shall be 5 years, which is renewable.

In the performance of their duties, the members of the Commission shall neither seek nor take instructions from any government or from any other body. Each Member State undertakes to respect this principle and not to seek to influence the Commission.

In addition and replaced by :
The Governments of the Member States shall nominate by common accord the President of the Commission, after consulting the European Parliament.

Replaced by :
The Governments of the Member States shall nominate by common accord the President of the Commission. The nomination will be approved by the European Parliament.

Treaty of Rome and Single European Act	Maastricht Treaty	Treaty of Amsterdam

(3) The Commission :
(Continued)

	In consultation with the President, they shall nominate the members of the Commission. The Commission shall be subject to approval by the European Parliament.	The governments of the Member States in common accord with the nominee for President will nominate the other members of the Commission.
The Commission shall act by a majority of its members.		*In addition*: The Commission will act under the political guidance if its President. (Article **219**).

(4) The Court of Justice :
(Articles **220** - **245**)

The Court of Justice shall ensure that the law is observed in the interpretation and application of the provisions of this Treaty.
The Court will consist of **15** judges and shall be assisted by **9** advocates-general, (*after the accession of Austria, Finland and Sweden*).
The Council, acting *unanimously*, may increase these numbers.
The Court shall sit in plenary session. It may form chambers **with three, five or seven** judges (*after the accession of Austria, Finland and Sweden*).
If a Member State or a Community institution is involved in a dispute, the court shall sit in plenary session.

The deliberations of the Court shall remain secret (Protocol, Article 32).

Changed to :
The Court will consist of 8 advocate-Generals and a ninth will be appointed from 1 January 1995 to 6 October 2000.
(Article **222**).

The Court may request the Council (acting *unanimously*) to attach a court of first instance, with the right of appeal to the Court of Justice on points of law.
The Council, acting *unanimously*, shall determine the composition of the Court of First Instance.
Judges will be appointed for a renewable term of six years; the court will be partially renewed every three years.
The areas of competence will be restricted to proceedings brought by individuals.

*The Maastricht Treaty has given a more formal structure to the **Court of First Instance**.*

Changed to :
A Court of First Instance shall be attached to the Court of Justice.
The Council, acting *unanimously*, shall determine the classes of action or proceedings on which the Court of First Instance shall adjudicate (Article **225**).

Treaty of Rome and Single European Act	Maastricht Treaty	Treaty of Amsterdam

(5) The Court of Justice :
(Continued)

If the Commission considers that a Member State has failed to fulfil an obligation under this Treaty and the Member State does not comply with an opinion of the Commission, then the Commission may bring the matter to the Court of Justice.
A Member State may bring a matter concerning an obligation of another Member State to the Court of Justice, but before this, the Commission shall deliver an opinion on the matter (Articles **226** - **227**).

Where the Court of Justice finds that a Member State has failed in an obligation, that Member State will be required to take the necessary measures to comply with the judgement.	*In addition :* If the Commission considers that the Member State has not complied with the obligation, it may specify the **lump sum or penalty payment** the Member State must make for non-compliance. The Court of Justice may also impose a **penalty** (Article **228**.2).
Regulations made by the Council may give the Court unlimited jurisdiction regarding **imposing penalties** (Article **229**).	*In addition :* Regulations adopted jointly by the Council and the European Parliament will give the Court unlimited jurisdiction on **penalties** (Article **229**).
The Court of Justice will review the legality of acts adopted by the Commission and the Council; where appropriate, the Court will declare the act to be void.	*In addition :* The Court will examine the acts adopted jointly by the Council and the European Parliament.
The Court will have jurisdiction to give preliminary rulings on: (a) The interpretation of the Treaty; (b) The validity and interpretation of the acts of the Community institutions; (c) The interpretation of statutes made by bodies created by the Council.	*In addition :* The Court will rule on the validity of acts by the ECB.

Treaty of Rome and Single European Act	Maastricht Treaty	Treaty of Amsterdam

(4) The Court of Justice :
    (Continued)

The Court will have jurisdiction in disputes concerning the European Investment Bank, with regard to the obligations of Member States and the obligations of the Board of Governors of the EIB.

In addition :
The Court will have jurisdiction over the ECB.
The Court will have jurisdiction over the fulfilment of the national central banks of their obligations. Where a central bank has failed in an obligation, that bank will be required to take the necessary measures to comply with the ruling of the Court.

(5) The Court of Auditors :
    (Articles **246** - **248**)

A Court of Auditors is hereby established and shall consist of **15** members (*after the accession of Austria, Finland and Sweden*).

The Court of Auditors has been included in the list of the Principal Institutions of the Community, shown in Article 6.

The members of the Court shall be appointed for a term of 6 years by the Council, acting *unanimously,* after consulting the European Parliament.

The powers and competencies of the Court of Auditors have not been changed in the Maastricht Treaty.

*The Articles relating to the Court have been moved from Articles 206 – 206a [old numbering] to **Articles 246 - 248**.*

The provisions of the protocol on the privileges and immunities of the Court of Justice will apply.

The Court shall examine the accounts of all revenue and expenditure of the Community and shall report to the European Parliament and the Council.

In addition:
The report (statement of assurance) will be published in the 'Official Journal of the European Communities'.
(Article **248**.1).
The Court shall report in particular on any cases of irregularity (Article **248**.2).
In addition :
The audit will be performed on the premises of any body which manages accounts on behalf of the Community or is in receipt of payments from the budget.

The audit will be performed at the location of the institutions of the Community and in the Member States.

In addition :
Any bodies managing funds will also forward any documents the Court of Auditors requires.

The institutions and the national bodies will provide any document or information necessary for the Court to carry out its tasks.

Treaty of Rome and Single European Act	Maastricht Treaty	Treaty of Amsterdam

(6)   The Court of Auditors :
(Continued)

The Court of Auditors will have access to the records of the EIB, with the right of access governed by an agreement between the Court, the EIB and the Commission.

The Court of Auditors may also, at any time, submit observations on specific questions and deliver opinions at the request of the Community.

(6)   Provisions Common to Several Institutions :
(Articles **249** - **256**)

In order to carry out their tasks, the Council and the Commission shall make regulations, directives, decisions, recommendations and opinions.

Replaced by :
In order to carry out their task and in accordance with the provisions of this Treaty, the European Parliament acting jointly with the Council, the Council and the Commission shall make regulations, directives, decisions, recommendations and opinions.

A **Regulation** shall be binding and apply to all Member States.
A **Directive** shall be binding to the Member State to which it is addressed, but the manner in which it is to be applied shall be left to the national authorities.
A **Decision** shall be binding to those it is addressed to.
Recommendations and **Opinions** have no binding force (Article **249**).

New procedures for the adoption of Acts of the Community have been introduced.
*(a) Article **250** concerns 'unanimous' voting.*
*(b) Articles **251** - **252** refer to the methods for **'qualified majority'** voting.*

Treaty of Rome and Single European Act	Maastricht Treaty	Treaty of Amsterdam
(7) Provisions Common to Several Institutions : (Continued)		

(7) Provisions Common to Several Institutions :
(Continued)

Article 250:

The Council shall vote *unanimously* to adopt an act which is an amendment to a proposal from the Commission, **subject to** the involvement of the Conciliation Committee (*described below under Article 251*). As long as the Council has not acted, the Commission may alter its proposal at any time until the proposal is adopted as an act.

Article 251 :

The Commission will submit a proposal to the Council.
The Council will act by **qualified majority** after obtaining the opinion of the European Parliament. The Council will inform the European Parliament of its opinion on the proposals.

If within 3 months, the European Parliament:
(a) Approves the Council's opinion, the act will become law;
(b) Has not made a decision, the Council will adopt the act;
(c) Rejects the opinion by an absolute majority, the Council may convene a Conciliation Committee;
(d) By an absolute majority, proposes amendments, the Council and the Commission will review the amendments. If the Commission rejects the amendments, the Council will act *unanimously* to vote on the amendments. If the Commission agrees the amendments, the Council will vote by **qualified majority**. If the Council rejects the amendments, a Conciliation Committee will be convened.

Article 251 replaced by :
The Council acting by **qualified majority** after obtaining the opinion of the European Parliament may adopt the proposal:
(a) If it approves all the amendments of the opinion of the European Parliament;
(b) If the European Parliament does not propose any amendments.

If there is a disagreement on the proposals with the European Parliament, the Council will form a common position and inform the European Parliament.

The European Parliament should reply within three months. If the European Parliament:
(a) agrees with the Council, the act will be adopted;
(b) rejects (by an absolute majority) the Council's comments, the act will not be adopted;
proposes amendments (by an absolute majority), the Council and the Commission will give an opinion on these amendments. If the amendments by the Parliament are approved by the Council, acting by a **qualified majority**, the act will be adopted in the form of the common position. If the Council does not approve all the amendments, the Council will convene the Conciliation Committee within six weeks.

Treaty of Rome and Single European Act	Maastricht Treaty	Treaty of Amsterdam
(6) Provisions Common to Several Institutions : (Continued)		

Maastricht Treaty:

Conciliation Committee :

The Conciliation Committee shall be composed of an equal number of representatives of the Council and the European Parliament.

The task of the Conciliation Committee is to reach agreement on a joint text and will be formed under the **'co-operation procedure'**, to discuss the differences between the European Parliament and the Council; if the Parliament confirms its rejection, the proposal shall **not** become law. (Article **251**.4).

Agreement shall be reached by a **qualified majority** for the Council members and by an absolute majority by the European Parliament members.

If the Conciliation Committee, within six weeks of being convened, agrees a joint text, the Council and the European Parliament shall have a period of six weeks to adopt the act.

The Council shall act by **qualified majority** and the European Parliament by an absolute majority.

The proposed act shall be considered not to have been adopted if one of the institutions does not approve it.

Treaty of Amsterdam:

In addition :
The Conciliation Committee shall examine the proposed law on the basis of the amendments of the Parliament.

If the Committee does not approve the proposed act, it shall not be adopted (Article **251**.6).

Amended by :
The European Parliament and the Council may increase the periods of three months (for the European Parliament to reply to the Council's proposals) and six weeks by a maximum of one month and two weeks respectively (Article **251**.7).

Changed to :
The proposed act shall be considered not to have been adopted if either of the two institutions does not approve it within six weeks of the Committee being convened.

Treaty of Rome and Single European Act	Maastricht Treaty	Treaty of Amsterdam

(6) Provisions Common to Several Institutions :
(Continued)

Article 252 :

The Council will act by a qualified majority on a proposal from the Commission after obtaining the opinion of the European Parliament. The opinion of the Council will be presented to the European Parliament. If the Parliament rejects the proposals, the Council shall either allow them to lapse or to adopt them, acting *unanimously.*

Where the Parliament proposes any amendments, these must be considered by the Council, before it votes on the proposed act.

Under both of these articles, the Commission shall re-examine its proposals where the Parliament has proposed any amendments.

The Council shall vote, acting *unanimously*, to adopt the amendments made by the Parliament which have been rejected by the Commission.

Regulations, directives and decisions of the Council and of the Commission shall state the reasons on which they are based (Article **253**).

Replaced by:
Regulations, directives and decisions adopted jointly by the Council and the European Parliament and such acts adopted by the Council or the Commission shall state the reasons on which they are based.

Regulations shall be published in the Official Journal of the Community. They shall enter force either on the date stated or 20 days following their publication.

In addition :
Regulations, directives and decisions adopted in accordance with Article **251** shall be signed by the President of the European Parliament and by the President of the Council.

Directives and decisions shall be notified to those to whom they are addressed and shall take effect from the time of notification (Article **254**).

Treaty of Rome and Single European Act	Maastricht Treaty	Treaty of Amsterdam

(6) Provisions Common to Several Institutions :
(Continued)

<table>
<tr><td></td><td></td><td>

In addition :
Transparency :
Any citizen of the Union and any body residing in a Member State shall have a right of access to documents of the European Parliament, the Council and the Commission.
General principles will be determined by the Council, acting by **qualified majority under Article 251**, within two years of the date of this Treaty (Article **255**).

</td></tr>
<tr><td>

Decisions of the Council or of the Commission which impose a pecuniary obligation on persons other than States shall be enforceable and this will be governed by the civil law in the relevant State. The State Government shall designate a national authority to enforce these Decisions and notify the Commission and the Court of Justice.
Once these formalities are completed, the decision may be enforced in accordance with national law.
Only the Court of Justice can suspend enforcement. The national courts shall have jurisdiction over complaints that the enforcement is being carried out in an irregular manner (Article **256**).

</td><td></td><td></td></tr>
</table>

(7)   The Economic and Social Committee :
(Articles **257 - 262**)

The Committee shall have advisory status and shall be consulted by the Council or the Commission, where they consider it to be appropriate. It will consist of representatives from each of the Member States (in a weighted proportion) drawn from the various categories of economic and social activity. The Committee shall consist of **222** members (*after the accession of Austria, Finland and Sweden*). The members shall be appointed by the Council, acting *unanimously*, for a period of 4 years.	*In addition :* The Committee may issue an opinion on its own initiative in cases where it considers such action appropriate.	

Treaty of Rome and Single European Act	Maastricht Treaty	Treaty of Amsterdam
(8) The Economic and Social Committee : (Continued)		
The Committee shall include specialised sections for the principal fields, especially agriculture and transport. The opinion of the Committee shall be forwarded to the Council or the Commission.		*In addition:* The Committee may be consulted by the European Parliament (Article **262**).
	(9) The Committee of the Regions: (Articles **263** - **265**)	
	The Committee shall have advisory status and shall be consulted by the Council or the Commission, where they consider it appropriate.	*In addition :* The Committee will in particular be consulted on cross-border co-operation and may be consulted by the European Parliament (Article **265**).
	It will consist of representatives of regional and local bodies from each Member State (in weighted pro-portion). The Committee shall consist of **222** members (*after the accession of Austria, Finland and Sweden*). The members shall be appointed for 4 years and must be completely independent.	*In addition :* No member of the Committee can be at the same time a member of the European Parliament (Article **263**).
	The Committee may issue an opinion on its own initiative, where it considers it to be appropriate.	
(8) European Investment Bank : (Articles **266** - **267**)		
The tasks of the EIB will be to contribute to the balanced and steady development of the Common Market.	*Changed to :* In carrying out its tasks, the EIB shall help the financing of the programmes with assistance from the structural Funds and other Community financial instruments.	
It shall grant loans and give guarantees for the following types of project : (a) developing less-developed reg-ions; (b) modernising or converting undertakings; (c) projects of common interest to several Member States.		

Treaty of Rome and Single European Act	Maastricht Treaty	Treaty of Amsterdam

(9) European Investment Bank :
(Continued)

There will be one Governor from each Member State plus **22** Directors - **21** from the Member States and one from the Commission (*after the accession of Austria, Finland and Sweden*).

Financial Provisions :
(Articles **268 - 280**)

The Budget for each year will include all income and expenditure of the Community, including the European Social Fund.

The Budget shall be in balance (Article **268**).

In addition:
Administrative expenditure in relation to the Foreign Policy and Justice & Home Affairs shall be charged to the Budget.
The operational expenditure relating to these policies may be charged to the Budget, if the Council decides *unanimously*, following the terms of Articles **28** and **41** of Titles V and VI of the TEU respectively.

Member States shall make financial contributions (*on a given scale*) to form the revenue of the Community, including contributions to cover the cost of the European Social Fund (*on a different given scale*).
The Council, acting *unanimously*, may modify these scales of contributions.

~ Article repealed.

The Commission shall examine how the Member States' contributions can be replaced by financing by the Community's 'Own Resources', in particular from the Common Customs Tariff.

Replaced by:
The Budget shall be financed wholly from 'Own Resources'.

The Commission shall submit proposals to the Council concerning the system of 'Own Resources'.

The Council, after consulting the European Parliament, may, acting *unanimously*, recommend provisions to the Member States for adoption in accordance with their respective constitutional requirements (Article **269**).

Treaty of Rome and Single European Act	Maastricht Treaty	Treaty of Amsterdam

Financial Provisions :
(Continued)

In addition:
In order to maintain budgetary discipline, the Commission shall ensure that any proposal which may affect the Budget will be able to be financed entirely by the 'Own Resources' (Article **270**).

Expenditure in the Budget will be authorised for one year, unless the Council, acting *unanimously* on a proposal from the Commission, decides to alter this (Article **271**).

Any appropriations (other than staff expenditure) which have not been used by the year end, may be carried forward to the next financial year.
Appropriations shall be categorised according to their nature.
Expenditure of the European Parliament, Council, Commission and the Court of Justice shall be set out in separate parts of the Budget (Article **271**).

The financial year will be 1 January to 31 December.
Each Institution of the Community will draw up its expenditure budget by 1 July before the start of the year; the Commission shall consolidate this into a draft budget and present this to the Council by 1 September preceding the financial year.

The Council, acting by **qualified majority**, shall agree the budget and pass it to the European Parliament before 5 October.

The European Parliament, acting by a majority, may amend the Budget and propose any changes to the Council, by an absolute majority.
The European Parliament should vote within 45 days of receiving the Budget; if it has not voted, the Budget will be assumed to be adopted.
The Council shall review the proposed changes to the Budget made by the European Parliament and may adopt these amendments by **qualified majority** (Article **272**.4).

Treaty of Rome and Single European Act	Maastricht Treaty	Treaty of Amsterdam

Financial Provisions :
(Continued)

The European Parliament, acting by a majority and ° of the votes cast, can reject the draft budget and ask for a new draft to be submitted, if it considers that there are important reasons to do so.
(Article **272**.8).

A maximum rate of increase to the expenditure for each new year, except for items requiring an increase owing to the provisions of this Treaty, will be determined by the Commission, after consulting the Economic Policy Committee.
This rate may be increased by the European Parliament, acting by a majority and ° of the votes cast, and by the Council, acting by **qualified majority**.

The European Parliament, voting by a majority and 3/5 of the votes cast, may alter the expenditure and this aspect of the Council's decision will be suspended until the European Parliament has taken its decision (Article **272**.6).

If the Budget has not been finalised before the beginning of the year, then the Council, acting *unanimously*, may allow 1/12 of the previous year's budget to be spent in each month.
The Council, acting by **qualified majority** authorise expenditure in excess of 1/12.
If part of the expenditure does not relate to areas covered by this Treaty, then the decision must be passed to the European Parliament (Article **273**).

In addition:
The Council shall adopt the decision on the expenditure after consulting the European Parliament and the Court of Auditors.

The Commission shall implement the Budget, on its own responsibility, following the regulations set out by the Council, acting *unanimously*.

In addition:
The Commission shall follow the principles of sound financial management.

In addition :
Member States shall co-operate in accordance with the principles of sound financial management (Article **274**).

The regulations will give detailed rules for each institution (Article **274**).

The Commission shall provide annual accounts to the Council and the European Parliament (Article **275**).

Treaty of Rome and Single European Act	Maastricht Treaty	Treaty of Amsterdam

Financial Provisions :
(Continued)

Articles 206 and 206a [old numbering] described the powers of the Court of Auditors. These are discussed in Articles 246 - 248.

The Council, acting by **qualified majority**, shall recommend to the European Parliament that the Commission shall be discharged in respect of the implementation of the Budget. The European Parliament and the Council shall examine the accounts and the annual report of the Court of Auditors before giving the discharge. (Article **276**).

In addition:
Before giving the discharge, the European Parliament may ask the Commission to report on how the expenditure was operated and on the financial controls systems.
The Commission shall act on the decisions of the European Parliament and the comments adopted by the Council.
The Commission will report to the European Parliament and the Council on the implementation of these decisions, in particular on the instructions given to the various departments responsible for the implementation of the Budget.

In addition :
The annual report by the Court of Auditors will include the Statement of Assurance (Article **276**.1)

The Council, acting *unanimously* on a proposal from the Commission, will determine the currency for the Budget.
(Article **207**).

The financial contributions will be paid by the Member States in their national currencies.
These contributions shall be deposited in the Treasuries of the Member States; the parity of these contributions shall be maintained with the currency adopted for the Budget.
The Commission and the Member States will agree the terms for the funds to be invested.
The Council, acting *unanimously*, will determine the conditions for the operation of the European Social Fund.
(Article 207 [old numbering]).

~ Paragraphs deleted.

The Commission may transfer holdings of one currency into another, after notifying the relevant Member States, so that the monies can be used for the purposes within the scope of the Treaty.

Treaty of Rome and Single European Act	Maastricht Treaty	Treaty of Amsterdam

Financial Provisions :
(Continued)

The Commission shall deal with each Member State through the authorities designated by that Member State and the Commission will employ the services of the national banks of the Member States.
(Article **278**).

The Council, acting *unanimously* on a proposal from the Commission, shall :
(a) make financial regulations for the Budget;
(b) determine the way for the revenue for Own Resources to be made available to the Commission;
(c) lay down rules for the responsibility of the regulation of the Budget (Article **279**).

In addition:
The Council shall consult the European Parliament and obtain the opinion of the Court of Auditors before it acts on the proposal.

In addition :
Member States shall take measures to counter fraud in the Community as they would in their own countries.
Member States shall co-ordinate their actions to counter fraud in the Community (Article **280**).

In addition :
The Council, acting by **qualified majority under Article 251** after consulting the Court of Auditors, shall counter fraud by adopting measures to deter and give protection in the Member States
Each year, the Commission will report to the Council on the measures taken against fraud (Article **280**.5).

General and Final Provisions :
(Articles **281 - 312**)

The Community shall have legal personality and shall enjoy all legal protection and capacity in the Member States; it will be represented by the Commission.

The Commission may collect any information and carry out any checks required for the performance of its tasks under the Treaty.

Treaty of Rome and Single European Act	Maastricht Treaty	Treaty of Amsterdam

General and Final Provisions :
(Continued)

In addition :
The Council, acting by **qualified majority under Article 251**, will adopt measures for statistics to be produced on the activities of the Community. The production of these statistics should be impartial, reliable, objective and not put unnecessary burdens on businesses (Article **285**).

From 1 January 1999, protection of data, currently for individuals, will apply to the Community institutions. (Article **286**).
An independent supervisory body responsible for data protection will be established from 1 January 1999 by the Council, acting by **qualified majority under Article 251**.

Member States undertake to resolve any disputes concerning the Treaty solely through the institutions of the Community (i.e. the Commission, the Council and the Court of Justice). (Article **292**).

The terms of the Treaty will not prevent the following:
(a) A Member State shall not be obliged to supply information to other Member States which it considers to be in the essential interests of its security.
(b) A Member State may take such measures necessary for the protection of the essential interests of its security, as long as these measures do not adversely affect competition in the Common Market for products which are not intended specifically for military purposes.
The Council, acting *unanimously* may alter these areas (Article **296**).

If the functioning of the Common Market is likely to be affected by measures which a Member State has to take in the event of an emergency, the Commission shall examine how these measures can be adjusted to the rules of the Treaty (Article **298**).

Treaty of Rome and Single European Act	Maastricht Treaty	Treaty of Amsterdam
General and Final Provisions : (Continued)		

During the transitional period, a Member State may apply for authorisation to take action where there is a serious deterioration in the economic situation.
The Commission shall determine the protective measures necessary.

The Treaty will apply to the Member States. There will be special arrangements for other territories of the Member States, stated in Annex **II** of the Treaty (and Article **299**.2 for the French outermost regions).

The Council, acting *unanimously*, will determine which of the other Treaty provisions will apply to the French outermost regions (Article **299**).

Changed to :
The Council, acting by **qualified majority** after consulting the European Parliament, will determine the conditions of the Treaty to apply to the French outermost regions (Article **299**.2).

Agreements between the Community and other countries shall be negotiated by the Commission and concluded by the Council.
The Council, the Commission or a Member State may ask the Court of Justice if the proposed agreement is compatible with the Treaty.
The agreements made shall be binding to the Community and the Member States (Article **300**).

In addition :
The Council, acting by **qualified majority**, shall adopt, by directives, a framework for the Commission to operate within and shall appoint special committees to consult with the Commission.
The Council may authorise the Commission to approve modifications to the agreements.
The Council may attach specific conditions to the authorisation.
The Council, the Commission or a Member State may ask the Court of Justice to rule if an agreement is compatible with the Treaty.

The Council, acting by **qualified majority**, shall break or reduce economic relations with a third country, where the articles of the Treaty on European Union relating to the common foreign and security policy, so provides (Article **301**).

Treaty of Rome and Single European Act	Maastricht Treaty	Treaty of Amsterdam

General and Final Provisions :
(Continued)

Where the Treaty has not provided the necessary powers to the Council, and action should prove to be needed to achieve one of the objectives of the Community, the Council, acting *unanimously* after consulting the European Parliament, shall take the appropriate measures (Article **308**).

In addition :
Where the voting rights of a Member State have been suspended under the Common Provisions (Article **7** *of Title I, Common Provisions*), the voting rights will also apply to the Treaty establishing the European Community.
In addition, the Council, acting by **qualified majority**, may decide to suspend certain rights from the State, although the obligations will remain.
The Council, acting by **qualified majority**, may vary or revoke these measures. The votes of the State in question will not be included (Article **309**).

A Member State or the Commission may make proposals to the Council to amend the Treaty.
The amendments shall take effect after being ratified by all the Member States.

Article repealed and replaced by ***Article 48***, *Title* ***VIII***, *Final Provisions of the TEU (see below).*

Any European state may apply to the Council for membership of the Union.
The conditions for admission will be agreed by each of the Member States with the applicant state and ratified by all of the contracting states.

Article repealed and replaced by ***Article 49***, *Title* ***VIII***, *Final Provisions of the TEU (see below).*

Treaty of Rome and Single European Act	Maastricht Treaty	Treaty of Amsterdam

Setting up of the Institutions :
(Articles 241 - 246 [old numbering])

*These articles refer to the arrangements for the **first** meetings of the institutions of the Community (the Council, the Commission, the European Parliament, the Court of Justice and the Court of Auditors) after the signing of the Treaty of Rome.*
As a result, although these articles have not been repealed, they are no longer relevant and do not affect the Maastricht Treaty amendments.

~ *Articles repealed.*

Final Provisions :
(Articles **313 - 314**)

The Treaty shall be ratified by the High Contracting Parties of each Member State and will come into force one month after the last signatory has signed the Treaty.

Effectively, these articles have been superseded by the Maastricht Treaty, although they have not been repealed.

*The Maastricht Treaty has a separate section for the Final Provisions, under **Title VIII of the TEU (Articles 46 - 48**), and this is an expanded and more detailed series of articles than in the Treaty of Rome.*
***Articles 46, 47** and **50** of Title VIII define the limitations of the amendments of the Maastricht Treaty to the provisions of the Treaty on European Union and repeal certain articles of previous treaties which have been superseded by the Maastricht Treaty.*

* * * * * * *

CXX

'THE TREATY ON EUROPEAN UNION'

The Treaty of Rome as amended by The Single European Act,
The Maastricht Treaty and **The Treaty of Amsterdam**

2

TREATY ON EUROPEAN UNION

SUBJECT CONTENTS

4

* * * * * * *

THE CONSOLIDATED TREATY ON EUROPEAN UNION

HIS MAJESTY THE KING OF THE BELGIANS,

HER MAJESTY THE QUEEN OF DENMARK,

THE PRESIDENT OF THE FEDERAL REPUBLIC OF GERMANY,

THE PRESIDENT OF THE HELLENIC REPUBLIC,

HIS MAJESTY THE KING OF SPAIN,

THE PRESIDENT OF THE FRENCH REPUBLIC,

THE PRESIDENT OF IRELAND,

THE PRESIDENT OF THE ITALIAN REPUBLIC,

HIS ROYAL HIGHNESS THE GRAND DUKE OF LUXEMBOURG,

HER MAJESTY THE QUEEN OF THE NETHERLANDS,

THE PRESIDENT OF THE PORTUGUESE REPUBLIC,

HER MAJESTY THE QUEEN OF THE UNITED KINGDOM OF GREAT BRITAIN AND NORTHERN IRELAND,

RESOLVED to mark a new stage in the process of European integration undertaken with the establishment of the European Communities,

RECALLING the historic importance of the ending of the division of the European continent and the need to create firm bases for the construction of the future Europe,

CONFIRMING their attachment to the principles of liberty, democracy and respect for human rights and fundamental freedoms and of the rule of law,

CONFIRMING their attachment to fundamental social rights as defined in the European Social Charter signed at Turin on 18 October 1961 and in the 1989 Community Charter of the Fundamental Social Rights of Workers,

DESIRING to deepen the solidarity between their peoples while respecting their history, their culture and their traditions,

DESIRING to enhance further the democratic and efficient functioning of the institutions so as to enable them better to carry out, within a single institutional framework, the tasks entrusted to them,

RESOLVED to achieve the strengthening and the convergence of their economies and to establish an economic and monetary union, in accordance with the provisions of this Treaty, a single and stable currency,

DETERMINED to promote economic and social progress for their peoples, **taking into account the principle of sustainable development and** within the context of the accomplishment of the internal market and of reinforced cohesion and environmental protection, and to implement policies ensuring that advances in economic integration are accompanied by parallel progress in other fields,

RESOLVED to establish a citizenship common to nationals of their countries,

RESOLVED to implement a common foreign and security policy including the **progressive** framing of a common defence policy, **which might lead** to a common defence **in accordance with the provisions of Article 17**, thereby reinforcing the European identity and its independence in order to promote peace, security and progress in Europe and in the world,

RESOLVED to facilitate the free movement of persons, while ensuring the safety and security of their peoples, by **establishing an area of freedom, security and justice, in accordance with the provisions of this Treaty,**

RESOLVED to continue the process of creating an ever closer union among the peoples of Europe, in which decisions are taken as closely as possible to the citizen in accordance with the principle of subsidiarity,

IN VIEW of further steps to be taken in order to advance European integration,

HAVE DECIDED to establish a European Union and to this end have designated as their plenipotentiaries:

HIS MAJESTY THE KING OF THE BELGIANS:

Mark EYSKENS,
Minister for Foreign Affairs;

Philippe MAYSTADT,
Minister for Finance;

HER MAJESTY THE QUEEN OF DENMARK:

Uffe ELLEMANN-JENSEN,
Minister for Foreign Affairs;

Anders FOGH RASMUSSEN,
Minister for Economic Affairs;

THE PRESIDENT OF THE FEDERAL REPUBLIC
OF GERMANY:

Hans-Dietrich GENSCHER,
Federal Minister for Foreign Affairs;

Theodor WAIGEL,
Federal Minister for Finance;

THE PRESIDENT OF THE HELLENIC REPUBLIC:

Antonios SAMARAS,
Minister for Foreign Affairs;

Efthymios CHRISTODOULOU,
Minister for Economic Affairs;

HIS MAJESTY THE KING OF SPAIN:

Francisco FERNÁNDEZ ORDÓÑEZ,
Minister for Foreign Affairs;

Carlos SOLCHAGA CATALÁN,
Minister for Economic Affairs and Finance;

THE PRESIDENT OF THE FRENCH REPUBLIC:

Roland DUMAS,
Minister for Foreign Affairs;

Pierre BEREGOVOY,
Minister for Economic and Financial Affairs
and the Budget;

THE PRESIDENT OF IRELAND:

Gerard COLLINS,
Minister for Foreign Affairs;

Bertie AHERN,
Minister for Finance;

THE PRESIDENT OF THE ITALIAN
REPUBLIC:

Gianni DE MICHELIS,
Minister for Foreign Affairs;

Guido CARLI,
Minister for the Treasury;

HIS ROYAL HIGHNESS THE GRAND
DUKE OF LUXEMBOURG:

Jacques F. POOS,
Deputy Prime Minister,
Minister for Foreign Affairs;

Jean-Claude JUNCKER,
Minister for Finance;

HER MAJESTY THE QUEEN OF THE
NETHERLANDS:

Hans van den BROEK,
Minister for Foreign Affairs;

Willem KOK,
Minister for Finance;

THE PRESIDENT OF THE
PORTUGUESE REPUBLIC:

João de Deus PINHEIRO,
Minister for Foreign Affairs;

Jorge BRAGA de MACEDO,
Minister for Finance;

HER MAJESTY THE QUEEN OF THE
UNITED KINGDOM OF GREAT
BRITAIN AND NORTHERN IRELAND:

The Rt. Hon. Douglas HURD,
Secretary of State for Foreign and
Commonwealth Affairs;

The Hon. Francis MAUDE,
Financial Secretary to the Treasury;

WHO, having exchanged their full powers, found in good and due form, have agreed as follows.

TITLE I

COMMON PROVISIONS

ARTICLE **1** (ex Article A)

By this Treaty, the HIGH CONTRACTING PARTIES establish among themselves a EUROPEAN UNION, hereinafter called 'the Union'.

This Treaty marks a new stage in the process of creating an ever closer union among the peoples of Europe, in which decisions are taken as **openly as possible and** closely as possible to the citizen.

The Union shall be founded on the European Communities, supplemented by the policies and forms of co-operation established by this Treaty. Its task shall be to organise, in a manner demonstrating consistency and solidarity, relations between the Member States and between their peoples.

ARTICLE **2** (ex Article B)

The Union shall set itself the following objectives:

- to promote economic and social progress **and a high level of employment and to achieve** balanced and sustainable **development**, in particular through the creation of an area without internal frontiers, through the strengthening of economic and social cohesion and through the establishment of economic and monetary union, ultimately including a single currency in accordance with the provisions of this Treaty;
- to assert its identity on the international scene, in particular through the implementation of a common foreign and security policy including the **progressive** framing of a common defence policy, which **might lead** to a common defence, **in accordance with the provisions of Article 17**;
- to strengthen the protection of the rights and interests of the nationals of its Member States through the introduction of a citizenship of the Union;
- **to maintain and develop the Union as an area of freedom, security and justice, in which the free movement of persons is assured in conjunction with appropriate measures with respect to external borders controls, immigration, asylum and the prevention and combating of crime;**
- to maintain in full the *acquis communautaire* and build on it with a view to **considering to** what extent the policies and forms of co-operation introduced by this Treaty may need to be revised with the aim of ensuring the effectiveness of the mechanisms and the institutions of the Community.

The objectives of the Union shall be achieved as provided in this Treaty and in accordance with the conditions and the timetable set out therein while respecting the principle of subsidiarity as defined in Article **5** of the Treaty establishing the European Community.

ARTICLE **3** (ex Article C)

The Union shall be served by a single institutional framework which shall ensure the consistency and the continuity of the activities carried out in order to attain its objectives while respecting and building upon the *acquis communautaire*.

The Union shall in particular ensure the consistency of its external activities as a whole in the context of its external relations, security, economic and development policies. The Council and the Commission shall be responsible for ensuring such consistency **and shall co-operate to this end**. They shall ensure the implementation of these policies, each in accordance with its respective powers.

ARTICLE **4** (ex Article D)

The European Council shall provide the Union with the necessary impetus for its development and shall define the general political guidelines thereof.

The European Council shall bring together the Heads of State or Government of the Member States and the President of the Commission. They shall be assisted by the Ministers for Foreign Affairs of the Member States and by a Member of the Commission. The European Council shall meet at least twice a year, under the chairmanship of the Head of State or Government of the Member State which holds the Presidency of the Council.

The European Council shall submit to the European Parliament a report after each of its meetings and a yearly written report on the progress achieved by the Union.

ARTICLE **5** (ex Article E)
The European Parliament, the Council, the Commission, the Court of Justice **and the Court of Auditors** shall exercise their powers under the conditions and for the purposes provided for, on the one hand, by the provisions of the Treaties establishing the European Communities and of the subsequent Treaties and Acts modifying and supplementing them and, on the other hand, by the other provisions of this Treaty.

ARTICLE **6** (ex Article F)
1. **The Union is founded on the principles of liberty, democracy, respect for human rights and fundamental freedoms, and the rule of law, principles which are common to the Member States.**

2. The Union shall respect fundamental rights, as guaranteed by the European Convention for the Protection of Human Rights and Fundamental Freedoms signed in Rome on 4 November 1950 and as they result from the constitutional traditions common to the Member States, as general principles of Community law.

3. **The Union shall respect the national identities of its Member States.**

4. The Union shall provide itself with the means necessary to attain its objectives and carry through its policics.

ARTICLE 7 (ex Article **F.1**)
1. **The Council, meeting in the composition of the Heads of State or Government and acting by unanimity on a proposal by one-third of the Member States or by the Commission and after obtaining the assent of the European Parliament, may determine the existence of a serious and persistent breach by a Member State of principles mentioned in Article 6(1), after inviting the government of the Member State in question to submit its observations.**

2. **Where such a determination has been made, the Council, acting by a qualified majority, may decide to suspend certain of the rights deriving from the application of this Treaty to the Member State in question, including the voting rights of the representative of the government of that Member State in the Council. In doing so, the Council shall take into account the possible consequences of such a suspension on the rights and obligations of natural and legal persons.**
The obligations of the Member State in question under this Treaty shall in any case continue to be binding on that State.

3. **The Council, acting by a qualified majority, may decide subsequently to vary or revoke measures taken under paragraph 2 in response to changes in the situation which led to their being imposed.**

4. **For the purposes of this Article, the Council shall act without taking into account the vote of the representative of the government of the Member State in question. Abstentions by members present in person or represented shall not prevent the adoption of decisions referred to in paragraph 1. A qualified majority shall be defined as the same proportion of the weighted votes of the members of the Council concerned as laid down in Article 205(2) of the Treaty establishing the European Community. This paragraph shall also apply in the event of voting rights being suspended pursuant to paragraph 2.**

5. **For the purposes of this Article, the European Parliament shall act by a two-thirds majority of the votes cast, representing a majority of its members.**

* * * * * * *

*The following three Articles form part of the Treaty on European Union and contain provisions from the Maastricht Treaty and the Treaty of Amsterdam which amend the Treaties establishing the European Community, the European Coal and Steel Community and the European Atomic Energy Community. The provisions in Article 8 have been consolidated into the treaty establishing the European Community, starting on page 25; the provisions amending Titles **III** and **IV** have not been reproduced (see pages VI and VIII for notes on these Titles).*

TITLE II

PROVISIONS AMENDING THE TREATY ESTABLISHING THE EUROPEAN ECONOMIC COMMUNITY WITH A VIEW TO ESTABLISHING THE EUROPEAN COMMUNITY

ARTICLE **8** (ex Article G)
Provisions amending the Treaty establishing the European Community.

TITLE III

PROVISIONS AMENDING THE TREATY ESTABLISHING THE EUROPEAN COAL AND STEEL COMMUNITY

ARTICLE **9** (ex Article H)
Provisions amending the Treaty establishing the European Coal and Steel Community.

TITLE IV

PROVISIONS AMENDING THE TREATY ESTABLISHING THE EUROPEAN ATOMIC ENERGY COMMUNITY

ARTICLE **10** (ex Article I)
Provisions amending the Treaty establishing the European Atomic Energy Community.

* * * * * * *

10

TITLE V

PROVISIONS ON A COMMON FOREIGN
AND
SECURITY POLICY

Article J shall be repealed.

ARTICLE **11** (ex Article **J.1**)
1.   **The Union** shall define and implement a common foreign and security policy **covering all areas of foreign and security policy, the objectives of which shall be:**
-    to safeguard the common values, fundamental interests, independence **and integrity** of the Union **in conformity with the principles of the United Nations Charter;**
-    to strengthen the security of **the Union** in all ways;
-    to preserve peace and strengthen international security, in accordance with the principles of the United Nations Charter, as well as the principles of the Helsinki Final Act and the objectives of the Paris Charter, **including those on external borders;**
-    to promote international co-operation;
-    to develop and consolidate democracy and the rule of law, and respect for human rights and fundamental freedoms.

2.   The Member States shall support the Union's external and security policy actively and unreservedly in a spirit of loyalty and mutual solidarity.
The Member States shall work together to enhance and develop their mutual political solidarity. They shall refrain from any action which is contrary to the interests of the Union or likely to impair its effectiveness as a cohesive force in international relations.
The Council shall ensure that these principles are complied with.

ARTICLE **12** (ex Article **J.2**)
The Union shall pursue the objectives set out in Article 11 by:
-    **defining the principles of and general guidelines for the common foreign and security policy;**
-    **deciding on common strategies;**
-    **adapting joint actions;**
-    **adopting common positions:**
-    **and strengthening systematic co-operation between Member States in the conduct of policy.**

ARTICLE **13** (ex Article **J.3**)
1.   The European Council shall define the principles of and general guidelines for the common foreign and security policy, **including for matters with defence implications.**

2.   **The European Council shall decide on common strategies to be implemented by the Union in areas where the Member States have important interests in common.**
Common strategies shall set out their objectives, duration and the means to be made available by the Union and the Member States.

3.   The Council shall take the decisions necessary for defining and implementing the common foreign and security policy on the basis of the general guidelines **defined** by the European Council.
The Council shall recommend common strategies to the European Council and shall implement them, in particular by adopting joint actions and common positions.
The Council shall ensure the unity, consistency and effectiveness of action by the Union.
(formally Article J.8(1-2))

ARTICLE 14 (ex Article J.4)

1. **The Council shall adopt joint actions. Joint actions shall address specific situations where operational action by the Union is deemed to be required. They shall lay down their objectives, scope, the means to be made available to the Union, if necessary their duration, and the conditions for their implementation.**

2. If there is a change in circumstances having a substantial effect on a question subject to joint action, the Council shall review the principles and objectives of that action and take the necessary decisions. As long as the Council has not acted, the joint action shall stand.

3. Joint actions shall commit the Member States in the positions they adopt and in the conduct of their activity.

4. **The Council may request the Commission to submit to it any appropriate proposals relating to the common foreign and security policy to ensure the implementation of a joint action.**

5. Whenever there is any plan to adopt a national position or take national action pursuant to a joint action, information shall be provided in time to allow, if necessary, for prior consultations within the Council. The obligation to provide prior information shall not apply to measures which are merely a national transposition of Council decisions.

6. In cases of imperative need arising from changes in the situation and failing a Council decision, Member States may take the necessary measures as a matter of urgency having regard to the general objectives of the joint action. The Member State concerned shall inform the Council immediately of any such measures.

7. Should there be any major difficulties in implementing a joint action, a Member State shall refer them to the Council which shall discuss them and seek appropriate solutions. Such solutions shall not run counter to the objectives of the joint action or impair its effectiveness.
(formally Article J.3(3-7))

ARTICLE 15 (ex Article J.5)
The Council shall adopt common positions. Common positions shall define the approach of the Union to a particular matter of a geographical or thematic nature. Member States shall ensure that their national policies conform to the common positions.

ARTICLE 16 (ex Article J.6)
Member States shall inform and consult one another within the Council on any matter of foreign and security policy of general interest in order to ensure that the Union's influence is exerted as effectively as possible by means of concerted and convergent action.
(formally Article J.2(1))

ARTICLE 17 (ex Article J.7)
1. The common foreign and security policy shall include all questions relating to the security of the Union, including **the progressive** framing of a common defence policy, **in accordance with the second sub-paragraph, which might lead** to a common defence, **should the European Council so decide. It shall in that case recommend to the Member States the adoption of such a decision in accordance with their respective constitutional requirements.**
The Western European Union (WEU) is an integral part of the development of the Union providing the Union with access to an operational capability notably in the context of paragraph 2. It supports the Union in framing the defence aspects of the common foreign and security policy as set out in this Article. The Union shall accordingly foster closer institutional relations with the WEU with a view to the possibility of the integration of the WEU into the Union, should the European Council so decide. It shall in that case recommend to the Member States the adoption of such a decision in accordance with their respective constitutional requirements.
The policy of the Union in accordance with this Article shall not prejudice the specific character of the security and defence policy of certain Member States and shall respect the obligations of certain Member States, **which see their common defence realised in the North Atlantic Treaty Organisation (NATO),** under the North Atlantic Treaty and be compatible with the common security and defence policy established within that framework.
The progressive framing of a common defence policy will be supported, as Member States consider appropriate, by co-operation between them in the field of armaments.

2. Questions referred to in this Article shall include humanitarian and rescue tasks, peacekeeping tasks and tasks of combat forces in crisis management, including peacemaking.

3. The Union will avail itself of the WEU to elaborate and implement decisions and actions of the Union which have defence implications.
The competence of the European Council to establish guidelines in accordance with Article 13 shall also obtain in respect of the WEU for those matters for which the Union avails itself of the WEU.
When the Union avails itself of the WEU to elaborate and implement decisions of the Union on the tasks referred to in paragraph 2, all Member States of the Union shall be entitled to participate fully in the tasks in question. The Council, in agreement with the institutions of the WEU, shall adopt the necessary practical arrangements to allow all Member States contributing to the tasks in question to participate fully and on an equal footing in planning and decision-taking in the WEU.
Decisions having defence implications dealt with under this paragraph shall be taken without prejudice to the policies and obligations referred to in paragraph 1, third sub-paragraph.

4. The provisions of this Article shall not prevent the development of closer co-operation between two or more Member States on a bilateral level, in the framework of the WEU and the Atlantic Alliance, provided such co-operation does not run counter to or impede that provided for in this Title.

5. With a view to furthering the objectives of this Article, **the provisions of this Article will be reviewed in accordance with Article 48**.
(formally Article J.4(1,4,5 and 6))

ARTICLE 18 (ex Article **J.8**)
1. The Presidency shall represent the Union in matters coming within the common foreign and security policy.

2. The Presidency shall be responsible for the implementation of **decisions taken under this Title**; in that capacity it shall in principle express the position of the Union in international organisations and international conferences.
(formally Article J.5(1-2))

3. **The Presidency shall be assisted by the Secretary-General of the Council who shall exercise the function of High Representative for the common foreign and security policy.**

4. **The Commission shall be fully associated in the tasks referred to in paragraphs 1 and 2. The Presidency shall be assisted in those tasks if need be by the next Member State to hold the Presidency.**

5. **The Council may, whenever it deems it necessary, appoint a special representative with a mandate in relation to particular policy issues.**

ARTICLE 19 (ex Article **J.9**)
1. Member States shall co-ordinate their action in international organisations and at international conferences. They shall uphold the common positions in such fora.
In international organisations and at international conferences where not all the Member States participate, those which do take part shall uphold the common positions.
(formally Article J.2(3))

2. Without prejudice to **paragraph 1 and Article 14(3)**. Member States represented in international organisations or international conferences where not all the Member States participate shall keep the latter informed of any matter of common interest.
Member States which are also members of the United Nations Security Council will concert and keep the other Member States fully informed. Member States which are permanent members of the Security Council will, in the execution of their functions, ensure the defence of the positions and the interests of the Union, without prejudice to their responsibilities under the provisions of the United Nations Charter.
(formally Article J.5(4))

ARTICLE 20 (ex Article **J.10**)
The diplomatic and consular missions of the Member States and the Commission Delegations in third countries and international conferences, and their representations to international organisations, shall co-operate in ensuring that the common positions and common measures adopted by the Council are complied with and implemented.

They shall step up co-operation by exchanging information, carrying out joint assessments and contributing to the implementation of the provisions referred to in Article **20** of the Treaty establishing the European Community.
(formally Article J.6)

ARTICLE 21 (ex Article **J.11**)
The Presidency shall consult the European Parliament on the main aspects and the basic choices of the common foreign and security policy and shall ensure that the views of the European Parliament are duly taken into consideration. The European Parliament shall be kept regularly informed by the Presidency and the Commission of the development of the Union's foreign and security policy.
The European Parliament may ask questions of the Council or make recommendations to it. It shall hold an annual debate on progress in implementing the common foreign and security policy.
(formally Article J.7)

ARTICLE 22 (ex Article **J.12**)
1. Any Member State or the Commission may refer to the Council any question relating to the common foreign and security policy and may submit proposals to the Council.

2. In cases requiring a rapid decision, the Presidency, of its own motion, or at the request of the Commission or a Member State, shall convene an extraordinary Council meeting within forty-eight hours or, in an emergency, within a shorter period.
(formally Article J.8(3-4))

ARTICLE 23 (ex Article **J.13**)
1. **Decisions under this Title shall be taken by the Council acting unanimously. Abstentions by members present in person or represented shall not prevent the adoption of such decisions.**
When abstaining in a vote, any member of the Council may qualify its abstention by making a formal declaration under the present sub-paragraph. In that case, it shall not be obliged to apply the decision, but shall accept that the decision commits the Union. In a spirit of mutual solidarity, the Member State concerned shall refrain from any action likely to conflict with or impede Union action based on that decision and the other Member States shall respect its position. If the members of the Council qualifying their abstention in this way represent more than one-third of the votes weighted in accordance with Article 205(2) of the Treaty establishing the European Community, the decision shall not be adopted.

2. **By derogation from the provisions of paragraph 1, the Council shall act by qualified majority:**
- **when adopting joint actions, common positions or taking any other decision on the basis of a common strategy;**
- **when adopting any decision implementing a joint action or a common position.**
If a member of the Council declares that, for important and stated reasons of national policy, it intends to oppose the adoption of a decision to be taken by qualified majority, a vote shall not be taken. The Council may, acting by a qualified majority, request that the matter be referred to the European Council for decision by unanimity.
The votes of the members of the Council shall be weighted in accordance with Article 205(2) of the Treaty establishing the European Community. For their adoption, decisions shall require at least 62 votes in favour, cast by at least 10 members.
This paragraph shall not apply to decisions having military or defence implications.

3. **For procedural questions, the Council shall act by a majority of its members.**

ARTICLE 24 (ex Article **J.14**)
When it is necessary to conclude an agreement with one or more States or international organisations in implementation of this Title, the Council, acting unanimously, may authorise the Presidency, assisted by the Commission as appropriate, to open negotiations to that effect. Such agreements shall be concluded by the Council acting unanimously on a recommendation from the Presidency. No agreement shall be binding on a Member State whose representative in the Council states that it has to comply with the requirements of its own constitutional procedure; the other members of the Council may agree that the agreement shall apply provisionally to them.
The provisions of this Article shall also apply to matters falling under Title VI.

ARTICLE 25 (ex Article **J.15**)

Without prejudice to Article **207** of the Treaty establishing the European Community, **a Political Committee shall monitor** the international situation in the areas covered by common foreign and security policy and contribute to the definition of policies by delivering opinions to the Council at the request of the Council or on its own initiative. It shall also monitor the implementation of agreed policies, without prejudice to the responsibility of the Presidency and the Commission.

(formally Article J.8(5))

ARTICLE 26 (ex Article **J.16**)

The Secretary-General of the Council, High Representative for the common foreign and security policy, shall assist the Council in matters coming within the scope of the common foreign and security policy, in particular through contributing to the formulation, preparation and implementation of policy decisions, and, when appropriate and acting on behalf of the Council at the request of the Presidency, through conducting political dialogue with third parties.

ARTICLE 27 (ex Article **J.17**)

The Commission shall be fully associated with the work carried out in the common foreign and security policy field.

(formally Article J.9)

ARTICLE 28 (ex Article **J.18**)

1.   The provisions referred to in Articles **189, 190, 196** to **199, 203, 204, 206** to **209, 213** to **219, 255** and **290** of the Treaty establishing the European Community shall apply to the provisions relating to the areas referred to in this Title.

2.   Administrative expenditure which the provisions relating to the areas referred to in this Title entail for the institutions shall be charged to the budget of the European Communities.

(formally Article J.11(1-2))

3.   **Operational expenditure to which the implementation of those provisions gives rise shall also be charged to the budget of the European Communities, except for such expenditure arising from operations having military or defence implications and cases where the Council acting unanimously decides otherwise.**

In cases where expenditure is not charged to the budget of the European Communities it shall be charged to the Member States in accordance with the gross national product scale, unless the Council acting unanimously decides otherwise. As for expenditure arising from operations having military or defence implications, Member States whose representatives in the Council have made a formal declaration under Article 23(1), second sub-paragraph, shall not be obliged to contribute to the financing thereof.

4.   **The budgetary procedure laid down in the Treaty establishing the European Community shall apply to the expenditure charged to the budget of the European Communities.**

* * * * * * *

TITLE VI

PROVISIONS ON POLICE AND JUDICIAL CO-OPERATION IN CRIMINAL MATTERS

Article K shall be repealed.

ARTICLE 29   (ex Article **K.1**)
Without prejudice to the powers of the European Community, the Union's objective shall be to provide citizens with a high level of safety within an area of freedom, security and justice by developing common action among the Member States in the fields of police and judicial co-operation in criminal matters and by preventing and combating racism and xenophobia.

That objective shall be achieved by preventing and combating crime, organised or otherwise, in particular terrorism, trafficking in persons and offences against children, illicit drug trafficking and illicit arms trafficking, corruption and fraud, through:

- closer co-operation between police forces, customs authorities and other competent authorities in the Member States, both directly and, through the European Police Office (Europol), in accordance with the provisions of Article 30 and 32;
- closer co-operation between judicial and other competent authorities of the Member States in accordance with the provisions of Articles 31(a) to (d) and 32;
- approximation, where necessary, of rules on criminal matters in the Member States, in accordance with the provisions of Article 31(e).

ARTICLE 30   (ex Article **K.2**)
1.   Common action in the field of police co-operation shall include:
(a)   operational co-operation between the competent authorities, including the police, customs and other specialised law enforcement services of the Member States in relation to the prevention, detection and investigation of criminal offences;
(b)   the collection, storage, processing, analysis and exchange of relevant information, including information held by law enforcement services of reports on suspicious financial transactions, in particular through Europol, subject to appropriate provisions on the protection of personal data;
(c)   co-operation and joint initiatives in training, the exchange of liaison officers, secondments, the use of equipment, and forensic research;
(d)   the common evaluation of particular investigative techniques in relation to the detection of serious forms of organised crime.

2.   The Council shall promote co-operation through Europol and shall in particular, within a period of five years after the date of entry into force of the Treaty of Amsterdam:
(a)   enable Europol to facilitate and support the preparation, and to encourage the co-ordination and carrying out of specific investigative actions by the competent authorities of the Member States, including operational actions of joint teams comprising representatives of Europol in a support capacity;
(b)   adopt measures allowing Europol to ask the competent authorities of the Member States to conduct and co-ordinate their investigations in specific cases and to develop specific expertise which may be put at the disposal of Member States to assist them in investigating cases of organised crime;
(c)   promote liaison arrangements between prosecuting/investigating officials specialising in the fight against organised crime in close co-operation with Europol;
(d)   establish a research, documentation and statistical network on cross-border crime.

ARTICLE 31   (ex Article **K.3**)
Common action on judicial co-operation in criminal matters shall include:
(a)   facilitating and accelerating co-operation between competent ministries and judicial or equivalent authorities of the Member States in relation to proceedings and the enforcement of decisions;
(b)   facilitating extradition between Member States;

(c) ensuring compatibility in rules applicable in the Member States, as may be necessary to improve such co-operation;

(d) preventing conflicts of jurisdiction between Member States;

(e) progressively adopting measures establishing minimum rules relating to the constituent elements of criminal acts and to penalties in the fields of organised crime, terrorism and drug trafficking.

ARTICLE 32 (ex Article K.4)

The Council shall lay down the conditions and limitations under which the competent authorities referred to in Articles 30 and 31 may operate in the territory of another Member State in liaison and in agreement with the authorities of that State.

ARTICLE 33 (ex Article K.5)

This Title shall not affect the exercise of the responsibilities incumbent upon Member States with regard to the maintenance of law and order and the safeguarding of internal security.
(*formally Article K.2(2)*)

ARTICLE 34 (ex Article K.6)

1. In the areas referred to **in this Title**, Member States shall inform and consult one another within the Council with a view to co-ordinating their action. To that end, they shall establish collaboration between the relevant departments of their administrations.
(*formally Article K.3(1)*)

2. The Council shall take measures and promote co-operation, using the appropriate form and procedures as set out in this Title, contributing to the pursuit of the objectives of the Union. To that end, acting unanimously on an initiative of any Member State or of the Commission, the Council may:

(a) adopt common positions defining the approach of the Union to a particular matter;

(b) adopt framework decisions for the purpose of approximation of the laws and regulations of the Member States. Framework decisions shall be binding upon the Member States as to the result to be achieved but shall leave to the national authorities the choice of form and methods. They shall not entail direct effect;

(c) adopt decisions for any other purpose consistent with the objectives of this Title, excluding any approximation of the laws and regulations of the Member States. These decisions shall be binding and shall not entail direct effect; the Council, acting by a qualified majority, shall adopt measures necessary to implement those decisions at the level of the Union;

(d) establish conventions which it shall recommend to the Member States for adoption in accordance with their respective constitutional requirements. Member States shall begin the procedures applicable within a time limit to be set by the Council.

Unless they provide otherwise, conventions shall, once adopted by at least half of the Member States, enter into force for those Member States. Measures implementing conventions shall be adopted within the Council by a majority of two-thirds of the Contracting Parties.

3. Where the Council is required to act by a qualified majority, the votes of its members shall be weighted as laid down in Article 205(2) of the Treaty establishing the European Community, and for their adoption acts of the Council shall require at least 62 votes in favour, cast by at least 10 members.

4. For procedural questions, the Council shall act by a majority of its members.

ARTICLE 35 (ex Article K.7)

1. The Court of Justice of the European Communities shall have jurisdiction, subject to the conditions laid down in this Article, to give preliminarily rulings on the validity and interpretation of framework decisions and decisions, on the interpretation of conventions established under this Title and on the validity and interpretation of the measures implementing them.

2. By a declaration made at the time of signature of the Treaty of Amsterdam or any time thereafter, any Member State shall be able to accept the jurisdiction of the Court of Justice to give preliminary rulings as specified in paragraph 1.

3. Where a Member State has made a declaration pursuant to paragraph 2 of this Article:

(a) any court or tribunal of that State against whose decisions there is no judicial remedy under national law may request the Court of Justice to give a preliminary ruling on a question raised in a case pending before it and concerning the validity or interpretation of an act referred to in paragraph 1 if that court or tribunal considers that a decision on the question is necessary to enable it to give judgement, or

(b) any court or tribunal of that State may request the Court of Justice to give a preliminary ruling on a question raised in a case pending before it and concerning the validity or interpretation of an act referred to in paragraph 1 if that court or tribunal considers that a decision on the question is necessary to enable it to give judgement.

4. Any Member State, whether or not it has made a declaration pursuant to paragraph 2, shall be entitled to submit statements of case or written observations to the Court in cases which arise under paragraph 1.

5. The Court of Justice shall have no jurisdiction to review the validity or proportionality of operations carried out by the police or other law enforcement agencies of a Member State or the exercise of the responsibilities incumbent upon Member States with regard to the maintenance of law and order and the safeguarding of internal security.

6. The Court of Justice shall have jurisdiction to review the legality of framework decisions and decisions in actions brought by a Member State or the Commission on grounds of lack of competence, infringement of an essential procedural requirement, infringement of this Treaty or of any rule of law relating to its application, or misuse of powers. The proceedings provided for in this paragraph shall be instituted within two months of the publication of the measure.

7. The Court of Justice shall have jurisdiction to rule on any dispute between Member States regarding the interpretation or the application of acts adopted under Article 34(2) whenever such dispute cannot be settled by the Council within six months of its being referred to the Council by one of its members. The Court shall also have jurisdiction to rule on any dispute between Member States and the Commission regarding the interpretation or the application of conventions established under Article 34(2)(d).

ARTICLE 36 (ex Article **K.8**)

1. A Co-ordinating Committee shall be set up consisting of senior officials. In addition to its co-ordinating role, it shall be the task of the Committee to:
- give opinions for the attention of the Council, either at the Council's request or on its own initiative;
- **contribute, without prejudice to Article 207 of the Treaty establishing the European Community, to the preparation of the Council's discussions in the areas referred to in Article 29**.

2. **The Commission shall be fully associated with the work in the areas referred to in this Title.**
(formally Article K.4(1-2))

ARTICLE 37 (ex Article **K.9**)

Within international organisations and at international conferences in which they take part, Member States shall defend the common positions adopted under the provisions of this Title.
Articles 18 and 19 shall apply as appropriate to matters falling under this Title.
(formally Article K.5)

ARTICLE 38 (ex Article **K.10**)

Agreements referred to in Article 24 may cover matters falling under this Title.

ARTICLE 39 (ex Article **K.11**)

1. **The Council shall consult the European Parliament before adopting any measure referred to in Article 34(2)(b), (c) and (d). The European Parliament shall deliver its opinion within a time-limit which the Council may lay down, which shall not be less than three months. In the absence of an opinion within that time-limit, the Council may act.**

2. The Presidency and the Commission shall regularly inform the European Parliament of discussions in the areas covered by this Title.

3. The European Parliament may ask questions of the Council or make recommendations to it. Each year, it shall hold a debate on the progress made in the areas referred to in this Title.
(formally Article K.6)

ARTICLE 40 (ex Article **K.12**)

1. **Member States which intend to establish closer co-operation between themselves may be authorised, subject to Articles 43 and 44, to make use of the institutions, procedures and mechanisms laid down by the Treaties provided that the co-operation proposed:**
(a) **respects the powers of the European Community, and the objectives laid down by this Title;**

(b)   has the aim of enabling the Union to develop more rapidly into an area of freedom, security and justice.

2.   The authorisation referred to in paragraph 1 shall be granted by the Council, acting by a qualified majority at the request of the Member States concerned and after inviting the Commission to present its opinion; the request shall also be forwarded to the European Parliament.
If a member of the Council declares that, for important and stated reasons of national policy, it intends to oppose the granting of an authorisation by qualified majority, a vote shall not be taken. The Council may, acting by a qualified majority, request that the matter be referred to the European Council for decision by unanimity.
The votes of the members of the Council shall be weighted in accordance with Article 205(2) of the Treaty establishing the European Community. For their adoption, decisions shall require at least 62 votes in favour, cast by at least 10 members.

3.   Any Member State which wishes to become a party to co-operation set up in accordance with this Article shall notify its intention to the Council and to the Commission, which shall give an opinion to the Council within three months of receipt of that notification, possibly accompanied by a recommendation for specific arrangements as it may deem necessary for that Member State to become a party to the co-operation in question. Within four months of the date of that notification, the Council shall decide on the request and on possible specific arrangements as it may deem necessary. The decision shall be deemed to be taken unless the Council, acting by a qualified majority, decides to hold it in abeyance; in this case, the Council shall state the reasons for its decision and set a deadline for re-examining it. For the purposes of this paragraph, the Council shall act under the conditions set out in Article 44.

4.   The provisions of Articles 29 to 41 shall apply to the closer co-operation provided for by this Article, save as otherwise provided for in this Article and in Articles 43 and 44.
The provisions of the Treaty establishing the European Community concerning the powers of the Court of Justice of the European Communities and the exercise of those powers shall apply to paragraphs 1, 2 and 3.

5.   This Article is without prejudice to the provisions of the Protocol integrating the Schengen *acquis* into the framework of the European Union.

ARTICLE 41   (ex Article K.13)
1.   Articles **189, 190, 195, 196** to **199, 203, 204, 205(3), 206** to **209, 213** to **219, 255** and **290** of the Treaty establishing the European Community shall apply to the provisions relating to the areas referred to in this Title.

2.   Administrative expenditure which the provisions relating to the areas referred to in this Title entail for the institutions shall be charged to the budget of the European Communities.

3.   Operational expenditure to which the implementation of those provisions gives rise shall also be charged to the budget of the European Communities, except where the Council acting unanimously decides otherwise. In cases where expenditure is not charged to the budget of the European Communities it shall be charged to the Member States in accordance with the gross national product scale, unless the Council acting unanimously decides otherwise.

4.   The budgetary procedure laid down in the Treaty establishing the European Community shall apply to the expenditure charged to the budget of the European Communities.
(formally Article K.8(1-2))

ARTICLE 42   (ex Article K.14)
The Council, acting unanimously on the initiative of the Commission or a Member State, **and after consulting the European Parliament, may decide that action in areas referred to in Article 29 shall fall under Title IV of the Treaty establishing the European Community**, and at the same time determine the relevant voting conditions relating to it. It shall recommend the Member States to adopt that decision in accordance with their respective constitutional requirements.
(formally Article K.9)

* * * * * * *

TITLE VII (ex Title VIa)

PROVISIONS ON CLOSER CO-OPERATION

ARTICLE 43 (ex Article **K.15**)

1.   Member States which intend to establish closer co-operation between themselves may make use of the institutions, procedures and mechanisms laid down by this Treaty and the Treaty establishing the European Community provided that the co-operation:

(a)   is aimed at furthering the objectives of the Union and at protecting and serving its interests;

(b)   respects the principles of the said Treaties and the single institutional framework of the Union;

(c)   is only used as a last resort, where the objectives of the said Treaties could not be attained by applying the relevant procedures laid down therein;

(d)   concerns at least a majority of Member States;

(e)   does not affect the *"acquis communautaire"* and the measures adopted under the other provisions of the said Treaties;

(f)   does not affect the competences, rights, obligations and interests of those Member States which do not participate therein;

(g)   is open to all Member States and allows them to become parties to the co-operation at any time, provided that they comply with the basic decision and with the decisions taken within that framework;

(h)   complies with the specific additional criteria laid down in Article 11 of the Treaty establishing the European Community and Article 40 of this Treaty, depending on the area concerned, and is authorised by the Council in accordance with the procedures laid down therein.

2.   Member States shall apply, as far as they are concerned, the acts and decisions adopted for the implementation of the co-operation in which they participate. Member States not participating in such co-operation shall not impede the implementation thereof by the participating Member States.

ARTICLE 44 (ex Article **K.16**)

1.   For the purposes of the adoption of the acts and decisions necessary for the implementation of the co-operation referred to in Article 43, the relevant institutional provisions of this Treaty and the Treaty establishing the European Community shall apply. However, while all members of the Council shall be able to take part in the deliberations, only those representing participating Member States shall take part in the adoption of decisions. The qualified majority shall be defined as the same proportion of the weighted votes of the members of the Council concerned as laid down in Article 205(2) of the Treaty establishing the European Community. Unanimity shall be constituted by only those Council members concerned.

2.   Expenditure resulting from implementation of the co-operation, other than administrative costs entailed for the institutions, shall be borne by the participating Member States, unless the Council, acting unanimously, decides otherwise.

ARTICLE 45 (ex Article **K.17**)

The Council and the Commission shall regularly inform the European Parliament of the development of closer co-operation established on the basis of this Title.

* * * * * * *

TITLE VIII (ex Title VII)

FINAL PROVISIONS

ARTICLE **46** (ex Article L)

The provisions of the Treaty establishing the European Community, the Treaty establishing the European Coal and Steel Community and the Treaty establishing the European Atomic Energy Community concerning the powers of the Court of Justice of the European Communities and the exercise of those powers shall apply only to the following provisions of this Treaty.

(a)   provisions amending the Treaty establishing the European Economic Community with a view to establishing the European Community, the Treaty establishing the European Coal and Steel Community and the Treaty establishing the European Atomic Energy Community;

(b)   provisions of Title VI, under the conditions provided for by Article 35;

(c)   provisions of Title VII, under the conditions provided for by Article 11 of the Treaty establishing the European Community and Article 40 of this Treaty;

(d)   Article 6(2) with regard to action of the institutions, insofar as the Court has jurisdiction under the Treaties establishing the European Communities and under this Treaty;

(e)   Articles **46** to **53**.

ARTICLE **47** (ex Article M)

Subject to the provisions amending the Treaty establishing the European Economic Community with a view to establishing the European Community, the Treaty establishing the European Coal and Steel Community and the Treaty establishing the European Atomic Energy Community, and to these final provisions, nothing in this Treaty shall affect the Treaties establishing the European Communities or the subsequent Treaties and Acts modifying or supplementing them.

ARTICLE **48** (ex Article N)

The government of any Member State or the Commission may submit to the Council proposals for the amendment of the Treaties on which the Union is founded.

If the Council, after consulting the European Parliament and, where appropriate, the Commission, delivers an opinion in favour of calling a conference of representatives of the governments of the Member States, the conference shall be convened by the President of the Council for the purpose of determining by common accord the amendments to be made to those Treaties. The European Central Bank shall also be consulted in the case of institutional changes in the monetary area.

The amendments shall enter into force after being ratified by all the Member States in accordance with their respective constitutional requirements.

Paragraph 2 shall be deleted.

ARTICLE **49** (ex Article O)

Any European State which respects the principles set out in Article 6(1) may apply to become a member of the Union. It shall address its application to the Council, which shall act unanimously after consulting the Commission and after receiving the assent of the European Parliament, which shall act by an absolute majority of its component members.

The conditions of admission and the adjustments to the Treaties on which the Union is founded which such admission entails shall be the subject of an agreement between the Member States and the applicant State. This agreement shall be submitted for ratification by all the contracting States in accordance with their respective constitutional requirements.

ARTICLE **50** (ex Article P)

1.   Articles 2 to 7 and 10 to 19 of the Treaty establishing a Single Council and a Single Commission of the European Communities, signed in Brussels on 8 April 1965, are hereby repealed.

2.   Article 2, Article 3(2) and Title III of the Single European Act signed in Luxembourg on 17 February 1986 and in The Hague on 28 February 1986 are hereby repealed.

ARTICLE **51** (ex Article Q)
This Treaty is concluded for an unlimited period.

ARTICLE **52** (ex Article R)
1.   This Treaty shall be ratified by the High Contracting Parties in accordance with their respective constitutional requirements. The instruments of ratification shall be deposited with the government of the Italian Republic.

2.   This Treaty shall enter into force on 1 January 1993, provided that all the instruments of ratification have been deposited, or, failing that, on the first day of the month following the deposit of the instrument of ratification by the last signatory State to take this step.

ARTICLE **53** (ex Article S)
This Treaty, drawn up in a single original in the Danish, Dutch, English, French, German, Greek, Irish, Italian, Portuguese and Spanish languages, the texts in each of these languages being equally authentic, shall be deposited in the archives of the government of the Italian Republic, which will transmit a certified copy to each of the governments of the other signatory States.

Pursuant to the Accession Treaty of 1994, the Finnish and Swedish versions of this Treaty shall also be authentic.

IN WITNESS WHEREOF the undersigned Plenipotentiaries have signed this Treaty.

Done at Maastricht on the seventh day of February in the year one thousand nine hundred and ninety-two.

* * * * * * *

CONSOLIDATED TREATY ESTABLISHING
THE EUROPEAN COMMUNITY

TITLE II

THE TREATY ESTABLISHING THE EUROPEAN COMMUNITY

The HIGH CONTRACTING PARTIES,

DETERMINED to lay the foundations of an ever-closer union among the peoples of Europe,

RESOLVED to ensure the economic and social progress of their countries by common action to eliminate the barriers which divide Europe,

AFFIRMING as the essential objective of their efforts the constant improvement of the living and working conditions of their peoples,

RECOGNISING that the removal of existing obstacles calls for concerted action in order to guarantee steady expansion, balanced trade and fair competition,

ANXIOUS to strengthen the unity of their economies and to ensure their harmonious development by reducing the differences existing between the various regions and the backwardness of the less-favoured regions,

DESIRING to contribute, by means of a common commercial policy, to the progressive abolition of restrictions on international trade,

INTENDING to confirm the solidarity which binds Europe and the overseas countries and desiring to ensure the development of their prosperity, in accordance with the principles of the Charter of the United Nations,

RESOLVED by thus pooling their resources to preserve and strengthen peace and liberty, and calling upon the other peoples of Europe who share their ideal to join in their efforts,

DETERMINED to promote the development of the highest possible level of knowledge for their peoples through a wide access to education and its continuous updating,

HAVE DECIDED to create a EUROPEAN COMMUNITY and to this end have designated their Plenipotentiaries,

WHO, having exchanged their Full Powers, found in good and due form, have agreed as follows.

PART ONE

PRINCIPLES

ARTICLE **1** (ex Article 1)
By this Treaty, the HIGH CONTRACTING PARTIES establish among themselves a EUROPEAN COMMUNITY.

ARTICLE **2** (ex Article 2)
The Community shall have as its task, by establishing a common market and an economic and monetary union and by implementing common policies or activities referred to in Articles **3** and **4**, to promote throughout the Community a harmonious and balanced **and sustainable** development of economic activities, **a high level of employment and social protection**, **equality between men and women,** sustainable and non-inflationary growth**, a high degree of **competitiveness and** convergence of economic performance, **a high level of protection and improvement of the quality of the environment**, the raising of the standard of living and quality of life, and economic and social cohesion and solidarity among Member States.

ARTICLE **3** (ex Article 3)

1. For the purposes set out in Article **2**, the activities of the Community shall include, as provided in this Treaty and in accordance with the timetable set out therein:

(a) the **prohibition**, as between Member States, of customs duties and quantitative restrictions on the import and export of goods, and of all other measures having equivalent effect;

(b) a common commercial policy;

(c) an internal market characterised by the abolition, as between Member States, of obstacles to the free movement of goods, persons, services and capital;

(d) measures concerning the entry and movement of **persons as** provided for in **Title IV**;

(e) a common policy in the sphere of agriculture and fisheries;

(f) a common policy in the sphere of transport;

(g) a system ensuring that competition in the internal market is not distorted;

(h) the approximation of the laws of Member States to the extent required for the functioning of the common market;

(i) **the promotion of co-ordination between employment policies of the Member States with a view to enhancing their effectiveness by developing a co-ordinated strategy for employment;**

(j) a policy in the social sphere comprising a European Social Fund;

(k) the strengthening of economic and social cohesion;

(l) a policy in the sphere of the environment;

(m) the strengthening of the competitiveness of Community industry;

(n) the promotion of research and technological development;

(o) encouragement for the establishment and development of trans-European networks;

(p) a contribution to the attainment of a high level of health protection;

(q) a contribution to education and training of quality and to the flowering of the cultures of the Member States;

(r) a policy in the sphere of development co-operation;

(s) the association of the overseas countries and territories in order to increase trade and promote jointly economic and social development;

(t) a contribution to the strengthening of consumer protection;

(u) measures in the spheres of energy, civil protection and tourism.

2. In all the activities referred to in this Article, the Community shall aim to eliminate inequalities, and to promote equality, between men and women.

ARTICLE **4** (ex Article 3 a)

1. For the purposes set out in Article **2**, the activities of the Member States and the Community shall include, as provided in this Treaty and in accordance with the timetable set out therein, the adoption of an economic policy which is based on the close co-ordination of Member States' economic policies, on the internal market and on the definition of common objectives, and conducted in accordance with the principle of an open market economy with free competition.

2. Concurrently with the foregoing, and as provided in this Treaty and in accordance with the timetable and the procedures set out therein, these activities shall include the irrevocable fixing of exchange rates leading to the introduction of a single currency, the ECU, and the definition and conduct of a single monetary policy and exchange rate policy the primary objective of both of which shall be to maintain price stability and, without prejudice to this objective, to support the general economic policies in the Community, in accordance with the principle of an open market economy with free competition.

3. These activities of the Member States and the Community shall entail compliance with the following guiding principles: stable prices, sound public finances and monetary conditions and a sustainable balance of payments.

ARTICLE **5** (ex Article 3 b)

The Community shall act within the limits of the powers conferred upon it by this Treaty and of the objectives assigned to it therein.

In areas which do not fall within its exclusive competence, the Community shall take action, in accordance with the principle of subsidiarity, only if and insofar as the objectives of the proposed action cannot be sufficiently achieved by the Member States and can therefore, by reason of the scale or effects of the proposed action, be better achieved by the Community.

Any action by the Community shall not go beyond what is necessary to achieve the objectives of this Treaty.

ARTICLE 6 (ex Article **3 c**)
Environmental protection requirements must be integrated into the definition and implementation of the Community policies and activities referred to in Article 3, in particular with a view to promoting sustainable development.

ARTICLE **7** (ex Article 4)
1.   The tasks entrusted to the Community shall be carried out by the following institutions:
-   a EUROPEAN PARLIAMENT,
-   a COUNCIL,
-   a COMMISSION,
-   a COURT OF JUSTICE,
-   a COURT OF AUDITORS.
Each institution shall act within the limits of the powers conferred upon it by this Treaty.

2.   The Council and the Commission shall be assisted by an Economic and Social Committee and a Committee of the Regions acting in an advisory capacity.

ARTICLE **8** (ex Article 4 a)
A European System of Central Banks (hereinafter referred to as 'ESCB') and a European Central Bank (hereinafter referred to as 'ECB') shall be established in accordance with the procedures laid down in this Treaty; they shall act within the limits of the powers conferred upon them by this Treaty and by the Statute of the ESCB and of the ECB (hereinafter referred to as 'Statute of the ESCB') annexed thereto.

ARTICLE **9** (ex Article 4 b)
A European Investment Bank is hereby established, which shall act within the limits of the powers conferred upon it by this treaty and the Statute annexed thereto.

ARTICLE **10** (ex Article 5)
Member States shall take all appropriate measures, whether general or particular, to ensure fulfilment of the obligations arising out of this Treaty or resulting from action taken by the institutions of the Community. They shall facilitate the achievement of the Community's tasks.
They shall abstain from any measure which could jeopardise the attainment of the objectives of this Treaty.

ARTICLE 11 (ex Article **5 a**)
1.   Member States which intend to establish closer co-operation between themselves may be authorised, subject to Articles 43 and 44 of the Treaty on European Union, to make use of the institutions, procedures and mechanisms laid down by this Treaty, provided that the co-operation proposed:
(a)   does not concern areas which fall within the exclusive competence of the Community;
(b)   does not affect Community policies, actions or programmes;
(c)   does not concern the citizenship of the Union or discriminate between nationals of Member States;
(d)   remains within the limits of the powers conferred upon the Community by this Treaty; and
(e)   does not constitute a discrimination or a restriction of trade between Member States and does not distort the conditions of competition between the latter.

2.   The authorisation referred to in paragraph 1 shall be granted by the Council, acting by a qualified majority on a proposal from the Commission and after consulting the European Parliament.
If a member of the Council declares that, for important and stated reasons of national policy, it intends to oppose the granting of an authorisation by qualified majority, a vote shall not be taken. The Council may, acting by a qualified majority, request that the matter be referred to the Council, meeting in the composition of the Heads of State or Government, for decision by unanimity.
Member States which intend to establish closer co-operation as referred to in paragraph 1 may address a request to the Commission, which may submit a proposal to the Council to that effect. In the event of the Commission not submitting a proposal, it shall inform the Member States concerned of the reasons for not doing so.

3.   Any Member State which wishes to become a party to co-operation set up in accordance with this Article shall notify its intention to the Council and to the Commission, which shall give an opinion to the Council within three months of receipt of that notification. Within four months of the date of that notification, the Commission shall decide on it and on possible specific arrangements as it may deem necessary.

4. The acts and decisions necessary for the implementation of co-operation activities shall be subject to all the relevant provisions of this Treaty, save as otherwise provided for in this Article and in Articles 43 and 44 of the Treaty on European Union.

5. This Article is without prejudice to the provisions of the Protocol integrating the Schengen *acquis* into the framework of the European Union.

ARTICLE **12** (ex Article 6)
Within the scope of application of this Treaty, and without prejudice to any special provisions contained therein, any discrimination on grounds of nationality shall be prohibited.
The Council, acting in accordance with the procedure referred to in **Article 251**, may adopt rules designed to prohibit such discrimination.

ARTICLE **13** (ex Article **6 a**)
Without prejudice to the other provisions of this Treaty and within the limits of the powers conferred by it upon the Community, the Council, acting unanimously on a proposal from the Commission and after consulting the European Parliament, may take appropriate action to combat discrimination based on sex, racial or ethnic origin, religion or belief, disability, age or sexual orientation.

ARTICLE 7 shall be repealed.

ARTICLE **14** (ex Article 7 a)
1. The Community shall adopt measures with the aim of progressively establishing the internal market over a period expiring on 31 December 1992, in accordance with the provisions of this Article and of **Articles 15, 26, 47(2), 49, 80, 93** and **95** and without prejudice to the other provisions of this Treaty.
2. The internal market shall comprise an area without internal frontiers in which the free movement of goods, persons, services and capital is ensured in accordance with the provisions of this Treaty.
3. The Council, acting by a qualified majority on a proposal from the Commission, shall determine the guidelines and conditions necessary to ensure balanced progress in all the sectors concerned.
(Formally paragraph 2 of Article 7b.)

ARTICLE 7 b shall be repealed.

ARTICLE **15** (ex Article 7 c)
When drawing up its proposals with a view to achieving the objectives set out in Article **14**, the Commission shall take into account the extent of the effort that certain economies showing differences in development will have to sustain during the period of establishment of the internal market and it may propose appropriate provisions.
If these provisions take the form of derogations, they must be of a temporary nature and must cause the least possible disturbance to the functioning of the common market.

ARTICLE **16** (ex Article **7 d**)
Without prejudice to Articles 73, 86 and 87, and given the place occupied by services of general economic interest in the shared values of the Union as well as their role in promoting social and territorial cohesion, the Community and the Member States, each within their respective powers and within the scope of application of this Treaty, shall take care that such services operate on the basis of principles and conditions which enable them to fulfil their missions.

PART TWO

CITIZENSHIP OF THE UNION

ARTICLE **17** (ex Article 8)
1.   Citizenship of the Union is hereby established. Every person holding the nationality of a Member State shall be a citizen of the Union. **Citizenship of the Union shall complement and not replace national citizenship.**

2.   Citizens of the Union shall enjoy the rights conferred by this Treaty and shall be subject to the duties imposed thereby.

ARTICLE **18** (ex Article 8 a)
1.   Every citizen of the Union shall have the right to move and reside freely within the territory of the Member States, subject to the limitations and conditions laid down in this Treaty and by the measures adopted to give it effect.

2.   The Council may adopt provisions with a view to facilitating the exercise of the rights referred to in paragraph 1; save as otherwise provided in this Treaty, the Council shall act **in accordance with the procedure referred to in Article 251. The Council shall act unanimously throughout this procedure.**

ARTICLE **19** (ex Article 8 b)
1.   Every citizen of the Union residing in a Member State of which he is not a national shall have the right to vote and to stand as a candidate at municipal elections in the Member State in which he resides, under the same conditions as nationals of that State. This right shall be exercised subject to detailed arrangements **adopted by** the Council, acting unanimously on a proposal from the Commission and after consulting the European Parliament; these arrangements may provide for derogations where warranted by problems specific to a Member State.

2.   Without prejudice to Article **190(4)** and to the provisions adopted for its implementation, every citizen of the Union residing in a Member State of which he is not a national shall have the right to vote and to stand as a candidate in elections to the European Parliament in the Member State in which he resides, under the same conditions as nationals of that State. This right shall be exercised subject to detailed arrangements **adopted by** the Council, acting unanimously on a proposal from the Commission and after consulting the European Parliament; these arrangements may provide for derogations where warranted by problems specific to a Member State.

ARTICLE **20** (ex Article 8 c)
Every citizen of the Union shall, in the territory of a third country in which the Member State of which he is a national is not represented, be entitled to protection by the diplomatic or consular authorities of any Member State, on the same conditions as the nationals of that State. **Member States** shall establish the necessary rules among themselves and start the international negotiations required to secure this protection.

ARTICLE **21** (ex Article 8 d)
Every citizen of the Union shall have the right to petition the European Parliament in accordance with Article **194**.
Every citizen of the Union may apply to the Ombudsman established in accordance with Article **195**.
Every citizen of the Union may write to any of the institutions or bodies referred to in this Article or in Article 7 in one of the languages mentioned in Article 314 and have an answer in the same language.

ARTICLE **22** (ex Article 8 e)
The Commission shall report to the European Parliament, to the Council and to the Economic and Social Committee **every three years** on the application of the provisions of this Part. This report shall take account of the development of the Union.
On this basis, and without prejudice to the other provisions of this Treaty, the Council, acting unanimously on a proposal from the Commission and after consulting the European Parliament, may adopt provisions to strengthen or to add to the rights laid down in this Part, which it shall recommend to the Member States for adoption in accordance with their respective constitutional requirements.

PART THREE

COMMUNITY POLICIES

TITLE I

FREE MOVEMENT OF GOODS

ARTICLE **23** (ex Article 9)

1. The Community shall be based upon a customs union which shall cover all trade in goods and which shall involve the prohibition between Member States of customs duties on imports and exports and of all charges having equivalent effect, and the adoption of a common customs tariff in their relations with third countries.

2. The provisions of **Article 25** and of Chapter 2 of this Title shall apply to products originating in Member States and to products coming from third countries which are in free circulation in Member States.

ARTICLE **24** (ex Article 10)

Products coming from a third country shall be considered to be in free circulation in a Member State if the import formalities have been complied with and any customs duties or charges having equivalent effect which are payable have been levied in that Member State, and if they have not benefited from a total or partial drawback of such duties or charges. *(Formally Paragraph 1).*
Paragraph 2 shall be repealed.

ARTICLE 11 shall be repealed.

CHAPTER 1

THE CUSTOMS UNION

SECTION HEADING (Section 1 – Elimination of customs duties between Member States) shall be deleted.

ARTICLE **25** (ex Article 12)

Customs duties on imports and exports and charges having equivalent effect shall be prohibited between Member States. This prohibition shall also apply to customs duties of a fiscal nature.

ARTICLES 13 to 17 shall be repealed.

SECTION HEADING (Section 2 – Setting up of the Common Customs Tariff) shall be deleted.

ARTICLES 18 to 27 shall be repealed.

ARTICLE **26** (ex Article 28)

Common Customs Tariff duties shall be **fixed** by the Council acting by a qualified majority on a proposal from the Commission.

ARTICLE **27** (ex Article 29)

In carrying out the tasks entrusted to it under this **Chapter** the Commission shall be guided by:
(a) the need to promote trade between Member States and third countries;
(b) developments in conditions of competition within the Community in so far as they lead to an improvement in the competitive capacity of undertakings;
(c) the requirements of the Community as regards the supply of raw materials and semi-finished goods; in this connection the Commission shall take care to avoid distorting conditions of competition between Member States in respect of finished goods;
(d) the need to avoid serious disturbances in the economies of Member States and to ensure rational development of production and an expansion of consumption within the Community.

CHAPTER 2

PROHIBITION OF QUANTITATIVE RESTRICTIONS
BETWEEN MEMBER STATES

ARTICLE **28** (ex Article 30)
Quantitative restrictions on imports and all measures having equivalent effect **shall be prohibited** between Member States.

ARTICLES 31 to 33 shall be repealed.

ARTICLE **29** (ex Article 34)
Quantitative restrictions on exports, and all measures having equivalent effect, shall be prohibited between Member States. *(formally Paragraph 1).*

Paragraph 2 shall be repealed.

ARTICLE 35 shall be repealed.

ARTICLE **30** (ex Article 36)
The provisions of Articles **28 and 29** shall not preclude prohibitions or restrictions on imports, exports or goods in transit justified on grounds of public morality, public policy or public security; the protection of health and life of humans, animals or plants; the protection of national treasures possessing artistic, historic or archaeological value; or the protection of industrial and commercial property. Such prohibitions or restrictions shall not, however, constitute a means of arbitrary discrimination or a disguised restriction on trade between Member States.

ARTICLE **31** (ex Article 37)
1.   Member States **shall adjust** any State monopolies of a commercial character so as to ensure **that no** discrimination regarding the conditions under which goods are procured and marketed exists between nationals of Member States.
The provisions of this Article shall apply to any body through which a Member State, in law or in fact, either directly or indirectly supervises, determines or appreciably influences imports or exports between Member States. These provisions shall likewise apply to monopolies delegated by the State to others.

2.   Member States shall refrain from introducing any new measure which is contrary to the principles laid down in paragraph 1 or which restricts the scope of the Articles dealing with the **prohibition** of customs duties and quantitative restrictions between Member States.

Paragraph 3 shall be repealed.

3.   If a State monopoly of a commercial character has rules which are designed to make it easier to dispose of agricultural products or obtain for them the best return, steps should be taken in applying the rules contained in this Article to ensure equivalent safeguards for the employment and standard of living of the producers concerned. ***Remainder of sentence shall be deleted.***

Paragraphs 5 and 6 shall be repealed.

TITLE II

AGRICULTURE

ARTICLE **32** (ex Article 38)
1.   The common market shall extend to agriculture and trade in agricultural products. 'Agricultural products' means the products of the soil, of stock farming and of fisheries and products of first-stage processing directly related to these products.

2.   Save as otherwise provided in Articles **33 to 38**, the rules laid down for the establishment of the common market shall apply to agricultural products.

3.   The products subject to the provisions of Articles **33 to 38** are listed in **Annex I** to this Treaty. ***Second Sentence shall be deleted.***

4.   The operation and development of the common market for agricultural products must be accompanied by the establishment of a common agricultural policy. ***Remainder of sentence shall be deleted.***

ARTICLE **33**   (ex Article 39)
1.   The objectives of the common agricultural policy shall be:
(a)   to increase agricultural productivity by promoting technical progress and by ensuring the rational development of agricultural production and the optimum utilisation of the factors of production, in particular labour;
(b)   thus to ensure a fair standard of living for the agricultural community, in particular by increasing the individual earnings of persons engaged in agriculture;
(c)   to stabilise markets;
(d)   to assure the availability of supplies;
(e)   to ensure that supplies reach consumers at reasonable prices.

2.   In working out the common agricultural policy and the special methods for its application, account shall be taken of:
(a)   the particular nature of agricultural activity, which results from the social structure of agriculture and from structural and natural disparities between the various agricultural regions;
(b)   the need to effect the appropriate adjustments by degrees;
(c)   the fact that in the Member States agriculture constitutes a sector closely linked with the economy as a whole.

ARTICLE **34**   (ex Article 40)
Paragraph 1 shall be repealed.

1.   In order to attain the objectives set out in Article **33**, a common organisation of agricultural markets shall be established.
This organisation shall take one of the following forms, depending on the product concerned:
(a)   common rules on competition;
(b)   compulsory co-ordination of the various national market organisations;
(c)   a European market organisation.

2.   The common organisation established in accordance with **paragraph 1** may include all measures required to attain the objectives set out in Article **33**, in particular regulation of prices, aids for the production and marketing of the various products, storage and carryover arrangements and common machinery for stabilising imports or exports.
The common organisation shall be limited to pursuit of the objectives set out in Article **33** and shall exclude any discrimination between producers or consumers within the Community.
Any common price policy shall be based on common criteria and uniform methods of calculation.

3.   In order to enable the common organisation referred to in **paragraph 1** to attain its objectives, one or more agricultural guidance and guarantee funds may be set up.

ARTICLE **35**   (ex Article 41)
To enable the objectives set out in Article **33** to be attained, provision may be made within the framework of the common agricultural policy for measures such as:
(a)   an effective co-ordination of efforts in the spheres of vocational training, of research and of the dissemination of agricultural knowledge; this may include joint financing of projects or institutions;
(b)   joint measures to promote consumption of certain products.

ARTICLE **36**   (ex Article 42)
The provisions of the Chapter relating to rules on competition shall apply to production of and trade in agricultural products only to the extent determined by the Council within the framework of Article **37**(2) and (3) and in accordance with the procedure laid down therein, account being taken of the objectives set out in Article **33**.
The Council may, in particular, authorise the granting of aid:
(a)   for the protection of enterprises handicapped by structural or natural conditions;
(b)   within the framework of economic development programmes.

ARTICLE **37**   (ex Article 43)
1.   In order to evolve the broad lines of a common agricultural policy, the Commission shall, immediately this Treaty enters into force, convene a conference of the Member States with a view to making a comparison of their agricultural policies, in particular by producing a statement of their resources and needs.

2.   Having taken into account the work of the conference provided for in paragraph 1, after consulting the Economic and Social Committee and within two years of the entry into force of this Treaty, the Commission shall submit proposals for working out and implementing the common agricultural policy, including the replacement of the national organisations by one of the forms of common organisation provided for in **Article 34(1)**, and for implementing the measures specified in this Title.

These proposals shall take account of the interdependence of the agricultural matters mentioned in this Title.

The Council shall, on a proposal from the Commission and after consulting the European Parliament, **acting by a qualified majority**, make regulations, issue directives, or take decisions, without prejudice to any recommendations it may also make.

3.   The Council may, acting by a qualified majority and in accordance with paragraph 2, replace the national market organisations by the common organisation provided for in **Article 34(1)** if:

(a)   the common organisation offers Member States which are opposed to this measure and which have an organisation of their own for the production in question equivalent safeguards for the employment and standard of living of the producers concerned, account being taken of the adjustments that will be possible and the specialisation that will be needed with the passage of time;

(b)   such an organisation ensures conditions for trade within the Community similar to those existing in a national market.

4.   If a common organisation for certain raw materials is established before a common organisation exists for the corresponding processed products, such raw materials as are used for processed products intended for export to third countries may be imported from outside the Community.

ARTICLES 44 and 45 shall be repealed.

ARTICLE **38** (ex Article 46)

Where in a Member State a product is subject to a national market organisation or to internal rules having equivalent effect which affect the competitive position of similar production in another Member State, a countervailing charge shall be applied by Member States to imports of this product coming from the Member State where such organisation or rules exist, unless that State applies a countervailing charge on export.

The Commission shall fix the amount of these charges at the level required to redress the balance; it may also authorise other measures, the conditions and details of which it shall determine.

ARTICLE 47 shall be repealed.

TITLE III

FREE MOVEMENT OF PERSONS, SERVICES AND CAPITAL

CHAPTER 1

WORKERS

ARTICLE **39** (ex Article 48)

1.   Freedom of movement for workers shall be secured within the Community. *Remainder of sentence shall be deleted.*

2.   Such freedom of movement shall entail the abolition of any discrimination based on nationality between workers of the Member States as regards employment, remuneration and other conditions of work and employment.

3.   It shall entail the right, subject to limitations justified on grounds of public policy, public security or public health:

(a)   to accept offers of employment actually made;

(b)   to move freely within the territory of Member States for this purpose;

(c)   to stay in a Member State for the purpose of employment in accordance with the provisions governing the employment of nationals of that State laid down by law, regulation or administrative action;

(d)   to remain in the territory of a Member State after having been employed in that State, subject to conditions which shall be embodied in implementing regulations to be drawn up by the Commission.

4.   The provisions of this Article shall not apply to employment in the public service.

ARTICLE **40** (ex Article 49)

The Council shall, acting in accordance with the procedure referred to in Article **251** and after consulting the Economic and Social Committee, issue directives or make regulations setting out the measures required to bring **about freedom** of movement for workers, as defined in Article **39**, in particular:

(a) by ensuring close co-operation between national employment services;

(b) **by abolishing** those administrative procedures and practices and those qualifying periods in respect of eligibility for available employment, whether resulting from national legislation or from agreements previously concluded between Member States, the maintenance of which would form an obstacle to liberalisation of the movement of workers;

(c) **by abolishing** all such qualifying periods and other restrictions provided for either under national legislation or under agreements previously concluded between Member States as imposed on workers of other Member States conditions regarding the free choice of employment other than those imposed on workers of the State concerned;

(d) by setting up appropriate machinery to bring offers of employment into touch with applications for employment and to facilitate the achievement of a balance between supply and demand in the employment market in such a way as to avoid serious threats to the standard of living and level of employment in the various regions and industries.

ARTICLE **41** (ex Article 50)

Member States shall, within the framework of a joint programme, encourage the exchange of young workers.

ARTICLE **42** (ex Article 51)

The Council shall, acting **in accordance with the procedure referred to in Article 251**, adopt such measures in the field of social security as are necessary to provide freedom of movement for workers; to this end, it shall make arrangements to secure for migrant workers and their dependants:

(a) aggregation, for the purpose of acquiring and retaining the right to benefit and of calculating the amount of benefit, of all periods taken into account under the laws of the several countries;

(b) payment of benefits to persons resident in the territories of Member States.

The Council shall act unanimously throughout the procedure referred to in Article 251.

CHAPTER 2

RIGHT OF ESTABLISHMENT

ARTICLE **43** (ex Article 52)

Within the framework of the provisions set out below, restrictions on the freedom of establishment of nationals of a Member State in the territory of another Member State shall be **prohibited**. Such **prohibition** shall also apply to restrictions on the setting up of agencies, branches or subsidiaries by nationals of any Member State established in the territory of any Member State.

Freedom of establishment shall include the right to take up and pursue activities as self-employed persons and to set up and manage undertakings, in particular companies or firms within the meaning of the second paragraph of Article **48**, under the conditions laid down for its own nationals by the law of the country where such establishment is effected, subject to the provisions of the Chapter relating to capital.

ARTICLE 53 shall be repealed.

ARTICLE 44 (ex Article 54)

Paragraph 1 shall be repealed.

1. In order **to attain** freedom of establishment as regards a particular activity, the Council, acting in accordance with the procedure referred to in Article **251** and after consulting the Economic and Social Committee, shall act by means of directives.

2. The Council and the Commission shall carry out the duties devolving upon them under the preceding provisions, in particular:

(a) by according, as a general rule, priority treatment to activities where freedom of establishment makes a particularly valuable contribution to the development of production and trade;

(b) by ensuring close co-operation between the competent authorities in the Member States in order to ascertain the particular situation within the Community of the various activities concerned;

(c) by abolishing those administrative procedures and practices, whether resulting from national legislation or from agreements previously concluded between Member States, the maintenance of which would form an obstacle to freedom of establishment;

(d) by ensuring that workers of one Member State employed in the territory of another Member State may remain in that territory for the purpose of taking up activities therein as self-employed persons, where they satisfy the conditions which they would be required to satisfy if they were entering that State at the time when they intended to take up such activities;

(e) by enabling a national of one Member State to acquire and use land and building situated in the territory of another Member State, insofar as this does not conflict with the principles laid down in Article 33(2);

(f) by effecting the progressive abolition of restrictions on freedom of establishment in every branch of activity under consideration, both as regards the conditions for setting up agencies, branches or subsidiaries in the territory of a Member State and as regards the subsidiaries in the territory of a Member State and as regards the conditions governing the entry of personnel belonging to the main establishment into managerial or supervisory posts in such agencies, branches or subsidiaries;

(g) by co-ordinating to the necessary extent the safeguards which, for the protection of the interests of members and others, are required by Member States of companies or firms within the meaning of the second paragraph of Article **48** with a view to making such safeguards equivalent throughout the Community;

(h) by satisfying themselves that the conditions of establishment are not distorted by aids granted by Member States.

ARTICLE **45** (ex Article 55)
The provisions of this Chapter shall not apply, so far as any given Member State is concerned, to activities which in that State are connected, even occasionally, with the exercise of official authority.
The Council may, acting by a qualified majority on a proposal from the Commission, rule that the provisions of this Chapter shall not apply to certain activities.

ARTICLE **46** (ex Article 56)
1.   The provisions of this Chapter and measures taken in pursuance thereof shall not prejudice the applicability of provisions laid down by law, regulation or administrative action providing for special treatment for foreign nationals on grounds of public policy, public security or public health.

2.   **The Council shall**, acting in accordance with the procedure referred to in Article **251**, issue directives for the co-ordination of **the above-mentioned provisions**.

ARTICLE **47** (ex Article 57)
1.   In order to make it easier for persons to take up and pursue activities as self-employed persons, the Council shall, acting in accordance with the procedure referred to in Article **251**, issue directives for the mutual recognition of diplomas, certificates and other evidence of formal qualifications.

2.   For the same purpose, the Council shall acting **in accordance with the procedure referred to in Article 251 issue** directives for the co-ordination of the provisions laid down by law, regulation or administrative action in Member States concerning the taking up and pursuit of activities as self-employed persons. The Council, acting unanimously **throughout the procedure referred to in Article 251, shall** decide on directives the implementation of which involves in at least one Member State amendment of the existing principles laid down by law governing the professions with respect to training and conditions of access for natural persons. **In other cases the Council shall act by qualified majority.**

3.   In the case of the medical and allied and pharmaceutical professions, the progressive abolition of restrictions shall be dependent upon co-ordination of the conditions for their exercise in the various Member States.

ARTICLE **48** (ex Article 58)
Companies or firms formed in accordance with the law of a Member State and having their registered office, central administration or principal place of business within the Community shall, for the purposes of this Chapter, be treated in the same way as natural persons who are nationals of the Member States.
'Companies or firms' means companies or firms constituted under civil or commercial law, including co-operative societies, and other legal persons governed by public or private law, save for those which are non-profit-making.

CHAPTER 3

SERVICES

ARTICLE **49** (ex Article 59)
Within the framework of the provisions set out below, restrictions on freedom to provide services within the Community shall be **prohibited** in respect of nationals of Member States who are established in a State of the Community other than that of the person for whom the services are intended.
The Council may, acting by a qualified majority on a proposal from the Commission, extend the provisions of the Chapter to nationals of a third country who provide services and who are established within the Community.

ARTICLE **50** (ex Article 60)
Services shall be considered to be 'services' within the meaning of this Treaty where they are normally provided for remuneration, insofar as they are not governed by the provisions relating to freedom of movement for goods, capital and persons.
'Services' shall in particular include:
(a)   activities of an industrial character;
(b)   activities of a commercial character;
(c)   activities of craftsmen;
(d)   activities of the professions.
Without prejudice to the provisions of the Chapter relating to the right of establishment, the person providing a service may, in order to do so, temporarily pursue his activity in the State where the service is provided, under the same conditions as are imposed by that State on its own nationals.

ARTICLE **51** (ex Article 61)
1.   Freedom to provide services in the field of transport shall be governed by the provisions of the Title relating to transport.

2.   The liberalisation of banking and insurance services connected with movements of capital shall be effected in step with **the liberalisation** of movement of capital.

ARTICLE 62 shall be repealed.

ARTICLE **52** (ex Article 63)
Paragraph 1 shall be repealed.

1.   In order **to achieve the** liberalisation of a specific service, the Council shall, on a proposal from the Commission and after consulting the Economic and Social Committee and the European Parliament, issue directives acting **by a qualified majority**.

2.   As regards the **directives** referred to in **paragraph 1**, priority shall as a general rule be given to those services which directly affect production costs or the liberalisation of which helps to promote trade in goods.

ARTICLE **53** (ex Article 64)
The Member States declare their readiness to undertake the liberalisation of services beyond the extent required by the directives issued pursuant to **Article 52(1)**, if their general economic situation and the situation of the economic sector concerned so permit.
To this end, the Commission shall make recommendations to the Member States concerned.

ARTICLE **54** (ex Article 65)
As long as restrictions on freedom to provide services have not been abolished, each Member State shall apply such restrictions without distinction on grounds of nationality or residence to all persons providing services within the meaning of the first paragraph of Article **49**.

ARTICLE **55** (ex Article 66)
The provisions of Articles **45** to **48** shall apply to the matters covered by this Chapter.

CHAPTER 4

CAPITAL AND PAYMENTS

ARTICLES 67 to 73a shall be repealed.

ARTICLE **56** (ex Article 73 b)
1.   Within the framework of the provisions set out in this Chapter, all restrictions on the movement of capital between Member States and between Member States and third countries shall be prohibited.

2.   Within the framework of the provisions set out in this Chapter, all restrictions on payments between Member States and between Member States and third countries shall be prohibited.

ARTICLE **57** (ex Article 73 c)
1.   The provisions of Article **56** shall be without prejudice to the application to third countries of any restrictions which exist on 31 December 1993 under national or Community law adopted in respect of the movement of capital to or from third countries involving direct investment - including in real estate - establishment, the provision of financial services or the admission of securities to capital markets.

2.   Whilst endeavouring to achieve the objective of free movement of capital between Member States and third countries to the greatest extent possible and without prejudice to the other Chapters of this Treaty, the Council may, acting by a qualified majority on a proposal from the Commission, adopt measures on the movement of capital to or from third countries involving direct investment - including investment in real estate - establishment, the provision of financial services or the admission of securities to capital markets. Unanimity shall be required for measures under this paragraph which constitute a step back in Community law as regards the liberalisation of the movement of capital to or from third countries.

ARTICLE **58** (ex Article 73 d)
1.   The provisions of Article **56** shall be without prejudice to the right of Member States:
(a)   to apply the relevant provisions of their tax law which distinguish between taxpayers who are not in the same situation with regard to their place of residence or with regard to the place where their capital is invested;
(b)   to take all requisite measures to prevent infringements of national law and regulations, in particular in the field of taxation and the prudential supervision of financial institutions, or to lay down procedures for the declaration of capital movements for purposes of administrative or statistical information, or to take measures which are justified on grounds of public policy or public security.

2.   The provisions of this Chapter shall be without prejudice to the applicability of restrictions on the right of establishment which are compatible with this Treaty.

3.   The measures and procedures referred to in paragraphs 1 and 2 shall not constitute a means of arbitrary discrimination or a disguised restriction on the free movement of capital and payments as defined in Article **56**.

ARTICLE 73 e shall be repealed.

ARTICLE **59** (ex Article 73 f)
Where, in exceptional circumstances, movements of capital to or from third countries cause, or threaten to cause, serious difficulties for the operation of economic and monetary union, the Council, acting by a qualified majority on a proposal from the Commission and after consulting the ECB, may take safeguard measures with regard to third countries for a period not exceeding six months if such measures are strictly necessary.

ARTICLE **60** (ex Article 73 g)
1.   If in the cases envisaged in Article **301**, action by the Community is deemed necessary, the Council may, in accordance with the procedure provided for in Article **301**, take the necessary urgent measures on the movement of capital and on payments as regards the third countries concerned.

2.   Without prejudice to Article **297** and as long as the Council has not taken measures pursuant to paragraph 1, a Member State may, for serious political reasons and on grounds of urgency, take unilateral measures against a third country with regard to capital movements and payments. The Commission and the other Member States shall be informed of such measures by the date of their entry into force at the latest.
The Council may, acting by a qualified majority on a proposal from the Commission, decide that the Member State concerned shall amend or abolish such measures. The President of the Council shall inform the European Parliament of any such decision taken by the Council.

ARTICLE 73 h shall be repealed.

TITLE IV (ex Title IIIa)

**VISAS, ASYLUM, IMMIGRATION AND OTHER POLICIES RELATED TO
FREE MOVEMENT OF PERSONS**

ARTICLE 61 (ex Article 73 i)
In order to establish progressively an area of freedom, security and justice, the Council shall adopt:
(a) within a period of five years after the entry into force of the Treaty of Amsterdam, measures aimed at ensuring the free movement of persons in accordance with Article 14, in conjunction with directly related flanking measures with respect to external borders controls, asylum and immigration, in accordance with the provisions of Article 62(2) and (3), 63(l)(a) and (2)(a), and measures to prevent and combat crime in accordance with the provisions of Article 31(e) of the Treaty on European Union;
(b) other measures in the fields of asylum, immigration and safeguarding the rights of third country nationals, in accordance with the provisions of Article 63;
(c) measures in the field of judicial co-operation in civil matters as provided for in Article 65;
(d) appropriate measures to encourage and strengthen administrative co-operation, as provided for in Article 66;
(e) measures in the field of police and judicial co-operation in criminal matters aimed at a high level of security by preventing and combating crime within the Union in accordance with the provisions of the Treaty on European Union.

ARTICLE 62 (ex Article 73 j)
The Council, acting in accordance with the procedure referred to in Article 67, shall, within a period of five years after the entry into force of the Treaty of Amsterdam, adopt:
(1) measures with a view to ensuring, in compliance with Article 14, the absence of any controls on persons, be they citizens of the Union or nationals of third countries, when crossing internal borders;

(2) measures on the crossing of the external borders of the Member States which shall establish:
    (a) standards and procedures to be followed by Member States in carrying out checks on persons at such borders;
    (b) rules on visas for intended stays of no more than three months, including:
        (i) the list of third countries whose nationals must be in possession of visas when crossing the external borders and those whose nationals are exempt from that requirement;
        (ii) the procedures and conditions for issuing visas by Member States;
        (iii) a uniform format for visas;
        (iv) rules on a uniform visa;

(3) measures setting out the conditions under which the nationals of third countries shall have the freedom to travel within the territory of the Member States during a period of no more than three months.

ARTICLE 63 (ex Article 73 k)
The Council, acting in accordance with the procedure referred to in Article 67, shall, within a period of five years after the entry into force of the Treaty of Amsterdam, adopt:
(1) measures on asylum, in accordance with the Convention of 28 July 1951 and the Protocol of 31 January 1967 relating to the status of refugees and other relevant treaties, within the following areas:
    (a) criteria and mechanisms for determining which Member State is responsible for considering an application for asylum submitted by a third country national in one of the Member States,
    (b) minimum standards on the reception of asylum seekers in Member States,
    (c) minimum standards with respect to the qualification of third country nationals as refugees,
    (d) minimum standards on procedures in Member States for granting or withdrawing refugee status;

(2) measures on refugees and displaced persons within the following areas:
    (a) minimum standards for giving temporary protection to displaced persons from third countries who cannot return to their country of origin and for persons who otherwise need international protection,

(b)   promoting a balance of effort between Member States in receiving and bearing the consequences of receiving refugees and displaced persons;

(3)   measures on immigration policy within the following areas:
    (a)   conditions of entry and residence, and standards on procedures for the issue by Member States of long term visas and residence permits, including those for the purpose of family reunion,
    (b)   illegal immigration and illegal residence, including repatriation of illegal residents;

(4)   measures defining the rights and conditions under which nationals of third countries who are legally resident in a Member State may reside in other Member States.

Measures adopted by the Council pursuant to points 3 and 4 shall not prevent any Member State from maintaining or introducing in the areas concerned national provisions which are compatible with this Treaty and with international agreements.

Measures to be adopted pursuant to points 2(b), 3(a) and 4 shall not be subject to the five year period referred to above.

ARTICLE 64   (ex Article 73 *l*)

1.   This Title shall not affect the exercise of the responsibilities incumbent upon Member States with regard to the maintenance of law and order and the safeguarding of internal security.

2.   In the event of one or more Member States being confronted with an emergency situation characterised by a sudden inflow of nationals from a third country and without prejudice to paragraph 1, the Council may, acting by qualified majority on a proposal from the Commission, adopt provisional measures of a duration not exceeding six months for the benefit of the Member States concerned.

ARTICLE 65   (ex Article 73 m)

Measures in the field of judicial co-operation in civil matters having cross-border implications, to be taken in accordance with Article 67 and insofar as necessary for the proper functioning of the internal market, shall include:
(a)   improving and simplifying:
    -   the system for cross-border service of judicial and extra-judicial documents;
    -   co-operation in the taking of evidence;
    -   the recognition and enforcement of decisions in civil and commercial cases, including extra-judicial cases;
(b)   promoting the compatibility of the rules applicable in the Member States concerning the conflict of laws and of jurisdiction;
(c)   eliminating obstacles to the good functioning of civil proceedings, if necessary by promoting the compatibility of the rules on civil procedure applicable in the Member States.

ARTICLE 66   (ex Article 73 n)

The Council, acting in accordance with the procedure referred to in Article 67, shall take measures to ensure co-operation between the relevant departments of the administrations of the Member States in the areas covered by this Title, as well as between those departments and the Commission.

ARTICLE 67   (ex Article 73 o)

1.   During a transitional period of five years following the entry into force of the Treaty of Amsterdam, the Council shall act unanimously on a proposal from the Commission or on an initiative of a Member State and after consulting the European Parliament.

2.   After this period of five years:
-   the Council shall act on proposals from the Commission; the Commission shall examine any request made by a Member State that it submit a proposal to the Council;
-   the Council, acting unanimously after consulting the European Parliament, shall take a decision with a view to making all or parts of the areas covered by this Title to be governed by the procedure referred to in Article 251 and adapting the provisions relating to the powers of the Court of Justice.

3.   By derogation from paragraphs 1 and 2, measures referred to in Article 62(2)(b)(i) and (iii) shall, from the entry into force of the Treaty of Amsterdam, be adopted by the Council acting by a qualified majority on a proposal from the Commission and after consulting the European Parliament.

4. By derogation from paragraph 2, measures referred to in Article 62(2)(b)(ii) and (iv) shall, after a period of five years following the entry into force of the Treaty of Amsterdam, be adopted by the Council acting in accordance with the procedure referred to in Article 251.

ARTICLE 68 (ex Article **73 p**)

1. Article 234 shall apply to this Title under the following circumstances and conditions: where a question on the interpretation of this Title or on the validity or interpretation of acts of the institutions of the Community based on this Title is raised in a case pending before a court or a tribunal of a Member State against whose decisions there is no judicial remedy under national law, that court or tribunal shall, if it considers that a decision on the question is necessary to enable it to give judgement, request the Court of Justice to give a ruling thereon.

2. In any event, the Court of Justice shall not have jurisdiction to rule on any measure or decision taken pursuant to Article 62(1) relating to the maintenance of law and order and the safeguarding of internal security.

3. The Council, the Commission or a Member State may request the Court of Justice to give a ruling on a question of interpretation of this Title or of acts of the institutions of the Community based on this Title. The ruling given by the Court of Justice in response to such a request shall not apply to judgements of courts or tribunals of the Member States which have become *res judicata*.

ARTICLE 69 (ex Article **73 q**)

The application of this Title shall be subject to the provisions of the Protocol on the position of the United Kingdom and Ireland and to the Protocol on the position of Denmark, without prejudice to the Protocol on the application of certain aspects of Article 14 of the Treaty establishing the European Community to the United Kingdom and to Ireland.

TITLE **V**   (ex Title IV)

TRANSPORT

ARTICLE 70 (ex Article 70)

The objectives of this Treaty shall, in matters governed by this Title, be pursued by Member States within the framework of a common transport policy.

ARTICLE 71 (ex Article 75)

1. For the purpose of implementing Article **70**, and taking into account the distinctive features of transport, the Council shall, acting in accordance with the procedure referred to in **Article 251** and after consulting the Economic and Social Committee **and the Committee of the Regions**, lay down:

(a) common rules applicable to international transport to or from the territory of a Member State or passing across the territory of one or more Member States;

(b) the conditions under which non-resident carriers may operate transport services within a Member State;

(c) measures to improve transport safety;

(d) any other appropriate provisions.

Paragraph 2 shall be repealed.

2. By way of derogation from the procedure provided for in paragraph 1, where the application of provisions concerning the principles of the regulatory system for transport would be liable to have a serious effect on the standard of living and on employment in certain areas and on the operation of transport facilities, they shall be laid down by the Council acting unanimously on a proposal from the Commission, after consulting the European Parliament and the Economic and Social Committee. In so doing, the Council shall take into account the need for adaptation to the economic development which will result from establishing the common market.

ARTICLE 72 (ex Article 76)

Until the provisions referred to in Article **71**(1) have been laid down, no Member State may, without the unanimous approval of the Council, make the various provisions governing the subject **on 1 January 1958 or, for acceding States, the date of their accession,** less favourable in their direct or indirect effect on carriers of other Member States as compared with carriers who are nationals of that State.

ARTICLE **73** (ex Article 77)

Aids shall be compatible with this Treaty if they meet the needs of co-ordination of transport or if they represent reimbursement for the discharge of certain obligations inherent in the concept of a public service.

ARTICLE **74** (ex Article 78)

Any measures taken within the framework of this Treaty in respect of transport rates and conditions shall take account of the economic circumstances of carriers.

ARTICLE **75** (ex Article 79)

1. In the case of transport within the Community, discrimination which takes the form of carriers charging different rates and imposing different conditions for the carriage of the same goods over the same transport links on grounds of the country of origin or of destination of the goods in question shall be abolished. *Rest of sentence shall be deleted.*

2. Paragraph 1 shall not prevent the Council from adopting other measures in pursuance of Article **71**(1).

3. **The Council** shall, acting by a qualified majority on a proposal from the Commission and after consulting the Economic and Social Committee, lay down rules for implementing the provisions of paragraph 1.

The Council may in particular lay down the provisions needed to enable the institutions of the Community to secure compliance with the rule laid down in paragraph 1 and to ensure that users benefit from it to the full.

4. The Commission shall, acting on its own initiative or on application by a Member State, investigate any cases of discrimination falling within paragraph 1 and after consulting any Member State concerned, shall take the necessary decisions within the framework of the rules laid down in accordance with the provisions of paragraph 3.

ARTICLE **76** (ex Article 80)

1. The imposition by a Member State, in respect of transport operations carried out within the Community, of rates and conditions involving any element of support or protection in the interest of one or more particular undertakings or industries shall be **prohibited, unless** authorised by the Commission.

2. The Commission shall, acting on its own initiative or on application by a Member State, examine the rates and conditions referred to in paragraph 1, taking account in particular of the requirements of an appropriate regional economic policy, the needs of underdeveloped areas and the problems of areas seriously affected by political circumstances on the one hand, and of the effects of such rates and conditions on competition between the different modes of transport on the other.

After consulting each Member State concerned, the Commission shall take the necessary decisions.

3. The prohibition provided for in paragraph 1 shall not apply to tariffs fixed to meet competition.

ARTICLE **77** (ex Article 81)

Charges or dues in respect of the crossing of frontiers which are charged by a carrier in addition to the transport rates shall not exceed a reasonable level after taking the costs actually incurred thereby into account. Member States shall endeavour to reduce these costs progressively.

The Commission may make recommendations to Member States for the application of this Article.

ARTICLE **78** (ex Article 82)

The provisions of this Title shall not form an obstacle to the application of measures taken in the Federal Republic of Germany to the extent that such measures are required in order to compensate for the economic disadvantages caused by the division of Germany to the economy of certain areas of the Federal Republic affected by that division.

ARTICLE **79** (ex Article 83)

An Advisory Committee consisting of experts designated by the Governments of Member States, shall be attached to the Commission. The Commission, whenever it considers it desirable, shall consult the Committee on transport matters without prejudice to the **powers of** the Economic and Social Committee.

ARTICLE **80** (ex Article 84)

1. The provisions of this Title shall apply to transport by rail, road and inland waterway.

2. The Council may, acting by a qualified majority, decide whether, to what extent and by what procedure appropriate provisions may be laid down for sea and air transport.

The procedural provisions of **Article 71** shall apply.

TITLE **VI** (ex Title V)

COMMON RULES ON COMPETITION, TAXATION AND APPROXIMATION OF LAWS

CHAPTER 1

RULES ON COMPETITION

Section 1

Rules applying to undertakings

ARTICLE **81** (ex Article 85)

1.   The following shall be prohibited as incompatible with the common market: all agreements between undertakings, decisions by associations of undertakings and concerted practices which may affect trade between Member States and which have as their object or effect the prevention, restriction or distortion of competition within the common market, and in particular those which:
(a)   directly or indirectly fix purchase or selling prices or any other trading conditions;
(b)   limit or control production, markets, technical development, or investment;
(c)   share markets or sources of supply;
(d)   apply dissimilar conditions to equivalent transactions with other trading parties, thereby placing them at a competitive disadvantage;
(e)   make the conclusion of contracts subject to acceptance by the other parties of supplementary obligations which, by their nature or according to commercial usage, have no connection with the subject of such contracts.

2.   Any agreements or decisions prohibited pursuant to this Article shall be automatically void.

3.   The provisions of paragraph 1 may, however, be declared inapplicable in the case of:
-        any agreement or category of agreements between undertakings;
-        any decision or category of decisions by associations of undertakings;
-        any concerted practice or category of concerted practices;
which contributes to improving the production or distribution of goods or to promoting technical or economic progress, while allowing consumers a fair share of the resulting benefit, and which does not:
(a)   impose on the undertakings concerned restrictions which are not indispensable to the attainment of these objectives;
(b)   afford such undertakings the possibility of eliminating competition in respect of a substantial part of the products in question.

ARTICLE **82** (ex Article 86)

Any abuse by one or more undertakings of a dominant position within the common market or in a substantial part of it shall be prohibited as incompatible with the common market insofar as it may affect trade between Member States.
Such abuse may, in particular, consist in:
(a)   directly or indirectly imposing unfair purchase or selling prices or other unfair trading conditions;
(b)   limiting production, markets or technical development to the prejudice of consumers;
(c)   applying dissimilar conditions to equivalent transactions with other trading parties, thereby placing them at a competitive disadvantage;
(d)   making the conclusion of contracts subject to acceptance by the other parties of supplementary obligations which, by their nature or according to commercial usage, have no connection with the subject of such contracts.

ARTICLE **83** (ex Article 87)

1.   **The appropriate** regulations or directives to give effect to the principles set out in **Articles 81 and 82 shall be** laid down by the Council, acting by a qualified majority on a proposal from the Commission and after consulting the European Parliament.

2.   The regulations or directives referred to in paragraph 1 shall be designed in particular:
(a)   to ensure compliance with the prohibitions laid down in Article **81**(1) and in Article **82** by making provision for fines and periodic penalty payments;
(b)   to lay down detailed rules for the application of Article **81**(3), taking into account the need to ensure effective supervision on the one hand, and to simplify administration to the greatest possible extent on the other;

(c) to define, if need be, in the various branches of the economy, the scope of the provisions of Articles **81** and **82**;

(d) to define the respective functions of the Commission and of the Court of Justice in applying the provisions laid down in this paragraph;

(e) to determine the relationship between national laws and the provisions contained in this Section or adopted pursuant to this Article.

ARTICLE **84** (ex Article 88)

Until the entry into force of the provisions adopted in pursuance of Article **83**, the authorities in Member States shall rule on the admissibility of agreements, decisions and concerted practices and on abuse of a dominant position in the common market in accordance with the law of their country and with the provisions of Article **81**, in particular paragraph 3, and of Article **82**.

ARTICLE **85** (ex Article 89)

1. Without prejudice to Article **84**, the Commission **shall ensure** the application of the principles laid down in Articles **81** and **82**. On application by a Member State or on its own initiative, and in co-operation with the competent authorities in the Member States, who shall give it their assistance, the Commission shall investigate cases of suspected infringement of these principles. If it finds that there has been an infringement, it shall propose appropriate measures to bring it to an end.

2. If the infringement is not brought to an end, the Commission shall record such infringement of the principles in a reasoned decision. The Commission may publish its decision and authorise Member States to take the measures, the conditions and details of which it shall determine, needed to remedy the situation.

ARTICLE **86** (ex Article 90)

1. In the case of public undertakings and undertakings to which Member States grant special or exclusive rights, Member States shall neither enact nor maintain in force any measure contrary to the rules contained in this Treaty, in particular to those rules provided for in Article **12** and Articles **81** to **89**.

2. Undertakings entrusted with the operation of services of general economic interest or having the character of a revenue-producing monopoly shall be subject to the rules contained in this Treaty, in particular to the rules on competition, insofar as the application of such rules does not obstruct the performance, in law or in fact, of the particular tasks assigned to them. The development of trade must not be affected to such an extent as would be contrary to the interests of the Community.

3. The Commission shall ensure the application of the provisions of this Article and shall, where necessary, address appropriate directives or decisions to Member States.

SECTION HEADING (Section 2 – Dumping) shall be deleted.

ARTICLE 91 shall be repealed.

Section 2

Aids granted by States

ARTICLE **87** (ex Article 92)

1. Save as otherwise provided in this Treaty, any aid granted by a Member State or through State resources in any form whatsoever which distorts or threatens to distort competition by favouring certain undertakings or the production of certain goods shall, in so far as it affects trade between Member States, be incompatible with the common market.

2. The following shall be compatible with the common market:

(a) aid having a social character, granted to individual consumers, provided that such aid is granted without discrimination related to the origin of the products concerned;

(b) aid to make good the damage caused by natural disasters or exceptional occurrences;

(c) aid granted to the economy of certain areas of the Federal Republic of Germany affected by the division of Germany, insofar as such aid is required in order to compensate for the economic disadvantages caused by that division.

3. The following may be considered to be compatible with the common market:
(a) aid to promote the economic development of areas where the standard of living is abnormally low or where there is serious underemployment;
(b) aid to promote the execution of an important project of common European interest or to remedy a serious disturbance in the economy of a Member State;
(c) aid to facilitate the development of certain economic activities or of certain economic areas, where such aid does not adversely affect trading conditions to an extent contrary to the common interest; *Second sentence shall be deleted.*
(d) aid to promote culture and heritage conservation where such aid does not affect trading conditions and competition in the Community to an extent that is contrary to the common interest;
(e) such other categories of aid as may be specified by decision of the Council acting by a qualified majority on a proposal from the Commission.

ARTICLE **88** (ex Article 93)
1. The Commission shall, in co-operation with Member States, keep under constant review all systems of aid existing in those States. It shall propose to the latter any appropriate measures required by the progressive development or by the functioning of the common market.

2. If, after giving notice to the parties concerned to submit their comments, the Commission finds that aid granted by a State or through State resources is not compatible with the common market having regard to Article **87**, or that such aid is being misused, it shall decide that the State concerned shall abolish or alter such aid within a period of time to be determined by the Commission.
If the State concerned does not comply with this decision within the prescribed time, the Commission or any other interested State may, in derogation from the provisions of Articles **226** and **227**, refer the matter to the Court of Justice direct.
On application by a Member State, the Council, may acting unanimously, decide that aid which that State is granting or intends to grant shall be considered to be compatible with the common market, in derogation from the provisions of Article **87** or from the regulations provided for in Article **89**, if such a decision is justified by exceptional circumstances. If, as regards the aid in question, the Commission has already initiated the procedure provided for in the first sub-paragraph of this paragraph, the fact that the State concerned has made its application to the Council shall have the effect of suspending that procedure until the Council has made its attitude known.
If, however, the Council has not made its attitude known within three months of the said application being made, the Commission shall give its decision on the case.

3. The Commission shall be informed, in sufficient time to enable it to submit its comments, of any plans to grant or alter aid. If it considers that any such plan is not compatible with the common market having regard to Article **87**, it shall without delay initiate the procedure provided for in paragraph 2. The Member State concerned shall not put its proposed measures into effect until this procedure has resulted in a final decision.

ARTICLE **89** (ex Article 94)
The Council, acting by a qualified majority on a proposal from the Commission and after consulting the European Parliament, make any appropriate regulations for the application of Articles **87** and **88** and may in particular determine the conditions in which Article **88**(3) shall apply and the categories of aid exempted from this procedure.

CHAPTER 2

TAX PROVISIONS

ARTICLE **90** (ex Article 95)
No Member State shall impose, directly or indirectly, on the products of other Member States any internal taxation of any kind in excess of that imposed directly or indirectly on similar domestic products.
Furthermore, no Member State shall impose on the products of other Member States any internal taxation of such a nature as to afford indirect protection to other products.

Third paragraph shall be repealed.

ARTICLE **91** (ex Article 96)
Where products are exported to the territory of any Member State, any repayment of internal taxation shall not exceed the internal taxation imposed on them whether directly or indirectly.

ARTICLE 97 shall be repealed.

ARTICLE **92** (ex Article 98)
In the case of charges other than turnover taxes, excise duties and other forms of indirect taxation, remissions and repayments in respect of exports to other Member States may not be granted and countervailing charges in respect of imports from Member States may not be imposed unless the measures contemplated have been previously approved for a limited period by the Council acting by a qualified majority on a proposal from the Commission.

ARTICLE **93** (ex Article 99)
The Council shall, acting unanimously on a proposal from the Commission and after consulting the European Parliament and the Economic and Social Committee, adopt provisions for the harmonisation of legislation concerning turnover taxes, excise duties and other forms of indirect taxation to the extent that such harmonisation is necessary to ensure the establishment and the functioning of the internal market within the time limit laid down in Article **14**.

CHAPTER 3

APPROXIMATION OF LAWS

ARTICLE **94** (ex Article 100)
The Council shall, acting unanimously on a proposal from the Commission and after consulting the European Parliament and the Economic and Social Committee, issue directives for the approximation of such laws, regulations or administrative provisions of the Member States as directly affect the establishment or functioning of the common market.

ARTICLE **95** (ex Article 100 a)
1.   By way of derogation from Article **94** and save where otherwise provided in this Treaty, the following provisions shall apply for the achievement of the objectives set out in Article **14**. The Council shall, acting in accordance with the procedure referred to in Article **251** and after consulting the Economic and Social Committee, adopt the measures for the approximation of the provisions laid down by law, regulation or administrative action in Member States which have as their object the establishment and functioning of the internal market.

2.   Paragraph 1 shall not apply to fiscal provisions, to those relating to the free movement of persons nor to those relating to the rights and interests of employed persons.

3.   The Commission, in its proposals envisaged in paragraph 1 concerning health, safety, environmental protection and consumer protection, will take as a base a high level of protection, **taking account in particular of any new development based on scientific facts. Within their respective powers, the European Parliament and the Council will also seek to achieve this objective.**

4.   If, after the adoption **by the Council or by the Commission** of a harmonisation measure, a Member State deems it necessary **to maintain** national provisions on grounds of major needs referred to in Article **30**, or relating to the protection of the environment or the working environment, it shall notify the Commission of these provisions **as well as the grounds for maintaining them.**

5.   **Moreover, without prejudice to paragraph 4, if, after the adoption by the Council or by the Commission of a harmonisation measure, a Member State deems it necessary to introduce national provisions based on new scientific evidence relating to the protection of the environment or the working environment on grounds of a problem specific to that Member State arising after the adoption of the harmonisation measure, it shall notify the Commission of the envisaged provisions as well as the grounds for introducing them.**

6.   **The Commission shall, within six months of the notifications as referred to in paragraphs 4 and 5, approve or reject the national provisions involved after having verified whether or not they are not a means of arbitrary discrimination or a disguised restriction on trade between Member States and whether or not they shall constitute an obstacle to the functioning of the internal market.**
In the absence of a decision by the Commission within this period the national provisions referred to in paragraphs 4 and 5 shall be deemed to have been approved.
When justified by the complexity of the matter and in the absence of danger for human health, the Commission may notify the Member State concerned that the period referred to in this paragraph may be extended for a further period of up to six months.

7.   When, pursuant to paragraph 6, a Member State is authorised to maintain or introduce national provisions derogating from a harmonisation measure, the Commission shall immediately examine whether to propose an adaptation to that measure.

8.   When a Member State raises a specific problem on public health in a field which has been the subject of prior harmonisation measures, it shall bring it to the attention of the Commission which shall immediately examine whether to propose appropriate measures to the Council.

9.   By way of derogation from the procedure laid down in Articles **226** and **227**, the Commission **and** any Member State may bring the matter directly before the Court of Justice if it considers that another Member State is making improper use of the powers provided for in this Article.

10.   The harmonisation measures referred to above shall, in appropriate cases, include a safeguard clause authorising the Member States to take, for one or more of the non-economic reasons referred to in Article **30**, provisional measures subject to a Community control procedure.

ARTICLES 100 b, 100c and 100d shall be repealed.

ARTICLE **96** (ex Article 101)
Where the Commission finds that a difference between the provisions laid down by law, regulation or administrative action in Member States is distorting the conditions of competition in the common market and that the resultant distortion needs to be eliminated, it shall consult the Member States concerned.
If such consultation does not result in an agreement eliminating the distortion in question, the Council shall, on a proposal from the Commission, **acting by a qualified majority**, issue the necessary directives. The Commission and the Council may take any other appropriate measures provided for in this Treaty.

ARTICLE **97** (ex Article 102)
1.   Where there is reason to fear that the adoption or amendment of a provision laid down by law, regulation or administrative action may cause distortion within the meaning of Article **96**, a Member State desiring to proceed therewith shall consult the Commission. After consulting the Member States, the Commission shall recommend to the States concerned such measures as may be appropriate to avoid the distortion in question.

2.   If a State desiring to introduce or amend its own provisions does not comply with the recommendation addressed to it by the Commission, other Member States shall not be required, in pursuance of Article **96**, to amend their own provisions in order to eliminate such distortion. If the Member State which has ignored the recommendation of the Commission causes distortion detrimental only to itself, the provisions of Article **96** shall not apply.

TITLE **VII**   (ex Title VI)

ECONOMIC AND MONETARY POLICY

CHAPTER 1

ECONOMIC POLICY

ARTICLE **98** (ex Article 102 a)
Member States shall conduct their economic policies with a view to contributing to the achievement of the objectives of the Community, as defined in Article **2**, and in the context of the broad guidelines referred to in Article **99**(2). The Member States and the Community shall act in accordance with the principle of an open market economy with free competition, favouring an efficient allocation of resources, and in compliance with the principles set out in Article **4**.

ARTICLE **99** (ex Article 103)
1.   Member States shall regard their economic policies as a matter of common concern and shall co-ordinate them within the Council, in accordance with the provisions of Article **98**.

2.   The Council shall, acting by a qualified majority on a recommendation from the Commission, formulate a draft for the broad guidelines of the economic policies of the Member States and of the Community, and shall report its findings to the European Council.
The European Council shall, acting on the basis of the report from the Council, discuss a conclusion on the broad guidelines of the economic policies of the Member States and of the Community.

On the basis of this conclusion, the Council shall, acting by a qualified majority, adopt a recommendation setting out these broad guidelines. The Council shall inform the European Parliament of its recommendation.

3. In order to ensure closer co-ordination of economic policies and sustained convergence of the economic performances of the Member States, the Council shall, on the basis of reports submitted by the Commission, monitor economic developments in each of the Member States and in the Community as well as the consistency of economic policies with the broad guidelines referred to in paragraph 2, and regularly carry out an overall assessment.

For the purpose of this multilateral surveillance, Member States shall forward information to the Commission about important measures taken by them in the field of their economic policy and such other information as they deem necessary.

4. Where it is established, under the procedure referred to in paragraph 3, that the economic policies of a Member State are not consistent with the broad guidelines referred to in paragraph 2 or that they risk jeopardising the proper functioning of economic and monetary union, the Council may, acting by a qualified majority on a recommendation from the Commission, make the necessary recommendations to the Member State concerned. The Council may, acting by a qualified majority on a proposal from the Commission, decide to make its recommendations public.

The President of the Council and the Commission shall report to the European Parliament on the results of multilateral surveillance. The President of the Council may be invited to appear before the competent Committee of the European Parliament if the Council has made its recommendations public.

5. The Council, acting in accordance with the procedure referred to in Article **252**, may adopt detailed rules for the multilateral surveillance procedure referred to in paragraphs 3 and 4 of this Article.

ARTICLE **100** (ex Article 103 a)

1. Without prejudice to any other procedures provided for in this Treaty, the Council may, acting unanimously on a proposal from the Commission, decide upon the measures appropriate to the economic situation, in particular if severe difficulties arise in the supply of certain products.

2. Where a Member State is in difficulties or is seriously threatened with severe difficulties caused by exceptional occurrences beyond its control, the Council may, acting unanimously on a proposal from the Commission, grant, under certain conditions, Community financial assistance to the Member State concerned. Where the severe difficulties are caused by natural disasters, the Council shall act by qualified majority. The President of the Council shall inform the European Parliament of the decision taken.

ARTICLE **101** (ex Article 104)

1. Overdraft facilities or any other type of credit facility with the ECB or with the central banks of the Member States (hereinafter referred to as 'national central banks') in favour of Community institutions or bodies, central governments, regional, local or other public authorities, other bodies governed by public law, or public undertakings of Member States shall be prohibited, as shall the purchase directly from them by the ECB or national central banks of debt instruments.

2. Paragraph 1 shall not apply to publicly-owned credit institutions which, in the context of the supply of reserves by central banks, shall be given the same treatment by national central banks and the ECB as private credit institutions.

ARTICLE **102** (ex Article 104 a)

1. Any measure, not based on prudential considerations, establishing privileged access by Community institutions or bodies, central governments, regional, local or other public authorities, other bodies governed by public law, or public undertakings of Member States to financial institutions shall be prohibited.

2. The Council, acting in accordance with the procedure referred to in Article **252**, shall, before 1 January 1994, specify definitions for the application of the prohibition referred to in paragraph 1.

ARTICLE **103** (ex Article 104 b)

1. The Community shall not be liable for or assume the commitments of central governments, regional, local or other public authorities, other bodies governed by public law, or public undertakings of any Member State, without prejudice to mutual financial guarantees for the joint execution of a specific project. A Member State shall not be liable for or assume the commitments of central governments, regional, local or other public authorities, other bodies governed by public law or public undertakings of another Member State, without prejudice to mutual financial guarantees for the joint execution of a specific project.

2. If necessary, the Council, acting in accordance with the procedure referred to in Article **252**, may specify definitions for the application of the prohibitions referred to in Article **101** and in this Article.

ARTICLE **104** (ex Article 104 c)
1.   Member States shall avoid excessive government deficits.

2.   The Commission shall monitor the development of the budgetary situation and of the stock of government debt in the Member States with a view to identifying gross errors. In particular it shall examine compliance with budgetary discipline on the basis of the following two criteria:
(a)   whether the ratio of the planned or actual government deficit to gross domestic product exceeds a reference value, unless:
-      either the ratio has declined substantially and continuously and reached a level that comes close to the reference value;
-      or, alternatively, the excess over the reference value is only exceptional and temporary and the ratio remains close to the reference value;
(b)   whether the ratio of government debt to gross domestic product exceeds a reference value, unless the ratio is sufficiently diminishing and approaching the reference value at a satisfactory pace.
The reference values are specified in the Protocol on the excessive deficit procedure annexed to this Treaty.

3.   If a Member State does not fulfil the requirements under one or both of these criteria, the Commission shall prepare a report. The report of the Commission shall also take into account whether the government deficit exceeds government investment expenditure and take into account all other relevant factors, including the medium-term economic and budgetary position of the Member State.
The Commission may also prepare a report if, notwithstanding the fulfilment of the requirements under the criteria, it is of the opinion that there is a risk of an excessive deficit in a Member State.

4.   The Committee provided for in Article **114** shall formulate an opinion on the report of the Commission.

5.   If the Commission considers that an excessive deficit in a Member State exists or may occur, the Commission shall address an opinion to the Council.

6.   The Council shall, acting by a qualified majority on a recommendation from the Commission, and having considered any observations which the Member State concerned may wish to make, decide after an overall assessment whether an excessive deficit exists.

7.   Where the existence of an excessive deficit is decided according to paragraph 6, the Council shall make recommendations to the Member State concerned with a view to bringing that situation to an end within a given period. Subject to the provisions of paragraph 8, these recommendations shall not be made public.

8.   Where it establishes that there has been no effective action in response to its recommendations within the period laid down, the Council may make its recommendations public.

9.   If a Member State persists in failing to put into practice the recommendations of the Council, the Council may decide to give notice to the Member State to take, within a specified time limit, measures for the deficit reduction which is judged necessary by the Council in order to remedy the situation.
In such a case, the Council may request the Member State concerned to submit reports in accordance with a specific timetable in order to examine the adjustment efforts of that Member State.

10.   The rights to bring actions provided for in Articles **226** and **227** may not be exercised within the framework of paragraphs 1 to 9 of this Article.

11.   As long as a Member State fails to comply with a decision taken in accordance with paragraph 9, the Council may decide to apply or, as the case may be, intensify one or more of the following measures:
-      to require the Member State concerned to publish additional information, to be specified by the Council, before issuing bonds and securities;
-      to invite the European Investment Bank to reconsider its lending policy towards the Member State concerned;
-      to require the Member State concerned to make a non-interest-bearing deposit of an appropriate size with the Community until the excessive deficit has, in the view of the Council, been corrected;
-      to impose fines of an appropriate size.
The President of the Council shall inform the European Parliament of the decisions taken.

12.   The Council shall abrogate some or all of its decisions referred to in paragraphs 6 to 9 and 11 to the extent that the excessive deficit in the Member State concerned has, in the view of the Council, been corrected. If the Council has previously made public recommendations, it shall, as soon as the decision under paragraph 8 has been abrogated, make a public statement that an excessive deficit in the Member State concerned no longer exists.

13.   When taking the decisions referred to in paragraphs 7 to 9, 11 and 12, the Council shall act on a recommendation from the Commission by a majority of two-thirds of the votes of its members weighted in accordance with Article **205**(2), excluding the votes of the representative of the Member State concerned.

14.   Further provisions relating to the implementation of the procedure described in this Article are set out in the Protocol on the excessive deficit procedure annexed to this Treaty.

The Council shall, acting unanimously on a proposal from the Commission and after consulting the European Parliament and the ECB, adopt the appropriate provisions which shall then replace the said Protocol.

Subject to the other provisions of this paragraph the Council shall, before 1 January 1994, acting by a qualified majority on a proposal from the Commission and after consulting the European Parliament, lay down detailed rules and definitions for the application of the provisions of the said Protocol.

CHAPTER 2

MONETARY POLICY

ARTICLE **105**   (ex Article 105)

1.   The primary objective of the ESCB shall be to maintain price stability. Without prejudice to the objective of price stability, the ESCB shall support the general economic policies in the Community with a view to contributing to the achievement of the objectives of the Community as laid down in Article **2**. The ESCB shall act in accordance with the principle of an open market economy with free competition, favouring an efficient allocation of resources, and in compliance with the principles set out in Article **4**.

2.   The basic tasks to be carried out through the ESCB shall be:
-    to define and implement the monetary policy of the Community;
-    to conduct foreign exchange operations consistent with the provisions of Article **111**;
-    to hold and manage the official foreign reserves of the Member States;
-    to promote the smooth operation of payment systems.

3.   The third indent of paragraph 2 shall be without prejudice to the holding and management by the governments of Member States of foreign exchange working balances.

4.   The ECB shall be consulted:
-    on any proposed Community act in its fields of competence;
-    by national authorities regarding any draft legislative provision in its fields of competence, but within the limits and under the conditions set out by the Council in accordance with the procedure laid down in Article **107**(6).

The ECB may submit opinions to the appropriate Community institutions or bodies or to national authorities on matters in its fields of competence.

5.   The ESCB shall contribute to the smooth conduct of policies pursued by the competent authorities relating to the prudential supervision of credit institutions and the stability of the Financial system.

6.   The Council may, acting unanimously on a proposal from the Commission and after consulting the ECB and after receiving the assent of the European Parliament, confer upon the ECB specific tasks concerning policies relating to the prudential supervision of credit institutions and other financial institutions with the exception of insurance undertakings.

ARTICLE **106**   (ex Article 105 a)

1.   The ECB shall have the exclusive right to authorise the issue of bank notes within the Community. The ECB and the national central banks may issue such notes. The bank notes issued by the ECB and the national central banks shall be the only such notes to have the status of legal tender within the Community.

2.   Member States may issue coins subject to approval by the ECB of the volume of the issue. The Council may, acting in accordance with the procedure referred to in Article **252** and after consulting the ECB, adopt measures to harmonise the denominations and technical specifications of all coins intended for circulation to the extent necessary to permit their smooth circulation within the Community.

ARTICLE **107**   (ex Article 106)

1.   The ESCB shall be composed of the ECB and of the national central banks.

2.   The ECB shall have legal personality.

3.   The ESCB shall be governed by the decision-making bodies of the ECB which shall be the Governing Council and the Executive Board.

4. The Statute of the ESCB is laid down in a Protocol annexed to this Treaty.

5. Articles 5.1, 5.2, 5.3, 17, 18, 19.1, 22, 23, 24, 26, 32.2, 32.3, 32.4, 32.6, 33.1(a) and 36 of the Statute of the ESCB may be amended by the Council, acting either by a qualified majority on a recommendation from the ECB and after consulting the Commission or unanimously on a proposal from the Commission and after consulting the ECB. In either case, the assent of the European Parliament shall be required.

6. The Council, acting by a qualified majority either on a proposal from the Commission and after consulting the European Parliament and the ECB or on a recommendation from the ECB and after consulting the European Parliament and the Commission, shall adopt the provisions referred to in Articles 4, 5.4, 19.2, 20, 28.1, 29.2, 30.4 and 34.3 of the Statute of the ESCB.

ARTICLE **108** (ex Article 107)
When exercising the powers and carrying out the tasks and duties conferred upon them by this Treaty and the Statute of the ESCB, neither the ECB, nor a national central bank, nor any member of their decision-making bodies shall seek or take instructions from Community institutions or bodies, from any government of a Member State or from any other body. The Community institutions and bodies and the governments of the Member States undertake to respect this principle and not to seek to influence the members of the decision-making bodies of the ECB or of the national central banks in the performance of their tasks.

ARTICLE **109** (ex Article 108)
Each Member State shall ensure, at the latest at the date of the establishment of the ESCB, that its national legislation including the statutes of its national central bank is compatible with this Treaty and the Statute of the ESCB.

ARTICLE **110** (ex Article 108 a)
1. In order to carry out the tasks entrusted to the ESCB, the ECB shall, in accordance with the provisions of this Treaty and under the conditions laid down in the Statute of the ESCB:
- make regulations to the extent necessary to implement the tasks defined in Article 3.1, first indent, Articles 19.1, 22 and 25.2 of the Statute of the ESCB and in cases which shall be laid down in the acts of the Council referred to in Article **107**(6);
- take decisions necessary for carrying out the tasks entrusted to the ESCB under this Treaty and the Statute of the ESCB;
- make recommendations and deliver opinions.

2. A regulation shall have general application. It shall be binding in its entirety and directly applicable in all Member States.
Recommendations and opinions shall have no binding force.
A decision shall be binding in its entirety upon those to whom it is addressed.
Articles **253** to **256** shall apply to regulations and decisions adopted by the ECB.
The ECB may decide to publish its decisions, recommendations and opinions.

3. Within the limits and under the conditions adopted by the Council under the procedure laid down in Article **107**(6), the ECB shall be entitled to impose fines or periodic penalty payments on undertakings for failure to comply with obligations under its regulations and decisions.

ARTICLE **111** (ex Article 109)
1. By way of derogation from Article **300**, the Council may, acting unanimously on a recommendation from the ECB or from the Commission, and after consulting the ECB in an endeavour to reach a consensus consistent with the objective of price stability, after consulting the European Parliament, in accordance with the procedure in paragraph 3 for determining the arrangements, conclude formal agreements on an exchange rate system for the ECU in relation to non-Community currencies. The Council may, acting by a qualified majority on a recommendation from the ECB or from the Commission, and after consulting the ECB in an endeavour to reach a consensus consistent with the objective of price stability, adopt, adjust or abandon the central rates of the ECU within the exchange rate system. The President of the Council shall inform the European Parliament of the adoption, adjustment or abandonment of the ECU central rates.

2. In the absence of an exchange rate system in relation to one or more non-Community currencies as referred to in paragraph 1, the Council, acting by a qualified majority either on a recommendation from the Commission and after consulting the ECB or on a recommendation from the ECB, may formulate general orientations for exchange rate policy in relation to these currencies. These general orientations shall be without prejudice to the primary objective of the ESCB to maintain price stability.

3.   By way of derogation from Article **300**, where agreements concerning monetary or foreign exchange regime matters need to be negotiated by the Community with one or more States or international organisations, the Council, acting by a qualified majority on a recommendation from the Commission and after consulting the ECB, shall decide the arrangements for the negotiation and for the conclusion of such agreements. These arrangements shall ensure that the Community expresses a single position. The Commission shall be fully associated with the negotiations.

Agreements concluded in accordance with this paragraph shall be binding on the institutions of the Community, on the ECB and on Member States.

4.   Subject to paragraph 1, the Council shall, on a proposal from the Commission and after consulting the ECB, acting by a qualified majority decide on the position of the Community at international level as regards issues of particular relevance to economic and monetary union and, acting unanimously, decide its representation in compliance with the allocation of powers laid down in Articles **99** and **105**.

5.   Without prejudice to Community competence and Community agreements as regards economic and monetary Union, Member States may negotiate in international bodies and conclude international agreements.

CHAPTER 3

INSTITUTIONAL PROVISIONS

ARTICLE **112** (ex Article 109 a)
1.   The Governing Council of the ECB shall comprise the members of the Executive Board of the ECB and the Governors of the national central banks.

2.   (a)   The Executive Board shall comprise the President, the Vice-President and four other members.
       (b)   The President, the Vice-President and the other members of the Executive Board shall be appointed from among persons of recognised standing and professional experience in monetary or banking matters by common accord of the Governments of the Member States at the level of Heads of State or of Government, on a recommendation from the Council, after it has consulted the European Parliament and the Governing Council of the ECB.
              Their term of office shall be eight years and shall not be renewable.
              Only nationals of Member States may be members of the Executive Board.

ARTICLE **113** (ex Article 109 b)
1.   The President of the Council and a member of the Commission may participate, without having the right to vote, in meetings of the Governing Council of the ECB.
The President of the Council may submit a motion for deliberation to the Governing Council of the ECB.

2.   The President of the ECB shall be invited to participate in Council meetings when the Council is discussing matters relating to the objectives and tasks of the ESCB.

3.   The ECB shall address an annual report on the activities of the ESCB and on the monetary policy of both the previous and current year to the European Parliament, the Council and the Commission, and also to the European Council. The President of the ECB shall present this report to the Council and to the European Parliament, which may hold a general debate on that basis.
The President of the ECB and the other members of the Executive Board may, at the request of the European Parliament or on their own initiative, be heard by the competent Committees of the European Parliament.

ARTICLE **114** (ex Article 109 c)
1.   In order to promote co-ordination of the policies of Member States to the full extent needed for the functioning of the internal market, a Monetary Committee with advisory status is hereby set up.
It shall have the following tasks:
-    to keep under review the monetary and financial situation of the Member States and of the Community and the general payments system of the Member States and to report regularly thereon to the Council and to the Commission;
-    to deliver opinions at the request of the Council or of the Commission, or on its own initiative for submission to those institutions;
-    without prejudice to Article **207**, to contribute to the preparation of the work of the Council referred to in Articles **59**, **60**, **99**(2), (3), (4) and (5), **100**, **102**, **103**, **104**, **116**(2), **117**(6), **119**, **120**, **121**(2) and **122**(1);

- to examine, at least once a year, the situation regarding the movement of capital and the freedom of payments, as they result from the application of this Treaty and of measures adopted by the Council; the examination shall cover all measures relating to capital movements and payments; the Committee shall report to the Commission and to the Council on the outcome of this examination.

The Member States and the Commission shall each appoint two members of the Monetary Committee.

2.   At the start of the third stage, an Economic and Financial Committee shall be set up. The Monetary Committee provided for in paragraph 1 shall be dissolved.

The Economic and Financial Committee shall have the following tasks:

- to deliver opinions at the request of the Council or of the Commission, or on its own initiative for submission to those institutions;

- to keep under review the economic and financial situation of the Member States and of the Community and to report regularly thereon to the Council and to the Commission, in particular on financial relations with third countries and international institutions;

- without prejudice to Article **207**, to contribute to the preparation of the work of the Council referred to in Articles **59**, **60**, **99**(2), (3), (4) and (5), **100**, **102**, **103**, **104**, **105**(6), **106**(2), **107**(5) and (6), **111**, **119**, **120**(2) and (3), **122**(2), **123**(4) and (5), and to carry out other advisory and preparatory tasks assigned to it by the Council;

- to examine, at least once a year, the situation regarding the movement of capital and the freedom of payments, as they result from the application of this Treaty and of measures adopted by the Council; the examination shall cover all measures relating to capital movements and payments; the Committee shall report to the Commission and to the Council on the outcome of this examination.

The Member States, the Commission and the ECB shall each appoint no more than two members of the Committee.

3.   The Council shall, acting by a qualified majority on a proposal from the Commission and after consulting the ECB and the Committee referred to in this Article, lay down detailed provisions concerning the composition of the Economic and Financial Committee. The President of the Council shall inform the European Parliament of such a decision.

4.   In addition to the tasks set out in paragraph 2, if and as long as there are Member States with a derogation as referred to in Articles **122** and **123**, the Committee shall keep under review the monetary and financial situation and the general payments system of those Member States and report regularly thereon to the Council and to the Commission.

ARTICLE **115**   (ex Article 109 d)

For matters within the scope of Articles **99**(4), **104** with the exception of paragraph 14, **111**, **121**, **122** and **123**(4) and (5), the Council or a Member State may request the Commission to make a recommendation or a proposal, as appropriate. The Commission shall examine this request and submit its conclusions to the Council without delay.

CHAPTER 4

TRANSITIONAL PROVISIONS

ARTICLE **116**   (ex Article 109 e)

1.   The second stage for achieving economic and monetary union shall begin on 1 January 1994.

2.   Before that date:

(a)   each Member State shall:

- adopt, where necessary, appropriate measures to comply with the prohibitions laid down in **Article 56 and in** Articles **101** and **102**(1);

- adopt, if necessary, with a view to permitting the assessment provided for in sub-paragraph (b), multiannual programmes intended to ensure the lasting convergence necessary for the achievement of economic and monetary union, in particular with regard to price stability and sound public finances;

(b)   the Council shall, on the basis of a report from the Commission, assess the progress made with regard to economic and monetary convergence, in particular with regard to price stability and sound public finances, and the progress made with the implementation of Community law concerning the internal market.

3.   The provisions of Articles **101**, **102**(1), **103**(1) and **104** with the exception of paragraphs 1, 9, 11 and 14 shall apply from the beginning of the second stage.

The provisions of Articles **100**(2), **104**(1), (9) and (11), **105**, **106**, **108**, **111**, **112**, **113** and **114**(2) and (4) shall apply from the beginning of the third stage.

4.   In the second stage, Member States shall endeavour to avoid excessive government deficits.

5.   During the second stage, each Member State shall, as appropriate, start the process leading to the independence of its central bank, in accordance with Article **109**.

ARTICLE **117**   (ex Article 109 f)
1.   At the start of the second stage, a European Monetary Institute (hereinafter referred to as 'EMI') shall be established and take up its duties; it shall have legal personality and be directed and managed by a Council, consisting of a President and the Governors of the national central banks, one of whom shall be Vice-President. The President shall be appointed by common accord of the Governments of the Member States at the level of Heads of State or of Government, **on a recommendation from the Council of the EMI**, and after consulting the European Parliament and the Council. The President shall be selected from among persons of recognised standing and professional experience in monetary or banking matters. Only nationals of Member States may be President of the EMI. The Council of the EMI shall appoint the Vice-President.
The Statute of the EMI is laid down in a Protocol annexed to this Treaty.

Fourth sub-paragraph shall be repealed.

2.   The EMI shall:
-    strengthen co-operation between the national central banks;
-    strengthen the co-ordination of the monetary policies of the Member States, with the aim of ensuring price stability;
-    monitor the functioning of the European Monetary System;
-    hold consultations concerning issues falling within the competence of the national central banks and affecting the stability of financial institutions and markets;
-    take over the tasks of the European Monetary Co-operation Fund, which shall be dissolved; the modalities of dissolution are laid down in the Statute of the EMI;
-    facilitate the use of the ECU and oversee its development, including the smooth functioning of the ECU clearing system.

3.   For the preparation of the third stage, the EMI shall:
-    prepare the instruments and the procedures necessary for carrying out a single monetary policy in the third stage;
-    promote the harmonisation, where necessary, of the rules and practices governing the collection, compilation and distribution of statistics in the areas within its field of competence;
-    prepare the rules for operations to be undertaken by the national central banks within the framework of the ESCB;
-    promote the efficiency of cross-border payments;
-    supervise the technical preparation of ECU bank notes.
At the latest by 31 December 1996, the EMI shall specify the regulatory, organisational and logistical framework necessary for the ESCB to perform its tasks in the third stage. This framework shall be submitted for decision to the ECB at the date of its establishment.
4.   The EMI, acting by a majority of two-thirds of the members of its Council, may:
-    formulate opinions or recommendations on the overall orientation of monetary policy and exchange rate policy as well as on related measures introduced in each Member State;
-    submit opinions or recommendations to Governments and to the Council on policies which might affect the internal or external monetary situation in the Community and, in particular, the functioning of the European Monetary System;
-    make recommendations to the monetary authorities of the Member States concerning the conduct of their monetary policy.

5.   The EMI, acting unanimously, may decide to publish its opinions and its recommendations.

6.   The EMI shall be consulted by the Council regarding any proposed Community act within its field of competence.
Within the limits and under the conditions set out by the Council, acting by a qualified majority on a proposal from the Commission and after consulting the European Parliament and the EMI, the EMI shall be consulted by the authorities of the Member States on any draft legislative provision within its field of competence.

7.   The Council may, acting unanimously on a proposal from the Commission and after consulting the European Parliament and the EMI, confer upon the EMI other tasks for the preparation of the third stage.

8.   Where this Treaty provides for a consultative role for the ECB, references to the ECB shall be read as referring to the EMI before the establishment of the ECB.

Second sub-paragraph shall be repealed.

9.   During the second stage, the term 'ECB' used in Articles **230**, **232**, **233**, **234**, **237** and **238** shall be read as referring to the EMI.

ARTICLE **118**   (ex Article 109g)
The currency composition of the ECU basket shall not be changed.
From the start of the third stage, the value of the ECU shall be irrevocably fixed in accordance with Article **123**(4).

ARTICLE **119**   (ex Article 109 h)
1.   Where a Member State is in difficulties or is seriously threatened with difficulties as regards its balance of payments either as a result of an overall disequilibrium in its balance of payments, or as a result of the type of currency at its disposal, and where such difficulties are liable in particular to jeopardise the functioning of the common market or the progressive implementation of the common commercial policy, the Commission shall immediately investigate the position of the State in question and the action which, making use of all the means at its disposal, that State has taken or may take in accordance with the provisions of this Treaty. The Commission shall state what measures it recommends the State concerned to take.
If the action taken by a Member State and the measures suggested by the Commission do not prove sufficient to overcome the difficulties which have arisen or which threaten, the Commission shall, after consulting the Committee referred to in Article **114**, recommend to the Council the granting of mutual assistance and appropriate methods therefor.
The Commission shall keep the Council regularly informed of the situation and of how it is developing.

2.   The Council, acting by a qualified majority, shall grant such mutual assistance; it shall adopt directives or decisions laying down the conditions and details of such assistance, which may take such forms as:
(a)   a concerted approach to or within any other international organisations to which Member States may have recourse;
(b)   measures needed to avoid deflection of trade where the State which is in difficulties maintains or reintroduces quantitative restrictions against third countries;
(c)   the granting of limited credits by other Member States, subject to their agreement.

3.   If the mutual assistance recommended by the Commission is not granted by the Council or if the mutual assistance granted and the measures taken are insufficient, the Commission shall authorise the State which is in difficulties to take protective measures, the conditions and details of which the Commission shall determine.
Such authorisation may be revoked and such conditions and details may be changed by the Council acting by a qualified majority.

4.   Subject to Article **112**(6), this Article shall cease to apply from the beginning of the third stage.

ARTICLE **120**   (ex Article 109 i)
1.   Where a sudden crisis in the balance of payments occurs and a decision within the meaning of Article **119**(2) is not immediately taken, the Member State concerned may, as a precaution, take the necessary protective measures. Such measures must cause the least possible disturbance in the functioning of the common market and must not be wider in scope than is strictly necessary to remedy the sudden difficulties which have arisen.

2.   The Commission and the other Member States shall be informed of such protective measures not later than when they enter into force. The Commission may recommend to the Council the granting of mutual assistance under Article **119**.

3.   After the Commission has delivered an opinion and the Committee referred to in Article **114** has been consulted, the Council may, acting by a qualified majority, decide that the State concerned shall amend, suspend or abolish the protective measures referred to above.

4.   Subject to Article **122**(6), this Article shall cease to apply from the beginning of the third stage.

ARTICLE **121**   (ex Article 109 j)
1.   The Commission and the EMI shall report to the Council on the progress made in the fulfilment by the Member States of their obligations regarding the achievement of economic and monetary union. These reports shall include an examination of the compatibility between each Member State's national legislation, including the statutes of its national central bank, and Articles **108** and **109** of this Treaty and the Statute of the ESCB.

The reports shall also examine the achievement of a high degree of sustainable convergence by reference to the fulfilment by each Member State of the following criteria:

- the achievement of a high degree of price stability; this will be apparent from a rate of inflation which is close to that of, at most, the three best performing Member States in terms of price stability;
- the sustainability of the government financial position; this will be apparent from having achieved a government budgetary position without a deficit that is excessive as determined in accordance with Article **104**(6);
- the observance of the normal fluctuation margins provided for by the Exchange Rate Mechanism of the European Monetary System, for at least two years, without devaluing against the currency of any other Member State;
- the durability of convergence achieved by the Member State and of its participation in the Exchange Rate Mechanism of the European Monetary System being reflected in the long-term interest rate levels.

The four criteria mentioned in this paragraph and the relevant periods over which they are to be respected are developed further in a Protocol annexed to this Treaty. The reports of the Commission and the EMI shall also take account of the development of the ECU, the results of the integration of markets, the situation and development of the balances of payments on current account and an examination of the development of unit labour costs and other price indices.

2.   On the basis of these reports, the Council, acting by a qualified majority on a recommendation from the Commission, shall assess:

- for each Member State, whether it fulfils the necessary conditions for the adoption of a single currency;
- whether a majority of the Member States fulfil the necessary conditions for the adoption of a single currency,

and recommend its findings to the Council, meeting in the composition of the Heads of State or of Government. The European Parliament shall be consulted and forward its opinion to the Council, meeting in the composition of the Heads of State or of Government.

3.   Taking due account of the reports referred to in paragraph 1 and the opinion of the European Parliament referred to in paragraph 2, the Council, meeting in the composition of Heads of State or of Government, shall, acting by a qualified majority, not later than 31 December 1996:

- decide, on the basis of the recommendations of the Council referred to in paragraph 2, whether a majority of the Member States fulfil the necessary conditions for the adoption of a single currency;
- decide whether it is appropriate for the Community to enter the third stage,

and if so:

- set the date for the beginning of the third stage.

4.   If by the end of 1997 the date for the beginning of the third stage has not been set, the third stage shall start on 1 January 1999. Before 1 July 1998, the Council, meeting in the composition of Heads of State or of Government, after a repetition of the procedure provided for in paragraphs 1 and 2, with the exception of the second indent of paragraph 2, taking into account the reports referred to in paragraph 1 and the opinion of the European Parliament, shall, acting by a qualified majority and on the basis of the recommendations of the Council referred to in paragraph 2, confirm which Member States fulfil the necessary conditions for the adoption of a single currency.

ARTICLE **122**   (ex Article 109 k)

1.   If the decision has been taken to set the date in accordance with Article **121**(3), the Council shall, on the basis of its recommendations referred to in Article **121**(2), acting by a qualified majority on a recommendation from the Commission, decide whether any, and if so which, Member States shall have a derogation as defined in paragraph 3 of this Article. Such Member States shall in this Treaty be referred to as 'Member States with a derogation'.

If the Council has confirmed which Member States fulfil the necessary conditions for the adoption of a single currency, in accordance with Article **121**(4), those Member States which do not fulfil the conditions shall have a derogation as defined in paragraph 3 of this Article. Such Member States shall in this Treaty be referred to as 'Member States with a derogation'.

2.   At least once every two years, or at the request of a Member State with a derogation, the Commission and the ECB shall report to the Council in accordance with the procedure laid down in Article **121**(1). After consulting the European Parliament and after discussion in the Council, meeting in the composition of the Heads of State or of Government, the Council shall, acting by a qualified majority on a proposal from the Commission, decide which Member States with a derogation fulfil the necessary conditions on the basis of the criteria set out in Article **121**(1), and abrogate the derogations of the Member States concerned.

3.   A derogation referred to in paragraph 1 shall entail that the following Articles do not apply to the Member State concerned: Articles **104**(9) and (11), **105**(1), (2), (3) and (5), **106**, **110**, **111**, and **112**(2)(b). The exclusion of such a Member State and its national central bank from rights and obligations within the ESCB is laid down in Chapter IX of the Statute of the ESCB.

4.   In Articles **105**(1), (2) and (3), **106**, **110**, **111** and **112**(2)(b), 'Member States' shall be read as 'Member States without a derogation'.

5.   The voting rights of Member States with a derogation shall be suspended for the Council decisions referred to in the Articles of this Treaty mentioned in paragraph 3. In that case, by way of derogation from Articles **205** and **250**(1), a qualified majority shall be defined as two thirds of the votes of the representatives of the Member States without a derogation weighted in accordance with Article **205**(2), and unanimity of those Member States shall be required for an act requiring unanimity.

6.   Articles **119** and **120** shall continue to apply to a Member State with a derogation.

ARTICLE **123**   (ex Article 109 *l*)
1.   Immediately after the decision on the date for the beginning of the third stage has been taken in accordance with Article **121**(3), or, as the case may be, immediately after 1 July 1998:
-   the Council shall adopt the provisions referred to in Article **107**(6);
-   the governments of the Member States without a derogation shall appoint, in accordance with the procedure set out in Article 50 of the Statute of the ESCB, the President, the Vice-President and the other members of the Executive Board of the ECB. If there are Member States with a derogation, the number of members of the Executive Board may be smaller than provided for in Article 11.1 of the Statute of the ESCB, but in no circumstances shall it be less than four.
As soon as the Executive Board is appointed, the ESCB and the ECB shall be established and shall prepare for their full operation as described in this Treaty and the Statute of the ESCB. The full exercise of their powers shall start from the first day of the third stage.

2.   As soon as the ECB is established, it shall, if necessary, take over the tasks of the EMI. The EMI shall go into liquidation upon the establishment of the ECB; the modalities of liquidation are laid down in the Statute of the EMI.

3.   If and as long as there are Member States with a derogation, and without prejudice to Article **107**(3) of this Treaty, the General Council of the ECB referred to in Article 45 of the Statute of the ESCB shall be constituted as a third decision-making body of the ECB.

4.   At the starting date of the third stage, the Council shall, acting with the unanimity of the Member States without a derogation, on a proposal from the Commission and after consulting the ECB, adopt the conversion rates at which their currencies shall be irrevocably fixed and at which irrevocably fixed rate the ECU shall be substituted for these currencies, and the ECU will become a currency in its own right. This measure shall by itself not modify the external value of the ECU. The Council shall, acting according to the same procedure, also take the other measures necessary for the rapid introduction of the ECU as the single currency of those Member States.

5.   If it is decided, according to the procedure set out in Article **122**(2), to abrogate a derogation, the Council shall, acting with the unanimity of the Member States without a derogation and the Member State concerned, on a proposal from the Commission and after consulting the ECB, adopt the rate at which the ECU shall be substituted for the currency of the Member State concerned, and take the other measures necessary for the introduction of the ECU as the single currency in the Member State concerned.

ARTICLE **124**   (ex Article 109 m)
1.   Until the beginning of the third stage, each Member State shall treat its exchange rate policy as a matter of common interest. In so doing, Member States shall take account of the experience acquired in co-operation within the framework of the European Monetary System (EMS) and in developing the ECU, and shall respect existing powers in this field.

2.   From the beginning of the third stage and for as long as a Member State has a derogation, paragraph 1 shall apply by analogy to the exchange rate policy of that Member State.

TITLE VIII (ex Title VI a)

EMPLOYMENT

ARTICLE 125 (ex Article **109 n**)
Member States and the Community shall, in accordance with this Title, work towards developing a co-ordinated strategy for employment and particularly for promoting a skilled, trained and adaptable workforce and labour markets responsive to economic change with a view to achieving the objectives defined in Article 2 of the Treaty on European Union and in Article 2 of this Treaty.

ARTICLE 126 (ex Article **109 o**)
1.   Member States, through their employment policies, shall contribute to the achievement of the objectives referred to in Article 125 in a way consistent with the broad guidelines of the economic policies of the Member States and of the Community adopted pursuant to Article 99(2).

2.   Member States, having regard to the national practices related to the responsibilities of management and labour, shall regard promoting employment as a matter of common concern and shall co-ordinate their action in this respect within the Council, in accordance with the provisions of Article 128.

ARTICLE 127 (ex Article **109 p**)
1.   The Community shall contribute to a high level of employment by encouraging co-operation between Member States and by supporting and, if necessary, complementing their action. In doing so, the competences of the Member States shall be respected.

2.   The objective of a high level of employment shall be taken into consideration in the formulation and implementation of Community policies and activities.

ARTICLE 128 (ex Article **109 q**)
1.   The European Council shall each year consider the employment situation in the Community and adopt conclusions thereon, on the basis of a joint annual report by the Council and the Commission.

2.   On the basis of the conclusions of the European Council, the Council, acting by a qualified majority on a proposal from the Commission and after consulting the European Parliament, the Economic and Social Committee, the Committee of the Regions and the Employment Committee referred to in Article 130, shall each year draw up guidelines which the Member States shall take into account in their employment policies. These guidelines shall be consistent with the broad guidelines adopted pursuant to Article 99(2).

3.   Each Member State shall provide the Council and the Commission with an annual report on the principal measures taken to implement its employment policy in the light of the guidelines for employment as referred to in paragraph 2.

4.   The Council, on the basis of the reports referred to in paragraph 3 and having received the views of the Employment Committee shall each year carry out an examination of the implementation of the employment policies of the Member States in the light of the guidelines for employment. The Council, acting by a qualified majority on a recommendation from the Commission, may, if it considers it appropriate in the light of that examination, make recommendations to Member States.

5.   On the basis of the results of that examination, the Council and the Commission shall make a joint annual report to the European Council on the employment situation in the Community and on the implementation of the guidelines for employment.

ARTICLE 129 (ex Article **109 r**)
The Council, acting in accordance with the procedure referred to in Article 251 and after consulting the Economic and Social Committee and the Committee of the Regions, may adopt incentive measures designed to encourage co-operation between Member States and to support their action in the field of employment through initiatives aimed at developing exchanges of information and best practices, providing comparative analysis and advice as well as promoting innovative approaches and evaluating experiences, in particular by recourse to pilot projects.
Those measures shall not include harmonisation of the laws and regulations of the Member States.

ARTICLE 130   (ex Article **109 s**)
The Council, after consulting the European Parliament, shall establish an Employment Committee with advisory status to promote co-ordination between Member States on employment and labour market policies. The tasks of the Committee shall be:
-   **to monitor the employment situation and employment policies in the Member States and the Community;**
-   **without prejudice to Article 207, to formulate opinions at the request of either the Council or the Commission or on its oven initiative, and to contribute to the preparation of the Council proceedings referred to in Article 128.**
In fulfilling its mandate, the Committee shall consult management and labour.
Each Member State and the Commission shall appoint two members of the Committee.

TITLE   **IX**   (ex Title VII)

COMMON COMMERCIAL POLICY

ARTICLE **131**   (ex Article 110)
By establishing a customs union between themselves Member States aim to contribute, in the common interest, to the harmonious development of world trade, the progressive abolition of restrictions on international trade and the lowering of customs barriers.
The common commercial policy shall take into account the favourable effect which the abolition of customs duties between Member States may have on the increase in the competitive strength of undertakings in those States.

[ARTICLE 111 repealed by the Maastricht Treaty.]

ARTICLE **132**   (ex Article 112)
1.   Without prejudice to obligations undertaken by them within the framework of other international organisations, Member States **shall progressively harmonise** the systems whereby they grant aid for exports to third countries, to the extent necessary to ensure that competition between undertakings of the Community is not distorted.
On a proposal from the Commission, the Council shall, **acting by a qualified majority**, issue any directives needed for this purpose.

2.   The preceding provisions shall not apply to such drawback of customs duties or charges having equivalent effect nor to such repayment of indirect taxation including turnover taxes, excise duties and other indirect taxes as is allowed when goods are exported from a Member State to a third country, insofar as such drawback or repayment does not exceed the amount imposed, directly or indirectly, on the products exported.

ARTICLE **133**   (ex Article 113)
1.   The common commercial policy shall be based on uniform principles, particularly in regard to changes in tariff rates, the conclusion of tariff and trade agreements, the achievement of uniformity in measures of liberalisation, export policy and measures to protect trade such as those to be taken in the event of dumping or subsidies.

2.   The Commission shall submit proposals to the Council for implementing the common commercial policy.

3.   Where agreements with one or more States or international organisations need to be negotiated, the Commission shall make recommendations to the Council, which shall authorise the Commission to open the necessary negotiations.
The Commission shall conduct these negotiations in consultation with a special committee appointed by the Council to assist the Commission in this task and within the framework of such directives as the Council may issue to it.
The relevant provisions of Article **300** shall apply.

4.   In exercising the powers conferred upon it by this Article, the Council shall act by a qualified majority.

5.   The Council, acting unanimously on a proposal from the Commission and after consulting the European Parliament, may extend the application of paragraphs 1 to 4 to international negotiations and agreements on services and intellectual property insofar as they are not covered by these paragraphs.

[ARTICLE 114 repealed by the Maastricht Treaty.]

ARTICLE **134** (ex Article 115)

In order to ensure that the execution of measures of commercial policy taken in accordance with this Treaty by any Member State is not obstructed by deflection of trade, or where differences between such measures lead to economic difficulties in one or more Member States, the Commission shall recommend the methods for the requisite co-operation between Member States. Failing this, the Commission may authorise Member States to take the necessary protective measures, the conditions and details of which it shall determine.

In case of urgency, Member States shall request authorisation to take the necessary measures themselves from the Commission, which shall take a decision as soon as possible; the Member States concerned shall then notify the measures to the other Member States. The Commission may decide at any time that the Member States concerned shall amend or abolish the measures in question.

In the selection of such measures, priority shall be given to those which cause the least disturbance to the functioning of the common market.

[ARTICLE 116 repealed by the Maastricht Treaty. *A new Article 116 was introduced by the Treaty of Amsterdam, in a new Title (Title X) shown below.*]

TITLE X (ex Title VII a)

CUSTOMS CO-OPERATION

ARTICLE **135** (ex Article **116**)

Within the scope of application of this Treaty, the Council, acting in accordance with the procedure referred to in Article 251, shall take measures in order to strengthen customs co-operation between Member States and between the latter and the Commission. These measures shall not concern the application of national criminal law and the national administration of justice.

TITLE XI (ex Title VIII)

SOCIAL POLICY, EDUCATION, VOCATIONAL TRAINING AND YOUTH

CHAPTER 1

SOCIAL PROVISIONS

ARTICLE **136** (ex Article 117)

The Community and the Member States, having in mind fundamental social rights such as those set out in the European Charter signed at Turin on 18 October 1961 and in the 1989 Community Charter of the Fundamental Social Rights of Workers, shall have as their objectives the promotion of employment, improved living and working conditions, so as to make possible their harmonisation while the improvement is being maintained, proper social protection, dialogue between management and labour, the development of human resources with a view to lasting high employment and the combating of exclusion.

To this end the Community and the Member States shall implement measures which take account of the diverse forms of national practices, in particular in the field of contractual relations, and the need to maintain the competitiveness of the Community economy.

They believe that such a development will ensue not only from the functioning of the common market, which will favour the harmonisation of social systems, but also from the procedures provided for in this Treaty and from the approximation of provisions laid down by law, regulation or administrative action.

ARTICLE **137** (ex Article **118**)

1. **With a view to achieving the objectives of Article 136, the Community shall support and complement the activities of the Member States in the following fields:**

- **improvement in particular of the working environment to protect workers' health and safety;**
- **working conditions;**
- **the information and consultation of workers;**
- **the integration of persons excluded from the labour market, without prejudice to Article 150;**
- **equality between men and women with regard to labour market opportunities and treatment at work.**

2.   To this end, the Council may adopt, by means of directives, minimum requirements for gradual implementation, having regard to the conditions and technical rules obtaining in each of the Member States. Such directives shall avoid imposing administrative, financial and legal constraints in a way which would hold back the creation and development of small and medium-sized undertakings.

The Council shall act in accordance with the procedure referred to in Article 251 after consulting the Economic and Social Committee and the Committee of the Regions.

The Council, acting in accordance with the same procedure, may adopt measures designed to encourage co-operation between Member States through initiatives aimed at improving knowledge, developing exchanges of information and best practices, promoting innovative approaches and evaluating experiences in order to combat social exclusion.

3.   However, the Council shall act unanimously on a proposal from the Commission, after consulting the European Parliament and the Economic and Social Committee and the Committee of the Regions, in the following areas:
-     social security and social protection of workers;
-     protection of workers where their employment contract is terminated;
-     representation and collective defence of the interests of workers and employers, including co-determination, subject to paragraph 6;
-     conditions of employment for third-country nationals legally residing in Community territory;
-     financial contributions for promotion of employment and job-creation, without prejudice to the provisions relating to the Social Fund.

4.   A Member State may entrust management and labour, at their joint request, with the implementation of directives adopted pursuant to paragraphs 2 and 3.

In this case, it shall ensure that, no later than the date on which a directive must be transposed in accordance with Article 249, management and labour have introduced the necessary measures by agreement, the Member State concerned being required to take any necessary measure enabling it at any time to be in a position to guarantee the results imposed by that directive.

5.   The provisions adopted pursuant to this Article shall not prevent any Member State from maintaining or introducing more stringent protective measures compatible with the Treaty.

6.   The provisions of this Article shall not apply to pay, the right of association, the right to strike or the right to impose lock-outs.

ARTICLE 138   (ex Article 118 a)
1.   The Commission shall have the task of promoting the consultation of management and labour at Community level and shall take any relevant measure to facilitate their dialogue by ensuring balanced support for the parties.

2.   To this end, before submitting proposals in the social policy field, the Commission shall consult management and labour on the possible direction of Community action.

3.   If, after such consultation, the Commission considers Community action advisable, it shall consult management and labour on the content of the envisaged proposal. Management and labour shall forward to the Commission an opinion or, where appropriate, a recommendation.

4.   On the occasion of such consultation, management and labour may inform the Commission of their wish to initiate the process provided for in Article 139. The duration of the procedure shall not exceed nine months, unless the management and labour concerned and the Commission decide jointly to extend it.

ARTICLE 139   (ex Article 118 b)
1.   Should management and labour so desire, the dialogue between them at Community level may lead to contractual relations, including agreements.

2.   Agreements concluded at Community level shall be implemented either in accordance with the procedures and practices specific to management and labour and the Member States or, in matters covered by Article 137, at the joint request of the signatory parties, by a Council decision on a proposal from the Commission.

The Council shall act by qualified majority, except where the agreement in question contains one or more provisions relating to one of the areas referred to in Article 137(3), in which case it shall act unanimously.

ARTICLE 140 (ex Article **118 c**)
With a view to achieving the objectives of Article 136 and without prejudice to the other provisions of this Treaty, the Commission shall encourage co-operation between the Member States and facilitate the co-ordination of their action in all social policy fields under this chapter, particularly in matters relating to:

- employment;
- labour law and working conditions;
- basic and advanced vocational training;
- social security;
- prevention of occupational accidents and diseases;
- occupational hygiene;
- the rights of association and collective bargaining between employers and workers.

To this end, the Commission shall act in close contact with Member States by making studies, delivering opinions and arranging consultations both on problems arising at national level and on those of concern to international organisations.

Before delivering the opinions provided for in this Article, the Commission shall consult the Economic and Social Committee.

ARTICLE 141 (ex Article 119)
1.   Each Member State shall ensure that the principle of equal pay for male and female workers for equal work or work of equal value is applied.

2.   For the purpose of this Article, 'pay' means the ordinary basic or minimum wage or salary and any other consideration, whether in cash or in kind, which the worker receives directly or indirectly, in respect of his employment, from his employer.

Equal pay without discrimination based on sex means:

(a)   that pay for the same work at piece rates shall be calculated on the basis of the same unit of measurement;
(b)   that pay for work at time rates shall be the same for the same job.

3.   The Council, acting in accordance with the procedure referred to in Article 251, and after consulting the Economic and Social Committee, shall adopt measures to ensure the application of the principle of equal opportunities and equal treatment of men and women in matters of employment and occupation, including the principle of equal pay for equal work or work of equal value.

4.   With a view to ensuring full equality in practice between men and women in working life, the principle of equal treatment shall not prevent any Member State from maintaining or adopting measures providing for specific advantages in order to make it easier for the under-represented sex to pursue a vocational activity or to prevent or compensate for disadvantages in professional careers.

ARTICLE 142 (ex Article **119 a**)
Member States shall endeavour to maintain the existing equivalence between paid holiday schemes.

ARTICLE 143 (ex Article **120**)
The Commission shall draw up a report each year on progress in achieving the objectives of Article 136, including the demographic situation in the Community. It shall forward the report to the European Parliament, the Council and the Economic and Social Committee.
The European Parliament may invite the Commission to draw up reports on particular problems concerning the social situation.

ARTICLE 144 (ex Article 121)
The Council may, acting unanimously and after consulting the Economic and Social Committee, assign to the Commission tasks in connection with the implementation of common measures, particularly as regards social security for the migrant workers, referred to in Articles **39** to **42**.

ARTICLE 145 (ex Article 122)
The Commission shall include a separate chapter on social developments within the Community in its annual report to the European Parliament.
The European Parliament may invite the Commission to draw up reports on any particular problems concerning social conditions.

CHAPTER 2

THE EUROPEAN SOCIAL FUND

ARTICLE **146** (ex Article 123)

In order to improve employment opportunities for workers in the internal market and to contribute thereby to raising the standard of living, a European Social Fund is hereby established in accordance with the provisions set out below; it shall aim to render the employment of workers easier and to increase their geographical and occupational mobility within the Community, and to facilitate their adaptation to industrial changes and to changes in production systems, in particular through vocational training and retraining.

ARTICLE **147** (ex Article 124)

The Fund shall be administered by the Commission.

The Commission shall be assisted in this task by a Committee presided over by a member of the Commission and composed of representatives of Governments, trade unions and employers' organisations.

ARTICLE **148** (ex Article 125)

The Council, acting in accordance with the procedure referred to in **Article 251** and after consulting the Economic and Social Committee **and the Committee of the Regions**, shall adopt implementing decisions relating to the European Social Fund.

CHAPTER 3

EDUCATION, VOCATIONAL TRAINING AND YOUTH

ARTICLE **149** (ex Article 126)

1.   The Community shall contribute to the development of quality education by encouraging co-operation between Member States and, if necessary, by supporting and supplementing their action, while fully respecting the responsibility of the Member States for the content of teaching and the organisation of education systems and their cultural and linguistic diversity.

2.   Community action shall be aimed at:

- developing the European dimension in education, particularly through the teaching and dissemination of the languages of the Member States;
- encouraging mobility of students and teachers, *inter alia* by encouraging the academic recognition of diplomas and periods of study;
- promoting co-operation between educational establishments;
- developing exchanges of information and experience on issues common to the education systems of the Member States;
- encouraging the development of youth exchanges and of exchanges of socio-educational instructors;
- encouraging the development of distance education.

3.   The Community and the Member States shall foster co-operation with third countries and the competent international organisations in the field of education, in particular the Council of Europe.

4.   In order to contribute to the achievement of the objectives referred to in this Article, the Council:

- acting in accordance with the procedure referred to in Article **251**, after consulting the Economic and Social Committee and the Committee of the Regions, shall adopt incentive measures, excluding any harmonisation of the laws and regulations of the Member States;
- acting by a qualified majority on a proposal from the Commission, shall adopt recommendations.

ARTICLE **150** (ex Article 127)

1.   The Community shall implement a vocational training policy which shall support and supplement the action of the Member States, while fully respecting the responsibility of the Member States for the content and organisation of vocational training.

2.   Community action shall aim to:

- facilitate adaptation to industrial changes, in particular through vocational training and retraining;
- improve initial and continuing vocational training in order to facilitate vocational integration and reintegration into the labour market;
- facilitate access to vocational training and encourage mobility of instructors and trainees and particularly young people;

- stimulate co-operation on training between educational or training establishments and firms;
- develop exchanges of information and experience on issues common to the training systems of the Member States.

3. The Community and the Member States shall foster co-operation with third countries and the competent international organisations in the sphere of vocational training.

4. The Council, acting in accordance with the procedure referred to in **Article 251** and after consulting the Economic and Social Committee **and the Committee of the Regions**, shall adopt measures to contribute to the achievement of the objectives referred to in this Article, excluding any harmonisation of the laws and regulations of the Member States.

TITLE **XII**   (ex Title IX)

CULTURE

ARTICLE **151** (ex Article 128)
1. The Community shall contribute to the flowering of the cultures of the Member States, while respecting their national and regional diversity and at the same time bringing the common cultural heritage to the fore.

2. Action by the Community shall be aimed at encouraging co-operation between Member States and, if necessary, supporting and supplementing their action in the following areas:
- improvement of the knowledge and dissemination of the culture and history of the European peoples;
- conservation and safeguarding of cultural heritage of European significance;
- non-commercial cultural exchanges;
- artistic and literary creation, including in the audio-visual sector.

3. The Community and the Member States shall foster co-operation with third countries and the competent international organisations in the sphere of culture, in particular the Council of Europe.

4. The Community shall take cultural aspects into account in its action under other provisions of this Treaty, **in particular in order to respect and to promote the diversity of its cultures.**

5. In order to contribute to the achievement of the objectives referred to in this Article, the Council:
- acting in accordance with the procedure referred to in Article **251** and after consulting the Committee of the Regions, shall adopt incentive measures, excluding any harmonisation of the laws and regulations of the Member States. The Council shall act unanimously throughout the procedures referred to in Article **251**;
- acting unanimously on a proposal from the Commission, shall adopt recommendations.

TITLE **XIII**   (ex Title X)

PUBLIC HEALTH

ARTICLE **152** (ex Article 129)
1. **A high level of human health protection shall be ensured in the definition and implementation of all Community policies and activities.**
Community action, **which shall complement national policies,** shall be directed towards **improving public health, preventing human illness and diseases, and obviating sources of danger to human health. Such action shall cover the fight against the major health scourges,** by promoting research into their causes, **their transmission and their prevention,** as well as health information and education.
The Community shall complement the Member States' action in reducing drugs-related health damage, including information and prevention.

2. **The Community shall encourage co-operation between the Member States in the areas referred to in this Article and, if necessary, lend support to their action.**
Member States shall, in liaison with the Commission, co-ordinate among themselves their policies and programmes in the areas referred to in paragraph 1. The Commission may, in close contact with the Member States, take any useful initiative to promote such co-ordination.

3. The Community and the Member States shall foster co-operation with third countries and the competent international organisations in the sphere of public health.

4. The Council, acting in accordance with the procedure referred to in Article 251 after consulting the Social and Economic Committee and the Committee of the Regions, shall contribute to the achievement of the objectives referred to in this Article through adopting:
(a) measures setting high standards of quality and safety of organs and substances of human origin, blood and blood derivatives; these measures shall not prevent any Member State from maintaining or introducing more stringent protective measures;
(b) by way of derogation from Article 37, measures in the veterinary and phytosanitary fields which have as their direct objective the protection of public health,
(c) incentive measures designed to protect and improve human health, excluding any harmonisation of the laws and regulations of the Member States.
The Council, acting by a qualified majority on a proposal from the Commission, may also adopt recommendations for the purposes set out in this Article.

5. Community action in the field of public health shall fully respect the responsibilities of the Member States for the organisation and delivery of health services and medical care. In particular, measures referred to in paragraph 4(a) shall not affect national provisions on the donation or medical use of organs and blood.

TITLE **XIV** (ex Title XI)

CONSUMER PROTECTION

ARTICLE **153** (ex Article 129 a)
1. **In order to promote the interests of consumers and to ensure a high level of consumer protection, the Community shall contribute to protecting the health, safety and economic interests of consumers, as well as to promoting their right to information, education and to organise themselves in order to safeguard their interests.**

2. **Consumer protection requirements shall be taken into account in defining and implementing other Community policies and activities.**

3. The Community shall contribute to the attainment of **the objectives referred to in paragraph 1** through:
(a) measures adopted pursuant to Article **95** in the context of the completion of the internal market;
(b) measures which support, supplement and monitor the policy pursued by the Member States.

4. The Council, acting in accordance with the procedure referred to in Article **251** and after consulting the Economic and Social Committee, shall adopt the **measures** referred to in paragraph **3(b)**.

5. **Measures** adopted pursuant to paragraph **4** shall not prevent any Member State from maintaining or introducing more stringent protective measures. Such measures must be compatible with this Treaty. The Commission shall be notified of them.

TITLE **XV** (ex Title XII)

TRANS-EUROPEAN NETWORKS

ARTICLE **154** (ex Article 129 b)
1. To help achieve the objectives referred to in Articles **14** and **158** and to enable citizens of the Union, economic operators and regional and local communities to derive full benefit from the setting up of an area without internal frontiers, the Community shall contribute to the establishment and development of trans-European networks in the areas of transport, telecommunications and energy infrastructures.

2. Within the framework of a system of open and competitive markets, action by the Community shall aim at promoting the interconnection and inter-operability of national networks as well as access to such networks. It shall take account in particular of the need to link island, landlocked and peripheral regions with the central regions of the Community.

ARTICLE **155** (ex Article 129 c)
1. In order to achieve the objectives referred to in Article **154**, the Community:
- shall establish a series of guidelines covering the objectives, priorities and broad lines of measures envisaged in the sphere of trans-European networks; these guidelines shall identify projects of common interest;

- shall implement any measures that may prove necessary to ensure the inter-operability of the networks, in particular in the field of technical standardisation;
- **may support projects of common interest supported by Member States, which are identified in the framework of guidelines** referred to in the first indent, particularly through feasibility studies, loan guarantees or interest rate subsidies; the Community may also contribute, through the **Cohesion Fund set up** pursuant to Article **161**, to the financing of specific projects in Member States in the area of transport infrastructure.

The Community's activities shall take into account the potential economic viability of the projects.

2.   Member States shall, in liaison with the Commission, co-ordinate among themselves the policies pursued at national level which may have a significant impact on the achievement of the objectives referred to in Article **154**. The Commission may, in close co-operation with the Member States, take any useful initiative to promote such co-ordination.

3.   The Community may decide to co-operate with third countries to promote projects of mutual interest and to ensure the inter-operability of networks.

ARTICLE **156**   (ex Article 129 d)
The guidelines **and other measures** referred to in Article **155**(1) shall be adopted by the Council, acting in accordance with the procedure referred to in Article **251** and after consulting the Economic and Social Committee and the Committee of the Regions.
Guidelines and projects of common interest which relate to the territory of a Member State shall require the approval of the Member State concerned.

Paragraph 3 shall be deleted.

TITLE **XVI**   (ex Title XIII)

INDUSTRY

ARTICLE **157**   (ex Article 130)
1.   The Community and the Member States shall ensure that the conditions necessary for the competitiveness of the Community's industry exist.
For that purpose, in accordance with a system of open and competitive markets, their action shall be aimed at:
- speeding up the adjustment of industry to structural changes;
- encouraging an environment favourable to initiative and to the development of undertakings throughout the Community, particularly small and medium-sized undertakings;
- encouraging an environment favourable to co-operation between undertakings;
- fostering better exploitation of the industrial potential of policies of innovation, research and technological development.

2.   The Member States shall consult each other in liaison with the Commission and, where necessary, shall co-ordinate their action. The Commission may take any useful initiative to promote such co-ordination.

3.   The Community shall contribute to the achievement of the objectives set out in paragraph 1 through the policies and activities it pursues under other provisions of this Treaty. The Council, acting unanimously on a proposal from the Commission, after consulting the European Parliament and the Economic and Social Committee, may decide on specific measures in support of action taken in the Member States to achieve the objectives set out in paragraph 1.
This Title shall not provide a basis for the introduction by the Community of any measure which could lead to a distortion of competition.

TITLE **XVII**   (ex Title XIV)

ECONOMIC AND SOCIAL COHESION

ARTICLE **158**   (ex Article 130 a)
In order to promote its overall harmonious development, the Community shall develop and pursue its actions leading to the strengthening of its economic and social cohesion.
In particular, the Community shall aim at reducing disparities between the levels of development of the various regions and the backwardness of the least-favoured regions **or islands**, including rural areas.

ARTICLE **159**   (ex Article 130 b)

Member States shall conduct their economic policies and shall co-ordinate them in such a way as, in addition, to attain the objectives set out in Article **158**. The formulation and implementation of the Community's policies and actions and the implementation of the internal market shall take into account the objectives set out in Article **158** and shall contribute to their achievement. The Community shall also support the achievement of these objectives by the action it takes through the structural Funds (European Agricultural Guidance and Guarantee Fund, Guidance Section; European Social Fund; European Regional Development Fund), the European Investment Bank and the other existing financial instruments.

The Commission shall submit a report to the European Parliament, the Council, the Economic and Social Committee and the Committee of the Regions every three years on the progress made towards achieving economic and social cohesion and on the manner in which the various means provided for in this Article have contributed to it. This report shall, if necessary, be accompanied by appropriate proposals.

If specific actions prove necessary outside the Funds and without prejudice to the measures decided upon within the framework of the other Community policies, such actions may be adopted by the Council acting unanimously on a proposal from the Commission and after consulting the European Parliament, the Economic and Social Committee and the Committee of the Regions.

ARTICLE **160**   (ex Article 130 c)

The European Regional Development Fund is intended to help to redress the main regional imbalances in the Community through participation in the development and structural adjustment of regions whose development is lagging behind and in the conversion of declining industrial regions.

ARTICLE **161**   (ex Article 130 d)

Without prejudice to Article **162**, the Council, acting unanimously on a proposal from the Commission and after obtaining the assent of the European Parliament and consulting the Economic and Social Committee and the Committee of the Regions, shall define the tasks, priority objectives and the organisation of the Structural Funds, which may involve grouping the Funds. The Council, acting by the same procedure, shall also define the general rules applicable to them and the provisions necessary to ensure their effectiveness and the co-ordination of the Funds with one another and with the other existing financial instruments.

A Cohesion Fund set up by the Council, acting in accordance with the same procedure, shall provide a financial contribution to projects in the fields of environment and trans-European networks in the area of transport infrastructure.

ARTICLE **162**   (ex Article 130 e)

Implementing decisions relating to the European Regional Development Fund shall be taken by the Council, acting in accordance with the procedure referred to in **Article 251** and after consulting the Economic and Social Committee and the Committee of the Regions.

With regard to the European Agricultural Guidance and Guarantee Fund, Guidance Section, and the European Social Fund, Articles **37** and **148** respectively shall continue to apply.

TITLE **XVIII**   (ex Title XV)

RESEARCH AND TECHNOLOGICAL DEVELOPMENT

ARTICLE **163**   (ex Article 130 f)

1.   The Community shall have the objective of strengthening the scientific and technological bases of Community industry and encouraging it to become more competitive at international level, while promoting all the research activities deemed necessary by virtue of other Chapters of this Treaty.

2.   For this purpose the Community shall, throughout the Community, encourage undertakings, including small and medium-sized undertakings, research centres and universities in their research and technological development activities of high quality; it shall support their efforts to co-operate with one another, aiming, notably, at enabling undertakings to exploit the internal market potential to the full, in particular through the opening up of national public contracts, the definition of common standards and the removal of legal and fiscal obstacles to that co-operation.

3.   All Community activities under this Treaty in the area of research and technological development, including demonstration projects, shall be decided on and implemented in accordance with the provisions of this Title.

ARTICLE **164** (ex Article 130 g)

In pursuing these objectives, the Community shall carry out the following activities, complementing the activities carried out in the Member States:

(a) implementation of research, technological development and demonstration programmes, by promoting co-operation with and between undertakings, research centres and universities;

(b) promotion of co-operation in the field of Community research, technological development and demonstration with third countries and international organisations;

(c) dissemination and optimisation of the results of activities in Community research, technological development and demonstration;

(d) stimulation of the training and mobility of researchers in the Community.

ARTICLE **165** (ex Article 130 h)

1.   The Community and the Member States shall co-ordinate their research and technological development activities so as to ensure that national policies and community policy are mutually consistent.

2.   In close co-operation with the Member States, the Commission may take any useful initiative to promote the co-ordination referred to in paragraph 1.

ARTICLE **166** (ex Article 130 i)

1.   A multiannual framework programme, setting out all the activities of the Community, shall be adopted by the Council, acting in accordance with the procedure referred to in Article **251** after consulting the Economic and Social Committee. *Next sentence shall be deleted.*

The framework programme shall:

-    establish the scientific and technological objectives to be achieved by the activities provided for in Article **164** and fix the relevant priorities;

-    indicate the broad lines of such activities;

-    fix the maximum overall amount and the detailed rules for Community financial participation in the framework programme and the respective shares in each of the activities provided for.

2.   The framework programme shall be adapted or supplemented as the situation changes.

3.   The framework programme shall be implemented through specific programmes developed within each activity. Each specific programme shall define the detailed rules for implementing it, fix its duration and provide for the means deemed necessary. The sum of the amounts deemed necessary, fixed in the specific programmes, may not exceed the overall maximum amount fixed for the framework programme and each activity.

4.   The Council, acting by a qualified majority on a proposal from the Commission and after consulting the European Parliament and the Economic and Social Committee, shall adopt the specific programmes.

ARTICLE **167** (ex Article 130 j)

For the implementation of the multiannual framework programme the Council shall:

-    determine the rules for the participation of undertakings, research centres and universities;

-    lay down the rules governing the dissemination of research results.

ARTICLE **168** (ex Article 130 k)

In implementing the multiannual framework programme, supplementary programmes may be decided on involving the participation of certain Member States only, which shall finance them subject to possible Community participation.

The Council shall adopt the rules applicable to supplementary programmes, particularly as regards the dissemination of knowledge and access by other Member States.

ARTICLE **169** (ex Article 130 l)

In implementing the multiannual framework programme the Community may make provision, in agreement with the Member States concerned, for participation in research and development programmes undertaken by several Member States, including participation in the structures created for the execution of those programmes.

ARTICLE **170** (ex Article 130 m)

In implementing the multiannual framework programme the Community may make provision for co-operation in Community research, technological development and demonstration with third countries or international organisations.

The detailed arrangements for such co-operation may be the subject of agreements between the Community and the third parties concerned, which shall be negotiated and concluded in accordance with Article **300**.

ARTICLE **171** (ex Article 130 n)

The Community may set up joint undertakings or any other structure necessary for the efficient execution of Community research, technological development and demonstration programmes.

ARTICLE **172** (ex Article 130 o)

The Council, acting **by qualified majority** on a proposal from the Commission and after consulting the European Parliament and the Economic and Social Committee, shall adopt the provisions referred to in Article **171**.

The Council, acting in accordance with the procedure referred to in **Article 251** and after consulting the Economic and Social Committee, shall adopt the provisions referred to in Articles **167, 168 and 169**. Adoption of the supplementary programmes shall require the agreement of the Member States concerned.

ARTICLE **173** (ex Article 130 p)

At the beginning of each year the Commission shall send a report to the European Parliament and the Council. The report shall include information on research and technological development activities and the dissemination of results during the previous year, and the work programme for the current year.

[ARTICLE 130 q repealed by the Maastricht Treaty.]

TITLE **XIX** (ex Title XVI)

ENVIRONMENT

ARTICLE **174** (ex Article 130 r)

1. Community policy on the environment shall contribute to pursuit of the following objectives:
-   preserving, protecting and improving the quality of the environment;
-   protecting human health;
-   prudent and rational utilisation of natural resources;
-   promoting measures at international level to deal with regional or world-wide environmental problems.

2. Community policy on the environment shall aim at a high level of protection taking into account the diversity of situations in the various regions of the Community. It shall be based on the precautionary principle and on the principles that preventive action should be taken, that environmental damage should as a priority be rectified at source and that the polluter should pay. *Next sentence shall be deleted.*

In this context, harmonisation measures answering **environmental protection** requirements shall include, where appropriate, a safeguard clause allowing Member States to take provisional measures, for non-economic environmental reasons, subject to a Community inspection procedure.

3. In preparing its policy on the environment, the Community shall take account of:
-   available scientific and technical data;
-   environmental conditions in the various regions of the Community;
-   the potential benefits and costs of action or lack of action;
-   the economic and social development of the Community as a whole and the balanced development of its regions.

4. Within their respective spheres of competence, the Community and the Member States shall co-operate with third countries and with the competent international organisations. The arrangements for Community co-operation may be the subject of agreements between the Community and the third parties concerned, which shall be negotiated and concluded in accordance with Article **300**.

The previous sub-paragraph shall be without prejudice to Member States' competence to negotiate in international bodies and to conclude international agreements.

ARTICLE **175** (ex Article 130 s)

1. The Council, acting in accordance with the procedure referred to in **Article 251** and after consulting the Economic and Social Committee **and the Committee of the Regions**, shall decide what action is to be taken by the Community in order to achieve the objectives referred to in Article **174**.

2. By way of derogation from the decision-making procedure provided for in paragraph 1 and without prejudice to Article **95**, the Council, acting unanimously on a proposal from the Commission and after consulting the European Parliament, the Economic and Social Committee **and the Committee of the Regions**, shall adopt:
-   provisions primarily of a fiscal nature;

- measures concerning town and country planning, land use with the exception of waste management and measures of a general nature, and management of water resources;
- measures significantly affecting a Member State's choice between different energy sources and the general structure of its energy supply.

The Council may, under the conditions laid down in the preceding sub-paragraph, define those matters referred to in this paragraph on which decisions are to be taken by a qualified majority.

3.   In other areas, general action programmes setting out priority objectives to be attained shall be adopted by the Council, acting in accordance with the procedure referred to in Article **251** and after consulting the Economic and Social Committee **and the Committee of the Regions**.

The Council, acting under the terms of paragraph 1 or paragraph 2 according to the case, shall adopt the measures necessary for the implementation of these programmes.

4.   Without prejudice to certain measures of a Community nature, the Member States shall finance and implement the environment policy.

5.   Without prejudice to the principle that the polluter should pay, if a measure based on the provisions of paragraph 1 involves costs deemed disproportionate for the public authorities of a Member State, the Council shall, in the act adopting that measure, lay down appropriate provisions in the form of:
- temporary derogations and/or
- financial support from the Cohesion Fund **set up pursuant to Article 161**.

ARTICLE **176**   (ex Article 130 t)

The protective measures adopted pursuant to Article **175** shall not prevent any Member State from maintaining or introducing more stringent protective measures. Such measures must be compatible with this Treaty. They shall be notified to the Commission.

TITLE **XX**   (ex Title XVII)

DEVELOPMENT CO-OPERATION

ARTICLE **177**   (ex Article 130 u)

1.   Community policy in the sphere of development co-operation, which shall be complementary to the policies pursued by the Member States, shall foster:
- the sustainable economic and social development of the developing countries, and more particularly the most disadvantaged among them;
- the smooth and gradual integration of the developing countries into the world economy;
- the campaign against poverty in the developing countries.

2.   Community policy in this area shall contribute to the general objective of developing and consolidating democracy and the rule of law, and to that of respecting human rights and fundamental freedoms.

3.   The Community and the Member States shall comply with the commitments and take account of the objectives they have approved in the context of the United Nations and other competent international organisations.

ARTICLE **178**   (ex Article 130 v)

The Community shall take account of the objectives referred to in Article **177** in the policies that it implements which are likely to affect developing countries.

ARTICLE **179**   (ex Article 130 w)

1.   Without prejudice to the other provisions of this Treaty the Council, acting in accordance with the procedure referred to in **Article 251**, shall adopt the measures necessary to further the objectives referred to in Article **177**. Such measures may take the form of multiannual programmes.

2.   The European Investment Bank shall contribute, under the terms laid down in its Statute, to the implementation of the measures referred to in paragraph 1.

3.   The provisions of this Article shall not affect co-operation with the African, Caribbean and Pacific countries in the framework of the ACP-**EC** Convention.

ARTICLE **180** (ex Article 130 x)

1. The Community and the Member States shall co-ordinate their policies on development co-operation and shall consult each other on their aid programmes, including in international organisations and during international conferences. They may undertake joint action. Member States shall contribute if necessary to the implementation of Community aid programmes.

2. The Commission may take any useful initiative to promote the co-ordination referred to in paragraph 1.

ARTICLE **181** (ex Article 130 y)

Within their respective spheres of competence, the Community and the Member States shall co-operate with third countries and with the competent international organisations. The arrangements for Community co-operation may be the subject of agreements between the Community and the third parties concerned, which shall be negotiated and concluded in accordance with Article **300**.

The previous paragraph shall be without prejudice to Member States' competence to negotiate in international bodies and to conclude international agreements.

PART FOUR

ASSOCIATION OF THE OVERSEAS COUNTRIES AND TERRITORIES

ARTICLE **182** (ex Article 131)

The Member States agree to associate with the Community the non-European countries and territories which have special relations with **Denmark, France, the Netherlands and the United Kingdom**. These countries and territories (hereinafter called the 'countries and territories') are listed in **Annex II** to this Treaty.

The purpose of association shall be to promote the economic and social development of the countries and territories and to establish close economic relations between them and the Community as a whole.

In accordance with the principles set out in the Preamble to this Treaty, association shall serve primarily to further the interests and prosperity of the inhabitants of these countries and territories in order to lead them to the economic, social and cultural development to which they aspire.

ARTICLE **183** (ex Article 132)

Association shall have the following objectives:

1. Member States shall apply to their trade with the countries and territories the same treatment as they accord each other pursuant to this Treaty.

2. Each country or territory shall apply to its trade with Member States and with the other countries and territories the same treatment as that which it applies to the European State with which it has special relations.

3. The Member States shall contribute to the investments required for the progressive development of these countries and territories.

4. For investments financed by the Community, participation in tenders and supplies shall be open on equal terms to all natural and legal persons who are nationals of a Member State or of one of the countries and territories.

5. In relations between Member States and the countries and territories the right of establishment of nationals and companies or firms shall be regulated in accordance with the provisions and procedures laid down in the Chapter relating to the right of establishment and on a non-discriminatory basis, subject to any special provisions laid down pursuant to Article **187**.

ARTICLE **184** (ex Article 133)

1. Customs duties on imports into the Member States of goods originating in the countries and territories shall be **prohibited** in conformity with the **prohibition** of customs duties between Member States in Accordance with the provisions of this Treaty.

2. Customs duties on imports into each country or territory from Member States or from the other countries or territories shall be **prohibited** in accordance with the provisions of **Article 25**.

3. The countries and territories may, however, levy customs duties which meet the needs of their development and industrialisation or produce revenue for their budget.

The duties referred to in the preceding sub-paragraph **may not exceed** the level of those imposed on imports of products from the Member State with which each country or territory has special relations. ***Second sentence shall be deleted.***

4.   Paragraph 2 shall not apply to countries and territories which, by reason of the particular international obligations by which they are bound, already apply a non-discriminatory customs tariff. ***Remainder of sentence shall be deleted.***

5.   The introduction of or any change in customs duties imposed on goods imported into the countries and territories shall not, either in law or in fact, give rise to any direct or indirect discrimination between imports from the various Member States.

ARTICLE **185**   (ex Article 134)
If the level of the duties applicable to goods from a third country on entry into a country or territory is liable, when the provisions of Article **184**(1) have been applied, to cause deflections of trade to the detriment of any Member State, the latter may request the Commission to propose to the other Member States the measures needed to remedy the situation.

ARTICLE **186**   (ex Article 135)
Subject to the provisions relating to public health, public security or public policy, freedom of movement within Member States for workers from the countries and territories, and within the countries and territories for workers from Member States, shall be governed by agreements to be concluded subsequently with the unanimous approval of Member States.

ARTICLE **187**   (ex Article 136)
The Council, acting unanimously, shall, on the basis of the experience acquired under the association of the countries and territories with the Community and of the principles set out in this Treaty, lay down provisions as regards the detailed rules and the procedure for the association of the countries and territories with the Community.

ARTICLE **188**   (ex Article 136 a)
The provisions of Articles **182** to **187** shall apply to Greenland, subject to the specific provisions for Greenland set out in the Protocol on special arrangements for Greenland, annexed to this Treaty.

PART FIVE

INSTITUTIONS OF THE COMMUNITY

TITLE I

PROVISIONS GOVERNING THE INSTITUTIONS

CHAPTER 1

THE INSTITUTIONS

Section 1

The European Parliament

ARTICLE **189**   (ex Article 137)
The European Parliament, which shall consist of representatives of the peoples of the States brought together in the Community, shall exercise the powers conferred upon it by this Treaty.
The number of Members of the European Parliament shall not exceed seven hundred.

ARTICLE **190**   (ex Article 138)
1.   The representatives in the European Parliament of the peoples of the States brought together in the Community shall be elected by direct universal suffrage.

2.   The number of representatives selected in each Member State is as follows:

Belgium **25**; Denmark 16; Germany **99**; Greece **25**; Spain **64**; France **87**; Ireland 15; Italy **87**; Luxembourg 6; Netherlands **31**; **Austria 21**; Portugal **25**; **Finland 16**; **Sweden 22**; United Kingdom **87**.

In the event of amendments to this paragraph, the number of representatives elected in each Member State must ensure appropriate representation of the peoples of the States brought together in the Community.

3.   **Representatives shall be elected for a term of five years.**

4.   The European Parliament shall draw up **a proposal** for elections by direct universal suffrage in accordance with a uniform procedure in all Member States **or in accordance with principles common to all Member States**.

The Council shall, acting unanimously after obtaining the assent of the European Parliament, which shall act by a majority of its component members, lay down the appropriate provisions, which it shall recommend to Member States for adoption in accordance with their respective constitutional requirements.

5.   **The European Parliament shall, after seeking an opinion from the Commission and with the approval of the Council acting by unanimity, lay down the regulations and general conditions governing the performance of the duties of its Members.**

ARTICLE **191**   (ex Article 138 a)

Political parties at European level are important as a factor for integration within the Union. They contribute to forming a European awareness and to expressing the political will of the citizens of the Union.

ARTICLE **192**   (ex Article 138 b)

Insofar as provided in this Treaty, the European Parliament shall participate in the process leading up to the adoption of Community acts by exercising its powers under the procedures laid down in Articles **251** and **252** and by giving its assent or delivering advisory opinions.

The European Parliament may, acting by a majority of its Members, request the Commission to submit any appropriate proposal on matters on which it considers that a Community act is required for the purpose of implementing this Treaty.

ARTICLE **193**   (ex Article 138 c)

In the course of its duties, the European Parliament may, at the request of a quarter of its Members, set up a temporary Committee of Inquiry to investigate, without prejudice to the powers conferred by this Treaty on other institutions or bodies, alleged contravention or maladministration in the implementation of Community law, except where the alleged facts are being examined before a court and while the case is still subject to legal proceedings.

The temporary Committee of Inquiry shall cease to exist on the submission of its report.

The detailed provisions governing the exercise of the right of inquiry shall be determined by common accord of the European Parliament, the Council and the Commission.

ARTICLE **194**   (ex Article 138 d)

Any citizen of the Union, and any natural or legal person residing or having its registered office in a Member State, shall have the right to address, individually or in association with other citizens or persons, a petition to the European Parliament on a matter which comes within the Community's fields of activity and which affects him, her or it directly.

ARTICLE **195**   (ex Article 138 e)

1.   The European Parliament shall appoint an Ombudsman empowered to receive complaints from any citizen of the Union or any natural or legal person residing or having its registered office in a Member State concerning instances of maladministration in the activities of the Community institutions or bodies, with the exception of the Court of Justice and the Court of First Instance acting in their judicial role.

In accordance with his duties, the Ombudsman shall conduct inquiries for which he finds grounds, either on his own initiative or on the basis of complaints submitted to him direct or through a Member of the European Parliament, except where the alleged facts are or have been the subject of legal proceedings. Where the Ombudsman establishes an instance of maladministration, he shall refer the matter to the institution concerned, which shall have a period of three months in which to inform him of its views. The Ombudsman shall then forward a report to the European Parliament and the institution concerned. The person lodging the complaint shall be informed of the outcome of such inquiries.

The Ombudsman shall submit an annual report to the European Parliament on the outcome of his inquiries.

2.   The Ombudsman shall be appointed after each election of the European Parliament for the duration of its term of office. The Ombudsman shall be eligible for reappointment.
The Ombudsman may be dismissed by the Court of Justice at the request of the European Parliament if he no longer fulfils the conditions required for the performance of his duties or if he is guilty of serious misconduct.

3.   The Ombudsman shall be completely independent in the performance of his duties. In the performance of those duties he shall neither seek nor take instructions from any body. The Ombudsman may not, during his term of office, engage in any other occupation, whether gainful or not.

4.   The European Parliament shall, after seeking an opinion from the Commission and with the approval of the Council acting by a qualified majority, lay down the regulations and general conditions governing the performance of the Ombudsman's duties.

ARTICLE **196** (ex Article 139)
The European Parliament shall hold an annual session. It shall meet, without requiring to be convened, on the second Tuesday in March.
The European Parliament may meet in extraordinary session at the request of a majority of its Members or at the request of a majority of its Members or at the request of the Council or of the Commission.

ARTICLE **197** (ex Article 140)
The European Parliament shall elect its President and its officers from among its Members.
Members of the Commission may attend all meetings and shall, at their request, be heard on behalf of the Commission.
The Commission shall reply orally or in writing to questions put to it by the European Parliament or by its Members.
The Council shall be heard by the European Parliament in accordance with the conditions laid down by the Council in its Rules of Procedure.

ARTICLE **198** (ex Article 141)
Save as otherwise provided in this Treaty, the European Parliament shall act by an absolute majority of the votes cast.
The rules of procedure shall determine the quorum.

ARTICLE **199** (ex Article 142)
The European Parliament shall adopt its Rules of Procedure, acting by a majority of its Members.
The proceedings of the European Parliament shall be published in the manner laid down in its Rules of Procedure.

ARTICLE **200** (ex Article 143)
The European Parliament shall discuss in open session the annual general report submitted to it by the Commission.

ARTICLE **201** (ex Article 144)
If a motion of censure on the activities of the Commission is tabled before it, the European Parliament shall not vote thereon until at least three days after the motion has been tabled and only by open vote.
If the motion of censure is carried by a two-thirds majority of the votes cast, representing a majority of the Members of the European Parliament, the Members of the Commission shall resign as a body. They shall continue to deal with current business until they are replaced in accordance with Article **214**. In this case, the term of office of the Members of the Commission appointed to replace them shall expire on the date on which the term of office of the Members of the Commission obliged to resign as a body would have expired.

Section 2

The Council

ARTICLE **202** (ex Article 145)
To ensure that the objectives set out in this Treaty are attained, the Council shall, in accordance with the provisions of this treaty:
-    ensure co-ordination of the general economic policies of the Member States;
-    have power to take decisions;

- confer on the Commission, in the acts which the Council adopts, powers for the implementation of the rules which the Council lays down. The Council may impose certain requirements in respect of the exercise of these powers. The Council may also reserve the right in specific cases, to exercise directly implementing powers itself. The procedures referred to above must be consonant with principles and rules to be laid down in advance by the Council, acting unanimously on a proposal from the Commission and after obtaining the Opinion of the European Parliament.

ARTICLE **203** (ex Article 146)

The Council shall consist of a representative of each Member State at ministerial level, authorised to commit the government of that Member State.

The office of President shall be held in turn by each Member State in the Council for a term of six months, in the order decided by the Council acting unanimously.

[*Second paragraph revised under the Act of Accession of Austria, Finland and Sweden in 1994.*]

ARTICLE **204** (ex Article 147)

The Council shall meet when convened by its President on his own initiative or at the request of one of its members or of the Commission.

ARTICLE **205** (ex Article 148)

1.   Save as otherwise provided in this Treaty, the Council shall act by a majority of its members.

2.   Where the Council is required to act by a qualified majority, the votes of its members shall be weighted as follows:

Belgium 5; Denmark 3; Germany 10; Greece 5; Spain 8; France 10; Ireland 3; Italy 10; Luxembourg 2; Netherlands 5; Austria 4; Portugal 5; Finland 3; Sweden 4; United Kingdom 10.

For their adoption, acts of the Council shall require at least:

- sixty-two votes in favour where this Treaty requires them to be adopted on a proposal from the Commission,
- sixty-two votes in favour, cast by at least ten members, in other cases.

[*Second paragraph revised as a consequence of the Act of Accession of Austria, Finland and Sweden in 1994.*]

3.   Abstentions by members present in person or represented shall not prevent the adoption by the Council of acts which require unanimity.

[ARTICLE 149 repealed by the Maastricht Treaty.]

ARTICLE **206** (ex Article 150)

Where a vote is taken, any member of the Council may also act on behalf of not more than one other member.

ARTICLE **207** (ex Article 151)

1.   A committee consisting of the Permanent Representatives of the Member States shall be responsible for preparing the work of the Council and for carrying out the tasks assigned to it by the Council. **The Committee may adopt procedural decisions in cases provided for in the Council's Rules of Procedure.**

2.   The Council shall be assisted by a General Secretariat, under the **responsibility** of a Secretary-General, **High Representative for the common foreign and security policy, who shall be assisted by a Deputy Secretary-General responsible for the running of the General Secretariat.** The Secretary-General **and the Deputy Secretary-General** shall be appointed by the Council acting unanimously.

The Council shall decide on the organisation of the General Secretariat.

3.   The Council shall adopt its Rules of Procedure.

For the purpose of applying Article 255(3), the Council shall elaborate in these Rules the conditions under which the public shall have access to Council documents. For the purpose of this paragraph, the Council shall define the cases in which it is to be regarded as acting in its legislative capacity, with a view to allowing greater access to documents in those cases, while at the same time preserving the effectiveness of its decision-making process. In any event, when the Council acts in its legislative capacity, the results of votes and explanations of vote as well as statements in the minutes shall be made public.

ARTICLE **208** (ex Article 152)

The Council may request the Commission to undertake any studies the Council considers desirable for the attainment of the common objectives, and to submit to it any appropriate proposals.

ARTICLE **209** (ex Article 153)
The Council shall, after receiving an opinion from the Commission, determine the rules governing the committees provided for in this Treaty.

ARTICLE **210** (ex Article 154)
The Council shall, acting by a qualified majority, determine the salaries, allowances and pensions of the President and Members of the Commission, and of the President, Judges, Advocates-General and Registrar of the Court of Justice. It shall also, again by a qualified majority, determine any payment to be made instead of remuneration.

Section 3

The Commission

ARTICLE **211** (ex Article 155)
In order to ensure the proper functioning and development of the common market, the Commission shall:
- ensure that the provisions of this Treaty and the measures taken by the institutions pursuant thereto are applied;
- formulate recommendations or deliver opinions on matters dealt with in this Treaty, if it expressly so provides or if the Commission considers it necessary;
- have its own power of decision and participate in the shaping of measures taken by the Council and by the European Parliament in the manner provided for in this Treaty;
- exercise the powers conferred on it by the Council for the implementation of the rules laid down by the latter.

ARTICLE **212** (ex Article 156)
The Commission shall publish annually, not later than one month before the opening of the session of the European Parliament, a general report on the activities of the Community.

ARTICLE **213** (ex Article 157)
1.   The Commission shall consist of twenty Members, who shall be chosen on the grounds of their general competence and whose independence is beyond doubt.
The number of Members of the Commission may be altered by the Council, acting unanimously.
Only nationals of Member States may be Members of the Commission.
The Commission must include at least one national of each of the Member States, but may not include more than two Members having the nationality of the same State.

2.   The Members of the Commission shall, in the general interest of the Community, be completely independent in the performance of their duties.
In the performance of these duties, they shall neither seek nor take instructions from any government or from any other body. They shall refrain from any action incompatible with their duties. Each Member State undertakes to respect this principle and not to seek to influence the Members of the Commission in the performance of their tasks.
The Members of the Commission may not, during their term of office, engage in any other occupation, whether gainful or not. When entering upon their duties they shall give a solemn undertaking that, both during and after their term of office, they will respect the obligations arising therefrom and in particular their duty to behave with integrity and discretion as regards the acceptance, after they have ceased to hold office, of certain appointments or benefits. In the event of any breach of these obligations, the Court of Justice may, on application by the Council or the Commission, rule that the Member concerned be, according to the circumstances, either compulsorily retired in accordance with Article **216** or deprived of his right to a pension or other benefits in its stead.

ARTICLE **214** (ex Article 158)
1.   The Members of the Commission shall be appointed, in accordance with the procedure referred to in paragraph 2, for a period of five years, subject, if need be, to Article **201**.
Their term of office shall be renewable.

2.   The governments of the Member States shall nominate by common accord **the person they intend to appoint as President of the Commission; the nomination shall be approved by the European Parliament.**
The governments of the Member States shall, **by common accord** with the nominee for President, nominate the other persons whom they intend to appoint as Members of the Commission.

The President and the other Members of the Commission thus nominated shall be subject as a body to a vote of approval by the European Parliament. After approval by the European Parliament, the President and the other Members of the Commission shall be appointed by common accord of the governments of the Member States.

Paragraph 3 shall be repealed.

ARTICLE **215** (ex Article 159)
Apart from normal replacement, or death, the duties of a Member of the Commission shall end when he resigns or is compulsorily retired.
The vacancy thus caused shall be filled for the remainder of the Member's term of office by a new Member appointed by common accord of the governments of the Member States. The Council may, acting unanimously, decide that such a vacancy need not be filled.
In the event of resignation, compulsory retirement or death, the President shall be replaced for the remainder of his term of office. The procedure laid down in Article **214**(2) shall be applicable for the replacement of the President.
Save in the case of compulsory retirement under Article **216**, Members of the Commission shall remain in office until they have been replaced.

ARTICLE **216** (ex Article 160)
If any Member of the Commission no longer fulfils the conditions required for the performance of his duties or if he has been guilty of serious misconduct, the Court of Justice may, on application by the Council or the Commission, compulsorily retire him.

ARTICLE **217** (ex Article 161)
The Commission may appoint a Vice-President or two Vice-Presidents from among its Members.

ARTICLE **218** (ex Article 162)
1.   The Council and the Commission shall consult each other and shall settle by common accord their methods of co-operation.

2.   The Commission shall adopt its rules of procedure so as to ensure that both it and its departments operate in accordance with the provisions of this Treaty. It shall ensure that these rules are published.

ARTICLE **219** (ex Article 163)
The Commission shall work under the political guidance of its President.
The Commission shall act by a majority of the number of Members provided for in Article **213**.
A meeting of the Commission shall be valid only if the number of Members laid down in its Rules of Procedure is present.

Section   4

The Court of Justice

ARTICLE **220** (ex Article 164)
The Court of Justice shall ensure that in the interpretation and application of this Treaty the law is observed.

ARTICLE **221** (ex Article 165)
The Court of Justice shall consist of fifteen Judges.
The Court of Justice shall sit in plenary session. It may, however, form chambers, each consisting of three, five or seven Judges, either to undertake certain preparatory inquiries or to adjudicate on particular categories of cases in accordance with rules laid down for these purposes.
The Court of Justice shall sit in plenary session when a Member State or a Community institution that is a party to the proceedings so requests.
Should the Court of Justice so request, the Council may, acting unanimously, increase the number of Judges and make the necessary adjustments to the second and third paragraphs of this Article and to the second paragraph of Article **223**.

ARTICLE **222** (ex Article 166)
The Court of Justice shall be assisted by eight Advocates-General. However, a ninth Advocate-General shall be appointed as from **1 January 1995** until 6 October 2000.
[Sentence added under the Act of Accession of Austria, Finland and Sweden in 1994.]

It shall be the duty of the Advocate-General, acting with complete impartiality and independence, to make, in open court, reasoned submissions on cases brought before the Court of Justice, in order to assist the Court in the performance of the task assigned to it in Article **220**.

Should the Court of Justice so request, the Council may, acting unanimously, increase the number of Advocates-General and make the necessary adjustments to the third paragraph of Article **223**.

ARTICLE **223** (ex Article 167)

The Judges and Advocates-General shall be chosen from persons whose independence is beyond doubt and who possess the qualifications required for appointment to the highest judicial offices in their respective countries or who are jurisconsults of recognised competence; they shall be appointed by common accord of the Governments of the Member States for a term of six years.

Every three years there shall be a partial replacement of the Judges. Eight and seven Judges shall be replaced alternately.

Every three years there shall be a partial replacement of the Advocates-General. Four Advocates-General shall be replaced on each occasion.

Retiring Judges and Advocates-General shall be eligible for reappointment.

The Judges shall elect the President of the Court of Justice from among their number for a term of three years. He may be re-elected.

ARTICLE **224** (ex Article 168)

The Court of Justice shall appoint its Registrar and lay down the rules governing his service.

ARTICLE **225** (ex Article 168a)

1.   A Court of First Instance shall be attached to the Court of Justice with jurisdiction to hear and determine at first instance, subject to a right of appeal to the Court of Justice on points of law only and in accordance with the conditions laid down by the Statute, certain classes of action or proceeding defined in accordance with the conditions laid down in paragraph 2. The Court of First Instance shall not be competent to hear and determine questions referred for a preliminary ruling under Article **234**.

2.   At the request of the Court of Justice and after consulting the European Parliament and the Commission, the Council, acting unanimously, shall determine the classes of action or proceeding referred to in paragraph 1 and the composition of the Court of First Instance and shall adopt the necessary adjustments and additional provisions to the statute of the Court of Justice. Unless the Council decides otherwise, the provisions of this Treaty relating to the Court of Justice, in particular the provisions of the Protocol on the Statute of the Court of Justice, shall apply to the Court of First Instance.

3.   The members of the Court of First Instance shall be chosen from persons whose independence is beyond doubt and who possess the ability required for appointment to judicial office; they shall be appointed by common accord of the governments of the Member States for a term of six years. The membership shall be partially renewed every three years. Retiring members shall be eligible for re-appointment.

4.   The Court of First Instance shall establish its Rules of Procedure, in agreement with the Court of Justice. Those rules shall require the unanimous approval of the Council.

ARTICLE **226** (ex Article 169)

If the Commission considers that a Member State has failed to fulfil an obligation under this Treaty, it shall deliver a reasoned opinion on the matter after giving the State concerned the opportunity to submit its observations.

If the State concerned does not comply with the opinion within the period laid down by the Commission, the latter may bring the matter before the Court of Justice.

ARTICLE **227** (ex Article 170)

A Member State which considers that another Member State has failed to fulfil an obligation under this Treaty may bring the matter before the Court of Justice.

Before a Member State brings an action against another Member State for an alleged infringement of an obligation under this Treaty, it shall bring the matter before the Commission.

The Commission shall deliver a reasoned opinion after each of the States concerned has been given the opportunity to submit its own case and its observations on the other party's case both orally and in writing.

If the Commission has not delivered an opinion within three months of the date on which the matter was brought before it, the absence of such opinion shall not prevent the matter from being brought before the Court of Justice.

ARTICLE **228** (ex Article 171)

1.   If the Court of Justice finds that a Member State has failed to fulfil an obligation under this Treaty, the State shall be required to take the necessary measures to comply with the judgement of the Court of Justice.

2.   If the Commission considers that the Member State concerned has not taken such measures it shall, after giving that State the opportunity to submit its observations, issue a reasoned opinion specifying the points on which the Member State concerned has not complied with the judgement of the Court of Justice.

If the Member State concerned fails to take the necessary measures to comply with the Court's judgement within the time-limit laid down by the Commission, the latter may bring the case before the Court of Justice. In so doing it shall specify the amount of the lump sum or penalty payment to be paid by the Member State concerned which it considers appropriate in the circumstances.

If the Court of Justice finds that the Member State concerned has not complied with its judgement it may impose a lump sum or penalty payment on it.

This procedure shall be without prejudice to Article **227**.

ARTICLE **229** (ex Article 172)

Regulations adopted jointly by the European Parliament and the Council, and by the Council, pursuant to the provisions of this Treaty, may give the Court of Justice unlimited jurisdiction with regard to the penalties provided for in such regulations.

ARTICLE **230** (ex Article 173)

The Court of Justice shall review the legality of acts adopted jointly by the European Parliament and the Council, of acts of the Council, of the Commission and of the ECB, other than recommendations and opinions, and of acts of the European Parliament intended to produce legal effects *vis-à-vis* third parties.

It shall for this purpose have jurisdiction in actions brought by a Member State, the Council or the Commission on grounds of lack of competence, infringement of an essential procedural requirement, infringement of this Treaty or of any rule of law relating to its application, or misuse of powers.

The Court shall have jurisdiction under the same conditions in actions brought by the European Parliament, **by the Court of Auditors** and by the ECB for the purpose of protecting their prerogatives.

Any natural or legal person may, under the same conditions, institute proceedings against a decision addressed to that person or against a decision which, although in the form of a regulation or a decision addressed to another person, is of direct and individual concern to the former.

The proceedings provided for in this Article shall be instituted within two months of the publication of the measure, or of its notification to the plaintiff, or, in the absence thereof, of the day on which it came to the knowledge of the latter, as the case may be.

ARTICLE **231** (ex Article 174)

If the action is well founded, the Court of Justice shall declare the act concerned to be void.

In the case of a regulation, however, the Court of Justice shall, if it considers this necessary, state which of the effects of the regulation which it has declared void shall be considered as definitive.

ARTICLE **232** (ex Article 175)

Should the European Parliament, the Council or the Commission, in infringement of this Treaty, fail to act, the Member States and the other institutions of the Community may bring an action before the Court of Justice to have the infringement established.

The action shall be admissible only if the institution concerned has first been called upon to act. If, within two months of being so called upon, the institution concerned has not defined its position, the action may be brought within a further period of two months.

Any natural or legal person may, under the conditions laid down in the preceding paragraphs, complain to the Court of Justice that an institution of the Community has failed to address to that person any act other than a recommendation or an opinion.

The Court of Justice shall have jurisdiction, under the same conditions, in actions or proceedings brought by the ECB in the areas falling within the latter's field of competence and in actions or proceedings brought against the latter.

ARTICLE **233** (ex Article 176)

The institution or institutions whose act has been declared void or whose failure to act has been declared contrary to this Treaty shall be required to take the necessary measures to comply with the judgement of the Court of Justice.

This obligation shall not affect any obligation which may result from the application of the second paragraph of Article **288**.

This Article shall also apply to the ECB.

ARTICLE **234** (ex Article 177)

The Court of Justice shall have jurisdiction to give preliminary rulings concerning:

(a)   the interpretation of this Treaty;

(b)   the validity and interpretation of acts of the institutions of the Community and of the ECB;

(c)   the interpretation of the statutes of bodies established by an act of the Council, where those statutes so provide.

Where such a question is raised before any court or tribunal of a Member State, that court or tribunal may, if it considers that a decision on the question is necessary to enable it to give judgement, request the Court of Justice to give a ruling thereon.

Where any such question is raised in a case pending before a court or tribunal of a Member State against whose decisions there is no judicial remedy under national law, that court or tribunal shall bring the matter before the Court of Justice.

ARTICLE **235** (ex Article 178)

The Court of Justice shall have jurisdiction in disputes relating to compensation for damage provided for in the second paragraph of Article **288**.

ARTICLE **236** (ex Article 179)

The Court of Justice shall have jurisdiction in any dispute between the Community and its servants within the limits and under the conditions laid down in the Staff Regulations or the Conditions of Employment.

ARTICLE **237** (ex Article 180)

The Court of Justice shall, within the limits hereinafter laid down, have jurisdiction in disputes concerning:

(a)   the fulfilment by Member States of obligations under the Statute of the European Investment Bank. In this connection, the Board of Directors of the Bank shall enjoy the powers conferred upon the Commission by Article **226**;

(b)   measures adopted by the Board of Governors of the European Investment Bank. In this connection, any Member State, the Commission or the Board of Directors of the Bank may institute proceedings under the conditions laid down in Article **230**;

(c)   measures adopted by the Board of Directors of the European Investment Bank. Proceedings against such measures may be instituted only by Member States or by the Commission, under the conditions laid down in Article **230**, and solely on the grounds of non-compliance with the procedure provided for in Article 21(2), (5), (6) and (7) of the Statute of the Bank;

(d)   the fulfilment by national central banks of obligations under this Treaty and the Statute of the ESCB. In this connection the powers of the Council of the ECB in respect of national central banks shall be the same as those conferred upon the Commission in respect of Member States by Article **226**. If the Court of Justice finds that a national central bank has failed to fulfil an obligation under this Treaty, that bank shall be required to take the necessary measures to comply with the judgement of the Court of Justice.

ARTICLE **238** (ex Article 181)

The Court of Justice shall have jurisdiction to give judgement pursuant to any arbitration clause contained in a contract concluded by or on behalf of the Community, whether that contract be governed by public or private law.

ARTICLE **239** (ex Article 182)

The Court of Justice shall have jurisdiction in any dispute between Member States which relates to the subject matter of this Treaty if the dispute is submitted to it under a special agreement between the parties.

ARTICLE **240** (ex Article 183)

Save where jurisdiction is conferred on the Court of Justice by this Treaty, disputes to which the Community is a party shall not on that ground be excluded from the jurisdiction of the courts or tribunals of the Member States.

ARTICLE **241** (ex Article 184)

Notwithstanding the expiry of the period laid down in the fifth paragraph of Article **230**, any party may, in proceedings in which a regulation adopted jointly by the European Parliament and the Council, or a regulation of the Council, of the Commission, or of the ECB is at issue, plead the grounds specified in the second paragraph of Article **230** in order to invoke before the Court of Justice the inapplicability of that regulation.

ARTICLE **242** (ex Article 185)

Actions brought before the Court of Justice shall not have suspensory effect. The Court of Justice may, however, if it considers that circumstances so require, order that application of the contested act be suspended.

ARTICLE **243** (ex Article 186)
The Court of Justice may in any cases before it prescribe any necessary interim measures.

ARTICLE **244** (ex Article 187)
The judgements of the Court of Justice shall be enforceable under the conditions laid down in Article **256**.

ARTICLE **245** (ex Article 188)
The Statute of the Court of Justice is laid down in a separate Protocol.
The Council may, acting unanimously at the request of the Court of Justice and after consulting the Commission and the European Parliament, amend the provisions of Title III of the Statute.
The Court of Justice shall adopt its rules of procedure. These shall require the unanimous approval of the Council.

Section 5

The Court of Auditors

ARTICLE **246** (ex Article 188 a)
The Court of Auditors shall carry out the audit.

ARTICLE **247** (ex Article 188 b)
1.   The Court of Auditors shall consist of fifteen Members.

2.   The Members of the Court of Auditors shall be chosen from among persons who belong or have belonged in their respective countries to external audit bodies or who are especially qualified for this office. Their independence must be beyond doubt.

3.   The Members of the Court of Auditors shall be appointed for a term of six years by the Council, acting unanimously after consulting the European Parliament.

Second sub-paragraph shall be deleted.

The Members of the Court of Auditors shall be eligible for reappointment.
They shall elect the President of the Court of Auditors from among their number for a term of three years. The President may be re-elected.

4.   The Members of the Court of Auditors shall, in the general interest of the Community, be completely independent in the performance of their duties.
In the performance of these duties, they shall neither seek nor take instructions from any government or from any other body. They shall refrain from any action incompatible with their duties.

5.   The Members of the Court of Auditors may not, during their term of office, engage in any other occupation, whether gainful or not. When entering upon their duties they shall give a solemn undertaking that, both during and after their term of office, they will respect the obligations arising therefrom and in particular their duty to behave with integrity and discretion as regards the acceptance, after they have ceased to hold office, of certain appointments or benefits.

6.   Apart from normal replacement, or death, the duties of a Member of the Court of Auditors shall end when he resigns, or is compulsorily retired by a ruling of the Court of Justice pursuant to paragraph 7.
The vacancy thus caused shall be filled for the remainder of the Member's term of office.
Save in the case of compulsory retirement, Members of the Court of Auditors shall remain in office until they have been replaced.

7.   A Member of the Court of Auditors may be deprived of his office or of his right to a pension or other benefits in its stead only if the Court of Justice, at the request of the Court of Auditors, finds that he no longer fulfils the requisite conditions or meets the obligations arising from his office.

8.   The Council, acting by a qualified majority, shall determine the conditions of employment of the President and the Members of the Court of Auditors and in particular their salaries, allowances and pensions. It shall also, by the same majority, determine any payment to be made instead of remuneration.

9.   The provisions of the Protocol on the Privileges and Immunities of the European Communities applicable to the judges of the Court of Justice shall also apply to the Members of the Court of Auditors.

ARTICLE **248** (ex Article 188 c)

1.   The Court of Auditors shall examine the accounts of all revenue and expenditure of the Community. It shall also examine the accounts of all revenue and expenditure of all bodies set up by the Community in so far as the relevant constituent instrument does not preclude such examination.

The Court of Auditors shall provide the European Parliament and the Council with a statement of assurance as to the reliability of the accounts and the legality and regularity of the underlying transactions **which shall be published in the** *Official Journal of the European Communities.*

2.   The Court of Auditors shall examine whether all revenue has been received and all expenditure incurred in a lawful and regular manner and whether the financial management has been sound. **In doing so, it shall report in particular on any cases of irregularity.**

The audit of revenue shall be carried out on the basis both of the amounts established as due and the amounts actually paid to the Community.

The audit of expenditure shall be carried out on the basis both of commitments undertaken and payments made.

These audits may be carried out before the closure of accounts for the financial year in question.

3.   The audit shall be based on records and, if necessary, performed on the spot in the other institutions of the Community, **on the premises of any body which manages revenue or expenditure on behalf of the Community** and in the Member States, **including on the premises of any natural or legal person in receipt of payments from the budget.** In the Member States the audit shall be carried out in liaison with national audit bodies or, if these do not have the necessary powers, with the competent national departments. **The Court of Auditors and the national audit bodies of the Member States shall co-operate in a spirit of trust while maintaining their independence.** These bodies or departments shall inform the Court of Auditors whether they intend to take part in the audit.

The other institutions of the Community, **any bodies managing revenue or expenditure on behalf of the Community, any natural or legal person in receipt of payments from the budget,** and the national audit bodies or, if these do not have the necessary powers, the competent national departments, shall forward to the Court of Auditors, at its request, any document or information necessary to carry out its task.

In respect of the European Investment Bank's activity in managing Community expenditure and revenue, the Court's rights of access to information held by the Bank shall be governed by an agreement between the Court, the Bank and the Commission. In the absence of an agreement, the Court shall nevertheless have access to information necessary for the audit of Community expenditure and revenue managed by the Bank.

4.   The Court of Auditors shall draw up an annual report after the close of each financial year. It shall be forwarded to the other institutions of the Community and shall be published, together with the replies of these institutions to the observations of the Court of Auditors, in the *Official Journal of the European Communities.*

The Court of Auditors may also, at any time, submit observations, particularly in the form of special reports, on specific questions and deliver opinions at the request of one of the other institutions of the Community.

It shall adopt its annual reports, special reports or opinions by a majority of its Members.

It shall assist the European Parliament and the Council in exercising their powers of control over the implementation of the budget.

CHAPTER 2

PROVISIONS COMMON TO SEVERAL INSTITUTIONS

ARTICLE **249**   (ex Article 189)

In order to carry out their task and in accordance with the provisions of this Treaty, the European Parliament acting jointly with the Council, the Council and the Commission shall make regulations and issue directives, take decisions, make recommendations or deliver opinions.

A regulation shall have general application. It shall be binding in its entirety and directly applicable in all Member States.

A directive shall be binding, as to the result to be achieved, upon each Member State to which it is addressed, but shall leave to the national authorities the choice of form and methods.

A decision shall be binding in its entirety upon those to whom it is addressed.

Recommendations and opinions shall have no binding force.

ARTICLE **250**   (ex Article 189 a)

1.   Where, in pursuance of this Treaty, the Council acts on a proposal from the Commission, unanimity shall be required for an act constituting an amendment to that proposal, subject to Article **251**(4) and (5).

2.   As long as the Council has not acted, the Commission may alter its proposal at any time during the procedures leading to the adoption of a Community act.

ARTICLE **251** (ex Article 189 b)

1.   Where reference is made in this Treaty to this Article for the adoption of an act, the following procedure shall apply.

2.   The Commission shall submit a proposal to the European Parliament and the Council.

The Council, acting by a qualified majority after obtaining the opinion of the European Parliament,

-    **if it approves all the amendments contained in the European Parliament's opinion, may adopt the proposed act thus amended;**
-    **if the European Parliament does not propose any amendments, may adopt the proposed act;**
-    **shall otherwise adopt a common position and communicate it to the European Parliament. The Council shall inform the European Parliament fully of the reasons which led it to adopt its common position. The Commission shall inform the European Parliament fully of its position.**

If, within three months of such communication, the European Parliament:

(a)   **approves the common position or has not taken a decision, the act in question shall be deemed to have been adopted in accordance with that common position;**

(b)   **rejects, by an absolute majority of its component members, the common position, the proposed act shall be deemed not to have been adopted;**

(c)   **proposes amendments to the common position by an absolute majority of its component members, the amended text shall be forwarded to the Council and to the Commission, which shall deliver an opinion on those amendments.**

3.   If, within three months of the matter being referred to it, the Council, acting by a qualified majority, approves all the amendments of the European Parliament, **the act in question shall be deemed to have been adopted in the form of the common position thus amended;** however, the Council shall act unanimously on the amendments on which the Commission has delivered a negative opinion. If the Council does not approve **all the amendments**, the President of the Council, in agreement with the President of the European Parliament, **shall within six weeks** convene a meeting of the Conciliation Committee.

4.   The Conciliation Committee, which shall be composed of the members of the Council or their representatives and an equal number of representatives of the European Parliament, shall have the task of reaching agreement on a joint text, by a qualified majority of the members of the Council or their representatives and by a majority of the representatives of the European Parliament. The Commission shall take part in the Conciliation Committee's proceedings and shall take all the necessary initiatives with a view to reconciling the positions of the European Parliament and the Council. **In fulfilling this task, the Conciliation Committee shall address the common position on the basis of the amendments proposed by the European Parliament.**

5.   If, within six weeks of its being convened, the Conciliation Committee approves a joint text, the European Parliament, acting by an absolute majority of the votes cast, and the Council, acting by a qualified majority, shall each have a period of six weeks from that approval in which to adopt the act in question in accordance with the joint text. If **either** of the two institutions fails to approve the proposed act **within that period**, it shall be deemed not to have been adopted.

6.   **Where the Conciliation Committee does not approve a joint text, the proposed act shall be deemed not to have been adopted.**

7.   The periods of three months and six weeks referred to in this Article **shall** be extended by a maximum of one month and two weeks respectively **at the initiative of the European Parliament or the Council.**

Paragraph 8 shall be repealed.

ARTICLE **252** (ex Article 189 c)

Where reference is made in this Treaty to this Article for the adoption of an act, the following procedure shall apply:

(a)   The Council, acting by a qualified majority on a proposal from the Commission and after obtaining the opinion of the European Parliament, shall adopt a common position.

(b)   The Council's common position shall be communicated to the European Parliament. The Council and the Commission shall inform the European Parliament fully of the reasons which led the Council to adopt its common position and also of the Commission's position.

    If, within three months of such communication, the European Parliament approves this common position or has not taken a decision within that period, the Council shall definitively adopt the act in question in accordance with the common position.

(c)   The European Parliament may, within the period of three months referred to in point (b), by an absolute majority of its component Members, propose amendments to the Council's common position. The European Parliament may also, by the same majority, reject the Council's common position. The result of the proceedings shall be transmitted to the Council and the Commission.

If the European Parliament has rejected the Council's common position, unanimity shall be required for the Council to act on a second reading.

(d)   The Commission shall, within a period of one month, re-examine the proposal on the basis of which the Council adopted its common position, by taking into account the amendments proposed by the European Parliament.

The Commission shall forward to the Council, at the same time as its re-examined proposal, the amendments of the European Parliament which it has not accepted, and shall express its opinion on them. The Council may adopt these amendments unanimously.

(e)   The Council, acting by a qualified majority, shall adopt the proposal as re-examined by the Commission. Unanimity shall be required for the Council to amend the proposal as re-examined by the Commission.

(f)   In the cases referred to in points (c), (d) and (e), the Council shall be required to act within a period of three months. If no decision is taken within this period, the Commission proposal shall be deemed not to have been adopted.

(g)   The periods referred to in points (b) and (f) may be extended by a maximum of one month by common accord between the Council and the European Parliament.

ARTICLE 253   (ex Article 190)

Regulations, directives and decisions adopted jointly by the European Parliament and the Council, and such acts adopted by the Council or the Commission, shall state the reasons on which they are based and shall refer to any proposals or opinions which were required to be obtained pursuant to this Treaty.

ARTICLE 254   (ex Article 191)

1.   Regulations, directives and decisions adopted in accordance with the procedure referred to in Article 251 shall be signed by the President of the European Parliament and by the President of the Council and published in the *Official Journal of the European Communities*. They shall enter into force on the date specified in them or, in the absence thereof, on the twentieth day following that of their publication.

2.   Regulations of the Council and of the Commission, as well as directives of those institutions which are addressed to all Member States, shall be published in the *Official Journal of the European Communities*. They shall enter into force on the date specified in them or, in the absence thereof, on the twentieth day following that of their publication.

3.   Other directives, and decisions, shall be notified to those to whom they are addressed and shall take effect upon such notification.

ARTICLE 255   (ex Article 191 a)

1.   **Any citizen of the Union, and any natural or legal person residing or having its registered office in a Member State, shall have a right of access to European Parliament, Council and Commission documents, subject to the principles and the conditions to be defined in accordance with paragraphs 2 and 3.**

2.   **General principles and limits on grounds of public or private interest governing this right of access to documents shall be determined by the Council, acting in accordance with the procedure referred to in Article 251 within two years of the entry into force of the Treaty of Amsterdam.**

3.   **Each institution referred to above shall elaborate in its own Rules of Procedure specific provisions regarding access to its documents.**

ARTICLE 256   (ex Article 192)

Decisions of the Council or of the Commission which impose a pecuniary obligation on persons other than States, shall be enforceable.

Enforcement shall be governed by the rules of civil procedure in force in the State in the territory of which it is carried out. The order for its enforcement shall be appended to the decision, without other formality than verification of the authenticity of the decision, by the national authority which the Government of each Member State shall designate for this purpose and shall make known to the Commission and to the Court of Justice.

When these formalities have been completed on application by the party concerned, the latter may proceed to enforcement in accordance with the national law, by bringing the matter directly before the competent authority.

Enforcement may be suspended only by a decision of the Court of Justice. However, the courts of the country concerned shall have jurisdiction over complaints that enforcement is being carried out in an irregular manner.

CHAPTER 3

THE ECONOMIC AND SOCIAL COMMITTEE

ARTICLE 257 (ex Article 193)
An Economic and Social Committee is hereby established. It shall have advisory status.
The Committee shall consist of representatives of the various categories of economic and social activity, in particular, representatives of producers, farmers, carriers, workers, dealers, craftsmen, professional occupations and representatives of the general public.

ARTICLE 258 (ex Article 194)
The number of members of the Economic and Social Committee shall be as follows:
Belgium 12; Denmark 9; Germany 24; Greece 12; Spain 21; France 24; Ireland 9; Italy 24; Luxembourg 6; Netherlands 12; Austria 12; Portugal 12; Finland 9; Sweden 12; United Kingdom 24.
The members of the Committee shall be appointed by the Council, acting unanimously, for four years. Their appointments shall be renewable.
The members of the Committee may not be bound by any mandatory instructions. They shall be completely independent in the performance of their duties, in the general interest of the Community.
The Council, acting by a qualified majority, shall determine the allowances of members of the Committee.

ARTICLE 259 (ex Article 195)
1.   For the appointment of the members of the Committee, each Member State shall provide the Council with a list containing twice as many candidates as there are seats allotted to its nationals.
The composition of the Committee shall take account of the need to ensure adequate representation of the various categories of economic and social activity.

2.   The Council shall consult the Commission. It may obtain the opinion of European bodies which are representative of the various economic and social sectors to which the activities of the Community are of concern.

ARTICLE 260 (ex Article 196)
The Committee shall elect its chairman and officers from among its members for a term of two years.
It shall adopt its Rules of Procedure.
The Committee shall be convened by its chairman at the request of the Council or of the Commission. It may also meet on its own initiative.

ARTICLE 261 (ex Article 197)
The Committee shall include specialised sections for the principal fields covered by this Treaty.

Second paragraph shall be deleted.

These specialised sections shall operate within the general terms of reference of the Committee. They may not be consulted independently of the Committee.
Sub-committees may also be established within the Committee to prepare on specific questions or in specific fields, draft opinions to be submitted to the Committee for its consideration.
The Rules of Procedure shall lay down the methods of composition and the terms of reference of the specialised sections and of the sub-committees.

ARTICLE 262 (ex Article 198)
The Committee must be consulted by the Council or by the Commission where this Treaty so provides. The Committee may be consulted by these institutions in all cases in which they consider it appropriate. It may issue an opinion on its own initiative in cases in which it considers such action appropriate.
The Council or the Commission shall, if it considers it necessary, set the Committee, for the submission of its opinion, a time-limit which may not be less than one month from the date on which the chairman receives notification to this effect. Upon expiry of the time-limit, the absence of an opinion shall not prevent further action.
The opinion of the Committee and that of the specialised section, together with a record of the proceedings, shall be forwarded to the Council and to the Commission.
The Committee may be consulted by the European Parliament.

CHAPTER 4

THE COMMITTEE OF THE REGIONS

ARTICLE **263** (ex Article 198 a)

A Committee consisting of representatives of regional and local bodies, hereinafter referred to as 'the Committee of the Regions', is hereby established with advisory status.

The number of members of the Committee of the Regions shall be as follows:

Belgium 12; Denmark 9; Germany 24; Greece 12; Spain 21; France 24; Ireland 9; Italy 24; Luxembourg 6; Netherlands 12; Austria 12; Portugal 12; Finland 9; Sweden 12; United Kingdom 24.

The members of the Committee and an equal number of alternate members shall be appointed for four years by the Council acting unanimously on proposals from the respective Member States. Their term of office shall be renewable. **No member of the Committee shall at the same time be a Member of the European Parliament.**

The members of the Committee may not be bound by any mandatory instructions. They shall be completely independent in the performance of their duties, in the general interest of the Community.

ARTICLE **264** (ex Article 198 b)

The Committee of the Regions shall elect its chairman and officers from among its members for a term of two years.

It shall adopt its Rules of Procedure.

The Committee shall be convened by its chairman at the request of the Council or of the Commission. It may also meet on its own initiative.

ARTICLE **265** (ex Article 198 c)

The Committee of the Regions shall be consulted by the Council or by the Commission where this Treaty so provides and in all other cases, **in particular those which concern cross-border co-operation,** in which one of these two institutions considers it appropriate.

The Council or the Commission shall, if it considers it necessary, set the Committee, for the submission of its opinion, a time-limit which may not be less than one month from the date on which the chairman receives notification to this effect. Upon expiry of the time-limit, the absence of an opinion shall not prevent further action.

Where the Economic and Social Committee is consulted pursuant to Article **262**, the Committee of the Regions shall be informed by the Council or the Commission of the request for an opinion. Where it considers that specific regional interests are involved, the Committee of the Regions may issue an opinion on the matter.

The Committee of the Regions may be consulted by the European Parliament.

It may issue an opinion on its own initiative in cases in which it considers such action appropriate.

The opinion of the Committee, together with a record of the proceedings, shall be forwarded to the Council and to the Commission.

CHAPTER 5

EUROPEAN INVESTMENT BANK

ARTICLE **266** (ex Article 198 d)

The European Investment Bank shall have legal personality.

The members of the European Investment Bank shall be the Member States.

The Statute of the European Investment Bank is laid down in a Protocol annexed to this Treaty.

ARTICLE **267** (ex Article 198 e)

The task of the European Investment Bank shall be to contribute, by having recourse to the capital market and utilising its own resources, to the balanced and steady development of the common market in the interest of the Community. For this purpose the Bank shall, operating on a non-profit-making basis, grant loans and give guarantees which facilitate the financing of the following projects in all sectors of the economy:

(a)   projects for developing less-developed regions;

(b)   projects for modernising or developing undertakings or for developing fresh activities called for by the progressive establishment of the common market, where these projects are of such a size or nature that they cannot be entirely financed by the various means available in the individual Member States;

(c)   projects of common interest to several Member States which are of such a size or nature that they cannot be entirely financed by the various means available in the individual Member States.

In carrying out its task, the Bank shall facilitate the financing of investment programmes in conjunction with assistance from the structural Funds and other Community financial instruments.

TITLE II

FINANCIAL PROVISIONS

ARTICLE **268** (ex Article 199)
All items of revenue and expenditure of the Community, including those relating to the European Social Fund, shall be included in estimates to be drawn up for each financial year and shall be shown in the budget.
Administrative expenditure occasioned for the institutions by the provisions of the Treaty on European Union relating to common foreign and security policy and to co-operation in the fields of justice and home affairs shall be charged to the budget. The operational expenditure occasioned by the implementation of the said provisions may, under the conditions referred to therein, be charged to the budget.
The revenue and expenditure shown in the budget shall be in balance.

[ARTICLE 200 repealed by the Maastricht Treaty.]

ARTICLE **269** (ex Article 201)
Without prejudice to other revenue, the budget shall be financed wholly from own resources.
The Council, acting unanimously on a proposal from the Commission and after consulting the European Parliament, shall lay down provisions relating to the system of own resources of the Community, which it shall recommend to the Member States for adoption in accordance with their respective constitutional requirements.

ARTICLE **270** (ex Article 201 a)
With a view to maintaining budgetary discipline, the Commission shall not make any proposal for a Community act, or alter its proposals, or adopt any implementing measure which is likely to have appreciable implications for the budget without providing the assurance that that proposal or that measure is capable of being financed within the limit of the Community's own resources arising under provisions laid down by the Council pursuant to Article **269**.

ARTICLE **271** (ex Article 202)
The expenditure shown in the budget shall be authorised for one financial year, unless the regulations made pursuant to Article **279** provide otherwise.
In accordance with conditions to be laid down pursuant to Article **279**, any appropriations, other than those relating to staff expenditure, that are unexpended at the end of the financial year may be carried forward to the next financial year only.
Appropriations shall be classified under different chapters grouping items of expenditure according to their nature or purpose and sub-divided, as far as may be necessary, in accordance with the regulations made pursuant to Article **279**.
The expenditure of the European Parliament, the Council, the Commission and the Court of Justice shall be set out in separate parts of the budget, without prejudice to special arrangements for certain common items of expenditure.

ARTICLE **272** (ex Article 203)
1.   The financial year shall run from 1 January to 31 December.

2.   Each institution of the Community shall, before 1 July, draw up estimates of its expenditure. The Commission shall consolidate these estimates in a preliminary draft budget. It shall attach thereto an opinion which may contain different estimates.
The preliminary draft budget shall contain an estimate of revenue and an estimate of expenditure.

3.   The Commission shall place the preliminary draft budget before the Council not later than 1 September of the year preceding that in which the budget is to be implemented.
The Council shall consult the Commission and, where appropriate, the other institutions concerned whenever it intends to depart from the preliminary draft budget.
The Council, acting by a qualified majority, shall establish the draft budget and forward it to the European Parliament.

4.   The draft budget shall be placed before the European Parliament not later than 5 October of the year preceding that in which the budget is to be implemented.

The European Parliament shall have the right to amend the draft budget, acting by a majority of its Members, and to propose to the Council, acting by an absolute majority of the votes cast, modifications to the draft budget relating to expenditure necessarily resulting from this Treaty or from acts adopted in accordance therewith.

If, within 45 days of the draft budget being placed before it, the European Parliament has given its approval, the budget shall stand as finally adopted. If within this period the European Parliament has not amended the draft budget nor proposed any modifications thereto, the budget shall be deemed to be finally adopted.

If within this period the European Parliament has adopted amendments or proposed modifications, the draft budget together with the amendments or proposed modifications shall be forwarded to the Council.

5.   After discussing the draft budget with the Commission and, where appropriate, with the other institutions concerned, the Council shall act under the following conditions:

(a)   The Council may, acting by a qualified majority, modify any of the amendments adopted by the European Parliament;

(b)   With regard to the proposed modifications:

-    where a modification proposed by the European Parliament does not have the effect of increasing the total amount of the expenditure of an institution, owing in particular to the fact that the increase in expenditure which it would involve would be expressly compensated by one or more proposed modifications correspondingly reducing expenditure, the Council may, acting by a qualified majority, reject the proposed modification. In the absence of a decision to reject it, the proposed modification shall stand as accepted;

-    where a modification proposed by the European Parliament has the effect of increasing the total amount of the expenditure of an institution, the Council may, acting by a qualified majority, accept this proposed modification. In the absence of a decision to accept it, the proposed modification shall stand as rejected;

-    where, in pursuance of one of the two preceding sub-paragraphs, the Council has rejected a proposed modification, it may, acting by a qualified majority, either retain the amount shown in the draft budget or fix another amount.

The draft budget shall be modified on the basis of the proposed modifications accepted by the Council.

If, within 15 days of the draft being placed before it, the Council has not modified any of the amendments adopted by the European Parliament and if the modifications proposed by the latter have been accepted, the budget shall be deemed to be finally adopted. The Council shall inform the European Parliament that it has not modified any of the amendments and that the proposed modifications have been accepted.

If within this period the Council has modified one or more of the amendments adopted by the European Parliament or if the modifications proposed by the latter have been rejected or modified, the modified draft budget shall again be forwarded to the European Parliament. The Council shall inform the European Parliament of the results of its deliberations.

6.   Within 15 days of the draft budget being placed before it, the European Parliament, which shall have been notified of the action taken on its proposed modifications, may, acting by a majority of its Members and three-fifths of the votes cast, amend or reject the modifications to its amendments made by the Council and shall adopt the budget accordingly. If within this period the European Parliament has not acted, the budget shall be deemed to be finally adopted.

7.   When the procedure provided for in this Article has been completed, the President of the European Parliament shall declare that the budget has been finally adopted.

8.   However, the European Parliament, acting by a majority of its Members and two-thirds of the votes cast, may, if there are important reasons, reject the draft budget and ask for a new draft to be submitted to it.

9.   A maximum rate of increase in relation to the expenditure of the same type to be incurred during the current year shall be fixed annually for the total expenditure other than that necessarily resulting from this Treaty or from acts adopted in accordance therewith.

The Commission shall, after consulting the Economic Policy Committee, declare what this maximum rate is as it results from:

-    the trend, in terms of volume, of the gross national product within the Community;

-    the average variation in the budgets of the Member States;

and

-    the trend of the cost of living during the preceding financial year.

The maximum rate shall be communicated, before 1 May, to all the institutions of the Community. The latter shall be required to conform to this during the budgetary procedure, subject to the provisions of the fourth and fifth sub-paragraphs of this paragraph.

If, in respect of expenditure other than that necessarily resulting from this Treaty or from acts adopted in accordance therewith, the actual rate of increase in the draft budget, established by the Council is over half the maximum rate, the European Parliament may, exercising its right of amendment, further increase the total amount of that expenditure to a limit not exceeding half the maximum rate.

Where the European Parliament, the Council or the Commission consider that the activities of the Communities require that the rate determined according to the procedure laid down in this paragraph should be exceeded, another rate may be fixed by agreement between the Council, acting by a qualified majority, and the European Parliament, acting by a majority of its Members and three-fifths of the votes cast.

10.   Each institution shall exercise the powers conferred upon it by this Article, with due regard for the provisions of the Treaty and for acts adopted in accordance therewith, in particular those relating to the Communities' own resources and to the balance between revenue and expenditure.

ARTICLE 273 (ex Article 204)

If at the beginning of a financial year, the budget has not yet been voted, a sum equivalent to not more than one-twelfth of the budget appropriations for the preceding financial year may be spent each month in respect of any chapter or other sub-division of the budget in accordance with the provisions of the Regulations made pursuant to Article 279; this arrangement shall not, however, have the effect of placing at the disposal of the Commission appropriations in excess of one-twelfth of those provided for in the draft budget in course of preparation.

The Council may, acting by a qualified majority, provided that the other conditions laid down in the first sub-paragraph are observed, authorise expenditure in excess of one-twelfth.

If the decision relates to expenditure which does not necessarily result from this Treaty or from acts adopted in accordance therewith, the Council shall forward it immediately to the European Parliament; within 30 days the European Parliament, acting by a majority of its Members and three-fifths of the votes cast, may adopt a different decision on the expenditure in excess of the one-twelfth referred to in the first sub-paragraph. This part of the decision by the Council shall be suspended until the European Parliament has taken its decision. If within the said period the European Parliament has not taken a decision which differs from the decision of the Council, the latter shall be deemed to be finally adopted.

The decisions referred to in the second and third sub-paragraphs shall lay down the necessary measures relating to resources to ensure application of this Article.

ARTICLE 274 (ex Article 205)

The Commission shall implement the budget, in accordance with the provisions of the regulations made pursuant to Article 279, on its own responsibility and within the limits of the appropriations, having regard to the principles of sound financial management. **Member States shall co-operate with the Commission to ensure that the appropriations are used in accordance with the principles of sound financial management.**

The regulations shall lay down detailed rules for each institution concerning its part in effecting its own expenditure.

Within the budget, the Commission may, subject to the limits and conditions laid down in the regulations made pursuant to Article 279, transfer appropriations from one chapter to another or from one sub-division to another.

ARTICLE 275 (ex Article 205 a)

The Commission shall submit annually to the Council and to the European Parliament the accounts of the preceding financial year relating to the implementation of the budget. The Commission shall also forward to them a financial statement of the assets and liabilities of the Community.

ARTICLE 276 (ex Article 206)

1.   The European Parliament, acting on a recommendation from the Council which shall act by a qualified majority, shall give a discharge to the Commission in respect of the implementation of the budget. To this end, the Council and the European Parliament in turn shall examine the accounts and the financial statement referred to in Article 275, the annual report by the Court of Auditors together with the replies of the institutions under audit to the observations of the Court of Auditors, **the statement of assurance referred to in Article 248(1), second sub-paragraph** and any relevant special reports by the Court of Auditors.

2.   Before giving a discharge to the Commission, or for any other purpose in connection with the exercise of its powers over the implementation of the budget, the European Parliament may ask to hear the Commission give evidence with regard to the execution of expenditure or the operation of financial control systems. The Commission shall submit any necessary information to the European Parliament at the latter's request.

3.   The Commission shall take all appropriate steps to act on the observations in the decisions giving discharge and on other observations by the European Parliament relating to the execution of expenditure, as well as on comments accompanying the recommendations on discharge adopted by the Council.

At the request of the European Parliament or the Council, the Commission shall report on the measures taken in the light of these observations and comments and in particular on the instructions given to the departments which are responsible for the implementation of the budget. These reports shall also be forwarded to the Court of Auditors.

[ARTICLES 206 a and 206 b repealed by the Maastricht Treaty.]

ARTICLE **277** (ex Article 207)

The budget shall be drawn up in the unit of account determined in accordance with the provisions of the regulations made pursuant to Article **279**.

Second, third, fourth and fifth paragraphs shall be deleted.

ARTICLE **278** (ex Article 208)

The Commission may, provided it notifies the competent authorities of the Member States concerned, transfer into the currency of one of the Member States its holdings in the currency of another Member State, to the extent necessary to enable them to be used for purposes which come within the scope of this Treaty. The Commission shall as far as possible avoid making such transfers if it possesses cash or liquid assets in the currencies which it needs.

The Commission shall deal with each Member State through the authority designated by the State concerned. In carrying out financial operations the Commission shall employ the services of the bank of issue of the Member State concerned or of any other financial institution approved by that State.

ARTICLE **279** (ex Article 209)

The Council, acting unanimously on a proposal from the Commission and after consulting the European Parliament and obtaining the opinion of the Court of Auditors, shall:

(a)   make Financial Regulations specifying in particular the procedure to be adopted for establishing and implementing the budget and for presenting and auditing accounts;

(b)   determine the methods and procedure whereby the budget revenue provided under the arrangements relating to the Community's own resources shall be made available to the Commission, and determine the measures to be applied, if need be, to meet cash requirements;

(c)   lay down rules concerning the responsibility of financial controllers, authorising officers and accounting officers, and concerning appropriate arrangements for inspection.

ARTICLE 280 (ex Article **209 a**)

1.   The Community and the Member States shall counter fraud and any other illegal activities affecting the financial interests of the Community through measures to be taken in accordance with this Article, which shall act as a deterrent and be such as to afford effective protection in the Member States.

2.   Member States shall take the same measures to counter fraud affecting the financial interests of the Community as they take to counter fraud affecting their own financial interests.

3.   Without prejudice to other provisions of this Treaty, the Member States shall co-ordinate their action aimed at protecting the financial interests of the Community against fraud. To this end they shall organise, together with the Commission, close and regular co-operation between the competent **authorities.**

4.   The Council, acting in accordance with the procedure referred to in Article 251, after consulting the Court of Auditors, shall adopt the necessary measures in the fields of the prevention of and fight against fraud affecting the financial interests of the Community with a view to affording effective and equivalent protection in the Member States. These measures shall not concern the application of national criminal law and the national administration of justice.

5.   The Commission, in co-operation with Member States, shall each year submit to the Council and to the European Parliament a report on the measures taken for the implementation of this Article.

PART SIX

GENERAL AND FINAL PROVISIONS

ARTICLE **281** (ex Article 210)
The Community shall have legal personality.

ARTICLE **282** (ex Article 211)
In each of the Member States, the Community shall enjoy the most extensive legal capacity accorded to legal persons under their laws; it may, in particular, acquire or dispose of movable and immovable property and may be a party to legal proceedings. To this end, the Community shall be represented by the Commission.

ARTICLE **283** (ex Article 212)
The Council shall, acting by a qualified majority on a proposal from the Commission and after consulting the other institutions concerned, lay down the Staff Regulations of officials of the European Communities and the Conditions of Employment of other servants of those Communities.

ARTICLE **284** (ex Article 213)
The Commission may, within the limits and under conditions laid down by the Council in accordance with the provisions of this Treaty, collect any information and carry out any checks required for the performance of the tasks entrusted to it.

ARTICLE **285** (ex Article **213 a**)
1. Without prejudice to Article 5 of the Protocol on the Statute of the European System of Central Banks and of the European Central Bank, the Council, acting in accordance with the procedure referred to in Article 251, shall adopt measures for the production of statistics where necessary for the performance of the activities of the Community.

2. The production of Community statistics shall conform to impartiality, reliability, objectivity, scientific independence, cost-effectiveness and statistical confidentiality; it shall not entail excessive burdens on economic operators.

ARTICLE **286** (ex Article **213 b**)
1. From 1 January 1999, Community acts on the protection of individuals with regard to the processing of personal data and the free movement of such data shall apply to the institutions and bodies set up by, or on the basis of, this Treaty.

2. Before the date referred to in paragraph 1, the Council, acting in accordance with the procedure referred to in Article 251, shall establish an independent supervisory body responsible for monitoring the application of such Community acts to Community institutions and bodies and shall adopt any other relevant provisions as appropriate.

ARTICLE **287** (ex Article 214)
The members of the institutions of the Community, the members of committees, and the officials and other servants of the Community shall be required, even after their duties have ceased, not to disclose information of the kind covered by the obligation of professional secrecy, in particular information about undertakings, their business relations or their cost components.

ARTICLE **288** (ex Article 215)
The contractual liability of the Community shall be governed by the law applicable to the contract in question.
In the case of non-contractual liability, the Community shall, in accordance with the general principles common to the laws of the Member States, make good any damage caused by its institutions or by its servants in the performance of their duties.
The preceding paragraph shall apply under the same conditions to damage caused by the ECB or by its servants in the performance of their duties.
The personal liability of its servants towards the Community shall be governed by the provisions laid down in their Staff Regulations or in the Conditions of Employment applicable to them.

ARTICLE **289** (ex Article 216)
The seat of the institutions of the Community shall be determined by common accord of the Governments of the Member States.

ARTICLE **290** (ex Article 217)
The rules governing the languages of the institutions of the Community shall, without prejudice to the provisions contained in the rules of procedure of the Court of Justice, be determined by the Council, acting unanimously.

ARTICLE **291** (ex Article 218)
The Community shall enjoy in the territories of the Member States such privileges and immunities as are necessary for the performance of their tasks, under the conditions laid down in the Protocol of 8 April 1965 on the privileges and immunities of the European Communities. The same shall apply to the European Central Bank, the European Monetary institute and the European Investment Bank.

ARTICLE **292** (ex Article 219)
Member States undertake not to submit a dispute concerning the interpretation of this Treaty to any method of settlement other than those provided for therein.

ARTICLE **293** (ex Article 220)
Member States shall, so far as is necessary, enter into negotiations with each other with a view to securing for the benefit of their nationals:
- the protection of persons and the enjoyment and protection of rights under the same conditions as those accorded by each State to its own nationals;
- the abolition of double taxation within the Community;
- the mutual recognition of companies or firms within the meaning of the second paragraph of Article **48**, the retention of legal personality in the event of transfer of their seat from one country to another, and the possibility of mergers between companies or firms governed by the laws of different countries;
- the simplification of formalities governing the reciprocal recognition and enforcement of judgements of courts or tribunals and of arbitration awards.

ARTICLE **294** (ex Article 221)
Member States shall accord nationals of the other Member States the same treatment as their own nationals as regards participation in the capital of companies or firms within the meaning of Article **48**, without prejudice to the application of the other provisions of this Treaty.

ARTICLE **295** (ex Article 222)
This Treaty shall in no way prejudice the rules in Member States governing the system of property ownership.

ARTICLE **296** (ex Article 223)
1.   The provisions of this Treaty shall not preclude the application of the following rules:
(a)   No Member State shall be obliged to supply information the disclosure of which it considers contrary to the essential interests of its security;
(b)   Any Member State may take such measures as it considers necessary for the protection of the essential interests of its security which are connected with the production of or trade in arms, munitions and war material; such measures shall not adversely affect the conditions of competition in the common market regarding products which are not intended for specifically military purposes.

2.   **The Council may, acting unanimously on a proposal from the Commission, make changes to the list which it drew up on 15 April 1958, of the** products to which the provisions of paragraph 1(b) **apply.**

ARTICLE **297** (ex Article 224)
Member States shall consult each other with a view to taking together the steps needed to prevent the functioning of the common market being affected by measures which a Member State may be called upon to take in the event of serious internal disturbances affecting the maintenance of law and order, in the event of war, serious international tension constituting a threat of war, or in order to carry out obligations it has accepted for the purpose of maintaining peace and international security.

ARTICLE **298** (ex Article 225)
If measures taken in the circumstances referred to in Articles **296** and **297** have the effect of distorting the conditions of competition in the common market, the Commission shall, together with the State concerned, examine how these measures can be adjusted to the rules laid down in this Treaty.
By way of derogation from the procedure laid down in Articles **226** and **227**, the Commission or any Member State may bring the matter directly before the Court of Justice if it considers that another Member State is making improper use of the powers provided for in Articles **296** and **297**. The Court of Justice shall give its ruling *in camera.*

ARTICLE 226 shall be repealed.

ARTICLE **299** (ex Article 227)

1. This Treaty shall apply to the Kingdom of Belgium, the Kingdom of Denmark, the Federal Republic of Germany, the Hellenic Republic, the Kingdom of Spain, the French Republic, Ireland, the Italian Republic, the Grand Duchy of Luxembourg, the Kingdom of the Netherlands, **the Republic of Austria**, the Portuguese Republic, **the Republic of Finland**, **the Kingdom of Sweden** and the United Kingdom of Great Britain and Northern Ireland.

2. The provisions of the Treaty establishing the European Community shall apply to the French overseas departments, the Azores, Madeira and the Canary Islands.

However, taking account of the structural social and economic situation of the French overseas departments, the Azores, Madeira and the Canary Islands, which is compounded by their remoteness, insularity, small size, difficult topography and climate, economic dependence on a few products, the permanence and combination of which severely restrain their development, the Council, acting by a qualified majority on a proposal from the Commission and after consulting the European Parliament, shall adopt specific measures aimed, in particular, at laying down the conditions of application of the present Treaty to those regions, including common policies.

The Council shall, when adopting the relevant measures referred to in the previous subparagraph, take into account areas such as customs and trade policies, fiscal policy, free zones, agriculture and fisheries policies, conditions for supply of raw materials and essential consumer goods, State aids and conditions of access to structural funds and to horizontal Community programmes.

The Council shall adopt the measures referred to in the second sub-paragraph taking into account the special characteristics and constraints of the outermost regions without undermining the integrity and the coherence of the Community legal order, including the internal market and common policies.

3. The special arrangements for association set out in Part Four of this Treaty shall apply to the overseas countries and territories listed in **Annex II** to this Treaty.

This Treaty shall not apply to those overseas countries and territories having special relations with the United Kingdom of Great Britain and Northern Ireland which are not included in the afore-mentioned list.

4. The provisions of this Treaty shall apply to the European territories for whose external relations a Member State is responsible.

5. The provisions of this Treaty shall apply to the Åland Islands in accordance with the provisions set out in Protocol No. 2 to the Act concerning the conditions of accession of the Republic of Austria, the Republic of Finland and the Kingdom of Sweden.

6. Notwithstanding the preceding paragraphs:

(a) This Treaty shall not apply to the Faeroe Islands;

(b) This Treaty shall not apply to the Sovereign Base Areas of the United Kingdom of Great Britain and Northern Ireland in Cyprus;

(c) This Treaty shall apply to the Channel Islands and the Isle of Man only to the extent necessary to ensure the implementation of the arrangements for those islands set out in the Treaty concerning the accession of new Member States to the European Economic Community and to the European Atomic Energy Community signed on 22 January 1972.

ARTICLE **300** (ex Article 228)

1. Where this Treaty provides for the conclusion of agreements between the Community and one or more States or international organisations, the Commission shall make recommendations to the Council, which shall authorise the Commission to open the necessary negotiations. The Commission shall conduct these negotiations in consultation with special committees appointed by the Council to assist it in this task and within the framework of such directives as the Council may issue to it.

In exercising the powers conferred upon it by this paragraph, the Council shall act by a qualified majority, except in the cases provided **where the first sub-paragraph** of paragraph 2 **provides that the Council** shall act unanimously.

2. Subject to the powers vested in the Commission in this field, **the signing, which may be accompanied by a decision on provisional application before entry into force, and the conclusion of the agreements shall be decided on by the Council, acting by a qualified majority on a proposal from the Commission.** The Council shall act unanimously when the agreement covers a field for which unanimity is required for the adoption of internal rules and for the agreements referred to in Article **310**.

By way of derogation from the rules laid down in paragraph 3, the same procedure shall apply for a decision to suspend the application of an international agreement, and for the purpose of establishing the position to be adopted on behalf of the Community in a body set up by an agreement based on Article 310, when that body is called upon to adopt decisions having legal effects, with the exception of decisions supplementing or amending the institutional framework of the agreement.

The European Parliament shall be immediately and fully informed on any decision under this paragraph concerning the provisional application or the suspension of agreements, or the establishment of the Community position in a body set up by an agreement based on Article 310.

3. The Council shall conclude agreements after consulting the European Parliament, except for the agreements referred to in Article **133**(3), including cases where the agreement covers a field for which the procedure referred to in Article **251** or that referred to in Article **252** is required for the adoption of internal rules. The European Parliament shall deliver its opinion within a time-limit which the Council may lay down according to the urgency of the matter. In the absence of an opinion within that time-limit, the Council may act.

By way of derogation from the previous sub-paragraph, agreements referred to in Article **310**, other agreements establishing a specific institutional framework by organising co-operation procedures, agreements having important budgetary implications for the Community and agreements entailing amendment of an act adopted under the procedure referred to in Article **251** shall be concluded after the assent of the European Parliament has been obtained.

The Council and the European Parliament may, in an urgent situation, agree upon a time-limit for the assent.

4. When concluding an agreement, the Council may, by way of derogation from paragraph 2, authorise the Commission to approve modifications on behalf of the Community where the agreement provides for them to be adopted by a simplified procedure or by a body set up by the agreement; it may attach specific conditions to such authorisation.

5. When the Council envisages concluding an agreement which calls for amendments to this Treaty, the amendments must first be adopted in accordance with the procedure laid down in Article **48** of the Treaty on European Union.

6. The Council, the Commission or a Member State may obtain the opinion of the Court of Justice as to whether an agreement envisaged is compatible with the provisions of this Treaty. Where the opinion of the Court of Justice is adverse, the agreement may enter into force only in accordance with Article **48** of the Treaty on European Union.

7. Agreements concluded under the conditions set out in this Article shall be binding on the institutions of the Community and on Member States.

ARTICLE **301** (ex Article 228 a)
Where it is provided, in a common position or in a joint action adopted according to the provisions of the Treaty on European Union relating to the common foreign and security policy, for an action by the Community to interrupt or to reduce, in part or completely, economic relations with one or more third countries, the Council shall take the necessary urgent measures. The Council shall act by a qualified majority on a proposal from the Commission.

ARTICLE **302** (ex Article 229)
It shall be for the Commission to ensure the maintenance of all appropriate relations with the organs of the United Nations **and** of its specialised agencies. *Remainder of sentence to be deleted.*
The Commission shall also maintain such relations as are appropriate with all international organisations.

ARTICLE **303** (ex Article 230)
The Community shall establish all appropriate forms of co-operation with the Council of Europe.

ARTICLE **304** (ex Article 231)
The Community shall establish close co-operation with the Organisation for Economic Co-operation and Development, the details to be determined by common accord.

ARTICLE **305** (ex Article 232)
1. The provisions of this Treaty shall not affect the provisions of the Treaty establishing the European Coal and Steel Community, in particular as regards the rights and obligations of Member States, the powers of the institutions of that Community and the rules laid down by that Treaty for the functioning of the common market in coal and steel.

2.   The provisions of this Treaty shall not derogate from those of the Treaty establishing the European Atomic Energy Community.

ARTICLE 306   (ex Article 233)
The provisions of this Treaty shall not preclude the existence or completion of regional unions between Belgium and Luxembourg, or between Belgium, Luxembourg and the Netherlands, to the extent that the objectives of these regional unions are not attained by application of this Treaty.

ARTICLE 307   (ex Article 234)
The rights and obligations arising from agreements concluded before **1 January 1958 or, for acceding States, before the date of their accession,** between one or more Member States on the one hand, and one or more third countries on the other, shall not be affected by the provisions of this Treaty.

To the extent that such agreements are not compatible with this Treaty, that Member State or States concerned shall take all appropriate steps to eliminate the incompatibilities established. Member States shall, where necessary, assist each other to this end and shall, where appropriate, adopt a common attitude.

In applying the agreements referred to in the first paragraph, Member States shall take into account the fact that the advantages accorded under this Treaty by each Member State form an integral part of the establishment of the Community and are thereby inseparably linked with the creation of common institutions, the conferring of powers upon them and the granting of the same advantages by all the other Member States.

ARTICLE 308   (ex Article 235)
If action by the Community should prove necessary to attain, in the course of the operation of the common market, one of the objectives of the Community and this Treaty has not provided the necessary powers, the Council shall, acting unanimously on a proposal from the Commission and after consulting the European Parliament, take the appropriate measures.

ARTICLE 309   (ex Article 236)
1.   Where a decision has been taken to suspend voting rights of a Member State in accordance with Article 7(2) of the Treaty on European Union, these voting rights shall also be suspended with regard to this Treaty.

2.   Moreover, and where the existence of a serious and persistent breach by a Member State of the principles mentioned in Article 6(1) of the Treaty on European Union has been determined in accordance with Article 7(1) of that Treaty, the Council, acting by a qualified majority, may decide to suspend certain of the rights deriving from the application of this Treaty to the State in question. In doing so, the Council shall take into account the possible consequences of such a suspension on the rights and obligations of natural and legal persons.
The obligations of the Member State in question under this Treaty shall in any case continue to be binding on that State.

3.   The Council, acting by a qualified majority, may decide subsequently to vary or revoke measures taken in accordance with paragraph 2 in response to changes in the situation which led to their being imposed.

4.   When taking decisions referred to in paragraphs 2 and 3, the Council shall act without taking into account the votes of the representative of the Member State in question. By way of derogation from Article 205(2), a qualified majority shall be defined as the same proportion of the weighted votes of the members of the Council concerned as laid down in Article 205(2).
The provisions of this paragraph shall also apply in the event of voting rights being suspended in accordance with paragraph 1. In such cases, a decision requiring unanimity shall be taken without the vote of the representative of the Member State in question.

[ARTICLE 237 repealed by the Maastricht Treaty.]

ARTICLE 310   (ex Article 238)
The Community may conclude with one or more States or international organisations agreements establishing an association involving reciprocal rights and obligations, common action and special procedures.

ARTICLE 311   (ex Article 239)
The Protocols annexed to this Treaty by common accord of the Member States shall form an integral part thereof.

ARTICLE **312** (ex Article 240)
This Treaty is concluded for an unlimited period.

HEADING ('Setting up of the institutions') shall be deleted.

ARTICLES 241 to 246 shall be repealed.

FINAL PROVISIONS

ARTICLE **313** (ex Article 247)
This Treaty shall be ratified by the High Contracting Parties in accordance with their respective constitutional requirements. The instruments of ratification shall be deposited with the Government of the Italian Republic.
This Treaty shall enter into force on the first day of the month following the deposit of the instrument of ratification by the last signatory State to take this step. If, however, such deposit is made less than fifteen days before the beginning of the following month, this Treaty shall not enter into force until the first day of the second month after the date of such deposit.

ARTICLE **314** (ex Article 248)
This Treaty, drawn up in a single original in the Dutch, French, German and Italian languages, all four texts being equally authentic, shall be deposited in the archives of the Government of the Italian Republic, which shall transmit a certified copy to each of the Governments of the other signatory States.
Pursuant to the Accession Treaties, the Danish, English, Finnish, Greek, Irish, Portuguese, Spanish and Swedish versions of this Treaty shall also be authentic.

IN WITNESS WHEREOF, the Plenipotentiaries have signed this Treaty.

Done in Rome, this twenty-fifth day of March in the year one thousand nine hundred and fifty seven.

* * * * * *

ANNEXES TO THE TREATY

There are two annexes to the Treaty establishing the European Community. These are are referred to in the text of Title II. For the sake of brevity, these lists have not been included and a summary of these lists follows.

ANNEX I   List referred to in Article **32** (ex Article 38).

This list consists of animal and vegetable produce.

ANNEX II   Overseas Countries and Territories to which the provisions of Part IV of the Treaty apply.

*This relates in particular to Article **299** and the list includes Greenland, British Indian Ocean Territory, British Antarctic Territory, French Southern and Antarctic Territories, Pitcairn, British Virgin Islands, Burmuda, Cayman Islands and the Falkland Islands.*

Under the Treaty of Amsterdam, the number of Annexes has been reduced from four to two. The Annexes concerning the tariff headings and the rates of duty (old Annex I) and the list of invisible trade (old Annex III) have been deleted.

PROTOCOLS

*The Protocols highlighted in **bold** have been introduced by the Treaty of Amsterdam.*

98

Protocol annexed to the Treaties establishing the European Community, the European Coal and Steel Community and the European Atomic Energy Community

* * * * * * *

PROTOCOL ANNEXED TO THE TREATY ON EUROPEAN UNION

1. **PROTOCOL ON ARTICLE 17 OF THE TREATY ON EUROPEAN UNION**

THE HIGH CONTRACTING PARTIES,

BEARING IN MIND the need to implement fully the provisions of Article 17(1), second sub-paragraph, and (3) of the Treaty on European Union,

BEARING IN MIND that the policy of the Union in accordance with Article 17 shall not prejudice the specific character of the security and defence policy of certain Member States and shall respect the obligations of certain Member States, which see their common defence realised in NATO, under the North Atlantic Treaty and be compatible with the common security and defence policy established within that framework,

HAVE AGREED UPON the following provision, which shall be annexed to the Treaty on European Union:

The European Union shall draw up, together with the Western European Union, arrangements for enhanced co-operation between them, within a year from the entry into force of the Treaty of Amsterdam.

* * * * * * *

PROTOCOLS ANNEXED TO THE TREATY ON EUROPEAN UNION AND TO THE TREATY ESTABLISHING THE EUROPEAN COMMUNITY

2. PROTOCOL INTEGRATING THE SCHENGEN *ACQUIS* INTO THE FRAMEWORK OF THE EUROPEAN UNION

THE HIGH CONTRACTING PARTIES,

NOTING that the Agreements on the gradual abolition of checks at common borders signed by some Member States of the European Union in Schengen on 14 June 1985 and on 19 June 1990, as well as related agreements and the rules adopted on the basis of these agreements, are aimed at enhancing European integration and, in particular, at enabling the European Union to develop more rapidly into an area of freedom, security and justice,

DESIRING to incorporate the above-mentioned agreements and rules into the framework of the European Union,

CONFIRMING that the provisions of the Schengen *acquis* are applicable only if and as far as they are compatible with the Union and Community law,

TAKING INTO ACCOUNT the special position of Denmark,

TAKING INTO ACCOUNT the fact that Ireland and the United Kingdom of Great Britain and Northern Ireland are not parties to and have not signed the above-mentioned agreements; that provision should, however, be made to allow those Member States to accept some or all of the provisions thereof,

RECOGNISING that, as a consequence, it is necessary to make use of the provisions of the Treaty on European Union and of the Treaty establishing the European Community concerning closer co-operation between some Member States and that those provisions should only be used as a last resort,

TAKING INTO ACCOUNT the need to maintain a special relationship with the Republic of Iceland and the Kingdom of Norway, both States which have confirmed their intention to become bound by the provisions mentioned above, on the basis of the Agreement signed in Luxembourg on 19 December 1996,

HAVE AGREED UPON the following provisions, which shall be annexed to the Treaty on European Union and to the Treaty establishing the European Community:

ARTICLE 1
The Kingdom of Belgium, the Kingdom of Denmark, the Federal Republic of Germany, the Hellenic Republic, the Kingdom of Spain, the French Republic, the Italian Republic, the Grand Duchy of Luxembourg, the Kingdom of the Netherlands, the Republic of Austria, the Portuguese Republic, the Republic of Finland and the Kingdom of Sweden, signatories to the Schengen agreements, are authorised to establish closer co-operation among themselves within the scope of those agreements and related provisions, as they are listed in the Annex to this Protocol, hereinafter referred to as the "Schengen *acquis*". This co-operation shall be conducted within the institutional and legal framework of the European Union and with respect for the relevant provisions of the Treaty on European Union and of the Treaty establishing the European Community.

ARTICLE 2

1.   From the date of entry into force of the Treaty of Amsterdam, the Schengen *acquis*, including the decisions of the Executive Committee established by the Schengen agreements which have been adopted before this date, shall immediately apply to the thirteen Member States referred to in Article 1, without prejudice to the provisions of paragraph 2 of this Article. From the same date, the Council will substitute itself for the said Executive Committee.

The Council, acting by the unanimity of its Members referred to in Article 1, shall take any measure necessary for the implementation of this paragraph. The Council, acting unanimously, shall determine, in conformity with the relevant provisions of the Treaties, the legal basis for each of the provisions or decisions which constitute the Schengen *acquis*.

With regard to such provisions and decisions and in accordance with that determination, the Court of Justice of the European Communities shall exercise the powers conferred upon it by the relevant applicable provisions of the Treaties. In any event, the Court of Justice shall have no jurisdiction on measures or decisions relating to the maintenance of law and order and the safeguarding of internal security.

As long as the measures referred to above have not been taken and without prejudice to Article 5(2), the provisions or decisions which constitute the Schengen *acquis* shall be regarded as acts based on Title VI of the Treaty on European Union.

2.   The provisions of paragraph 1 shall apply to the Member States which have signed accession protocols to the Schengen agreements from the dates decided by the Council, acting with the unanimity of its Members mentioned in Article 1, unless the conditions for the accession of any of those States to the Schengen *acquis* are met before the date of the entry into force of the Treaty of Amsterdam.

ARTICLE 3

Following the determination referred to in Article 2(1), second sub-paragraph, Denmark shall maintain the same rights and obligations in relation to the other signatories to the Schengen agreements, as before the said determination with regard to those parts of the Schengen *acquis* that are determined to have legal basis in Title IV of the Treaty establishing the European Community.

With regard to those parts of the Schengen *acquis* that are determined to have legal base in Title VI of the Treaty on European Union, Denmark shall continue to have the same rights and obligations as the other signatories to the Schengen agreements.

ARTICLE 4

Ireland and the United Kingdom of Great Britain and Northern Ireland, which are not bound by the Schengen *acquis*, may at any time request to take part in some or all of the provisions of this *acquis*.

The Council shall decide on the request with the unanimity if its members referred to in Article 1 and of the representative of the Government of the State concerned.

ARTICLE 5

1.   Proposals and initiatives to build upon the Schengen *acquis* shall be subject to the relevant provisions of the Treaties.

In this context, where either Ireland or the United Kingdom or both have not notified the President of the Council in writing within a reasonable period that they wish to take part, the authorisation referred to in Article 11 of the Treaty establishing the European Community or Article 40 of the Treaty on European Union shall be deemed to have been granted to the Members States referred to in Article 1 and to Ireland or the United Kingdom where either of them wishes to take part in the areas of co-operation in question.

2.   The relevant provisions of the Treaties referred to in the first sub-paragraph of paragraph 1 shall apply even if the Council has not adopted the measures referred to in Article 2(1), second sub-paragraph.

ARTICLE 6
The Republic of Iceland and the Kingdom of Norway shall be associated with the implementation of the Schengen *acquis* and its further development on the basis of the Agreement signed in Luxembourg on 19 December 1996. Appropriate procedures shall be agreed to that effect in an Agreement to be concluded with those States by the Council, acting by the unanimity of its Members mentioned in Article 1. Such Agreement shall include provisions on the contribution of Iceland and Norway to any financial consequences resulting from the implementation of this Protocol.
A separate Agreement shall be concluded with Iceland and Norway by the Council, acting unanimously, for the establishment of rights and obligations between Ireland and the United Kingdom of Great Britain and Northern Ireland on the one hand, and Iceland and Norway on the other, in domains of the Schengen *acquis* which apply to these States.

ARTICLE 7
The Council shall, acting by a qualified majority, adopt the detailed arrangements for the integration of the Schengen Secretariat into the General Secretariat of the Council.

ARTICLE 8
For the purposes of the negotiations for the admission of new Member States into the European Union, the Schengen *acquis* and further measures taken by the institutions within its scope shall be regarded as an *acquis* which must be accepted in full by all States candidates for admission.

ANNEX

SCHENGEN *ACQUIS*

1.   The Agreement, signed in Schengen on 14 June 1985, between the Governments of the States of the Benelux Economic Union, the Federal Republic of Germany and the French Republic on the gradual abolition of checks at their common borders.

2.   The Convention, signed in Schengen on 19 June 1990, between the Kingdom of Belgium, the Federal Republic of Germany, the French Republic, the Grand Duchy of Luxembourg and the Kingdom of Netherlands, implementing the Agreement on the gradual abolition of checks at their common borders, signed in Schengen on 14 June 1985, with related Final Act and common declarations.

3.   The Accession Protocols and Agreements to the 1985 Agreement and the 1990 Implementation Convention with Italy (signed in Paris on 27 November 1990), Spain and Portugal (both signed in Bonn on 25 June 1991), Greece (signed in Madrid on 6 November 1992), Austria (signed in Brussels on 28 April 1995) and Denmark, Finland and Sweden (all signed in Luxembourg on 19 December 1996), with related Final Acts and declarations.

4.   Decisions and declarations adopted by the Executive Committee established by the 1990 Implementation Convention, as well as acts adopted for the implementation of the Convention by the organs upon which the Executive Committee has conferred decision-making powers.

3.   **PROTOCOL ON THE APPLICATION OF CERTAIN ASPECTS OF ARTICLE 14 OF THE TREATY ESTABLISHING THE EUROPEAN COMMUNITY TO THE UNITED KINGDOM AND TO IRELAND**

THE HIGH CONTRACTING PARTIES,

DESIRING to settle certain questions relating to the United Kingdom and Ireland,

HAVING REGARD to the existence for many years of special travel arrangements between the United Kingdom and Ireland,

HAVE AGREED UPON the following provisions, which shall be annexed to the Treaty establishing the European Community and to the Treaty on European Union:

ARTICLE 1
The United Kingdom shall be entitled, notwithstanding Article 14 of the Treaty establishing the European Community, any other provision of this Treaty or of the Treaty on European Union, any measure adopted under those Treaties, or any international agreement concluded by the Community or by the Community and its Member States with one or more third States, to exercise at its frontiers with other Member States such controls on persons seeking to enter the United Kingdom as it may consider necessary for the purpose:
(a)   of verifying the right to enter the United Kingdom of citizens of States which are Contracting Parties to the Agreement on the European Economic Area and of their dependants exercising rights conferred by Community law, as well as citizens of other States on whom such rights have been conferred by an agreement to which the United Kingdom is bound; and
(b)   of determining whether or not to grant other persons permission to enter the United Kingdom.
Nothing in Article 14 of the Treaty establishing the European Community or in any other provision of that Treaty or the Treaty on European Union or in any measure adopted under them shall prejudice the right of the United Kingdom to adopt or exercise any such controls. References to the United Kingdom in this Article shall include territories for whose external relations the United Kingdom is responsible.

ARTICLE 2
The United Kingdom and Ireland may continue to make arrangements between themselves relating to the movement of persons between their territories ("the Common Travel Area"), while fully respecting the rights of persons referred to in Article 1, first paragraph, point (a) of this Protocol. Accordingly, as long as they maintain such arrangements, the provisions of Article 1 of this Protocol shall apply to Ireland with the same terms and conditions as for the United Kingdom. Nothing in Article 14 of the Treaty establishing the European Community, in any other provision of that Treaty or of the Treaty on European Union or in any measure adopted under them, shall affect any such arrangements.

ARTICLE 3
The other Member States shall be entitled to exercise at their frontiers or at any point of entry into their territory such controls on persons seeking to enter their territory from the United Kingdom or any territories whose external relations are under its responsibility for the same purposes stated in Article 1 of this Protocol, or from Ireland as long as the provisions of Article 1 of this Protocol apply to Ireland.

Nothing in Article 14 of the Treaty establishing the European Community or in any other provision of that Treaty or of the Treaty on European Union or in any measure adopted under them shall prejudice the right of the other Member States to adopt or exercise any such controls.

4. PROTOCOL ON THE POSITION OF THE UNITED KINGDOM AND IRELAND

THE HIGH CONTRACTING PARTIES,

DESIRING to settle certain questions relating to the United Kingdom and Ireland,

HAVING REGARD to the Protocol on the application of certain aspects of Article 14 of the Treaty establishing the European Community to the United Kingdom and to Ireland,

HAVE AGREED UPON the following provisions which shall be annexed to the Treaty establishing the European Community and to the Treaty on European Union:

ARTICLE 1
Subject to Article 3, the United Kingdom and Ireland shall not take part in the adoption by the Council of proposed measures pursuant to Title IV of the Treaty establishing the European Community. By way of derogation from Article 205(2) of the Treaty establishing the European Community, a qualified majority shall be defined as the same proportion of the weighted votes of the members of the Council concerned as laid down in the said Article 205(2). The unanimity of the members of the Council, with the exception of the representatives of the governments of the United Kingdom and Ireland, shall be necessary for decisions of the Council which must be adopted unanimously.

ARTICLE 2
In consequence of Article 1 and subject to Articles 3, 4 and 6, none of the provisions of Title IV of the Treaty establishing the European Community, no measure adopted pursuant to that Title, no provision of any international agreement concluded by the Community pursuant to that Title, and no decision of the Court of Justice interpreting any such provision or measure shall be binding upon or applicable in the United Kingdom or Ireland; and no such provision, measure or decision shall in any way affect the competences, rights and obligations of those States; and no such provision, measure or decision shall in any way affect the *acquis communautaire* nor form part of Community law as they apply to the United Kingdom or Ireland.

ARTICLE 3
1.   The United Kingdom or Ireland may notify the President of the Council in writing, within three months after a proposal or initiative has been presented to the Council pursuant to Title IV of the Treaty establishing the European Community, that it wishes to take part in the adoption and application of any such proposed measure, whereupon that State shall be entitled to do so. By way of derogation from Article 205(2) of the Treaty establishing the European Community, a qualified majority shall be defined as the same proportion of the weighted votes of the members of the Council concerned as laid down in the said Article 205(2).
The unanimity of the members of the Council, with the exception of a member which has not made such a notification, shall be necessary for decisions of the Council which must be adopted unanimously. A measure adopted under this paragraph shall be binding upon all Member States which took part in its adoption.

2.   If after a reasonable period of time a measure referred to in paragraph 1 cannot be adopted with the United Kingdom or Ireland taking part, the Council may adopt such measure in accordance with Article 1 without the participation of the United Kingdom or Ireland. In that case Article 2 applies.

ARTICLE 4

The United Kingdom or Ireland may at any time after the adoption of a measure by the Council pursuant to Title IV of the Treaty establishing the European Community notify its intention to the Council and to the Commission that it wishes to accept that measure. In that case, the procedure provided for in Article 11(3) of the Treaty establishing the European Community shall apply *mutatis mutandis*.

ARTICLE 5

A Member State which is not bound by a measure adopted pursuant to Title IV of the Treaty establishing the European Community shall bear no financial consequences of that measure other than administrative costs entailed for the institutions.

ARTICLE 6

Where, in cases referred to in this Protocol, the United Kingdom or Ireland is bound by a measure adopted by the Council pursuant to Title IV of the Treaty establishing the European Community, the relevant provisions of that Treaty, including Article 68, shall apply to that State in relation to that measure.

ARTICLE 7

Articles 3 and 4 shall be without prejudice to the Protocol integrating the Schengen *acquis* into the framework of the European Union.

ARTICLE 8

Ireland may notify the President of the Council in writing that it no longer wishes to be covered by the terms of this Protocol. In that case, the normal Treaty provisions will apply to Ireland.

5.   PROTOCOL ON THE POSITION OF DENMARK

THE HIGH CONTRACTING PARTIES,

RECALLING the Decision of the Heads of State or Government, meeting within the European Council at Edinburgh on 12 December 1992, concerning certain problems raised by Denmark on the Treaty on European Union,

HAVING NOTED the position of Denmark with regard to Citizenship, Economic and Monetary Union, Defence Policy and Justice and Home Affairs as laid down in the Edinburgh Decision,

BEARING IN MIND Article 3 of the Protocol integrating the Schengen *acquis* into the framework of the European Union,

HAVE AGREED UPON the following provisions, which shall be annexed to the Treaty establishing the European Community and to the Treaty on European Union:

PART I

ARTICLE 1

Denmark shall not take part in the adoption by the Council of proposed measures pursuant to Title IV of the Treaty establishing the European Community. By way of derogation from Article 205(2) of the Treaty establishing the European Community, a qualified majority shall be defined as the same proportion of the weighted votes of the members of the Council concerned as laid down in the said Article 205(2). The unanimity of the members of the Council, with the exception of the representative of the government of Denmark, shall be necessary for the decisions of the Council which must be adopted unanimously.

ARTICLE 2
None of the provisions of Title IV of the Treaty establishing the European Community, no measure adopted pursuant to that Title, no provision of any international agreement concluded by the Community pursuant to that Title, and no decision of the Court of Justice interpreting any such provision or measure shall be binding upon or applicable in Denmark; and no such provision, measure or decision shall in any way affect the competences, rights and obligations of Denmark; and no such provision, measure or decision shall in any way affect the *acquis communautaire* nor form part of Community law as they apply to Denmark.

ARTICLE 3
Denmark shall bear no financial consequences of measures referred to in Article 1, other than administrative costs entailed for the institutions.

ARTICLE 4
Articles 1, 2 and 3 shall not apply to measures determining the third countries whose nationals must be in possession of a visa when crossing the external borders of the Member States, or measures relating to a uniform format for visas.

ARTICLE 5
1.   Denmark shall decide within a period of 6 months after the Council has decided on a proposal or initiative to build upon the Schengen *acquis* under the provisions of Title IV of the Treaty establishing the European Community, whether it will implement this decision in its national law. If it decides to do so, this decision will create an obligation under international law between Denmark and the other Member States referred to in Article 1 of the Protocol integrating the Schengen *acquis* into the framework of the European Union as well as with Ireland or the United Kingdom if those Member States take part in the areas of co-operation in question.

2.   If Denmark decides not to implement a decision of the Council as referred to in paragraph 1, the Member States referred to in Article 1 of the Protocol integrating the Schengen *acquis* into the framework of the European Union will consider appropriate measures to be taken.

PART II

ARTICLE 6
With regard to measures adopted by the Council in the field of Articles 13(1) and 17 of the Treaty on European Union, Denmark does not participate in the elaboration and the implementation of decisions and actions of the Union which have defence implications, but will not prevent the development of closer co-operation between Member States in this area. Therefore Denmark shall not participate in their adoption. Denmark shall not be obliged to contribute to the financing of operational expenditure arising from such measures.

PART III

ARTICLE 7
At any time Denmark may, in accordance with its constitutional requirements, inform other Member States that it no longer wishes to avail itself of all or part of this Protocol. In that event, Denmark will apply in full all relevant measures then in force taken within the framework of the European Union.

* * * * * * *

PROTOCOLS ANNEXED TO
THE TREATY ON EUROPEAN UNION AND TO THE TREATIES
ESTABLISHING THE EUROPEAN COMMUNITY, THE EUROPEAN COAL
AND STEEL COMMUNITY AND THE EUROPEAN ATOMIC ENERGY
COMMUNITY

6.   PROTOCOL ANNEXED TO THE TREATY ON EUROPEAN UNION AND TO THE TREATIES ESTABLISHING THE EUROPEAN COMMUNITIES

THE HIGH CONTRACTING PARTIES,

HAVE AGREED upon the following provision, which shall be annexed to the Treaty on European Union and to the Treaties establishing the European Communities:

Nothing in the Treaty on European Union, or in the Treaties establishing the European Communities, or in the Treaties or Acts modifying or supplementing those Treaties, shall affect the application in Ireland of Article 40.3.3. of the Constitution of Ireland.
(This protocol was introduced by the Maastricht Treaty.)

Declaration of 1 May 1992

On 1 May 1992, in Guimarães (Portugal), the High Contracting Parties to the Treaty on European Union adopted the following Declaration:

DECLARATION
OF THE HIGH CONTRACTING PARTIES
TO THE TREATY ON EUROPEAN UNION

The High Contracting Parties to the Treaty on European Union signed at Maastricht on the seventh day of February 1992,

Having considered the terms of Protocol No. **6** to the said Treaty on European Union which is annexed to that Treaty and to the Treaties establishing the European Communities,

Hereby give the following legal interpretation:

That it was and is their intention that the Protocol shall not limit freedom to travel between Member States or, in accordance with conditions which may be laid down, in conformity with Community law, by Irish legislation, to obtain or make available in Ireland information relating to services lawfully available in Member States.
At the same time the High Contracting Parties solemnly declare that, in the event of a future constitutional amendment in Ireland which concerns the subject matter of Article 40.3.3 of the Constitution of Ireland and which does not conflict with the intention of the High Contracting Parties herein before expressed, they will, following the entry into force of the Treaty on European Union, be favourably disposed to amending the said Protocol so as to extend its application to such constitutional amendment if Ireland so requests.

7. PROTOCOL ON THE INSTITUTIONS WITH THE PROSPECT OF ENLARGEMENT OF THE EUROPEAN UNION

THE HIGH CONTRACTING PARTIES,

HAVE AGREED UPON the following provisions, which shall be annexed to the Treaty on European Union and to the Treaties establishing the European Communities:

ARTICLE 1
At the date of entry into force of the first enlargement of the Union, notwithstanding Article 207(1) of the Treaty establishing the European Community, Article 9(1) of the Treaty establishing the European Coal and Steel Community and Article 126(1) of the Treaty establishing the European Atomic Energy Community, the Commission shall comprise one national of each of the Member States, provided that, by that date, the weighting of the votes in the Council has been modified, whether by reweighting of the votes or by dual majority, in a manner acceptable to all Member States, taking into account all relevant elements, notably compensating those Member States which give up the possibility of nominating a second member of the Commission.

ARTICLE 2
At least one year before the membership of the European Union exceeds twenty, a conference of representatives of the governments of Member States shall be convened in order to carry out a comprehensive review of the provisions of the Treaties on the composition and functioning of the institutions.

8. PROTOCOL ON THE LOCATION OF THE SEATS OF THE INSTITUTIONS AND OF CERTAIN BODIES AND DEPARTMENTS OF THE EUROPEAN COMMUNITIES AND OF EUROPOL

THE REPRESENTATIVES OF THE GOVERNMENTS OF THE MEMBER STATES,

HAVING REGARD to Article 289 of the Treaty establishing the European Community, Article 77 of the Treaty establishing the European Coal and Steel Community and Article 189 of the Treaty establishing the European Atomic Energy Community,

HAVING REGARD to the Treaty on European Union,

RECALLING AND CONFIRMING the Decision of 8 April 1965, and without prejudice to the decisions concerning the seat of future institutions, bodies and departments,

HAVE AGREED UPON the following provisions, which shall be annexed to the Treaty on European Union and the Treaties establishing the European Communities,

SOLE ARTICLE
(a) The European Parliament shall have its seat in Strasbourg where the 12 periods of monthly plenary sessions, including the budget session, shall be held. The periods of additional plenary sessions shall be held in Brussels. The committees of the European Parliament shall meet in Brussels. The General Secretariat of the European Parliament and its departments shall remain in Luxembourg.
(b) The Council shall have its seat in Brussels. During the months of April, June and October, the Council shall hold its meetings in Luxembourg.
(c) The Commission shall have its seat in Brussels. The departments listed in Articles 7, 8 and 9 of the Decision of 8 April 1965 shall be established in Luxembourg.
(d) The Court of Justice and the Court of First Instance shall have their seats in Luxembourg.
(e) The Court of Auditors shall have its seat in Luxembourg.
(f) The Economic and Social Committee shall have its seat in Brussels.
(g) The Committee of the Regions shall have its seat in Brussels.
(h) The European Investment Bank shall have its seat in Luxembourg.
(i) The European Monetary Institute and the European Central Bank shall have their seat in Frankfurt.
(j) The European Police Office (Europol) shall have its seat in The Hague.

9. PROTOCOL ON THE ROLE OF NATIONAL PARLIAMENTS IN THE EUROPEAN UNION

THE HIGH CONTRACTING PARTIES,

RECALLING that scrutiny by individual national parliaments of their own government in relation to the activities of the Union is a matter for the particular constitutional organisation and practice of each Member State,

DESIRING, however, to encourage greater involvement of national parliaments in the activities of the European Union and to enhance their ability to express their views on matters which may be of particular interest to them,

HAVE AGREED UPON the following provisions, which shall be annexed to the Treaty on European Union and the Treaties establishing the European Communities:

I.   Information for national Parliaments of Member States

1.   All Commission consultation documents (green and white papers and communications) shall be promptly forwarded to national parliaments of the Member States.

2.   Commission proposals for legislation as defined by the Council in accordance with Article 207(3) of the Treaty establishing the European Community, shall be made available in good time so that the Government of each Member State may ensure that its own national parliament receives them as appropriate.

3.   A six-week period shall elapse between a legislative proposal or a proposal for a measure to be adopted under Title VI of the Treaty on European Union being made available in all languages to the European Parliament and the Council by the Commission and the date when it is placed on a Council agenda for decision either for the adoption of an act or for adoption of a common position pursuant to Article 251 or 252 of the Treaty establishing the European Community, subject to exceptions on grounds of urgency, the reasons for which shall be stated in the act or common position.

II.   The Conference of European Affairs Committees

4.   The Conference of European Affairs Committees, hereinafter referred to as COSAC, established in Paris on 16-17 November 1989, may make any contribution it deems appropriate for the attention of the institutions of the European Union, in particular on the basis of draft legal texts which representatives of governments of the Member States may decide by common accord to forward to it, in view of the nature of their subject matter.

5.   COSAC may examine any legislative proposal or initiative in relation to the establishment of an area of freedom, security and justice which might have a direct bearing on the rights and freedoms of individuals. The European Parliament, the Council and the Commission shall be informed of any contribution made by COSAC under this point.

6.   COSAC may address to the European Parliament, the Council and the Commission any contribution which it deems appropriate on the legislative activities of the Union, notably in relation to the application of the principle of subsidiarity, the area of freedom, security and justice as well as questions regarding fundamental rights.

7.   Contributions made by COSAC shall in no way bind national parliaments or prejudge their position.

* * * * * * *

PROTOCOLS ANNEXED TO
THE TREATY ESTABLISHING THE EUROPEAN COMMUNITY

10. PROTOCOL ON THE STATUTE OF THE EUROPEAN INVESTMENT BANK

The High Contracting Parties, desiring to lay down the Statute of the European Investment Bank provided for in Article **266** of this Treaty, have agreed upon the following provisions, which shall be annexed to this Treaty:

ARTICLE 1
The European Investment Bank established by Article **266** of this Treaty (hereinafter called the 'Bank') is hereby constituted; it shall perform its functions and carry on its activities in accordance with the provisions of this Treaty and of this Statute.
The seat of the Bank shall be determined by common accord of the Governments of the Member States.

ARTICLE 2
The task of the Bank shall be that defined in Article **267** of this Treaty.

ARTICLE 3
In accordance with Article **266** of this Treaty, the following shall be members of the Bank:
- the Kingdom of Belgium;
- the Kingdom of Denmark;
- the Federal Republic of Germany;
- the Hellenic Republic;
- the Kingdom of Spain;
- the French Republic;
- Ireland;
- the Italian Republic;
- the Grand Duchy of Luxembourg;
- the Kingdom of the Netherlands;
- the Republic of Austria;
- the Portuguese Republic;
- the Republic of Finland;
- the Kingdom of Sweden;
- the United Kingdom of Great Britain and Northern Ireland.

ARTICLE 4
1.   The capital of the Bank shall be 62,013 million ECU, subscribed by the Member States as follows:
Germany, France, Italy and United Kingdom: 11,017,450,000; Spain: 4,049,856,000; Belgium and Netherlands: 3,053,960,000; Sweden: 2,026,000,000; Denmark: 1,546,308,000; Austria: 1,516,000,000; Finland: 871,000,000; Greece: 828,380,000; Portugal: 533,844,000; Ireland: 386,576,000; Luxembourg: 77,316,000.
The unit of account shall be defined as being the ECU used by the European Communities. The Board of Governors, acting unanimously on a proposal from the Board of Directors, may alter the definition of the unit of account.
The Member States shall be liable only up to the amount of their share of the capital subscribed and not paid up.

2.   The admission of a new member shall entail an increase in the subscribed capital corresponding to the capital brought in by the new member.

3.   The Board of Governors may, acting unanimously, decide to increase the subscribed capital.

4.   The share of a member in the subscribed capital may not be transferred, pledged or attached.

ARTICLE 5
1.   The subscribed capital shall be paid in by Member States to the extent of 7.50162895 per cent on average of the amounts laid down in Article 4(1).

2.   In the event of an increase in the subscribed capital, the Board of Governors, acting unanimously, shall fix the percentage to be paid up and the arrangements for payment.

3.   The Board of Directors may require payment of the balance of the subscribed capital, to such extent as may be required for the Bank to meet its obligations towards those who have made loans to it.

Each Member State shall make this payment in proportion to its share of the subscribed capital in the currencies required by the Bank to meet these obligations.

ARTICLE 6

1.   The Board of Governors may, acting by a qualified majority on a proposal from the Board of Directors, decide that Member States shall grant the Bank special interest bearing loans if and to the extent that the Bank requires such loans to finance specific projects and the Board of Directors shows that the Bank is unable to obtain the necessary funds on the capital markets on terms appropriate to the nature and purpose of the projects to be financed.

2.   Special loans may not be called for until the beginning of the fourth year after the entry into force of this Treaty. They shall not exceed 400 million units of account in the aggregate or 100 million units of account per annum.

3.   The term of special loans shall be related to the term of the loans or guarantees which the Bank proposes to grant by means of the special loans; it shall not exceed twenty years. The Board of Governors may, acting by a qualified majority on a proposal from the Board of Directors, decide upon the prior repayment of special loans.

4.   Special loans shall bear interest at 4 per cent per annum, unless the Board of Governors, taking into account the trend and level of interest rates on the capital markets, decides to fix a different rate.

5.   Special loans shall be granted by Member States in proportion to their share in the subscribed capital; payment shall be made in national currency within six months of such loans being called for.

6.   Should the Bank go into liquidation, special loans granted by Member States shall be repaid only after the other debts of the Bank have been settled.

ARTICLE 7

1.   Should the value of the currency of a Member State in relation to the unit of account defined in Article 4 be reduced, that State shall adjust the amount of its capital share paid in its own currency in proportion to the change in value by making a supplementary payment to the Bank.

2.   Should the value of the currency of a Member State in relation to the unit of account defined in Article 4 be increased, the bank shall adjust the amount of the capital share paid in by that State in its own currency in proportion to the change in value by making a repayment to that State.

3.   For the purpose of this Article, the value of the currency of a Member State in relation to the unit of account, defined in Article 4, shall correspond to the rate for converting the unit of account into this currency and vice versa based on market rates.

4.   The Board of Governors, acting unanimously on a proposal from the Board of Directors, may alter the method of converting sums expressed in units of account into national currencies and vice versa.

Furthermore, acting unanimously on a proposal from the Board of Directors, it may define the method for adjusting the capital referred to in paragraphs 1 and 2 of this Article; adjustment payments must be made at least once a year.

ARTICLE 8

The Bank shall be directed and managed by a Board of Governors, a Board of Directors and a Management Committee.

ARTICLE 9

1.   The Board of Governors shall consist of the Ministers designated by the Member States.

2.   The Board of Governors shall lay down general directives for the credit policy of the Bank, with particular reference to the objectives to be pursued as progress is made in the attainment of the common market.

The Board of Governors shall ensure that these directives are implemented.

3.   The Board of Governors shall in addition:
    (a)   decide whether to increase the subscribed capital in accordance with Article 4(3) and Article 5(2);
    (b)   exercise the powers provided in Article 6 in respect of special loans;
    (c)   exercise the powers provided in Articles 11 and 13 in respect of the appointment and the compulsory retirement of the members of the Board of Directors and of the Management Committee, and those powers provided in the second sub-paragraph of Article 13(1);

(d)   authorise the derogation provided for in Article 18(1);

(e)   approve the annual report of the Board of Directors;

(f)   approve the annual balance sheet and profit and loss account;

(g)   exercise the powers and functions provided in Articles 4, 7, 14, 17, 26 and 27;

(h)   approve the rules of procedure of the Bank.

4.   Where the framework of this Treaty and this Statute the Board of Governors shall be competent to take, acting unanimously, any decisions concerning the suspension of the operations of the Bank and, should the event arise, its liquidation.

ARTICLE 10

Save as otherwise provided for in this Statute, decisions of the Board of Governors shall be taken by a majority of its members. This majority must represent at least 50 per cent of the subscribed capital. Voting by the Board of Governors shall be in accordance with the provisions of Article **205** of this Treaty.

ARTICLE 11

1.   The Board of Directors shall have sole power to take decisions in respect of granting loans and guarantees and raising loans; it shall fix the interest rates on loans granted and the commission on guarantees; it shall see that the Bank is properly run; it shall ensure that the Bank is managed in accordance with the provisions of this Treaty and of this Statute and with the general directives laid down by the Board of Governors.

At the end of the financial year the Board of Directors shall submit a report to the Board of Governors and shall publish it when approved.

2.   The Board of Directors shall consist of 25 directors and 13 alternates.

The directors shall be appointed by the Board of Governors for five years as shown below:

- three directors nominated by the Federal Republic of Germany,
- three directors nominated by the French Republic,
- three directors nominated by the Italian Republic,
- three directors nominated by the United Kingdom of Great Britain and Northern Ireland,
- two directors nominated by the Kingdom of Spain,
- one director nominated by the Kingdom of Belgium,
- one director nominated by the Kingdom of Denmark,
- one director nominated by the Hellenic Republic,
- one director nominated by Ireland,
- one director nominated by the Grand Duchy of Luxembourg,
- one director nominated by the Kingdom of the Netherlands,
- one director nominated by the Republic of Austria,
- one director nominated by the Portuguese Republic,
- one director nominated by the Republic of Finland,
- one director nominated by the Kingdom of Sweden,
- one director nominated by the Commission.

The alternates shall be appointed by the Board of Governors for five years as shown below:

- two alternates nominated by the Federal Republic of Germany,
- two alternates nominated by the French Republic,
- two alternates nominated by the Italian Republic,
- two alternates nominated by the United Kingdom of Great Britain and Northern Ireland,
- one alternate nominated by common accord of the Kingdom of Spain and the Portuguese Republic,
- one alternate nominated by common accord of the Benelux countries,
- one alternate nominated by common accord of the Kingdom of Denmark, the Hellenic Republic and Ireland,
- one alternate nominated by common accord of the Republic of Austria, the Republic of Finland and the Kingdom of Sweden,
- one alternate nominated by the Commission.

The appointments of the directors and the alternates shall be renewable.

Alternates may take part in the meetings of the Board of Directors. Alternates nominated by a State, or by common accord of several States, or by the Commission, may replace directors nominated by that State, by one of those States or by the Commission respectively. Alternates shall have no right of vote except where they replace one director or more than one director or where they have been delegated for this purpose in accordance with Article 12(1).

The President of the Management Committee or, in his absence, one of the Vice-Presidents, shall preside over meetings of the Board of Directors but shall not vote.

Members of the Board of Directors shall be chosen from persons whose independence and competence are beyond doubt; they shall be responsible only to the Bank.

3.   A director may be compulsorily retired by the Board of Governors only if he no longer fulfils the conditions required for the performance of his duties; the Board must act by a qualified majority.
If the annual report is not approved, the Board of Directors shall resign.

4.   Any vacancy arising as a result of death, voluntary resignation, compulsory retirement or collective resignation shall be filled in accordance with paragraph 2. A member shall be replaced for the remainder of his term of office, save where the entire Board of Directors is being replaced.

5.   The Board of Governors shall determine the remuneration of members of the Board of Directors. The Board of Governors shall, acting unanimously, lay down what activities are incompatible with the duties of a director or an alternate.

ARTICLE 12
1.   Each director shall have one vote on the Board of Directors. He may delegate his vote in all cases, according to procedures to be laid down in the rules of procedure of the Bank.

2.   Save as otherwise provided in this Statute, decisions of the Board of Directors shall be taken by a simple majority of the members entitled to vote. A qualified majority shall require seventeen votes in favour. The rules of procedure of the Bank shall lay down how many members of the Board of Directors constitute a quorum for the needed for the adoption of decisions.

ARTICLE 13
1.   The Management Committee shall consist of a President and six Vice-Presidents appointed for a period of six years by the Board of Governors on a proposal from the Board of Directors. These appointments shall be renewable.
The Board of Governors, acting unanimously, may vary the number of members on the Management Committee.

2.   On a proposal from the Board of Directors adopted by a qualified majority, the Board of Governors may, acting in its turn by a qualified majority, compulsorily retire a member of the Management Committee.

3.   The Management Committee shall be responsible for the current business of the Bank, under the authority of the President and the supervision of the Board of Directors.
It shall prepare the decisions of the Board of Directors, in particular decisions on the raising of loans and the granting of loans and guarantees; it shall ensure that these decisions are implemented.

4.   The Management Committee shall act by a majority when delivering opinions on proposals for raising loans or granting loans and guarantees.

5.   The Board of Governors shall determine the remuneration of members of the Management Committee and shall lay down what activities are incompatible with their duties.

6.   The President or, if he is prevented, a Vice-President shall represent the Bank in judicial and other matters.

7.   The officials and other employees of the Bank shall be under the authority of the President. They shall be engaged and discharged by him. In the selection of staff, account shall be taken not only of personal ability and qualifications but also of an equitable representation of nationals of Member States.

8.   The Management Committee and the staff of the Bank shall be responsible only to the Bank and shall be completely independent in the performance of their duties.

ARTICLE 14
1.   A Committee consisting of three members, appointed on the grounds of their competence by the Board of Governors, shall annually verify that the operations of the Bank have been conducted and its books kept in a proper manner.

2.   The Committee shall confirm that the balance sheet and profit and loss account are in agreement with the accounts and faithfully reflect the position of the Bank in respect of its assets and liabilities.

ARTICLE 15
The Bank shall deal with each Member State through the authority designated by that State. In the conduct of financial operations the Bank shall have recourse to the bank of issue of the Member State concerned or to other financial institutions approved by that State.

ARTICLE 16

1.   The Bank shall co-operate with all international organisations active in fields similar to its own.

2.   The Bank shall seek to establish all appropriate contacts in the interests of co-operation with banking and financial institutions in the countries to which its operations extend.

ARTICLE 17

At the request of a Member State or of the Commission, or on its own initiative, the Board of Governors shall, in accordance with the same provisions as governed their adoption, interpret or supplement the directives laid down by it under Article 9 of this Statute.

ARTICLE 18

1.   Within the framework of the task set out in Article **267** of this Treaty, the Bank shall grant loans to its members or to private or public undertakings for investment projects to be carried out in the European territories of Member States, to the extent that funds are not available from other sources on reasonable terms. However, by way of derogation authorised by the Board of Governors, acting unanimously on a proposal from the Board of Directors, the Bank may grant loans for investment projects to be carried out, in whole or in part, outside the European territories of Member States.

2.   As far as possible, loans shall be granted only on condition that other sources of finance are also used.

3.   When granting a loan to an undertaking or to a body other than a Member State, the Bank shall make the loan conditional either on a guarantee from the Member State in whose territory the project will be carried out or on other adequate guarantees.

4.   The Bank may guarantee loans contracted by public or private undertakings or other bodies for the purpose of carrying out projects provided for in Article **267** of this Treaty.

5.   The aggregate amount outstanding at any time of loans and guarantees granted by the Bank shall not exceed 250 per cent of its subscribed capital.

6.   The Bank shall protect itself against exchange risks by including in contracts for loans and guarantees such clauses as it considers appropriate

ARTICLE 19

1.   Interest rates on loans to be granted by the Bank and Commission on guarantees shall be adjusted to conditions prevailing on the capital market and shall be calculated in such a way that the income therefrom shall enable the Bank to meet its obligations, to cover its expenses and to build up a reserve fund as provided for in Article 24.

2.   The Bank shall not grant any reduction in interest rates. Where a reduction in the interest rate appears desirable in view of the nature of the project to be financed, the Member State concerned or some other agency may grant aid towards the payment of interest to the extent that this is compatible with Article **86** of this Treaty.

ARTICLE 20

In its loan and guarantee operations, the Bank shall observe the following principles:
1.   It shall ensure that its funds are employed as rationally as possible in the interests of the Community.
It may grant loans or guarantees only:
  (a)   where, in the case of projects carried out by undertakings in the production sector, interest and amortisation payments are covered out of operating profits, or, in other cases, either by a commitment entered into by the State in which the project is carried out or by some other means; and
  (b)   where the execution of the project contributes to an increase in economic productivity in general and promotes the attainment of the common market.

2.   It shall neither acquire any interest in an undertaking nor assume any responsibility in its management unless this is required to safeguard the rights of the Bank in ensuring recovery of funds lent.

3.   It may dispose of its claims on the capital market and may, to this end, require its debtors to issue bonds or other securities.

4.   Neither the Bank nor the Member States shall impose conditions requiring funds lent by the Bank to be spent within a specified Member State.

5.   The Bank may make its loans conditional on international invitations to tender being arranged.

6.   The Bank shall not finance, in whole or in part, any project opposed by the Member State in whose territory it is to be carried out.

ARTICLE 21

1.   Applications for loans or guarantees may be made to the Bank either through the Commission or through the Member State in whose territory the project will be carried out. An undertaking may also apply direct to the Bank for a loan or guarantee.

2.   Applications made through the Commission shall be submitted for an opinion to the Member State in whose territory the project will be carried out. Applications made through a Member State shall be submitted to the Commission for an opinion. Applications made direct by an undertaking shall be submitted to the Member State concerned and to the Commission.

The Member State concerned and the Commission shall deliver their opinions within two months. If no reply is received within this period, the Bank may assume that there is no objection to the project in question.

3.   The Board of Directors shall rule on applications for loans or guarantees submitted to it by the Management Committee.

4.   The Management Committee shall examine whether applications for loans or guarantees submitted to it comply with the provisions of this Statute, in particular with Article 20. Where the Management Committee is in favour of granting the loan or guarantee, it shall submit the draft contract to the Board of Directors; the Committee may make its favourable opinion subject to such conditions as it considers essential. Where the Management Committee is against granting the loan or guarantee, it shall submit the relevant documents together with its opinion to the Board of Directors.

5.   Where the Management Committee delivers an unfavourable opinion, the Board of Directors may not grant the loan or guarantee concerned unless its decision is unanimous.

6.   Where the Commission delivers an unfavourable opinion, the Board of Directors may not grant the loan or guarantee concerned unless its decision is unanimous, the director nominated by the Commission abstaining.

7.   Where both the Management Committee and the Commission deliver an unfavourable opinion, the Board of Directors may not grant the loan or guarantee.

ARTICLE 22

1.   The Bank shall borrow on the international capital markets the funds necessary for the performance of its tasks.

2.   The Bank may borrow on the capital market of a Member State either in accordance with the legal provisions applying to internal issues or, if there are no such provisions in a Member State, after the Bank and the Member State concerned have conferred together and reached agreement on the proposed loan.

The competent authorities in the Member State concerned may refuse to give their assent only if there is reason to fear serious disturbances on the capital market of that State.

ARTICLE 23

1.   The Bank may employ any available funds which it does not immediately require to meet its obligations in the following ways:
    (a)   it may invest on the money markets;
    (b)   it may, subject to the provisions of Article 20(2), buy and sell securities issued by itself or by those who have borrowed from it;
    (c)   it may carry out any other financial operation linked with its objectives.

2.   Without prejudice to the provisions of Article 25, the Bank shall not, in managing its investments, engage in any currency arbitrage not directly required to carry out its lending operations or fulfil commitments arising out of loans raised or guarantees granted by it.

3.   The Bank shall, in the fields covered by this Article, act in agreement with the competent authorities or with the bank of issue of the Member State concerned.

ARTICLE 24

1.   A reserve fund of up to 10 per cent of the subscribed capital shall be built up progressively. If the state of the liabilities of the Bank should so justify, the Board of Directors may decide to set aside additional reserves. Until such time as the reserve fund has been fully built up, it shall be fed by:
    (a)   interest received on loans granted by the Bank out of sums to be paid up by the Member States pursuant to Article 5;

(b) interest received on loans granted by the Bank out of funds derived from repayment of the loans referred to in (a);

to the extent that this income is not required to meet the obligations of the Bank or to cover its expenses.

2. The resources of the reserve fund shall be so invested as to be available at any time to meet the purpose of the fund.

ARTICLE 25

1. The Bank shall at all times be entitled to transfer its assets in the currency of one Member State into the currency of another Member State in order to carry out financial operations corresponding to the task set out in Article **267** of this Treaty, taking into account the provisions of Article 23 of this Statute. The Bank shall, as far as possible, avoid making such transfers if it has cash or liquid assets in the currency required.

2. The Bank may not convert its assets in the currency of a Member State into the currency of a third country without the agreement of the Member State concerned.

3. The Bank may freely dispose of that part of its capital which is paid up in gold or convertible currency and of any currency borrowed on markets outside the Community.

4. The Member States undertake to make available to the debtors of the Bank the currency needed to repay the capital and pay the interest on loans or commission on guarantees granted by the Bank for projects to be carried out in their territory.

ARTICLE 26

If a Member State fails to meet the obligations of membership arising from this Statute, in particular the obligation to pay its share of the subscribed capital, to grant its special loans or to service its borrowings, the granting of loans or guarantees to that Member State or its nationals may be suspended by a decision of the Board of Governors, acting by a qualified majority.

Such decision shall not release either the State or its nationals from their obligations towards the Bank.

ARTICLE 27

1. If the Board of Governors decides to suspend the operations of the Bank, all its activities shall cease forthwith, except those required to ensure the due realisation, protection and preservation of its assets and the settlement of its liabilities.

2. In the event of liquidation, the Board of Governors shall appoint the liquidators and give them instructions for carrying out the liquidation.

ARTICLE 28

1. In each of the Member States, the Bank shall enjoy the most extensive legal capacity accorded to legal persons under their laws; it may, in particular, acquire or dispose of movable or immovable property and may be a party to legal proceedings.

(Second sub-paragraph repealed by the second paragraph of Article 28 of the Merger Treaty)
[See the first paragraph of Article 28 of the Merger Treaty, which reads as follows:
The European Communities shall enjoy in the territories of the Member States such privileges and immunities as are necessary for the performance of their tasks, under the conditions laid down in the Protocol annexed to this Treaty. The same shall apply to the European Investment Bank.]

2. The property of the Bank shall be exempt from all forms of requisition or expropriation.

ARTICLE 29

Disputes between the Bank on the one hand, and its creditors, debtors or any other person on the other, shall be decided by the competent national courts, save where jurisdiction has been conferred on the Court of Justice.

The Bank shall have an address for service in each Member State. It may, however, in any contract, specify a particular address for service or provide for arbitration.

The property and assets of the Bank shall not be liable to attachment or to seizure by way of execution except by decision of a court.

ARTICLE 30

1. The Board of Governors may, acting unanimously, decide to establish a European Investment Fund, which shall have legal personality and financial autonomy, and of which the Bank shall be a founding member.

2.   The Board of Governors shall establish the Statute of the European Investment Fund by unanimous decision. The Statute shall define, in particular, its objectives, structure, capital, membership, financial resources, means of intervention and auditing arrangements, as well as the relationship between the organs of the Bank and those of the Fund.

3.   Notwithstanding the provisions of Article 20(2), the Bank shall be entitled to participate in the management of the Fund and contribute to its subscribed capital up to the amount determined by the Board of Governors acting unanimously.

4.   The European Community may become a member of the Fund and contribute to its subscribed capital. Financial institutions with an interest in the objectives of the Fund may be invited to become members.

5.   The Protocol on the privileges and immunities of the European Communities shall apply to the Fund, to the members of its organs in the performance of their duties as such and to its staff.
The Fund shall in addition be exempt from any form of taxation or imposition of a like nature on the occasion of any increase in its capital and from the various formalities which may be connected therewith in the State where the Fund has its seat. Similarly, its dissolution or liquidation shall not give rise to any imposition. Finally, the activities of the Fund and of its organs carried out in accordance with its statute shall not be subject to any turnover tax.
Those dividends, capital gains or other forms of revenue stemming from the Fund to which the members, other than the European Community and the Bank, are entitled, shall however remain subject to the fiscal provisions of the applicable legislation.

6.   The Court of Justice shall, within the limits hereinafter laid down, have jurisdiction in disputes concerning measures in adopted by organs of the Fund. Proceedings against such measures may be instituted by any member of the Fund in its capacity as such or by Member States under the conditions laid down in Article 230 of this Treaty.

Done at Rome this twenty-fifth day of March in the year one thousand nine hundred and fifty-seven.

11.   PROTOCOL ON THE STATUTE OF THE COURT OF JUSTICE OF THE EUROPEAN COMMUNITY

The High Contracting Parties to the Treaty establishing the European Community, desiring to lay down the Statute of the Court provided for in Article 245 of this Treaty, have agreed upon the following provisions, which shall be annexed to the Treaty establishing the European Community.

ARTICLE 1
The Court established by Article 7 of this Treaty shall be constituted and shall function in accordance with the provisions of this Treaty and of this Statute.

TITLE I

JUDGES AND ADVOCATES-GENERAL

ARTICLE 2
Before taking up his duties each Judge shall, in open court, take an oath to perform his duties impartially and conscientiously and to preserve the secrecy of the deliberations of the Court.

ARTICLE 3
The Judges shall be immune from legal proceedings. After they have ceased to hold office, they shall continue to enjoy immunity in respect of acts performed by them in their official capacity including words spoken or written.
The Court, sitting in plenary session, may waive the immunity.
Where immunity has been waived and criminal proceedings are instituted against a Judge, he shall be tried, in any of the Member States, only by the Court competent to judge the members of the highest national judiciary.

Articles 12 to 15 and 18 of the Protocol on the privileges and immunities of the European Communities shall apply to the Judges, Advocates-General, Registrar and Assistant Rapporteurs of the Court of Justice, without prejudice to the provisions relating to immunity from legal proceedings of Judges which are set out in the preceding paragraphs.

ARTICLE 4

The Judges may not hold any political or administrative office.

They may not engage in any occupation, whether gainful or not, unless exemption is exceptionally granted by the Council.

When taking up their duties, they shall give a solemn undertaking that, both during and after their term of office, they will respect the obligations arising therefrom, in particular the duty to behave with integrity and discretion as regards the acceptance, after they have ceased to hold office, of certain appointments or benefits. Any doubt on this point shall be settled by decision of the Court.

ARTICLE 5

Apart from normal replacement, or death, the duties of a Judge shall end when he resigns.

Where a Judge resigns, his letter of resignation shall be addressed to the President of the Court for transmission to the President of the Council. Upon this notification a vacancy shall arise on the bench.

Save where Article 6 applies, a Judge shall continue to hold office until his successor takes up his duties.

ARTICLE 6

A Judge may be deprived of his office or of his right to a pension or other benefits in its stead only if, in the unanimous opinion of the Judges and Advocates-General of the Court, he no longer fulfils the requisite conditions or meets the obligations arising from his office. The Judge concerned shall not take part in any such deliberations.

The Registrar of the Court shall communicate the decision of the Court to the President of the European Parliament and to the President of the Commission and shall notify it to the President of the Council.

In the case of a decision depriving a Judge of his office, a vacancy shall arise on the bench upon this latter notification.

ARTICLE 7

A Judge who is to replace a member of the Court whose term of office has not expired shall be appointed for the remainder of his predecessor's term.

ARTICLE 8

The provisions of Articles 2 to 7 shall apply to the Advocates-General.

TITLE II

ORGANISATION

ARTICLE 9

The registrar shall take an oath before the Court to perform his duties impartially and conscientiously and to preserve the secrecy of the deliberations of the Court.

ARTICLE 10

The Court shall arrange for replacement of the Registrar on occasions when he is prevented from attending the Court.

ARTICLE 11

Officials and other servants shall be attached to the Court to enable it to function. They shall be responsible to the Registrar under the authority of the President.

ARTICLE 12

On a proposal from the Court, the Council may, acting unanimously, provide for the appointment of Assistant Rapporteurs and lay down the rules governing their service. The Assistant Rapporteurs may be required, under conditions laid down in the rules of procedure, to participate in preparatory inquiries in cases pending before the Court and to co-operate with the Judge who acts as Rapporteur.

The Assistant Rapporteurs shall be chosen from persons whose independence is beyond doubt and who possess the necessary legal qualifications; they shall be appointed by the Council. They shall take an oath before the Court to perform their duties impartially and conscientiously to preserve the secrecy of the deliberations of the Court.

ARTICLE 13

The Judges, the Advocates-General and the Registrar shall be required to reside at the place where the Court has its seat.

ARTICLE 14

The Court shall remain permanently in session. The duration of the judicial vacations shall be determined by the Court with due regard to the needs of its business.

ARTICLE 15

Decisions of the Court shall be valid only when an uneven number of its members is sitting in the deliberations. Decisions of the full Court shall be valid if nine members are sitting. Decisions of the Chambers consisting of three or five Judges shall be valid only if three Judges are sitting. Decisions of the Chambers consisting of seven Judges shall be valid only if five Judges are sitting. In the event of one of the Judges of a Chamber being prevented from attending, a Judge of another Chamber may be called upon to sit in accordance with conditions laid down in the Rules of Procedure.

ARTICLE 16

No Judge or Advocate-General may take part in the disposal of any case in which he has previously taken part as agent or adviser or has acted for one of the parties, or in which he has been called upon to pronounce as a Member of a court or tribunal, of a commission of inquiry or in any other capacity.

If, for some special reason, any Judge or Advocate-General considers that he should not take part in the judgement or examination of a particular case, he shall so inform the President. If, for some special reason, the President considers that any Judge or Advocate-General should not sit or make submissions in a particular case, he shall notify him accordingly.

Any difficulty arising as to the application of this Article shall be settled by decision of the Court.

A party may not apply for a change in the composition of the Court or of one of its Chambers on the grounds of either the nationality of a Judge or the absence from the Court or from the Chamber of a Judge of the nationality of that party.

TITLE III

PROCEDURE

ARTICLE 17

The States and the institutions of the Community shall be represented before the Court by an agent appointed for each case; the agent may be assisted by an adviser or by a lawyer.

The States, other than the Member States, which are parties to the Agreement on the European Economic Area, and also the EFTA Surveillance Authority referred to in that Agreement, shall be represented in same manner.

Other parties must be represented by a lawyer.

Only a lawyer authorised to practise before a court of a Member State or of another State which is a party to the Agreement on the European Economic Area may represent or assist a party before the Court.

Such agents, advisers and lawyers shall, when they appear before the Court, enjoy the rights and immunities necessary to the independent exercise of their duties, under conditions laid down in the rules of procedure.

As regards such advisers and lawyers who appear before it, the Court shall have the powers normally accorded to courts of law, under conditions laid down in the rules of procedure.

University teachers being nationals of a Member State whose law accords them a right of audience shall have the same rights before the Court as are accorded by this Article to lawyers entitled to practise before a court of a Member State.

ARTICLE 18

The procedure before the Court shall consist of two parts: written and oral.

The written procedure shall consist of the communication to the parties and to the institutions of the Community whose decisions are in dispute, of applications, statements of case, defences and observations, and of replies, if any, as well as of all papers and documents in support or of certified copies of them.

Communications shall be made by the Registrar in the order and within the time laid down in the rules of procedure.

The oral procedure shall consist of the reading of the report presented by a Judge acting as Rapporteur, the hearing by the Court of agents, advisers and lawyers entitled to practise before a court of a Member State and of the submissions of the Advocate-General, as well as the hearing, if any, of witnesses and experts.

ARTICLE 19

A case shall be brought before the Court by a written application addressed to the Registrar. The application shall contain the applicant's name and permanent address and the description of the signatory, the name of the party or names of the parties against whom the application is made, the subject-matter of the dispute, the form of order sought and a brief statement of the pleas in law on which the application is based.

The application shall be accompanied, where appropriate, by the measure the annulment of which is sought or, in the circumstances referred to in Article **232** of this Treaty, by documentary evidence of the date on which an institution was, in accordance with that Article, requested to act. If the documents are not submitted with the application, the Registrar shall ask the party concerned to produce them within a reasonable period, but in that event the rights of the party shall not lapse even if such documents are produced after the time limit for bringing proceedings.

ARTICLE 20

In the cases governed by Article **234** of this Treaty, the decision of the court or tribunal of a Member State which suspends its proceedings and refers a case to the Court shall be notified to the Court by the court or tribunal concerned. The decision shall then be notified by the Registrar of the Court to the parties, to the Member States and to the Commission, and also to the Council or to the European Central Bank if the act the validity or interpretation of which is in dispute originates from one of them, and to the European Parliament and the Council if the act the validity or interpretation of which is in dispute was adopted jointly by those two institutions.

Within two months of this notification, the parties, the Member State, the Commission and, where appropriate, the European Parliament, the Council and the European Central Bank, shall be entitled to submit statements of case or written observations to the Court.

The decision of the aforesaid Court or tribunal shall, moreover, be notified by the Registrar of the Court to the States, other than the Member States, which are parties to the Agreement on the European Economic Area and also to the EFTA Surveillance Authority referred to in that Agreement which may, within two months of notification, where one of the fields of application of that Agreement is concerned, submit statements of case or written observations to the Court.

ARTICLE 21

The Court may require the parties to produce all documents and to supply all information which the Court considers desirable. Formal note shall be taken of any refusal.

The Court may also require the Member States and institutions not being parties to the case to supply all information which the Court considers necessary for the proceedings.

ARTICLE 22

The Court may at any time entrust any individual, body authority, committee or other organisation it chooses with the task of giving expert opinion.

ARTICLE 23

Witnesses may be heard under conditions laid down in the rules of procedure.

ARTICLE 24

With respect to defaulting witnesses the Court shall have the powers generally granted to courts and tribunals and may impose pecuniary penalties under conditions laid down in the rules of procedure.

ARTICLE 25

Witnesses and experts may be heard on oath taken in the form laid down in the rules of procedure or in the manner laid down by the law of the country of the witness or expert.

ARTICLE 26

The Court may order that a witness or expert be heard by the judicial authority of his place of permanent residence.

The order shall be sent for implementation to the competent judicial authority under conditions laid down in the rules of procedure. The documents drawn up in compliance with the letters rogatory shall be returned to the Court under the same conditions.

The Court shall defray the expenses, without prejudice to the right to charge them, where appropriate, to the parties.

ARTICLE 27

A Member State shall treat any violation of an oath by a witness or expert in the same manner as if the offence had been committed before one of its courts with jurisdiction in civil proceedings. At the instance of the Court, the Member State concerned shall prosecute the offender before its competent court.

ARTICLE 28

The hearing in court shall be in public, unless the Court, of its own motion or on application by the parties, decides otherwise for serious reasons.

ARTICLE 29

During the hearings the Court may examine the experts, the witnesses and the parties themselves. The latter, however, may address the Court only through their representatives.

ARTICLE 30

Minutes shall be made of each hearing and signed by the President and the Registrar.

ARTICLE 31

The case list shall be established by the President.

ARTICLE 32

The deliberations of the Court shall be and shall remain secret.

ARTICLE 33

Judgements shall state the reasons on which they are based. They shall contain the names of the Judges who took part in the deliberations.

ARTICLE 34

Judgements shall be signed by the President and the Registrar. They shall be read in open court.

ARTICLE 35

The Court shall adjudicate upon costs.

ARTICLE 36

The President of the Court may, by way of summary procedure, which may, in so far as necessary, differ from some of the rules contained in this Statute and which shall be laid down in the rules of procedure, adjudicate upon applications to suspend execution, as provided for in Article **242** of this Treaty, or to prescribe interim measures in pursuance of Article **243**, or to suspend enforcement in accordance with the last paragraph of Article **256**.

Should the President be prevented from attending, his place shall be taken by another Judge under conditions laid down in the rules of procedure.

The ruling of the President or of the Judge replacing him shall be provisional and shall in no way prejudice the decision of the Court on the substance of the case.

ARTICLE 37

Member States and institutions of the Community may intervene in cases before the Court.

The same right shall be open to any other person establishing an interest in the result of any case submitted to the Court, save in cases between Member States, between institutions of the Community or between Member States and institutions of the Community.

Without prejudice to the preceding paragraph, the States, other than the Member States, which are parties to the Agreement on the European Economic Area, and also the EFTA Surveillance Authority referred to in that Agreement, may intervene in cases before the Court where one of the fields of application of that Agreement is concerned.

An application to intervene shall be limited to supporting the form of order sought by one of the parties.

ARTICLE 38

Where the defending party, after having been duly summoned, fails to file written submissions in defence, judgement shall be given against that party by default. An objection may be lodged against the judgement within one month of it being notified. The objection shall not have the effect of staying enforcement of the judgement by default unless the Court decides otherwise.

ARTICLE 39

Member States, institutions of the Community and any other natural or legal persons may, in cases and under conditions to be determined by the rules of procedure, institute third-party proceedings to contest a judgement rendered without there being heard, where the judgement is prejudicial to their rights.

ARTICLE 40

If the meaning or scope of a judgement is in doubt, the Court shall construe it on application by any party or any institution of the Community establishing an interest therein.

ARTICLE 41

An application for revision of a judgement may be made to the Court only on discovery of a fact which is of such a nature as to be a decisive factor, and which, when the judgement was given, was unknown to the Court and to the party claiming the revision.

The revision shall be opened by a judgement of the Court expressly recording the existence of a new fact, recognising that it is of such a character as to lay the case open to revision and declaring the application admissible on this ground.

No application for revision may be made after the lapse of ten years from the date of the judgement.

ARTICLE 42

Periods of grace based on considerations of distance shall be determined by the rules of procedure.

No right shall be prejudiced in consequence of the expiry of a time limit if the party concerned proves the existence of unforeseeable circumstances or of *force majeure*.

ARTICLE 43

Proceedings against the Community in matters arising from non-contractual liability shall be barred after a period of five years from the occurrence of the event giving rise thereto. The period of limitation shall be interrupted if proceedings are instituted before the Court or if prior to such proceedings an application is made by the aggrieved party to the relevant institution of the Community. In the latter event the proceedings must be instituted within the period of two months provided for in Article **230**; the provisions of the second paragraph of Article **232** shall apply where appropriate.

TITLE IV

THE COURT OF FIRST INSTANCE OF THE EUROPEAN COMMUNITIES

ARTICLE 44

Articles 2 to 8 and 13 to 16 of this Statute shall apply to the Court of First Instance and its members. The oath referred to in Article 2 shall be taken before the Court of Justice and the decisions referred to in Articles 3, 4 and 6 shall be adopted by that Court after hearing the Court of First Instance.

ARTICLE 45

The Court of First Instance shall appoint its Registrar and lay down the rules governing his service. Articles 9, 10 and 13 of this Statute shall apply to the Registrar of the Court of First Instance *mutatis mutandis*.

The President of the Court of Justice and the President of the Court of First Instance shall determine, by common accord, the conditions under which officials and other servants attached to the Court of Justice shall render their services to the Court of First Instance to enable it to function. Certain officials or other servants shall be responsible to the Registrar of the Court of First Instance under the authority of the President of the Court of First Instance.

ARTICLE 46

The procedure before the Court of First Instance shall be governed by Title III of this Statute, with the exception of Article 20.

Such further and more detailed provisions as may be necessary shall be laid down in the Rules of Procedure established in accordance with Article **225**(4) of this Treaty.

Notwithstanding the fourth paragraph of Article 18 of this Statute, the Advocate-General may make his reasoned submissions in writing.

ARTICLE 47

Where an application or other procedural document addressed to the Court of First Instance is lodged by mistake with the Registrar of the Court of Justice, it shall be transmitted immediately by that Registrar to the Registrar of the Court of First Instance; likewise, where an application or other procedural document addressed to the Court of Justice is lodged by mistake with the Registrar of the Court of First Instance, it shall be transmitted immediately by that Registrar to the Registrar of the Court of Justice.

Where the Court of First Instance finds that it does not have jurisdiction to hear and determine an action in respect of which the Court of Justice has jurisdiction, it shall refer that action to the Court of Justice; likewise, where the Court of Justice finds that an action falls within the jurisdiction of the Court of First Instance, it shall refer that action to the Court of First Instance, whereupon that Court may not decline jurisdiction.

Where the Court of Justice and the Court of First Instance are seized of cases in which the same relief is sought, the same issue of interpretation is raised or the validity of the same act is called in question, the Court of First Instance may, after hearing the parties, stay the proceedings before it until such time as the Court of Justice shall have delivered judgement. Where applications are made for the same act to be declared void, the Court of First Instance may also decline jurisdiction in order that the Court of Justice may rule on such applications. In the cases referred to in this subparagraph, the Court of Justice may also decide to stay the proceedings before it; in that event, the proceedings before the Court of First Instance shall continue.

ARTICLE 48

Final decisions of the Court of First Instance, decisions disposing of the substantive issues in part only or disposing of a procedural issue concerning a plea of lack of competence or inadmissibility, shall be notified by the Registrar of the Court of First Instance to all parties as well as Member States and the Community institutions even if they did not intervene in the case before the Court of First Instance.

ARTICLE 49

An appeal may be brought before the Court of Justice, within two months of the notification of the decision appealed against, against final decisions of the Court of First Instance and decisions of that Court disposing of the substantive issues in part only or disposing of a procedural issue concerning a plea of lack of competence or inadmissibility.

Such an appeal may be brought by any party which has been unsuccessful, in whole or in part, in its submissions. However, interveners other than the Member States and the Community institutions may bring such an appeal only where the decision of the Court of First Instance directly affects them.

With the exception of cases relating to disputes between the Community and its servants, an appeal may also be brought by Member States and Community institutions which did not intervene in the proceedings before the Court of First Instance. Such Member States and institutions shall be in the same position as Member States or institutions which intervened at first instance.

ARTICLE 50

Any person whose application to intervene has been dismissed by the Court of First Instance may appeal to the Court of Justice within two weeks of the notification of the decision dismissing the application.

The parties to the proceedings may appeal to the Court of Justice against any decision of the Court of First Instance made pursuant to Articles **242** or **243** or the fourth paragraph of Article **256** of this Treaty within two months from their notification.

The appeal referred to in the first two paragraphs of this Article shall be heard and determined under the procedure referred to in Article 36 of this Statute.

ARTICLE 51

An appeal to the Court of Justice shall be limited to points of law. It shall lie on the grounds of lack of competence of the Court of First Instance, a breach of procedure before it which adversely affects the interests of the appellant as well as the infringement of Community law by the Court of First Instance.

No appeal shall lie regarding only the amount of the costs or the party ordered to pay them.

ARTICLE 52

Where an appeal is brought against a decision of the Court of First Instance, the procedure before the Court of Justice shall consist of a written part and an oral part. In accordance with conditions laid down in the Rules of Procedure the Court of Justice, having heard the Advocate-General and the parties, may dispense with the oral procedure.

ARTICLE 53

Without prejudice to Articles **242** and **243** of this Treaty, an appeal shall not have suspensory effect.

By way of derogation from Article **244** of this Treaty, decisions of the Court of First Instance declaring a regulation to be void shall take effect only as from the date of expiry of the period referred to in the first paragraph of Article 49 of this Statute or, if an appeal shall have been brought within that period, as from the date of dismissal of the appeal, without prejudice, however, to the right of a party to apply to the Court of Justice, pursuant to Articles **242** and **243** of this Treaty, for the suspension of the effects of the regulation which has been declared void or for the prescription of any other interim measure.

ARTICLE 54

If the appeal is well founded, the Court of Justice shall quash the decision of the Court of First Instance. It may itself give final judgement in the matter, where the state of the proceedings so permits, or refer the case back to the Court of First Instance for judgement.

Where a case is referred back to the Court of First Instance, that Court shall be bound by the decision of the Court of Justice on points of law.

When an appeal brought by a Member State or a Community institution, which did not intervene in the proceedings before the Court of First Instance, is well founded the Court of Justice may, if it considers this necessary, state which of the effects of the decision of the Court of First Instance which has been quashed shall be considered as definitive in respect of the parties to the litigation.

ARTICLE 55

The Rules of Procedure of the Court provided for in Article **245** of this Treaty shall contain, apart from the provisions contemplated by this Statute, any other provisions necessary for applying and, where required, supplementing it.

ARTICLE 56

The Council may, acting unanimously, make such further adjustments to the provisions of this Statute as may be required by reason of measures taken by the Council in accordance with the last paragraph of Article **221** of this Treaty.

ARTICLE 57 shall be repealed.

Done at Brussels this seventeenth day of April in the year one thousand nine hundred and fifty-seven.

12.   PROTOCOL ON ITALY

THE HIGH CONTRACTING PARTIES,

DESIRING to settle certain particular problems relating to Italy,

HAVE AGREED upon the following provisions, which shall be annexed to this Treaty:

THE MEMBER STATES OF THE COMMUNITY,

TAKE NOTE of the fact that the Italian Government is carrying out a ten-year programme of economic expansion designed to rectify the disequilibria in the structure of the Italian economy, in particular by providing an infrastructure for the less developed areas in southern Italy and in the Italian islands and by creating new jobs in order to eliminate unemployment;

RECALL that the principles and objectives of this programme of the Italian Government have been considered and approved by organisations for international co-operation of which the Member States are members;

RECOGNISE that it is in their common interest that the objectives of the Italian programme should be attained;

AGREE, in order to facilitate the accomplishment of this task by the Italian Government, to recommend to the institutions of the Community that they should employ all the methods and procedures provided in this Treaty and, in particular, make appropriate use of the resources of the European Investment Bank and the European Social Fund;

ARE OF THE OPINION that the institutions of the Community should, in applying this Treaty, take account of the sustained effort to be made by the Italian economy in the coming years and of the desirability of avoiding dangerous stresses in particular within the balance of payments or the level of employment, which might jeopardise the application of this Treaty in Italy;

RECOGNISE that in the event of Articles **119** and **120** being applied it will be necessary to take care that any measures required of the Italian Government do not prejudice the completion of its programme for economic expansion and for raising the standard of living of the population.

Done at Rome this twenty-fifth day of March in the year one thousand nine hundred and fifty-seven.

13. PROTOCOL ON GOODS ORIGINATING IN AND COMING FROM CERTAIN COUNTRIES AND ENJOYING SPECIAL TREATMENT WHEN IMPORTED INTO A MEMBER STATE

THE HIGH CONTRACTING PARTIES,

DESIRING to define in greater detail the application of this Treaty to certain goods originating in and coming from certain countries and enjoying special treatment when imported into a Member State,

HAVE AGREED upon the following provisions, which shall be annexed to this Treaty;

1.   The application of the Treaty establishing the European Economic Community shall not require any alteration in the customs treatment **applicable on 1 January 1958**, to **imports into** the Benelux countries of goods originating in and coming from Surinam or the Netherlands Antilles.
Points (a), (b) and (c) shall be deleted.

2.   Goods imported into a Member State and benefiting from the treatment referred to above shall not be considered to be in free circulation in that State within the meaning of Article **24** of this Treaty when re-exported to another Member State.

3.   **Member States** shall communicate to the Commission and to the other Member States their rules governing the special treatment referred to in this Protocol, together with a list of the goods entitled to such treatment.
They shall also inform the Commission and the other Member States of any changes subsequently made in those lists or in the treatment.

4.   The Commission shall ensure that the application of these rules cannot be prejudicial to other Member States; to this end it may take any appropriate measures as regards relations between Member States.

Done at Rome this twenty-fifth day of March in the year one thousand nine hundred and fifty-seven.

14. PROTOCOL CONCERNING IMPORTS INTO THE EUROPEAN COMMUNITY OF PETROLEUM PRODUCTS REFINED IN THE NETHERLANDS ANTILLES

THE HIGH CONTRACTING PARTIES,

BEING DESIROUS of giving fuller details about the system of trade applicable to imports into the European Economic Community of petroleum products refined in the Netherlands Antilles,

HAVE AGREED on the following provisions to be appended to that Treaty:

ARTICLE 1

This Protocol is applicable to petroleum products coming under the Brussels Nomenclature numbers 27.10, 27.11, 27.12, ex 27.13 (paraffin wax, petroleum or shale wax and paraffin residues) and 27.14, imported for use in Member States.

ARTICLE 2

Member States shall undertake to grant to petroleum products refined in the Netherlands Antilles the tariff preferences resulting from the association of the latter with the Community, under the conditions provided for in this Protocol. These provisions shall hold good whatever may be the rules of origin applied by the Member States.

ARTICLE 3

1.   When the Commission, at the request of a Member State or on its own initiative, establishes that imports into the Community of petroleum products refined in the Netherlands Antilles under the system provided for in Article 2 above are giving rise to real difficulties on the market of one or more Member States, it shall decide that customs duties on the said imports shall be introduced, increased or re-introduced by the Member States in question, to such an extent and for such a period as may be necessary to meet that situation. The rates of the customs duties thus introduced, increased or re-introduced may not exceed the customs duties applicable to third countries for these same products.

2.   The provisions of paragraph 1 can in any case be applied when imports into the Community of petroleum products refined in the Netherlands Antilles reach two million metric tonnes a year.

3.   The Council shall be informed of decisions taken by the Commission in pursuance of paragraphs 1 and 2, including those directed at rejecting the request of a Member State. The Council shall, at the request of any Member State, assume responsibility for the matter and may at any time amend or revoke them by a decision taken by a qualified majority.

ARTICLE 4

1.   If a Member State considers that imports of petroleum products refined in the Netherlands Antilles, made either directly or through another Member State under the system provided for in Article 2 above, are giving rise to real difficulties on its market and that immediate action is necessary to meet them, it may on its own initiative decide to apply customs duties to such imports, the rate of which may not exceed those of the customs duties applicable to third countries in respect of the same products. It shall notify its decision to the Commission which shall decide within one month whether the measures taken by the State should be maintained or must be amended or cancelled. The provisions of Article 3(3) shall be applicable to such decision of the Commission.

2.   When the quantities of petroleum products refined in the Netherlands Antilles imported either directly or through another Member State, under the system provided for in Article 2 above, into a Member State or States of the EEC exceed during a calendar year the tonnage shown in the Annex to this Protocol, the measures taken in pursuance of paragraph 1 by that or those Member States for the current year shall be considered to be justified; the Commission shall, after assuring itself that the tonnage fixed has been reached, formally record the measures taken. In such a case the other Member States shall abstain from formally placing the matter before the Council.

ARTICLE 5

If the Community decides to apply quantitative restrictions to petroleum products, no matter whence they are imported, these restrictions may also be applied to imports of such products from the Netherlands Antilles. In such a case preferential treatment shall be granted to the Netherlands Antilles as compared with third countries.

ARTICLE 6

1.   The provisions of Articles 2 to 5 shall be reviewed by the Council, by unanimous decision, after consulting the European Parliament and the Commission, when a common definition of origin for petroleum products from third countries and associated countries is adopted, or when decisions are taken within the framework of a common commercial policy for the products in question or when a common energy policy is established.

2.   When such revision is made, however, equivalent preferences must in any case be maintained in favour of the Netherlands Antilles in a suitable form and for a minimum quantity of 2½ million tonnes of petroleum products.

3.   The Community's commitments in regard to equivalent preferences as mentioned in paragraph 2 of this Article may, if necessary, be broken down country by country taking into account the tonnage indicated in the Annex to this Protocol.

ARTICLE 7
For the implementation of this Protocol, the Commission is responsible for following the pattern of imports into the Member States of petroleum products refined in the Netherlands Antilles. Member States shall communicate to the Commission, which shall see that it is circulated, all useful information to that end in accordance with the administrative conditions recommended by it.

Done at Brussels, the thirteenth day of November, one thousand nine hundred and sixty-two.

ANNEX TO THE PROTOCOL

For the implementation of Article 4(2) of the Protocol concerning imports into the European Community of petroleum products refined in the Netherlands Antilles, the High Contracting Parties have decided that the quantity of 2 million metric tonnes of petroleum products from the Antilles shall be allocated among the Member States as follows:

Germany	625,000 metric tonnes
Belgo/Luxembourg Economic Union	200,000 metric tonnes
France	75,000 metric tonnes
Italy	100,000 metric tonnes
Netherlands	1,000,000 metric tonnes

15.   PROTOCOL ON SPECIAL ARRANGEMENTS FOR GREENLAND

ARTICLE 1
1.   The treatment on import into the Community of products subject to the common organisation of the market in fishery products, originating in Greenland, shall, while complying with the mechanisms of the common market organisation, involve exemption from customs duties and charges having equivalent effect and the absence of quantitative restrictions or measures having equivalent effect if the possibilities for access to Greenland fishing zones granted to the Community pursuant to an agreement between the Community and the authority responsible for Greenland are satisfactory to the Community.

2.   All measures relating to the import arrangements for such products, including those relating to the adoption of such measures, shall be adopted in accordance with the procedure laid down in Article 37 of the Treaty establishing the European Economic Community.

ARTICLE 2
The Commission shall make proposals to the Council, which shall act by a qualified majority, for the transitional measures which it considers necessary, by reason of the entry into force of the new arrangements, with regard to the maintenance of rights acquired by natural or legal persons during the period when Greenland was part of the Community and the regularisation of the situation with regard to financial assistance granted by the Community to Greenland during that period.

ARTICLE 3 shall be repealed.

16.   PROTOCOL ON THE ACQUISITION OF PROPERTY IN DENMARK

THE HIGH CONTRACTING PARTIES,

DESIRING to settle certain particular problems relating to Denmark,

HAVE AGREED UPON the following provision, which shall be annexed to the Treaty establishing the European Community:

Notwithstanding the provisions of this Treaty, Denmark may maintain the existing legislation on the acquisition of second homes.
(This protocol was introduced by the Maastricht Treaty.)

17. PROTOCOL CONCERNING ARTICLE 141 OF THE TREATY ESTABLISHING THE EUROPEAN COMMUNITY

THE HIGH CONTRACTING PARTIES,

HAVE AGREED UPON the following provision, which shall be annexed to the Treaty establishing the European Community:

For the purposes of Article **141** of this Treaty, benefits under occupational social security schemes shall not be considered as remuneration if and in so far as they are attributable to periods of employment prior to 17 May 1990, except in the case of workers or those claiming under them who have before that date initiated legal proceedings or introduced an equivalent claim under the applicable national law.
(This protocol was introduced by the Maastricht Treaty.)

18. PROTOCOL ON THE STATUTE OF THE EUROPEAN SYSTEM OF CENTRAL BANKS AND OF THE EUROPEAN CENTRAL BANK

THE HIGH CONTRACTING PARTIES,

DESIRING to lay down the Statute of the European System of Central Banks and of the European Central Bank provided for in Article **8** of the Treaty establishing the European Community,

HAVE AGREED UPON the following provisions, which shall be annexed to the Treaty establishing the European Community:

CHAPTER I

CONSTITUTION OF THE ESCB

ARTICLE 1
The European System of Central Banks
1.1. The European System of Central Banks (ESCB) and the European Central Bank (ECB) shall be established in accordance with Article **8** of this Treaty; they shall perform their tasks and carry on their activities in accordance with the provisions of this Treaty and of this Statute.

1.2. In accordance with Article **107**(1) of this Treaty, the ESCB shall be composed of the ECB and of the central banks of the Member States ('national central banks'). The Institut monétaire luxembourgeois will be the central bank of Luxembourg.

CHAPTER II

OBJECTIVES AND TASKS OF THE ESCB

ARTICLE 2
Objectives
In accordance with Article **105**(1) of this Treaty, the primary objective of the ESCB shall be to maintain price stability. Without prejudice to the objective of price stability, it shall support the general economic policies in the Community with a view to contributing to the achievement of the objectives of the Community as laid down in Article **2** of this Treaty. The ESCB shall act in accordance with the principle of an open market economy with free competition, favouring an efficient allocation of resources, and in compliance with the principles set out in Article **4** of this Treaty.

ARTICLE 3
Tasks
3.1. In accordance with Article **105**(2) of this Treaty, the basic tasks to be carried out through the ESCB shall be:
- to define and implement the monetary policy of the Community;
- to conduct foreign exchange operations consistent with the provisions of Article **111** of this Treaty;
- to hold and manage the official foreign reserves of the Member States;
- to promote the smooth operation of payment systems.

3.2. In accordance with Article **105**(3) of this Treaty, the third indent of Article 3.1 shall be without prejudice to the holding and management by the governments of Member States of foreign exchange working balances.

3.3. In accordance with Article **105**(5) of this Treaty, the ESCB shall contribute to the smooth conduct of policies pursued by the competent authorities relating to the prudential supervision of credit institutions and the stability of the financial system.

ARTICLE 4
Advisory functions
In accordance with Article **105**(4) of this Treaty:
(a) the ECB shall be consulted:
  - on any proposed Community act in its fields of competence;
  - by national authorities regarding any draft legislative provision in its fields of competence, but within the limits and under the conditions set out by the Council in accordance with the procedure laid down in Article 42;
(b) the ECB may submit opinions to the appropriate Community institutions or bodies or to national authorities on matters in its fields of competence.

ARTICLE 5
Collection of statistical information
5.1. In order to undertake the tasks of the ESCB, the ECB, assisted by the national central banks, shall collect the necessary statistical information either from the competent national authorities or directly from economic agents. For these purposes it shall co-operate with the Community institutions or bodies and with the competent authorities of the Member States or third countries and with international organisations.

5.2. The national central banks shall carry out, to the extent possible, the tasks described in Article 5.1.

5.3. The ECB shall contribute to the harmonisation, where necessary, of the rules and practices governing the collection, compilation and distribution of statistics in the areas within its fields of competence.

5.4. The Council, in accordance with the procedure laid down in Article 42, shall define the natural and legal persons subject to reporting requirements, the confidentiality regime and the appropriate provisions for enforcement.

ARTICLE 6
International co-operation
6.1. In the field of international co-operation involving the tasks entrusted to the ESCB, the ECB shall decide how the ESCB shall be represented.

6.2. The ECB and, subject to its approval, the national central banks may participate in international monetary institutions.

6.3. Articles 6.1 and 6.2 shall be without prejudice to Article **111**(4) of this Treaty.

CHAPTER III

ORGANISATION OF THE ESCB

ARTICLE 7
Independence
In accordance with Article **108** of this Treaty, when exercising the powers and carrying out the tasks and duties conferred upon them by this Treaty and this Statute, neither the ECB, nor a national central bank, nor any member of their decision-making bodies shall seek or take instructions from Community institutions or bodies, from any government of a Member State or from any other body. The Community institutions and bodies and the governments of the Member States undertake to respect this principle and not to seek to influence the members of the decision-making bodies of the ECB or of the national central banks in the performance of their tasks.

ARTICLE 8
General principle
The ESCB shall be governed by the decision-making bodies of the ECB.

ARTICLE 9

The European Central Bank

9.1. The ECB which, in accordance with Article **107**(2) of this Treaty, shall have legal personality, shall enjoy in each of the Member States the most extensive legal capacity accorded to legal persons under its law; it may, in particular, acquire or dispose of movable and immovable property and may be a party to legal proceedings.

9.2. The ECB shall ensure that the tasks conferred upon the ESCB under Article **105**(2), (3) and (5) of this Treaty are implemented either by its own activities pursuant to this Statute or through the national central banks pursuant to Articles 12.1 and 14.

9.3. In accordance with Article **107**(3) of this Treaty, the decision-making bodies of the ECB shall be the Governing Council and the Executive Board.

ARTICLE 10

The Governing Council

10.1. In accordance with Article **112**(l) of this Treaty, the Governing Council shall comprise the members of the Executive Board of the ECB and the Governors of the national central banks.

10.2. Subject to Article 10.3, only members of the Governing Council present in person shall have the right to vote. By way of derogation from this rule, the Rules of Procedure referred to in Article 12.3 may lay down that members of the Governing Council may cast their vote by means of teleconferencing. These rules shall also provide that a member of the Governing Council who is prevented from voting for a prolonged period may appoint an alternate as a member of the Governing Council.

Subject to Articles 10.3 and 11.3, each member of the Governing Council shall have one vote. Save as otherwise provided for in this Statute, the Governing Council shall act by a simple majority. In the event of a tie, the President shall have the casting vote.

In order for the Governing Council to vote, there shall be a quorum of two-thirds of the members. If the quorum is not met, the President may convene an extraordinary meeting at which decisions may be taken without regard to the quorum.

10.3. For any decisions to be taken under Articles 28, 29, 30, 32, 33 and 5l, the votes in the Governing Council shall be weighted according to the national central banks' shares in the subscribed capital of the ECB. The weights of the votes of the members of the Executive Board shall be zero. A decision requiring a qualified majority shall be adopted if the votes cast in favour represent at least two-thirds of the subscribed capital of the ECB and represent at least half of the shareholders. If a Governor is unable to be present, he may nominate an alternate to cast his weighted vote.

10.4. The proceedings of the meetings shall be confidential. The Governing Council may decide to make the outcome of its deliberations public.

10.5. The Governing Council shall meet at least ten times a year.

ARTICLE 11

The Executive Board

11.1. In accordance with Article **112**(2)(a) of this Treaty, the Executive Board shall comprise the President, the Vice-President and four other members.

The members shall perform their duties on a full-time basis. No member shall engage in any occupation, whether gainful or not, unless exemption is exceptionally granted by the Governing Council.

11.2. In accordance with Article **112**(2)(b) of this Treaty, the President, the Vice-President and the other Members of the Executive Board shall be appointed from among persons of recognised standing and professional experience in monetary or banking matters by common accord of the governments of the Member States at the level of the Heads of State or of Government, on a recommendation from the Council after it has consulted the European Parliament and the Governing Council.

Their term of office shall be 8 years and shall not be renewable.

Only nationals of Member States may be members of the Executive Board.

11.3. The terms and conditions of employment of the members of the Executive Board, in particular their salaries, pensions and other social security benefits shall be the subject of contracts with the ECB and shall be fixed by the Governing Council on a proposal from a Committee comprising three members appointed by the Governing Council and three members appointed by the Council. The members of the Executive Board shall not have the right to vote on matters referred to in this paragraph.

11.4. If a member of the Executive Board no longer fulfils the conditions required for the performance of his duties or if he has been guilty of serious misconduct, the Court of Justice may, on application by the Governing Council or the Executive Board, compulsorily retire him.

11.5. Each member of the Executive Board present in person shall have the right to vote and shall have, for that purpose, one vote. Save as otherwise provided, the Executive Board shall act by a simple majority of the votes cast. In the event of a tie, the President shall have the casting vote. The voting arrangements shall be specified in the Rules of Procedure referred to in Article 12.3.

11.6. The Executive Board shall be responsible for the current business of the ECB.

11.7. Any vacancy on the Executive Board shall be filled by the appointment of a new member in accordance with Article 11.2.

ARTICLE 12
Responsibilities of the decision-making bodies
12.1. The Governing Council shall adopt the guidelines and take the decisions necessary to ensure the performance of the tasks entrusted to the ESCB under this Treaty and this Statute. The Governing Council shall formulate the monetary policy of the Community including, as appropriate, decisions relating to intermediate monetary objectives, key interest rates and the supply of reserves in the ESCB, and shall establish the necessary guidelines for their implementation.
The Executive Board shall implement monetary policy in accordance with the guidelines and decisions laid down by the Governing Council. In doing so the Executive Board shall give the necessary instructions to national central banks. In addition the Executive Board may have certain powers delegated to it where the Governing Council so decides.
To the extent deemed possible and appropriate and without prejudice to the provisions of this Article, the ECB shall have recourse to the national central banks to carry out operations which form part of the tasks of the ESCB.

12.2. The Executive Board shall have responsibility for the preparation of meetings of the Governing Council.

12.3. The Governing Council shall adopt Rules of Procedure which determine the internal organisation of the ECB and its decision-making bodies.

12.4. The Governing Council shall exercise the advisory functions referred to in Article 4.

12.5. The Governing Council shall take the decisions referred to in Article 6.

ARTICLE 13
The President
13.1. The President or, in his absence, the Vice-President shall chair the Governing Council and the Executive Board of the ECB.

13.2. Without prejudice to Article 39, the President or his nominee shall represent the ECB externally.

ARTICLE 14
National central banks
14.1. In accordance with Article **109** of this Treaty, each Member State shall ensure, at the latest at the date of the establishment of the ESCB, that its national legislation, including the statutes of its national central bank, is compatible with this Treaty and this Statute.

14.2. The statutes of the national central banks shall, in particular, provide that the term of office of a Governor of a national central bank shall be no less than 5 years.
A Governor may be relieved from office only if he no longer fulfils the conditions required for the performance of his duties or if he has been guilty of serious misconduct. A decision to this effect may be referred to the Court of Justice by the Governor concerned or the Governing Council on grounds of infringement of this Treaty or of any rule of law relating to its application. Such proceedings shall be instituted within two months of the publication of the decision or of its notification to the plaintiff or, in the absence thereof, of the day on which it came to the knowledge of the latter, as the case may be.

14.3. The national central banks are an integral part of the ESCB and shall act in accordance with the guidelines and instructions of the ECB. The Governing Council shall take the necessary steps to ensure compliance with the guidelines and instructions of the ECB, and shall require that any necessary information be given to it.

14.4. National central banks may perform functions other than those specified in this Statute unless the Governing Council finds, by a majority of two-thirds of the votes cast, that these interfere with the objectives and tasks of the ESCB. Such functions shall be performed on the responsibility and liability of national central banks and shall not be regarded as being part of the functions of the ESCB.

ARTICLE 15
Reporting commitments
15.1. The ECB shall draw up and publish reports on the activities of the ESCB at least quarterly.

15.2. A consolidated financial statement of the ESCB shall be published each week.

15.3. In accordance with Article **113**(3) of this Treaty, the ECB shall address an annual report on the activities of the ESCB and on the monetary policy of both the previous and the current year to the European Parliament, the Council and the Commission, and also to the European Council.

15.4. The reports and statements referred to in this Article shall be made available to interested parties free of charge.

ARTICLE 16
Bank Notes
In accordance with Article **106**(1) of this Treaty, the Governing Council shall have the exclusive right to authorise the issue of bank notes within the Community. The ECB and the national central banks may issue such notes. The bank notes issued by the ECB and the national central banks shall be the only such notes to have the status of legal tender within the Community.
The ECB shall respect as far as possible existing practices regarding the issue and design of bank notes.

CHAPTER IV

MONETARY FUNCTIONS AND OPERATIONS OF THE ESCB

ARTICLE 17
Accounts with the ECB and the national central banks
In order to conduct their operations, the ECB and the national central banks may open accounts for credit institutions, public entities and other market participants and accept assets, including book-entry securities, as collateral.

ARTICLE 18
Open market and credit operations
18.1. In order to achieve the objectives of the ESCB and to carry out its tasks, the ECB and the national central banks may:
- operate in the financial markets by buying and selling outright (spot and forward) or under repurchase agreement and by lending or borrowing claims and marketable instruments, whether in Community or in non-Community currencies, as well as precious metals;
- conduct credit operations with credit institutions and other market participants, with lending being based on adequate collateral.

18.2. The ECB shall establish general principles for open market and credit operations carried out by itself or the national central banks, including for the announcement of conditions under which they stand ready to enter into such transactions.

ARTICLE 19
Minimum reserves
19.1. Subject to Article 2, the ECB may require credit institutions established in Member States to hold minimum reserves on accounts with the ECB and national central banks in pursuance of monetary policy objectives. Regulations concerning the calculation and determination of the required minimum reserves may be established by the Governing Council. In cases of non-compliance the ECB shall be entitled to levy penalty interest and to impose other sanctions with comparable effect.

19.2. For the application of this Article, the Council shall, in accordance with the procedure laid down in Article 42, define the basis for minimum reserves and the maximum permissible ratios between those reserves and their basis, as well as the appropriate sanctions in cases of non-compliance.

ARTICLE 20
Other instruments of monetary control
The Governing Council may, by a majority of two-thirds of the votes cast, decide upon the use of such other operational methods of monetary control as it sees it, respecting Article 2.
The Council shall, in accordance with the procedure laid down in Article 42, define the scope of such methods if they impose obligations on third parties.

ARTICLE 21
Operations with public entities
21.1. In accordance with Article **101** of this Treaty, overdrafts or any other type of credit facility with the ECB or with the national central banks in favour of Community institutions or bodies, central governments, regional, local or other public authorities, other bodies governed by public law, or public undertakings of Member States shall be prohibited, as shall the purchase directly from them by the ECB or national central banks of debt instruments.

21.2. The ECB and national central banks may act as fiscal agents for the entities referred to in Article 21.1.

21.3. The provisions of this Article shall not apply to publicly-owned credit institutions which, in the context of the supply of reserves by central banks, shall be given the same treatment by national central banks and the ECB as private credit institutions.

ARTICLE 22
Clearing and payment systems
The ECB and national central banks may provide facilities, and the ECB may make regulations, to ensure efficient and sound clearing and payment systems within the Community and with other countries.

ARTICLE 23
External operations
The ECB and national central banks may:
- establish relations with central banks and financial institutions in other countries and, where appropriate, with international organisations;
- acquire and sell spot and forward all types of foreign exchange assets and precious metals; the term 'foreign exchange asset' shall include securities and all other assets in the currency of any country or units of account and in whatever form held;
- hold and manage the assets referred to in this Article;
- conduct all types of banking transactions in relations with third countries and international organisations, including borrowing and lending operations.

ARTICLE 24
Other operations
In addition to operations arising from their tasks, the ECB and national central banks may enter into operations for their administrative purposes or for their staff.

CHAPTER V

PRUDENTIAL SUPERVISION

ARTICLE 25
Prudential supervision
25.1. The ECB may offer advice to and be consulted by the Council, the Commission and the competent authorities of the Member States on the scope and implementation of Community legislation relating to the prudential supervision of credit institutions and to the stability of the financial system.

25.2. In accordance with any decision of the Council under Article **105**(6) of this Treaty, the ECB may perform specific tasks concerning policies relating to the prudential supervision of credit institutions and other financial institutions with the exception of insurance undertakings.

CHAPTER VI

FINANCIAL PROVISIONS OF THE ESCB

ARTICLE 26

Financial accounts

26.1. The financial year of the ECB and national central banks shall begin on the first day of January and end on the last day of December.

26.2. The annual accounts of the ECB shall be drawn up by the Executive Board, in accordance with the principles established by the Governing Council. The accounts shall be approved by the Governing Council and shall thereafter be published.

26.3. For analytical and operational purposes, the Executive Board shall draw up a consolidated balance sheet of the ESCB, comprising those assets and liabilities of the national central banks that fall within the ESCB.

26.4. For the application of this Article, the Governing Council shall establish the necessary rules for standardising the accounting and reporting of operations undertaken by the national central banks.

ARTICLE 27

Auditing

27.1. The accounts of the ECB and national central banks shall be audited by independent external auditors recommended by the Governing Council and approved by the Council. The auditors shall have full power to examine all books and accounts of the ECB and national central banks and obtain full information about their transactions.

27.2. The provisions of Article **248** of this Treaty shall only apply to an examination of the operational efficiency of the management of the ECB.

ARTICLE 28

Capital of the ECB

28.1. The capital of the ECB, which shall become operational upon its establishment, shall be ECU 5,000 million. The capital may be increased by such amounts as may be decided by the Governing Council acting by the qualified majority provided for in Article 10.3, within the limits and under the conditions set by the Council under the procedure laid down in Article 42.

28.2. The national central banks shall be the sole subscribers to and holders of the capital of the ECB. The subscription of capital shall be according to the key established in accordance with Article 29.

28.3. The Governing Council, acting by the qualified majority provided for in Article 10.3, shall determine the extent to which and the form in which the capital shall be paid up.

28.4. Subject to Article 28.5, the shares of the national central banks in the subscribed capital of the ECB may not be transferred, pledged or attached.

28.5. If the key referred to in Article 29 is adjusted, the national central banks shall transfer among themselves capital shares to the extent necessary to ensure that the distribution of capital shares corresponds to the adjusted key. The Governing Council shall determine the terms and conditions of such transfers.

ARTICLE 29

Key for capital subscription

29.1. When in accordance with the procedure referred to in Article **123**(1) of this Treaty the ESCB and the ECB have been established, the key for subscription of the ECB's capital shall be established. Each national central bank shall be assigned a weighting in this key which shall be equal to the sum of:
-   50% of the share of its respective Member State in the population of the Community in the penultimate year preceding the establishment of the ESCB;
-   50% of the share of its respective Member State in the gross domestic product at market prices of the Community as recorded in the last five years preceding the penultimate year before the establishment of the ESCB;

The percentages shall be rounded up to the nearest multiple of 0.05 percentage points.

29.2. The statistical data to be used for the application of this Article shall be provided by the Commission in accordance with the rules adopted by the Council under the procedure provided for in Article 42.

29.3. The weightings assigned to the national central banks shall be adjusted every five years after the establishment of the ESCB by analogy with the provisions laid down in Article 29.1. The adjusted key shall apply with effect from the first day of the following year.

29.4. The Governing Council shall take all other measures necessary for the application of this Article.

ARTICLE 30

Transfer of foreign reserve assets to the ECB

30.1. Without prejudice to Article 28, the ECB shall be provided by the national central banks with foreign reserve assets, other than Member States' currencies, ECUs, IMF reserve positions and SDRs, up to an amount equivalent to ECU 50,000 million. The Governing Council shall decide upon the proportion to be called up by the ECB following its establishment and the amounts called up at later dates. The ECB shall have the full right to hold and manage the foreign reserves that are transferred to it and to use them for the purposes set out in this Statute.

30.2. The contributions of each national central bank shall be fixed in proportion to its share in the subscribed capital of the ECB.

30.3. Each national central bank shall be credited by the ECB with a claim equivalent to its contribution. The Governing Council shall determine the denomination and remuneration of such claims.

30.4. Further calls of foreign reserve assets beyond the limit set in Article 30.1 may be effected by the ECB, in accordance with Article 30.2, within the limits and under the conditions set by the Council in accordance with the procedure laid down in Article 42.

30.5. The ECB may hold and manage IMF reserve positions and SDRs and provide for the pooling of such assets.

30.6. The Governing Council shall take all other measures necessary for the application of this Article.

ARTICLE 31

Foreign reserve assets held by national central banks

31.1. The national central banks shall be allowed to perform transactions in fulfilment of their obligations towards international organisations in accordance with Article 23.

31.2. All other operations in foreign reserve assets remaining with the national central banks after the transfers referred to in Article 30, and Member States' transactions with their foreign exchange working balances shall, above a certain limit to be established within the framework of Article 31.3, be subject to approval by the ECB in order to ensure consistency with the exchange rate and monetary policies of the Community.

31.3. The Governing Council shall issue guidelines with a view to facilitating such operations.

ARTICLE 32

Allocation of monetary income of national central banks

32.1. The income accruing to the national central banks in the performance of the ESCB's monetary policy function (hereinafter referred to as 'monetary income') shall be allocated at the end of each financial year in accordance with the provisions of this Article.

32.2. Subject to Article 32.3, the amount of each national central bank's monetary income shall be equal to its annual income derived from its assets held against notes in circulation and deposit liabilities to credit institutions. These assets shall be earmarked by national central banks in accordance with guidelines to be established by the Governing Council.

32.3. If, after the start of the third stage, the balance sheet structures of the national central banks do not, in the judgement of the Governing Council, permit the application of Article 32.2, the Governing Council, acting by a qualified majority, may decide that, by way of derogation from Article 32.2, monetary income shall be measured according to an alternative method for a period of not more than five years.

32.4. The amount of each national central bank's monetary income shall be reduced by an amount equivalent to any interest paid by that central bank on its deposit liabilities to credit institutions in accordance with Article 19.

The Governing Council may decide that national central banks shall be indemnified against costs incurred in connection with the issue of bank notes or in exceptional circumstances for specific losses arising from monetary policy operations undertaken for the ESCB. Indemnification shall be in a form deemed appropriate in the judgement of the Governing Council; these amounts may be offset against the national central banks' monetary income.

32.5. The sum of the national central banks' income shall be allocated to the national central banks in proportion to their paid-up shares in the capital of the ECB, subject to any decision taken by the Governing Council pursuant to Article 33.2.

32.6. The clearing and settlement of the balances arising from the allocation of monetary income shall be carried out by the ECB in accordance with guidelines established by the Governing Council.

32.7. The Governing Council shall take all other measures necessary for the application of this Article.

ARTICLE 33
Allocation of net profits and losses of the ECB
33.1. The net profit of the ECB shall be transferred in the following order:
(a)   an amount to be determined by the Governing Council, which may not exceed 20% of the net profit, shall be transferred to the general reserve fund subject to a limit equal to 100% of the capital;
(b)   the remaining net profit shall be distributed to the shareholders of the ECB in proportion to their paid-up shares.

33.2. In the event of a loss incurred by the ECB, the shortfall may be offset against the general reserve fund of the ECB and, if necessary, following a decision by the Governing Council, against the monetary income of the relevant financial year in proportion and up to the amounts allocated to the national central banks in accordance with Article 32.5.

CHAPTER VII

GENERAL PROVISIONS

ARTICLE 34
Legal acts
34.1. In accordance with Article **110** of this Treaty, the ECB shall:
-    make regulations to the extent necessary to implement the tasks defined in Article 3.1, first indent, Articles 19.1, 22 or 25.2 and in cases which shall be laid down in the acts of the Council referred to in Article 42;
-    take decisions necessary for carrying out the tasks entrusted to the ESCB under this Treaty and this Statute;
-    make recommendations and deliver opinions.

34.2. A regulation shall have general application. It shall be binding in its entirety and directly applicable in all Member States.
Recommendations and opinions shall have no binding force.
A decision shall be binding in its entirety upon those to whom it is addressed.
Articles **253** to **256** of this Treaty shall apply to regulations and decisions adopted by the ECB.
The ECB may decide to publish its decisions, recommendations and opinions.

34.3. Within the limits and under the conditions adopted by the Council under the procedure laid down in Article 42, the ECB shall be entitled to impose fines or periodic penalty payments on undertakings for failure to comply with obligations under its regulations and decisions.

ARTICLE 35
Judicial control and related matters
35.1. The acts or omissions of the ECB shall be open to review or interpretation by the Court of Justice in the cases and under the conditions laid down in this Treaty. The ECB may institute proceedings in the cases and under the conditions laid down in this Treaty.

35.2. Disputes between the ECB, on the one hand, and its creditors, debtors or any other person, on the other, shall be decided by the competent national courts, save where jurisdiction has been conferred upon the Court of Justice.

35.3. The ECB shall be subject to the liability regime provided for in Article **288** of this Treaty. The national central banks shall be liable according to their respective national laws.

35.4. The Court of Justice shall have jurisdiction to give judgement pursuant to any arbitration clause contained in a contract concluded by or on behalf of the ECB, whether that contract be governed by public or private law.

35.5. A decision of the ECB to bring an action before the Court of Justice shall be taken by the Governing Council.

35.6. The Court of Justice shall have jurisdiction in disputes concerning the fulfilment by a national central bank of obligations under this Statute. If the ECB considers that a national central bank has failed to fulfil an obligation under this Statute, it shall deliver a reasoned opinion on the matter after giving the national central bank concerned the opportunity to submit its observations. If the national central bank concerned does not comply with the opinion within the period laid down by the ECB, the latter may bring the matter before the Court of Justice.

ARTICLE 36
Staff
36.1. The Governing Council, on a proposal from the Executive Board, shall lay down the conditions of employment of the staff of the ECB.

36.2. The Court of Justice shall have jurisdiction in any dispute between the ECB and its servants within the limits and under the conditions laid down in the conditions of employment.

ARTICLE 37
Seat
Before the end of 1992, the decision as to where the seat of the ECB will be established shall be taken be common accord of the governments of the Member States at the level of Heads of State or of Government.

ARTICLE 38
Professional secrecy
38.1. Members of the governing bodies and the staff of the ECB and the national central banks shall be required, even after their duties have ceased, not to disclose information of the kind covered by the obligation of professional secrecy.

38.2. Persons having access to data covered by Community legislation imposing an obligation of secrecy shall be subject to such legislation.

ARTICLE 39
Signatories
The ECB shall be legally committed to third parties by the President or by two members of the Executive Board or by the signatures of two members of the staff of the ECB who have been duly authorised by the President to sign on behalf of the ECB.

ARTICLE 40
Privileges and immunities
The ECB shall enjoy in the territories of the Member States such privileges and immunities as are necessary for the performance of its tasks, under the conditions laid down in the Protocol on the Privileges and Immunities of the European Communities. *Remainder of sentence deleted by the Treaty of Amsterdam.*

CHAPTER VIII

AMENDMENT OF THE STATUTE AND COMPLEMENTARY LEGISLATION

ARTICLE 41
Simplified amendment procedure
41.1. In accordance with Article **107**(5) of this Treaty, Articles 5.1, 5.2, 5.3, 17, 18, 19.1, 22, 23, 24, 26, 32.2, 32.3, 32.4, 32.6, 33.1(a) and 36 of this Statute may be amended by the Council, acting either by a qualified majority on a recommendation from the ECB and after consulting the Commission, or unanimously on a proposal from the Commission and after consulting the ECB. In either case the assent of the European Parliament shall be required.

41.2. A recommendation made by the ECB under this Article shall require a unanimous decision by the Governing Council.

ARTICLE 42
Complementary legislation
In accordance with Article **107**(6) of this Treaty, immediately after the decision on the date for the beginning of the third stage, the Council, acting by a qualified majority either on a proposal from the Commission and after consulting the European Parliament and the ECB or on a recommendation from the ECB and after consulting the European Parliament and the Commission, shall adopt the provisions referred to in Articles 4, 5.4, 19.2, 20, 28. 1, 29.2, 30.4 and 34.3 of this Statute.

CHAPTER IX

TRANSITIONAL AND OTHER PROVISIONS FOR THE ESCB

ARTICLE 43
General provisions
43.1. A derogation as referred to in Article **122**(l) of this Treaty shall entail that the following Articles of this Statute shall not confer any rights or impose any obligations on the Member State concerned: 3, 6, 9.2, 12.1, 14.3, 16, 18, 19, 20, 22, 23, 26.2, 27, 30, 31, 32, 33, 34, 50 and 52.

43.2. The central banks of Member States with a derogation as specified in Article **122**(l) of this Treaty shall retain their powers in the field of monetary policy according to national law.

43.3. In accordance with Article **122**(4) of this Treaty, 'Member States' shall be read as 'Member States without a derogation' in the following Articles of this Statute: 3, 11.2, 19, 34.2 and 50.

43.4. 'National central banks' shall be read as 'central banks of Member States without a derogation' in the following Articles of this Statute: 9.2, 10.1, 10.3, 12.1, 16, 17, 18, 22, 23, 27, 30, 31, 32, 33.2 and 52.

43.5. 'Shareholders' shall be read as 'central banks of Member States without a derogation' in Articles 10.3 and 33.1.

43.6. 'Subscribed capital of the ECB' shall be read as 'capital of the ECB subscribed by the central banks of Member States without a derogation' in Articles 10.3 and 30.2.

ARTICLE 44
Transitional tasks of the ECB
The ECB shall take over those tasks of the EMI which, because of the derogations of one or more Member States, still have to be performed in the third stage.
The ECB shall give advice in the preparations for the abrogation of the derogations specified in Article 109k of this Treaty.

ARTICLE 45
The General Council of the ECB
45.1. Without prejudice to Article **107**(3) of this Treaty, the General Council shall be constituted as a third decision-making body of the ECB.

45.2. The General Council shall comprise the President and Vice-President of the ECB and the Governors of the national central banks. The other members of the Executive Board may participate, without having the right to vote, in meetings of the General Council.

45.3. The responsibilities of the General Council are listed in full in Article 47 of this Statute.

ARTICLE 46
Rules of procedure of the General Council
46.1. The President or, in his absence, the Vice-President of the ECB shall chair the General Council of the ECB.

46.2. The President of the Council and a member of the Commission may participate, without having the right to vote, in meetings of the General Council.

46.3. The President shall prepare the meetings of the General Council.

46.4. By way of derogation from Article 12.3, the General Council shall adopt its Rules of Procedure.

46.5. The Secretariat of the General Council shall be provided by the ECB.

ARTICLE 47
Responsibilities of the General Council
47.1. The General Council shall:
- perform the tasks referred to in Article 44;
- contribute to the advisory functions referred to in Articles 4 and 25.1.

47.2. The General Council shall contribute to:
- the collection of statistical information as referred to in Article 5;
- the reporting activities of the ECB as referred to in Article 15;
- the establishment of the necessary rules for the application of Article 26 as referred to in Article 26.4;
- the taking of all other measures necessary for the application of Article 29 as referred to in Article 29.4;
- the laying down of the conditions of employment of the staff of the ECB as referred to in Article 36.

47.3. The General Council shall contribute to the necessary preparations for irrevocably fixing the exchange rates of the currencies of Member States with a derogation against the currencies, or the single currency, of the Member States without a derogation, as referred to in Article 123(5) of this Treaty.

47.4. The General Council shall be informed by the President of the ECB of decisions of the Governing Council.

ARTICLE 48
Transitional provisions for the capital of the ECB
In accordance with Article 29.1 each national central bank shall be assigned a weighting in the key for subscription of the ECB's capital. By way of derogation from Article 28.3, central banks of Member States with a derogation shall not pay up their subscribed capital unless the General Council, acting by a majority representing at least two-thirds of the subscribed capital of the ECB and at least half of the shareholders, decides that a minimal percentage has to be paid up as a contribution to the operational costs of the ECB.

ARTICLE 49
Deferred payment of capital, reserves and provisions of the ECB
49.1 The central bank of a Member State whose derogation has been abrogated shall pay up its subscribed share of the capital of the ECB to the same extent as the central banks of other Member States without a derogation, and shall transfer to the ECB foreign reserve assets in accordance with Article 30.1. The sum to be transferred shall be determined by multiplying the ECU value at current exchange rates of the foreign reserve assets which have already been transferred to the ECB in accordance with Article 30.1, by the ratio between the number of shares subscribed by the national central bank concerned and the number of shares already paid up by the other national central banks.

49.2. In addition to the payment to be made in accordance with Article 49.1, the central bank concerned shall contribute to the reserves of the ECB, to those provisions equivalent to reserves, and to the amount still to be appropriated to the reserves and provisions corresponding to the balance of the profit and loss account as at 31 December of the year prior to the abrogation of the derogation. The sum to be contributed shall be determined by multiplying the amount of the reserves, as defined above and as stated in the approved balance sheet of the ECB, by the ratio between the number of shares subscribed by the central bank concerned and the number of shares already paid up by the other central banks.

ARTICLE 50
Initial appointment of the members of the Executive Board
When the Executive Board of the ECB is being established, the President, the Vice-President and the other members of the Executive Board shall be appointed by common accord of the governments of the Member States at the level of Heads of State or of Government, on a recommendation from the Council and after consulting the European Parliament and the Council of the EMI. The President of the Executive Board shall be appointed for eight years. By way of derogation from Article 11.2, the Vice-President shall be appointed for four years and the other members of the Executive Board for terms of office of between five and eight years. No term of office shall be renewable. The number of members of the Executive Board may be smaller than provided for in Article 11.1, but in no circumstance shall it be less than four.

ARTICLE 51
Derogation from Article 32
51.1. If, after the start of the third stage, the Governing Council decides that the application of Article 32 results in significant changes in national central banks' relative income positions, the amount of income to be allocated pursuant to Article 32 shall be reduced by a uniform percentage which shall not exceed 60% in the first financial year after the start of the third stage and which shall decrease by at least 12 percentage points in each subsequent financial year.

51.2. Article 51.1 shall be applicable for not more than five financial years after the start of the third stage.

ARTICLE 52
Exchange of bank notes in Community currencies
Following the irrevocable fixing of exchange rates, the Governing Council shall take the necessary measures to ensure that bank notes denominated in currencies with irrevocably fixed exchange rates are exchanged by the national central banks at their respective par values.

ARTICLE 53
Applicability of the transitional provisions
If and as long as there are Member States with a derogation Articles 43 to 48 shall be applicable.
(This protocol was introduced by the Maastricht Treaty.)

19. PROTOCOL ON THE STATUTE OF THE EUROPEAN MONETARY INSTITUTE

THE HIGH CONTRACTING PARTIES,

DESIRING TO lay down the Statute of the European Monetary Institute,

HAVE AGREED UPON the following provisions, which shall be annexed to the Treaty establishing the European Community:

ARTICLE 1
Constitution and name
1.1. The European Monetary Institute (EMI) shall be established in accordance with Article **117** of this Treaty; it shall perform its functions and carry out its activities in accordance with the provisions of this Treaty and of this Statute.

1.2. The members of the EMI shall be the central banks of the Member States ('national central banks'). For the purposes of this Statute, the Institut monétiare luxembourgeois shall be regarded as the central bank of Luxembourg.

1.3. Pursuant to Article **117** of this Treaty, both the Committee of Governors and the European Monetary Co-operation Fund (EMCF) shall be dissolved. All assets and liabilities of the EMCF shall pass automatically to the EMI.

ARTICLE 2
Objectives
The EMI shall contribute to the realisation of the conditions necessary for the transition to the third stage of Economic and Monetary Union, in particular by:
- strengthening the co-ordination of monetary policies with a view to ensuring price stability;
- making the preparations required for the establishment of the European System of Central Banks (ESCB), and for the conduct of a single monetary policy and the creation of a single currency in the third stage;
- overseeing the development of the ECU.

ARTICLE 3
General principles
3.1. The EMI shall carry out the tasks and functions conferred upon it by this Treaty and this Statute without prejudice to the responsibility of the competent authorities for the conduct of the monetary policy within the respective Member States.

3.2. The EMI shall act in accordance with the objectives and principles stated in Article 2 of the Statute of the ESCB.

ARTICLE 4
Primary tasks
4.1. In accordance with Article **117**(2) of this Treaty, the EMI shall:
- strengthen co-operation between the national central banks;

- strengthen the co-ordination of the monetary policies of the Member States with the aim of ensuring price stability;
- monitor the functioning of the European Monetary System (EMS);
- hold consultations concerning issues falling within the competence of the national central banks and affecting the stability of financial institutions and markets;
- take over the tasks of the EMCF; in particular it shall perform the functions referred to in Articles 6.1, 6.2 and 6.3;
- facilitate the use of the ECU and oversee its development, including the smooth functioning of the ECU clearing system.

The EMI shall also:
- hold regular consultations concerning the course of monetary policies and the use of monetary policy instruments;
- normally be consulted by the national monetary authorities before they take decisions on the course of monetary policy in the context of the common framework for *ex ante* co-ordination.

4.2. At the latest by 31 December 1996, the EMI shall specify the regulatory, organisational and logistical framework necessary for the ESCB to perform its tasks in the third stage, in accordance with the principle of an open market economy with free competition. This framework shall be submitted by the Council of the EMI for decision to the ECB at the date of its establishment.

In accordance with Article **117**(3) of this Treaty, the EMI shall in particular:
- prepare the instruments and the procedures necessary for carrying out a single monetary policy in the third stage;
- promote the harmonisation, where necessary, of the rules and practices governing the collection, compilation and distribution of statistics in the areas within its field of competence;
- prepare the rules for operations to be undertaken by the national central banks in the framework of the ESCB;
- promote the efficiency of cross-border payments;
- supervise the technical preparation of ECU bank notes.

ARTICLE 5
Advisory functions

5.1. In accordance with Article **117**(4) of this Treaty, the Council of the EMI may formulate opinions or recommendations on the overall orientation of monetary policy and exchange rate policy as well as on related measures introduced in each Member State. The EMI may submit opinions or recommendations to governments and to the Council on policies which might affect the internal or external monetary situation in the Community and, in particular, the functioning of the EMS.

5.2. The Council of the EMI may also make recommendations to the monetary authorities of the Member States concerning the conduct of their monetary policy.

5.3. In accordance with Article **117**(6) of this Treaty, the EMI shall be consulted by the Council regarding any proposed Community act within its field of competence. Within the limits and under the conditions set out by the Council acting by a qualified majority on a proposal from the Commission and after consulting the European Parliament and the EMI, the EMI shall be consulted by the authorities of the Member States on any draft legislative provision within its field of competence, in particular with regard to Article 4.2.

5.4. In accordance with Article **117**(5) of this Treaty, the EMI may decide to publish its opinions and its recommendations.

ARTICLE 6
Operational and technical functions
6.1. The EMI shall;
- provide for the multilateralisation of positions resulting from interventions by the national central banks in Community currencies and the multilateralisation of intra-Community settlements;
- administer the very short-term financing mechanism provided for by the Agreement of 13 March 1979 between the central banks of the Member States of the European Economic Community laying down the operating procedures for the European Monetary System (hereinafter referred to as 'EMS Agreement') and the short-term monetary support mechanism provided for in the Agreement between the central banks of the Member States of the European Economic Community of 9 February 1970, as amended;
- perform the functions referred to in Article 11 of Council Regulation (EEC) No. 1969/88 of 24 June 1988 establishing a single facility providing medium-term financial assistance for Member States' balances of payments.

6.2.   The EMI may receive monetary reserves from the national central banks and issue ECUs against such assets for the purpose of implementing the EMS Agreement. These ECUs may be used by the EMI and the national central banks as a means of settlement and for transactions between them and the EMI. The EMI shall take the necessary administrative measures for the implementation of this paragraph.

6.3.   The EMI may grant to the monetary authorities of third countries and to international monetary institutions the status of 'other holders' of ECUs and fix the terms and conditions under which such ECUs may be acquired, held or used by other holders.

6.4.   The EMI shall be entitled to hold and manage foreign exchange reserves as an agent for and at the request of national central banks. Profits and losses regarding these reserves shall be for the account of the national central bank depositing the reserves. The EMI shall perform this function on the basis of bilateral contracts in accordance with rules laid down in a decision of the EMI. These rules shall ensure that transactions with these reserves shall not interfere with the monetary policy and exchange rate policy of the competent monetary authority of any Member State and shall be consistent with the objectives of the EMI and the proper functioning of the Exchange Rate Mechanism of the EMS.

ARTICLE 7
Other tasks
7.1.   Once a year the EMI shall address a report to the Council on the state of the preparations for the third stage. These reports shall include an assessment of the progress towards convergence in the Community, and cover in particular the adaptation of monetary policy instruments and the preparation of the procedures necessary for carrying out a single monetary policy in the third stage, as well as the statutory requirements to be fulfilled for national central banks to become an integral part of the ESCB.

7.2.   In accordance with the Council decisions referred to in Article **117**(7) of this Treaty, the EMI may perform other tasks for the preparation of the third stage.

ARTICLE 8
Independence
The members of the Council of the EMI who are the representatives of their institutions shall, with respect to their activities, act according their own responsibilities. In exercising the powers and performing the tasks and duties conferred upon them by this Treaty and this Statute, the Council of the EMI may not seek or take any instructions from Community institutions or bodies or governments of Member States. The Community institutions and bodies as well as the governments of the Member States undertake to respect this principle and not to seek to influence the Council of the EMI in the performance of its tasks.

ARTICLE 9
Administration
9.1.   In accordance with Article **117**(l) of this Treaty, the EMI shall be directed and managed by the Council of the EMI.

9.2.   The Council of the EMI shall consist of a President and the Governors of the national central banks, one of whom shall be Vice-President. If a Governor is prevented from attending a meeting, he may nominate another representative of his institution.

9.3.   The President shall be appointed by common accord of the governments of the Member States at the level of Heads of State or of Government, on a recommendation from, as the case may be, the Committee of Governors or the Council of the EMI, and after consulting the European Parliament and the Council. The President shall be selected from among persons of recognised standing and professional experience in monetary or banking matters. Only nationals of Member States may be President of the EMI. The Council of the EMI shall appoint the Vice-President. The President and Vice-President shall be appointed for a period of three years.

9.4.   The President shall perform his duties on a full-time basis. He shall not engage in any occupation, whether gainful or not, unless exemption is exceptionally granted by the Council of the EMI.

9.5.   The President shall:
-    prepare and chair the meetings of the Council of the EMI;
-    without prejudice to Article 22, present the views of the EMI externally;
-    be responsible for the day-today management of the EMI.
In the absence of the President, his duties shall be performed by the Vice-President.

9.6. The terms and conditions of employment of the President, in particular his salary, pension and other social security benefits, shall be the subject of a contract with the EMI and shall be fixed by the Council of the EMI on a proposal from a Committee comprising three members appointed by the Committee of Governors or the Council of the EMI, as the case may be, and three members appointed by the Council. The President shall not have the right to vote on matters referred to in this paragraph.

9.7. If the President no longer fulfils the conditions required for the performance of his duties or if he has been guilty of serious misconduct, the Court of Justice may, on application by the Council of the EMI, compulsorily retire him.

9.8. The Rules of Procedure of the EMI shall be adopted by the Council of the EMI.

ARTICLE 10
Meetings of the Council of the EMI and voting procedures
10.1. The Council of the EMI shall meet at least ten times a year. The proceedings of Council meetings shall be confidential. The Council of the EMI may, acting unanimously, decide to make the outcome of its deliberations public.

10.2. Each member of the Council of the EMI or his nominee shall have one vote.

10.3. Save as otherwise provided for in this Statute, the Council of the EMI shall act by a simple majority of its members.

10.4. Decisions to be taken in the context of Articles 4.2, 5.4, 6.2 and 6.3 shall require unanimity of the members of the Council of the EMI.
The adoption of opinions and recommendations under Articles 5.1 and 5.2, the adoption of decisions under Articles 6.4, 16 and 23.6 and the adoption of guidelines under Article 15.3 shall require a qualified majority of two-thirds of the members of the Council of the EMI.

ARTICLE 11
Inter-institutional co-operation and reporting requirements
11.1. The President of the Council and a member of the Commission may participate, without having the right to vote, in meetings of the Council of the EMI.

11.2. The President of the EMI shall be invited to participate in Council meetings when the Council is discussing matters relating to the objectives and tasks of the EMI.

11.3. At a date to be established in the Rule of Procedure, the EMI shall prepare an annual report on its activities and on monetary and financial conditions in the Community. The annual report, together with the annual accounts of the EMI, shall be addressed to the European Parliament, the Council and the Commission and also to the European Council.
The President of the EMI may, at the request of the European Parliament or on his own initiative, be heard by the competent Committees of the European Parliament.

11.4. Reports published by the EMI shall be made available to interested parties free of charge.

ARTICLE 12
Currency denomination
The operations of the EMI shall be expressed in ECUs.

ARTICLE 13
Seat
Before the end of 1992, the decision as to where the seat of the EMI will be established shall be taken by common accord of the governments of the Member States at the level of Heads of State or of Government.

ARTICLE 14
Legal capacity
The EMI, which in accordance with Article **117**(1) of this Treaty shall have legal personality, shall enjoy in each of the Member States the most extensive legal capacity accorded to legal persons under their law; it may, in particular, acquire or dispose of movable or immovable property and may be a party to legal proceedings.

ARTICLE 15
Legal acts
15.1. In the performance of its tasks, and under the conditions laid down in this Statute, the EMI shall:
-    deliver opinions;

- make recommendations;
- adopt guidelines, and take decisions, which shall be addressed to the national central banks.

15.2. Opinions and recommendations of the EMI shall have no binding force.

15.3. The Council of the EMI may adopt guidelines laying down the methods for the implementation of the conditions necessary for the ESCB to perform its functions in the third stage. EMI guidelines shall have no binding force; they shall be submitted for decision to the ECB.

15.4. Without prejudice to Article 3.1, a decision of the EMI shall be binding in its entirety upon those to whom it is addressed. Articles **253** and **254** of this Treaty shall apply to these decisions.

ARTICLE 16
Financial resources
16.1. The EMI shall be endowed with its own resources. The size of the resources of the EMI shall be determined by the Council of the EMI with a view to ensuring the income deemed necessary to cover the administrative expenditure incurred in the performance of the tasks and functions of the EMI.

16.2. The resources of the EMI determined in accordance with Article 16.1 shall be provided out of contributions by the national central banks in accordance with the key referred to in Article 29.1 of the Statute of the ESCB and be paid up at the establishment of the EMI. For this purpose, the statistical data to be used for the determination of the key shall be provided by the Commission, in accordance with the rules adopted by the Council, acting by a qualified majority on a proposal from the Commission and after consulting the European Parliament, the Committee of Governors and the Committee referred to in Article **114** of this Treaty.

16.3. The Council of the EMI shall determine the form in which contributions shall be paid up.

ARTICLE 17
Annual accounts and auditing
17.1. The financial year of the EMI shall begin on the first day of January and end on the last day of December.

17.2. The Council of the EMI shall adopt an annual budget before the beginning of each financial year.

17.3. The annual accounts shall be drawn up in accordance with the principles established by the Council of the EMI. The annual accounts shall be approved by the Council of the EMI and shall thereafter be published.

17.4. The annual accounts shall be audited by independent external auditors approved by the Council of the EMI. The auditors shall have full power to examine all books and accounts of the EMI and to obtain full information about its transactions.
The provisions of Article **247** of this Treaty shall only apply to an examination of the operational efficiency of the management of the EMI.

17.5. Any surplus of the EMI shall be transferred in the following order:
(a) an amount to be determined by the Council of the EMI shall be transferred to the general reserve fund of the EMI;
(b) any remaining surplus shall be distributed to the national central banks in accordance with the key referred to in Article 16.2.

17.6. In the event of a loss incurred by the EMI, the shortfall shall be offset against the general reserve fund of the EMI. Any remaining shortfall shall be made good by contributions from the national central banks, in accordance with the key as referred to in Article 16.2.

ARTICLE 18
Staff
18.1. The Council of the EMI shall lay down the conditions of employment of the staff of the EMI.

18.2. The Court of Justice shall have jurisdiction in any dispute between the EMI and its servants within the limits and under the conditions laid down in the conditions of employment.

ARTICLE 19
Judicial control and related matters
19.1. The acts or omissions of the EMI shall be open to review or interpretation by the Court of Justice in the cases and under the conditions laid down in the Treaty. The EMI may institute proceedings in the cases and under the conditions laid down in this Treaty.

19.2. Disputes between the EMI, on the one hand, and its creditors, debtors or any other person, on the other, shall fall within the jurisdiction of the competent national courts, save where jurisdiction has been conferred upon the Court of Justice.

19.3. The EMI shall be subject to the liability regime provided for in Article **288** of this Treaty.

19.4. The Court of Justice shall have jurisdiction to give judgement pursuant to any arbitration clause contained in a contract concluded by or on behalf of the EMI, whether that contract be governed by public or private law.

19.5. A decision of the EMI to bring an action before the Court of Justice shall be taken by the Council of the EMI.

ARTICLE 20
Professional secrecy
20.1. Members of the Council of the EMI and the staff of the EMI shall be required, even after their duties have ceased, not to disclose information of the kind covered by the obligation of professional secrecy.

20.2. Persons having access to data covered by Community legislation imposing an obligation of secrecy shall be subject to such legislation.

ARTICLE 21
Privileges and immunities
The EMI shall enjoy in the territories of the Member States such privileges and immunities as are necessary for the performance of its tasks, under the conditions laid down in the Protocol on the Privileges and Immunities of the European Communities. ***Remainder of sentence deleted by the Treaty of Amsterdam.***

ARTICLE 22
Signatories
The EMI shall be legally committed to third parties by the President or the Vice-President or by the signatures of two members of the staff of the EMI who have been duly authorised by the President to sign on behalf of the EMI.

ARTICLE 23
Liquidation of the EMI
23.1. In accordance with Article **123** of this Treaty, the EMI shall go into liquidation on the establishment of the ECB. All assets and liabilities of the EMI shall then pass automatically to the ECB. The latter shall liquidate the EMI according to the provisions of this Article. The liquidation shall be completed by the beginning of the third stage.

23.2. The mechanism for the creation of ECUs against gold and US dollars as provided for by Article 17 of the EMS Agreement shall be unwound by the first day of the third stage in accordance with Article 20 of the said Agreement.

23.3. All claims and liabilities arising from the very short-term financing mechanism and the short-term monetary support mechanism, under the Agreements referred to in Article 6.1, shall be settled by the first day of the third stage.

23.4. All remaining assets of the EMI shall be disposed of and all remaining liabilities of the EMI shall be settled.

23.5. The proceeds of the liquidation described in Article 23.4 shall be distributed to the national central banks in accordance with the key referred to in Article 16.2.

23.6. The Council of the EMI may take the measures necessary for the application of Articles 23.4 and 23.5.

23.7. Upon the establishment of the ECB, the President of the EMI shall relinquish his office.
(This protocol was introduced by the Maastricht Treaty.)

20. PROTOCOL ON THE EXCESSIVE DEFICIT PROCEDURE

THE HIGH CONTRACTING PARTIES,

DESIRING TO lay down the details of the excessive deficit procedure referred to in Article **104** of the Treaty establishing the European Community,

HAVE AGREED upon the following provisions, which shall be annexed to the Treaty establishing the European Community:

ARTICLE 1
The reference values referred to in Article **104**(2) of this Treaty are:
- 3% for the ratio of the planned or actual government deficit to gross domestic product at market prices;
- 60% for the ratio of government debt to gross domestic product at market prices.

ARTICLE 2
In Article **104** of this Treaty and in this Protocol:
- government means general government, that is central government, regional or local government and social security funds, to the exclusion of commercial operations, as defined in the European System of Integrated Economic Accounts;
- deficit means net borrowing as defined in the European System of Integrated Economic Accounts;
- investment means gross fixed capital formation as defined in the European System of Integrated Economic Accounts;
- debt means total gross debt at nominal value outstanding at the end of the year and consolidated between and within the sectors of general government as defined in the first indent.

ARTICLE 3
In order to ensure the effectiveness of the excessive deficit procedure, the governments of the Member States shall be responsible under this procedure for the deficits of general government as defined in the first indent of Article 2. The Member States shall ensure that national procedures in the budgetary area enable them to meet their obligations in this area deriving from this Treaty. The Member States shall report their planned and actual deficits and the levels of their debt promptly and regularly to the Commission.

ARTICLE 4
The statistical data to be used for the application of this Protocol shall be provided by the Commission.
(This protocol was introduced by the Maastricht Treaty.)

21. PROTOCOL ON THE CONVERGENCE CRITERIA REFERRED TO IN ARTICLE 121 OF THE TREATY ESTABLISHING THE EUROPEAN COMMUNITY

THE HIGH CONTRACTING PARTIES,

DESIRING to lay down the details of the convergence criteria which shall guide the Community in taking decisions on the passage to the third stage of economic and monetary union, referred to in Article **121**(l) of this Treaty,

HAVE AGREED upon the following provisions, which shall be annexed to the Treaty establishing the European Community:

ARTICLE 1
The criterion on price stability referred to in the first indent of Article **121**(l) of this Treaty shall mean that a Member State has a price performance that is sustainable and an average rate of inflation, observed over a period of one year before the examination, that does not exceed by more than 1½ percentage points that of, at most, the three best performing Member States in terms of price stability. Inflation shall be measured by means of the consumer price index on a comparable basis, taking into account differences in national definitions.

ARTICLE 2
The criterion on the government budgetary position referred to in the second indent of Article **121**(l) of this Treaty shall mean that at the time of the examination the Member State is not the subject of a Council decision under Article **104**(6) of this Treaty that an excessive deficit exists.

ARTICLE 3
The criterion on participation in the Exchange Rate Mechanism of the European Monetary System referred to in the third indent of Article **121**(l) of this Treaty shall mean that a Member State has respected the normal fluctuation margins provided for by the Exchange Rate Mechanism of the European Monetary System without severe tensions for at least the last two years before the examination. In particular, the Member State shall not have devalued its currency's bilateral central rate against any other Member State's currency on its own initiative for the same period.

ARTICLE 4
The criterion on the convergence of interest rates referred to in the fourth indent of Article **121**(l) of this Treaty shall mean that, observed over a period of one year before the examination, a Member State has had an average nominal long-term interest rate that does not exceed by more than 2 percentage points that of, at most, the three best performing Member States in terms of price stability. Interest rates shall be measured on the basis of long term government bonds or comparable securities, taking into account differences in national definitions.

ARTICLE 5
The statistical data to be used for the application of this Protocol shall be provided by the Commission.

ARTICLE 6
The Council shall, acting unanimously on a proposal from the Commission and after consulting the European Parliament, the EMI or the ECB as the case may be, and the Committee referred to in Article **114**, adopt appropriate provisions to lay down the details of the convergence criteria referred to in Article **121** of this Treaty, which shall then replace this Protocol.
(This protocol was introduced by the Maastricht Treaty.)

22.   PROTOCOL ON DENMARK

THE HIGH CONTRACTING PARTIES,

DESIRING to settle certain particular problems relating to Denmark,

HAVE AGREED UPON the following provisions, which shall be annexed to the Treaty establishing the European Community:

The provisions of Article 14 of the Protocol on the Statute of the European System of Central Banks and of the European Central Bank shall not affect the right of the National Bank of Denmark to carry out its existing tasks concerning those parts of the Kingdom of Denmark which are not part of the Community.
(This protocol was introduced by the Maastricht Treaty.)

23.   PROTOCOL ON PORTUGAL

THE HIGH CONTRACTING PARTIES,

DESIRING TO settle certain particular problems relating to Portugal,

HAVE AGREED upon the following provisions, which shall be annexed to the Treaty establishing the European Community:

1.   Portugal is hereby authorised to maintain the facility afforded to the Autonomous Regions of Azores and Madeira to benefit from an interest-free credit facility with the Banco de Portugal under the terms established by existing Portuguese law.

2.   Portugal commits itself to pursue its best endeavours in order to put an end to the above-mentioned facility as soon as possible.
(This protocol was introduced by the Maastricht Treaty.)

24.   PROTOCOL ON THE TRANSITION TO THE THIRD STAGE OF ECONOMIC AND MONETARY UNION

THE HIGH CONTRACTING PARTIES,

Declare the irreversible character of the Community's movement to the third stage of Economic and Monetary Union by signing the new Treaty provision on Economic and Monetary Union.

Therefore all Member States shall, whether they fulfil the necessary conditions for the adoption of a single currency or not, respect the will for the Community to enter swiftly into the third stage, and therefore no Member State shall prevent the entering into the third stage.

If by the end of 1997 the date of the beginning of the third stage has not been set, the Member States concerned, the Community institutions and other bodies involved shall expedite all preparatory work during 1998, in order to enable the Community to enter the third stage irrevocably on 1 January 1999 and to enable the ECB and the ESCB to start their full functioning from this date.

This Protocol shall be annexed to the Treaty establishing the European Community.
(This protocol was introduced by the Maastricht Treaty.)

25.   PROTOCOL ON CERTAIN PROVISIONS RELATING TO THE UNITED KINGDOM OF GREAT BRITAIN AND NORTHERN IRELAND

THE HIGH CONTRACTING PARTIES,

RECOGNISING that the United Kingdom shall not be obliged or committed to move to the third stage of Economic and Monetary Union without a separate decision to do so by its government and Parliament,

NOTING the practice of the government of the United Kingdom to fund its borrowing requirement by the sale of debt to the private sector,

HAVE AGREED the following provisions, which shall be annexed to the Treaty establishing the European Community:

1.   The United Kingdom shall notify the Council whether it intends to move to the third stage before the Council makes its assessment under Article **121**(2) of this Treaty.
Unless the United Kingdom notifies the Council that it intends to move to the Third Stage, it shall be under no obligation to do so.
If no date is set for the beginning of the third stage under Article **121**(3) of this Treaty, the United Kingdom may notify its intention to move to the third stage before 1 January 1998.

2.   Paragraphs 3 to 9 shall have effect if the United Kingdom notifies the Council that it does not intend to move to the third stage.

3.   The United Kingdom shall not be included among the majority of Member States which fulfil the necessary conditions referred to in the second indent of Article **121**(2) and the first indent of Article **121**(3) of this Treaty.

4.   The United Kingdom shall retain its powers in the field of monetary policy according to national law.

5.   Articles **4**(2), **104**(l), (9) and (11), **105**(1) to (5), **106**, **108**, **109**, **110**, **111**, **112**(l) and (2)(b) and **123**(4) and (5) of this Treaty shall not apply to the United Kingdom. In these provisions references to the Community or the Member States shall not include the United Kingdom and references to national central banks shall not include the Bank of England.

6.   Articles **116**(4) and **119** and **120** of this Treaty shall continue to apply to the United Kingdom. Articles **114**(4) and **124** shall apply to the United Kingdom as if it had a derogation.

7.   The voting rights of the United Kingdom shall be suspended in respect of acts of the Council referred to in the Articles listed in paragraph 5. For this purpose the weighted votes of the United Kingdom shall be excluded from any calculation of a qualified majority under Article **122**(5) of this Treaty.
The United Kingdom shall also have no right to participate in the appointment of the President, the Vice-President and the other members of the Executive Board of the ECB under Articles **112**(2)(b) and **123**(1) of this Treaty.

8.   Articles, 3, 4, 6, 7, 9.2, 10.1, 10.3, 11.2, 12.1, 14, 16, 18 to 20, 22, 23, 26, 27, 30 to 34, 50 and 52 of the Protocol on the Statute of the European System of Central Banks and of the European Central Bank ('the Statute') shall not apply to the United Kingdom.
In those Articles, references to the Community or the Member States shall not include the United Kingdom and references to national central banks or shareholders shall not include the Bank of England.
References in Articles 10.3 and 30.2 of the Statute to 'subscribed capital of the ECB' shall not include capital subscribed by the Bank of England.

9.   Article **123**(3) of this Treaty and Articles 44 to 48 of the Statute shall have effect, whether or not there is any Member State with a derogation, subject to the following amendments:
(a)   References in Article 44 to the tasks of the ECB and the EMI shall include those tasks that still need to be performed in the third stage owing to any decision of the United Kingdom not to move to that stage.
(b)   In addition to the tasks referred to in Article 47 the ECB shall also give advice in relation to and contribute to the preparation of any decision of the Council with regard to the United Kingdom taken in accordance with paragraphs 10(a) and 10(c).
(c)   The Bank of England shall pay up its subscription to the capital of the ECB as a contribution to its operational costs on the same basis as national central banks of Member States with a derogation.

10.   If the United Kingdom does not move to the third stage, it may change its notification at any time after the beginning of that stage. In that event:
(a)   The United Kingdom shall have the right to move to the third stage provided only that it satisfies the necessary conditions. The Council, acting at the request of the United Kingdom and under the conditions and in accordance with the procedure laid down in Article **122**(2) of this Treaty, shall decide whether it fulfils the necessary conditions.
(b)   The Bank of England shall pay up its subscribed capital, transfer to the ECB foreign reserve assets and contribute to its reserves on the same basis as the national central bank of a Member State whose derogation has been abrogated.
(c)   The Council, acting under the conditions and in accordance with the procedure laid down in Article **123**(5) of this Treaty, shall take all other necessary decisions to enable the United Kingdom to move to the third stage.

If the United Kingdom moves to the third stage pursuant to the provisions of this protocol, paragraphs 3 to 9 shall cease to have effect.

11.   Notwithstanding Articles **101** and **116**(3) of this Treaty and Article 21.1 of the Statute, the government of the United Kingdom may maintain its 'Ways and Means' facility with the Bank of England if and so long as the United Kingdom does not move to the third stage.
(This protocol was introduced by the Maastricht Treaty.)

26. PROTOCOL ON CERTAIN PROVISIONS RELATING TO DENMARK

THE HIGH CONTRACTING PARTIES,

DESIRING to settle, in accordance with the general objectives of the Treaty establishing the European Community, certain particular problems existing at the present time,

TAKING INTO ACCOUNT that the Danish Constitution contains provisions which may imply a referendum in Denmark prior to Danish participation in the third stage of Economic and Monetary Union,

HAVE AGREED on the following provisions, which shall be annexed to the Treaty establishing the European Community:

1. The Danish Government shall notify the Council of its position concerning participation in the third stage before the Council makes its assessment under Article **121**(2) of this Treaty.

2. In the event of a notification that Denmark will not participate in the third stage, Denmark shall have an exemption. The effect of the exemption shall be that all Articles and provisions of this Treaty and the Statute of the ESCB referring to a derogation shall be applicable to Denmark.

3. In such case, Denmark shall not be included among the majority of Member States which fulfil the necessary conditions referred to in the second indent of Article **121**(2) and the first indent of Article **121**(3) of this Treaty.

4. As for the abrogation of the exemption, the procedure referred to in Article **122**(2) shall only be initiated at the request of Denmark.

5. In the event of abrogation of the exemption status, the provisions of the Protocol shall cease to apply.
(This protocol was introduced by the Maastricht Treaty.)

27. PROTOCOL ON FRANCE

THE HIGH CONTRACTING PARTIES,

DESIRING TO take into account a particular point relating to France,

HAVE AGREED upon the following provisions, which shall be annexed to the Treaty establishing the European Community:

France will keep the privilege of monetary emission in its overseas territories under the terms established by its national laws, and will be solely entitled to determine the parity of the CFP franc.
(This protocol was introduced by the Maastricht Treaty.)

28. PROTOCOL ON ECONOMIC AND SOCIAL COHESION

THE HIGH CONTRACTING PARTIES,

RECALLING that the Union has set itself the objective of promoting economic and social progress, *inter alia*, through the strengthening of economic and social cohesion;

RECALLING that Article **2** of the Treaty establishing the European Community includes the task of promoting economic and social cohesion and solidarity between Member States and that the strengthening of economic and social cohesion figures among the activities of the Community listed in Article **3**;

RECALLING that the provisions of Part Three, Title **XVII**, on economic and social cohesion as a whole provide the legal basis for consolidating and further developing the Community's action in the field of economic and social cohesion, including the creation of a new fund;

RECALLING that the provisions of Part Three, Title **XV** on trans-European networks and Title **XIX** on environment envisage a Cohesion Fund to be set up before 31 December 1993;

STATING their belief that progress towards Economic and Monetary Union will contribute to the economic growth of all Member States;

NOTING that the Community's Structural Funds are being doubled in real terms between 1987 and 1993, implying large transfers, especially as a proportion of GDP of the less prosperous Member States;

NOTING that the European Investment Bank is lending large and increasing amounts for the benefit of the poorer regions;

NOTING the desire for greater flexibility in the arrangements for allocations from the Structural Funds;

NOTING the desire for modulation of the levels of Community participation in programmes and projects in certain countries;

NOTING the proposal to take greater account of the relative prosperity of Member States in the system of own resources,

REAFFIRM that the promotion of economic and social cohesion is vital to the full development and enduring success of the Community, and underline the importance of the inclusion of economic and social cohesion in Articles 2 and 3 of this Treaty;

REAFFIRM their conviction that the Structural Funds should continue to play a considerable part in the achievement of Community objectives in the field of cohesion;

REAFFIRM their conviction that the European Investment Bank should continue to devote the majority of its resources to the promotion of economic and social cohesion, and declare their willingness to review the capital needs of the European Investment Bank as soon as this is necessary for that purpose;

REAFFIRM the need for a thorough evaluation of the operation and effectiveness of the Structural Funds in 1992, and the need to review on that occasion, the appropriate size of these Funds in the light of the tasks of the Community in the area of economic and social cohesion;

AGREE that the Cohesion Fund to be set up before 31 December 1993 will provide Community financial contributions to projects in the fields of environment and trans-European networks in Member States with a *per capita* GNP of less than 90% of the Community average which have a programme leading to the fulfilment of the conditions of economic convergence as set out in Article **104**;

DECLARE their intention of allowing a greater margin of flexibility in allocating financing from the Structural Funds to specific needs not covered under the present Structural Funds regulations;

DECLARE their willingness to modulate the levels of Community participation in the context of programmes and projects of the Structural Funds, with a view to avoiding excessive increases in budgetary expenditure in the less prosperous Member States;

RECOGNISE the need to monitor regularly the progress made towards achieving economic and social cohesion and state their willingness to study all necessary measures in this respect;

DECLARE their intention of taking greater account of the contributive capacity of individual Member States in the system of own resources, and of examining means of correcting, for the less prosperous Member States, regressive elements existing in the present own resources system;

AGREE to annex this Protocol to the Treaty establishing the European Community.
(This protocol was introduced by the Maastricht Treaty.)

29. PROTOCOL ON ASYLUM FOR NATIONALS OF MEMBER STATES OF THE EUROPEAN UNION

THE HIGH CONTRACTING PARTIES,

WHEREAS pursuant to the provisions of Article 6(2) of the Treaty on European Union, the Union shall respect fundamental rights as guaranteed by the European Convention for the Protection of Human Rights and Fundamental Freedoms signed in Rome on 4 November 1950;

WHEREAS the Court of Justice of the European Communities has jurisdiction to ensure that in the interpretation and application of Article 6(2) of the Treaty on European Union the law is observed by the European Community;

WHEREAS pursuant to Article 49 of the Treaty on European Union any European State, when applying to become a Member of the Union, must respect the principles set out in Article 6(1) of the Treaty on European Union;

BEARING IN MIND that Article 309 of the Treaty establishing the European Community establishes a mechanism for the suspension of certain rights in the event of a serious and persistent breach by a Member State of those principles;

RECALLING that each national of a Member State, as a citizen of the Union, enjoys a special status and protection which shall be guaranteed by the Member States in accordance with the provisions of Part Two of the Treaty establishing the European Community;

BEARING IN MIND that the Treaty establishing the European Community establishes an area without internal frontiers and grants every citizen of the Union the right to move and reside freely within the territory of the Member States;

RECALLING that the question of extradition of nationals of Member States of the Union is addressed in the European Convention on Extradition of 13 December 1957 and the Convention of 27 September 1996 drawn up on the basis of Article 31 of the Treaty on European Union relating to extradition between the Member States of the European Union;

WISHING to prevent that the institution of asylum is resorted to for purposes alien to those for which it is intended;

WHEREAS this Protocol respects the finality and the objectives of the Geneva Convention of 28 July 1951 relating to the status of refugees;

HAVE AGREED UPON the following provisions which shall be annexed to the Treaty establishing the European Community:

SOLE ARTICLE
Given the level of protection of fundamental rights and freedoms by the Member States of the European Union, Member States shall be regarded as constituting safe countries of origin in respect of each other for all legal and practical purposes in relation to asylum matters. Accordingly, any application for asylum made by a national of a Member State may be taken into consideration or declared admissible for processing by another Member State only in the following cases:
(a) if the Member State of which the applicant is a national proceeds after the entry into force of the Treaty of Amsterdam, availing itself of the provisions of Article 15 of the Convention for the Protection of Human Rights and Fundamental Freedoms, to take measures derogating in its territory from its obligations under that Convention;
(b) if the procedure referred to Article 7(1) of the Treaty on European Union has been initiated and until the Council takes a decision in respect thereof;
(c) if the Council, acting on the basis of Article 7(1) of the Treaty on European Union, has determined, in respect of the Member State which the applicant is a national, the existence of a serious and persistent breach by that Member State of principles mentioned in Article 6(1);
(d) if a Member State should so decide unilaterally in respect of the application of a national of another Member State; in that case the Council shall be immediately informed; the application shall be dealt with on the basis of the presumption that it is manifestly unfounded without affecting in any way, whatever the cases may be, the decision-making power of the Member State.

30. PROTOCOL ON THE APPLICATION OF THE PRINCIPLES OF SUBSIDIARITY AND PROPORTIONALITY

THE HIGH CONTRACTING PARTIES,

DETERMINED to establish the conditions for the application of the principles of subsidiarity and proportionality enshrined in Article 5 of the Treaty establishing the European Community with a view to defining more precisely the criteria for applying them and to ensure their strict observance and consistent implementation by all institutions;

WISHING to ensure that decisions are taken as closely as possible to the citizens of the Union;

TAKING ACCOUNT of the Inter-institutional Agreement of 28 October 1993 between the European Parliament, the Council and the Commission on procedures for implementing the principle of subsidiarity;

HAVE CONFIRMED that the conclusions of the Birmingham European Council on 16 October 1992 and the overall approach to the application of the subsidiarity principle agreed by the European Council meeting in Edinburgh on 11-12 December 1992 will continue to guide the action of the Union's institutions as well as the development of the application of the principle of subsidiarity, and, for this purpose,

HAVE AGREED ON the following provisions which shall be annexed to the Treaty establishing the European Community:

(1)   In exercising the powers conferred on it, each institution shall ensure that the principle of subsidiarity is complied with. It shall also ensure compliance with the principle of proportionality, according to which any action by the Community shall not go beyond what is necessary to achieve the objectives of the Treaty.

(2)   The application of the principles of subsidiarity and proportionality shall respect the general provisions and the objectives of the Treaty, particularly as regards the maintaining in full of the *acquis communautaire* and the institutional balance; it shall not affect the principles developed by the Court of Justice regarding the relationship between national and Community law, and it should take into account Article 6(4) of the Treaty on European Union, according to which "the Union shall provide itself with the means necessary to attain its objectives and carry through its policies".

(3)   The principle of subsidiarity does not call into question the powers conferred on the European Community by the Treaty, as interpreted by the Court of Justice. The criteria referred to in the second paragraph of Article 5 of the Treaty shall relate to areas for which the Community does not have exclusive competence. The principle of subsidiarity provides a guide as to how those powers are to be exercised at the Community level. Subsidiarity is a dynamic concept and should be applied in the light of the objectives set out in the Treaty. It allows Community action within the limits of its powers to be expanded where circumstances so require, and conversely, to be restricted or discontinued where it is no longer justified.

(4)   For any proposed Community legislation, the reasons on which it is based shall be stated with a view to justifying its compliance with the principles of subsidiarity and proportionality; the reasons for concluding that a Community objective can be better achieved by the Community must be substantiated by qualitative or, wherever possible, quantitative indicators.

(5)   For Community action to be justified, both aspects of the subsidiarity principle shall be met: the objectives of the proposed action cannot be sufficiently achieved by Member States' action in the framework of their national constitutional system and can therefore be better achieved by action on the part of the Community.
The following guidelines should be used in examining whether the above-mentioned condition is fulfilled:
-     the issue under consideration has trans-national aspects which cannot be satisfactorily regulated by action by Member States;
-     actions by Member States alone or lack of Community action would conflict with the requirements of the Treaty (such as the need to correct distortion of competition or avoid disguised restrictions on trade or strengthen economic and social cohesion) or would otherwise significantly damage Member States' interests;

- action at Community level would produce clear benefits by reason of its scale or effects compared with action at the level of the Member States.

(6) The form of Community action shall be as simple as possible, consistent with satisfactory achievement of the objective of the measure and the need for effective enforcement. The Community shall legislate only to the extent necessary. Other things being equal, directives should be preferred to regulations and framework directives to detailed measures. Directives as provided for in Article 249 of the Treaty, while binding upon each Member State to which they are addressed as to the result to be achieved, shall leave to the national authorities the choice of form and methods.

(7) Regarding the nature and the extent of Community action, Community measures should leave as much scope for national decision as possible, consistent with securing the aim of the measure and observing the requirements of the Treaty. While respecting Community law, care should be taken to respect well-established national arrangements and the organisation and working of Member States' legal systems. Where appropriate and subject to the need for proper enforcement, Community measures should provide Member States with alternative ways to achieve the objectives of the measures.

(8) Where the application of the principle of subsidiarity leads to no action being taken by the Community, Member States are required in their action to comply with the general rules laid down in Article 10 of the Treaty, by taking all appropriate measures to ensure fulfilment of their obligations under the Treaty and by abstaining from any measure which could jeopardise the attainment of the objectives of the Treaty.

(9) Without prejudice to its right of initiative, the Commission should:
- except in cases of particular urgency or confidentiality, consult widely before proposing legislation and, wherever appropriate, publish consultation documents;
- justify the relevance of its proposals with regard to the principle of subsidiarity; whenever necessary, the explanatory memorandum accompanying a proposal will give details in this respect. The financing of Community action in whole or in part from the Community budget shall require an explanation;
- take duly into account the need for any burden, whether financial or administrative, falling upon the Community, national governments, local authorities, economic operators and citizens, to be minimised and proportionate to the objective to be achieved;
- submit an annual report to the European Council, the European Parliament and the Council on the application of Article 5 of the Treaty. This annual report shall also be sent to the Committee of the Regions and to the Economic and Social Committee.

(10) The European Council shall take account of the Commission report referred in the fourth indent of point 9 within the report on the progress achieved by the Union which it is required to submit to the European Parliament in accordance with Article 4 of the Treaty on European Union.

(11) While fully observing the procedures applicable, the European Parliament and the Council shall, as an integral part of the overall examination of Commission proposals, consider their consistency with Article 5 of the Treaty. This concerns the original Commission proposal as well as amendments which the European Parliament and the Council envisage making to the proposal.

(12) In the course of the procedures referred to in Articles 251 and 252, the European Parliament shall be informed of the Council's position on the application of Article 5, by way of a statement of the reasons which led the Council to adopt its common position. The Council shall inform the European Parliament of the reasons on the basis of which all or part of a Commission proposal is deemed to be inconsistent with Article 5 of the Treaty.

(13) Compliance with the principle of subsidiarity shall be reviewed in accordance with the rules laid down by the Treaty.

31. PROTOCOL ON EXTERNAL RELATIONS OF THE MEMBER STATES WITH REGARD TO THE CROSSING OF EXTERNAL BORDERS

THE HIGH CONTRACTING PARTIES,

TAKING INTO ACCOUNT the need of the Member States to ensure effective controls at their external borders, in co-operation with third countries where appropriate,

HAVE AGREED UPON the following provisions, which shall be annexed to the Treaty establishing the European Community:

The provisions on the measures on the crossing of external borders included in Article 62(2)(a) of Title IV of the Treaty shall be without prejudice to the competence of Member States to negotiate or conclude agreements with third countries as long as they respect Community law and other relevant international agreements.

32. PROTOCOL ON THE SYSTEM OF PUBLIC SERVICE BROADCASTING IN THE MEMBER STATES

THE HIGH CONTRACTING PARTIES,

CONSIDERING that the system of public broadcasting in the Member States is directly related to the democratic, social and cultural needs of each society and to the need to preserve media pluralism;

HAVE AGREED UPON the following interpretative provisions, which shall be annexed to the Treaty establishing the European Community:

The provisions of this Treaty establishing the European Community shall be without prejudice to the competence of Member States to provide for the funding of public service broadcasting insofar as such funding is granted to broadcasting organisations for the fulfilment of the public service remit as conferred, defined and organised by each Member State, and insofar as such funding does not affect trading conditions and competition in the Community to an extent which would be contrary to the common interest, while the realisation of the remit of that public service shall be taken into account.

33. PROTOCOL ON PROTECTION AND WELFARE OF ANIMALS

THE HIGH CONTRACTING PARTIES,

DESIRING to ensure improved protection and respect for the welfare of animals as sentient beings;

HAVE AGREED UPON the following provision which shall be annexed to the Treaty establishing the European Community:

In formulating and implementing the Community's agriculture, transport, internal market and research policies, the Community and the Member States shall pay full regard to the welfare requirements of animals, while respecting the legislative or administrative provisions and customs of the Member States relating in particular to religious rites, cultural traditions and regional heritage.

* * * * * * *

PROTOCOL ANNEXED TO
THE TREATIES ESTABLISHING THE EUROPEAN COMMUNITY,
THE EUROPEAN COAL AND STEEL COMMUNITY AND
THE EUROPEAN ATOMIC ENERGY COMMUNITY

34.   PROTOCOL ON THE PRIVILEGES AND IMMUNITIES OF THE EUROPEAN COMMUNITIES

THE HIGH CONTRACTING PARTIES,

CONSIDERING that, in accordance with Article 28 of the Treaty establishing a Single Council and a Single Commission of the European Communities, these Communities and the European Investment Bank shall enjoy in the territories of the Member States such privileges and immunities as are necessary for the performance of their tasks,

HAVE AGREED upon the following provisions, which shall be annexed to this Treaty:

CHAPTER I

PROPERTY, FUNDS, ASSETS AND OPERATIONS OF THE EUROPEAN COMMUNITIES

ARTICLE 1
The premises and buildings of the Communities shall be inviolable. They shall be exempt from search, requisition, confiscation or expropriation. The property and assets of the Communities shall not be the subject of any administrative or legal measure of constraint without the authorisation of the Court of Justice.

ARTICLE 2
The archives of the Communities shall be inviolable.

ARTICLE 3
The Communities, their assets, revenues and other property shall be exempt from all direct taxes.
The Governments of the Member States shall, wherever possible, take the appropriate measures to remit or refund the amount of indirect taxes or sales taxes included in the price of movable or immovable property, where the Communities make, for their official use, substantial purchases the price of which includes taxes of this kind. These provisions shall not be applied, however, so as to have the effect of distorting competition within the Communities.
No exemption shall be granted in respect of taxes and dues which amount merely to charges for public utility services.

ARTICLE 4
The Communities shall be exempt from all customs duties, prohibitions and restrictions on imports and exports in respect of articles intended for their official use: articles so imported shall not be disposed of, whether or not in return for payment, in the territory of the country into which they have been imported, except under conditions approved by the Government of that country.
The Communities shall also be exempt from any customs duties and any prohibitions and restrictions on imports and exports in respect of their publications.

ARTICLE 5
The European Coal and Steel Community may hold currency of any kind and operate accounts in any currency.

CHAPTER II

COMMUNICATIONS AND *LAISSEZ-PASSER*

ARTICLE 6

For their official communications and the transmission of all their documents, the institutions of the Communities shall enjoy in the territory of each Member State the treatment accorded by that State to diplomatic missions.

Official correspondence and other official communications of the institutions of the Communities shall not be subject to censorship.

ARTICLE 7

1.   *Laissez-passer* in a form to be prescribed by the Council, which shall be recognised as valid travel documents by the authorities of the Member States, may be issued to Members and servants of the institutions of the Communities by the Presidents of these institutions. These *laissez-passer* shall be issued to officials and other servants under conditions laid down in the Staff Regulations of officials and the Conditions of Employment of other servants of the Communities.

The Commission may conclude agreements for these *laissez-passer* to be recognised as valid travel documents within the territory of third countries.

2.   The provisions of Article 6 of the Protocol on the Privileges and Immunities of the European Coal and Steel Community shall, however, remain applicable to Members and servants of the institutions who are at the date of entry into force of this Treaty in possession of the *laissez-passer* provided for in that Article, until the provisions of paragraph 1 of this Article are applied.

CHAPTER III

MEMBERS OF THE EUROPEAN PARLIAMENT

ARTICLE 8

No administrative or other restriction shall be imposed on the free movement of Members of the European parliament travelling to or from the place of meeting of the European Parliament.

Members of the European Parliament shall, in respect of customs and exchange control, be accorded:

(a)   by their own Government, the same facilities as those accorded to senior officials travelling abroad on temporary official missions;

(b)   by the Governments of other Member States, the same facilities as those accorded to representatives of foreign Governments on temporary official missions.

ARTICLE 9

Members of the European Parliament shall not be subject to any form of inquiry, detention or legal proceedings in respect of opinions expressed or votes cast by them in the performance of their duties.

ARTICLE 10

During the sessions of the European Parliament, its Members shall enjoy:

(a)   in the territory of their own State, the immunities accorded to Members of their Parliament;

(b)   in the territory of any other Member State, immunity from any measure of detention and from legal proceedings.

Immunity shall likewise apply to Members while they are travelling to and from the place of meeting of the European Parliament.

Immunity cannot be claimed when a member is found in the act of committing an offence and shall not prevent the European Parliament from exercising its right to waive the immunity of one of its Members.

CHAPTER IV

REPRESENTATIVES OF MEMBER STATES TAKING PART IN THE WORK OF THE INSTITUTIONS OF THE EUROPEAN COMMUNITIES

ARTICLE 11

Representatives of Member States taking part in the work of the institutions of the Communities, their advisors and technical experts shall, in the performance of their duties and during their travel to and from the place of meeting, enjoy the customary privileges, immunities and facilities.
This Article shall also apply to Members of the advisory bodies of the Communities.

CHAPTER V

OFFICIALS AND OTHER SERVANTS OF THE EUROPEAN COMMUNITIES

ARTICLE 12

In the territory of each Member State and whatever their nationality, officials and other servants of the Communities shall:

(a) subject to the provisions of the Treaties relating, on the one hand, to the rules on the liability of officials and other servants towards the Communities and, on the other hand, to the jurisdiction of the Court in disputes between the Communities and their officials and other servants, be immune from legal proceedings in respect of acts performed by them in their official capacity, including their words spoken or written. They shall continue to enjoy this immunity after they have ceased to hold office;

(b) together with their spouses and dependent Members of their families, not be subject to immigration restrictions or to formalities for the registration of aliens;

(c) in respect of currency or exchange regulations, be accorded the same facilities as are customarily accorded to officials of international organisations;

(d) enjoy the right to import free of duty their furniture and effects at the time of first taking up their post in the country concerned, and the right to re-export free of duty their furniture and effects, on termination of their duties in that country, subject in either case to the conditions considered to be necessary by the Government of the country in which this fight is exercised;

(e) have the right to import free of duty a motor car for their personal use, acquired either in the country of their last residence or in the country of which they are nationals on the terms ruling in the home market in that country, and to re-export it free of duty, subject in either case to the conditions considered to be necessary by the Government of the country concerned.

ARTICLE 13

Officials and other servants of the Communities shall be liable to a tax for the benefit of the Communities on salaries, wages and emoluments paid to them by the Communities, in accordance with the conditions and procedure laid down by the Council, acting on a proposal from the Commission.
They shall be exempt from national taxes on salaries, wages and emoluments paid by the Communities.

ARTICLE 14

In the application of income tax, wealth tax and death duties and in the application of conventions on the avoidance of double taxation concluded between Member States of the Communities, officials and other servants of the Communities who, solely by reason of the performance of their duties in the service of the Communities, establish their residence in the territory of a Member State other than their country of domicile for tax purposes at the time of entering the service of the Communities, shall be considered, both in the country of their actual residence and in the country of domicile for tax purposes, as having maintained their domicile in the latter country provided that it is a member of the Communities. This provision shall also apply to a spouse, to the extent that the latter is not separately engaged in a gainful occupation, and to children dependent on and in the care of the persons referred to in this Article.
Movable property belonging to persons referred to in the preceding paragraph and situated in the territory of the country where they are staying shall be exempt from death duties in that country; such property shall for the assessment of such duty, be considered as being in the country of domicile for tax purposes, subject to the rights of third countries and to the possible application of provisions of international conventions on double taxation.

Any domicile acquired solely by reason of the performance of duties in the service of other international organisations shall not be taken into consideration in applying the provisions of this Article.

ARTICLE 15
The Council shall, acting unanimously on a proposal from the Commission lay down the scheme of social security benefits for officials and other servants of the Communities.

ARTICLE 16
The Council shall, acting on a proposal from the Commission and after consulting the other institutions concerned, determine the categories of officials and other servants of the Communities to whom the provisions of Article 12, the second paragraph of Article 13, and Article 14 shall apply, in whole or in part.
The names, grades and addresses of officials and other servants included in such categories shall be communicated periodically to the Governments of the Member States.

CHAPTER VI

PRIVILEGES AND IMMUNITIES OF MISSIONS OF THIRD COUNTRIES
ACCREDITED TO THE EUROPEAN COMMUNITIES

ARTICLE 17
The Member State in whose territory the Communities have their seat shall accord the customary diplomatic immunities and privileges to missions of third countries accredited to the Communities.

CHAPTER VII

GENERAL PROVISIONS

ARTICLE 18
Privileges, immunities and facilities shall be accorded to officials and other servants of the Communities solely in the interests of the Communities.
Each institution of the Communities shall be required to waive the immunity accorded to an official or other servant wherever that institution considers that the waiver of such immunity is not contrary to the interests of the Communities.

ARTICLE 19
The institutions of the Communities shall, for the purpose of applying this Protocol, co-operate with the responsible authorities of the Member States concerned.

ARTICLE 20
Articles 12 to 15 and Article 18 shall apply to Members of the Commission.

ARTICLE 21
Articles 12 to 15 and Article 18 shall apply to the Judges, the Advocates-General, the Registrar and the Assistant Rapporteurs of the Court of Justice, without prejudice to the provisions of Article 3 of the Protocols on the Statute of the Court of Justice concerning immunity from legal proceedings of Judges and Advocates-General.

ARTICLE 22
This Protocol shall also apply to the European Investment Bank, to the Members of its organs, to its staff and to the representatives of the Member States taking part in its activities, without prejudice to the provisions of the Protocol on the Statute of the Bank.
The European Investment Bank shall in addition be exempt from any form of taxation or imposition of a like nature on the occasion of any increase in its capital and from the various formalities which may be connected therewith in the State where the Bank has its seat. Similarly, its dissolution or liquidation shall not give rise to any imposition. Finally, the activities of the Bank and of its organs carried on in accordance with its Statute shall not be subject to any turnover tax.

ARTICLE 23

This Protocol shall also apply to the European Central Bank, to the Members of its organs and to its staff, without prejudice to the provisions of the Protocol on the Statute of the European System of Central Banks and the European Central Bank.

The European Central Bank shall, in addition, be exempt from any form of taxation or imposition of a like nature on the occasion of any increase in its capital and from the various formalities which may be connected therewith in the State where the bank has its seat. The activities of the Bank and of its organs carried on in accordance with the Statute of the European System of Central Banks and of the European Central Bank shall not be subject to any turnover tax.

The above provisions shall also apply to the European Monetary Institute. Its dissolution or liquidation shall not give rise to any imposition.'

*(Article 23 added by the Maastricht Treaty and confirmed by **Article 9 of the Treaty of Amsterdam**.)*

Done at Brussels this eighth day of April in the year one thousand nine hundred and sixty-five.

* * * * * * *

THE TREATY OF AMSTERDAM

HIS MAJESTY THE KING OF THE BELGIANS,

HER MAJESTY THE QUEEN OF DENMARK,

THE PRESIDENT OF THE FEDERAL REPUBLIC OF GERMANY,

THE PRESIDENT OF THE HELLENIC REPUBLIC,

HIS MAJESTY THE KING OF SPAIN,

THE PRESIDENT OF THE FRENCH REPUBLIC,

THE COMMISSION AUTHORISED BY ARTICLE 14 OF THE CONSTITUTION OF IRELAND TO EXERCISE AND PERFORM THE POWERS AND FUNCTIONS OF THE PRESIDENT OF IRELAND,

THE PRESIDENT OF THE ITALIAN REPUBLIC,

HIS ROYAL HIGHNESS THE GRAND DUKE OF LUXEMBOURG,

HER MAJESTY THE QUEEN OF THE NETHERLANDS,

THE FEDERAL PRESIDENT OF THE REPUBLIC OF AUSTRIA,

THE PRESIDENT OF THE PORTUGUESE REPUBLIC,

THE PRESIDENT OF THE REPUBLIC OF FINLAND,

HIS MAJESTY THE KING OF SWEDEN,

HER MAJESTY THE QUEEN OF THE UNITED KINGDOM OF GREAT BRITAIN AND NORTHERN IRELAND,

HAVE RESOLVED to amend the Treaty on European Union, the Treaties establishing the European Communities and certain related acts,

And to this end have designated as their Plenipotentiaries:

HIS MAJESTY THE KING OF THE BELGIANS:

Mr Erik Derycke, Minister for Foreign Affairs;

HER MAJESTY THE QUEEN OF DENMARK:

Mr Niels Helveg Petersen, Minister for Foreign Affairs;

THE PRESIDENT OF THE FEDERAL REPUBLIC OF GERMANY:

Dr Klaus Kinkel, Federal Minister for Foreign Affairs and Deputy Federal Chancellor;

THE PRESIDENT OF THE HELLENIC REPUBLIC:

Mr Theodoros Pangalos, Minister for Foreign Affairs;

HIS MAJESTY THE KING OF SPAIN:

Mr Juan Abel Matutes, Minister for Foreign Affairs;

THE PRESIDENT OF THE FRENCH REPUBLIC:

Mr Hubert Védrine, Minister for Foreign Affairs;

THE COMMISSION AUTHORISED BY ARTICLE 14 OF THE CONSTITUTION OF IRELAND TO EXERCISE AND PERFORM THE POWERS OF THE PRESIDENT OF IRELAND:

Mr Raphael P. Burke, Minister for Foreign Affairs;

THE PRESIDENT OF THE ITALIAN REPUBLIC:

Mr Lamberto Dini, Minister for Foreign Affairs;

HIS ROYAL HIGHNESS THE GRAND DUKE OF LUXEMBOURG:

Mr Jacques F. Poos, Deputy Prime Minister,
Minister for Foreign Affairs, Foreign Trade and Co-operation;

HER MAJESTY THE QUEEN OF THE NETHERLANDS:

Mr Hans van Mierlo, Deputy Prime Minister and Minister for Foreign Affairs;

THE FEDERAL PRESIDENT OF THE REPUBLIC OF AUSTRIA:

Mr Wolfgang Schüssel, Federal Minister for foreign Affairs and Vice Chancellor;

THE PRESIDENT OF THE PORTUGUESE REPUBLIC:

Mr Jaime Gama, Minister for Foreign Affairs;

THE PRESIDENT OF THE REPUBLIC OF FINLAND:

Ms Tarja Halonen, Minister for Foreign Affairs;

HIS MAJESTY THE KING OF SWEDEN:

Ms Lena Hjelm-Wallén, Minister for Foreign Affairs;

HER MAJESTY THE QUEEN OF THE UNITED KINGDOM OF GREAT BRITAIN AND NORTHERN IRELAND:

Mr Douglas Henderson, Secretary of State, Foreign and Commonwealth Office;

WHO, having exchanged their full powers, found in good and due form,

HAVE AGREED AS FOLLOWS:

PART ONE

SUBSTANTIVE AMENDMENTS

ARTICLES 1 – 5
These concern the major amendments to the Treaty on European Union and the Treaties establishing the European Communities and have been incorporated into the main text of the consolidated Treaties.

PART TWO

SIMPLIFICATION

ARTICLES 6 – 8
These concern amendments to delete lapsed provisions and to adapt the text where appropriate in the Treaty on European Union and the Treaties establishing the European Communities. They have been incorporated into the main text of the consolidated Treaties.

ARTICLE 9
1.   Without prejudice to the paragraphs following hereinafter, which have as their purpose to retain the essential elements of their provisions, the Convention of 25 March 1957 on certain institutions common to the European Communities and the Treaty of 8 April 1965 establishing a Single Council and a Single Commission of the European Communities, but with the exception of the Protocol referred to in paragraph 5, shall be repealed.

2.   The powers conferred on the European Parliament, the Council, the Commission, the Court of Justice and the Court of Auditors by the Treaty establishing the European Community, the Treaty establishing the European Coal and Steel Community and the Treaty establishing the European Atomic Energy Community shall be exercised by the single institutions under the conditions laid down respectively by the said Treaties and this Article.

The functions conferred on the Economic and Social Committee by the Treaty establishing the European Community and the Treaty establishing the European Atomic Energy Community shall be exercised by a single committee under the conditions laid down respectively by the said Treaties. The provisions of Articles **257** and **261** of the Treaty establishing the European Community shall apply to that Committee.

3.   The officials and other staff of the European Communities shall form part of the single administration of those Communities and shall be governed by the provisions adopted pursuant to Article **283** of the Treaty establishing the European Community.

4.   The European Communities shall enjoy in the territories of the Member States such privileges and immunities as are necessary for the performance of their tasks under the conditions set out in the Protocol referred to in paragraph 5. The position shall be the same as regards the European Central Bank, the European Monetary Institute and the European Investment Bank.

5.   In the Protocol of 8 April 1965 on the privileges and immunities of the European Communities there shall be inserted an Article 23, as laid down in the Protocol amending the said Protocol; that Article reads as follows:

"*Article 23*
This Protocol shall also apply to the European Central Bank, to the members of its organs and to its staff, without prejudice to the provisions of the Protocol on the Statute of the European System of Central Banks and the European Central Bank.

The European Central Bank shall, in addition, be exempt from any form of taxation or imposition of a like nature on the occasion of any increase in its capital and from the various formalities which may be connected therewith in the State where the Bank has its seat. The activities of the Bank and of its organs carried on in accordance with the Statute of the European System of Central Banks and of the European Central Bank shall not be subject to any turnover tax.

The above provisions shall also apply to the European Monetary Institute. Its dissolution or liquidation shall not give rise to any imposition."

6. The revenue and expenditure of the European Community, the administrative expenditure of the European Coal and Steel Community and the revenue relating thereto and the revenue and expenditure of the European Atomic Energy Community, except for those of the Supply Agency and Joint Undertakings, shall be shown in the budget of the European Communities, under the conditions laid down respectively in the Treaties establishing the three Communities.

7. Without prejudice to the application of Article **289** of the Treaty establishing the European Community, Article 77 of the Treaty establishing the European Coal and Steel Community, Article 189 of the Treaty establishing the European Atomic Energy Community and the second paragraph of Article 1 of the Protocol on the Statute of the European Investment Bank, the representatives of the Governments of the Member States shall adopt by common accord the necessary provisions for the purpose of dealing with certain problems particular to the Grand Duchy of Luxembourg which arise from the creation of a Single Council and a Single Commission of the European Communities.

ARTICLE 10
1. The repeal or deletion in this Part of lapsed provisions of the Treaty establishing the European Community, the Treaty establishing the European Coal and Steel Community and the Treaty establishing the European Atomic Energy Community as in force before the entry into force of this Treaty of Amsterdam and the adaptation of certain of their provisions shall not bring about any change in the legal effects of the provisions of those Treaties, in particular the legal effects arising from the time limits laid down by the said Treaties, nor of Accession Treaties.

2. There shall be no change in the legal effects of the acts in force adopted on the basis of the said Treaties.

3. The position shall be the same as regards the repeal of the Convention of 25 March 1957 on certain institutions common to the European Communities and the repeal of the Treaty of 8 April 1965 establishing a Single Council and a Single Commission of the European Communities.

ARTICLE 11
The provisions of the Treaty establishing the European Community, the Treaty establishing the European Coal and Steel Community and the Treaty establishing the European Atomic Energy Community relating to the powers of the Court of Justice of the European Communities and to the exercise of those powers shall apply to the provisions of this Part and to the Protocol on privileges and immunities referred to in Article 9(5).

PART THREE

GENERAL AND FINAL PROVISIONS

ARTICLE 12
1. The Articles, Titles and Sections of the Treaty on European Union and of the Treaty establishing the European Community, as amended by the provisions of this Treaty, shall be renumbered in accordance with the tables of equivalences set out in the Annex to this Treaty, which shall form an integral part thereof.

2. The cross references to Articles, Titles and Sections in the Treaty on European Union and in the Treaty establishing the European Community, as well as between them, shall be adapted in consequence. The same shall apply as regards references to Articles, titles and Sections of those Treaties contained in the other Community Treaties.

3. The references to the Articles, Titles and Sections of the Treaties referred to in paragraph 2 contained in other instruments or acts shall be understood as references to the Articles, Titles and Sections of the Treaties as renumbered pursuant to paragraph 1 and, respectively, to the paragraphs of the said Articles, as renumbered by certain provisions of Article 6.

4.   References, contained in other instruments or acts, to paragraphs of Articles of the Treaties referred to in Articles 7 and 8 shall be understood as referring to those paragraphs as renumbered by certain provisions of the said Articles 7 and 8.

[Note: the Annex shows the Table of equivalents referred to in Article 12 and is not shown as the references have been made in the text of the main Treaty and the associated Protocols, declarations and Acts.]

ARTICLE 13
This Treaty is concluded for an unlimited period.

ARTICLE 14
1.   This Treaty shall be ratified by the High Contracting Parties in accordance with their respective constitutional requirements. The instruments of ratification shall be deposited with the Government of the Italian Republic.

2.   This Treaty shall enter into force on the first day of the second month following that in which the instrument of ratification is deposited by the last signatory State to fulfil that formality.

ARTICLE 15
This Treaty, drawn up in a single original in the Danish, Dutch, English, Finnish, French, German, Greek, Irish, Italian, Portuguese, Spanish and Swedish languages, the texts in each of these languages being equally authentic, shall be deposited in the archives of the Government of the Italian Republic, which will transmit a certified copy to each of the governments of the other signatory States.

EN FE DE LO CUAL, los plenipotenciarios abajo firmantes suscriben el presente Tratado.

TIL BEKRÆFTELSE HERAF har undertegnede befuldmægtigede underskrevet denne traktat.

ZU URKUND DESSEN haben die unterzeichneten Bevollmächtigten ihre Unterschriften unter diesen Vertrag gesetzt.

ΕΙΣ ΠΙΣΤΩΣΗ ΤΩΝ ΑΝΩΕΡΩ, οι υπογεγραμμενοι πληρεξουσιοι υπεγραψαν την παρυσα Συνθηκη.

IN WITNESS WHEREOF the undersigned Plenipotentiaries have signed this Treaty.

EN FOI DE QUOI, les plénipotentiares soussignés ont apposé leurs signatures au bas du présent traité.

DÁ FHIANÚ SIN, chuir na Lánchumhachtaigh thíos-sínithe a lámh leis an gConradh seo.

IN FEDE DI CHE, i plenipotenziari sottoscritti hanno apposto le loro firme in calce al presnte trattato.

TEN BLIJKE WAARVAN de ondergetekende gevolmachtigden hun handtekening onder dit Verdrag hebben gesteld.

EM FÉ DO QUE, os plenipotenciários abaixo assinados apuseram as suas assinaturas no presente Tratado.

TÄMÄN VAKUUDEKSI aala mainitut täysivaltaisset edusajat ovat allekirjoittaneet tämän sopimuksen.

TIL BEVIS HÄRPÅ har undertecknade befullmäktgade undertecknat detta fördrag.

Hecho en Amsterdam, el dos de octubre de mil novecientos noventa y siete.

Udfærdiget i Amsterdam, den anden oktober nitten hundrede og syvoghalvfems.

Geschehen zu Amsterdam am zweiten Oktober neunzehnhundertsiebenundneunzig.

Εγινε στο Αμοτερνταμ, οτιζ δυο Οκτωβριου του ετουζ χιλια εννιακοσια ενενηντα επτα.

Done in Amsterdam on the second day of October in the year one thousand nine hundred and ninety-seven.

Fait à Amsterdam, le deux octobre de l'an mil neuf cent quatre-vingt-dix-sept.

Arna dhéanamh in Amsterdam ar an dara lá de dheireadh Fómhair sa bhlain míle naoi gcéad nócha a seacht.

Fatto ad Amsterdam, addì due ottobre nell'anno millenovecentonovantasette.

Gedaan te Amsterdam, de tweede oktober negentienhonderd zevenennegentig.

Feito em Amsterdão, em dois Outubro de mil novecentos e noventa e sete.

Tehty Amsterdamissa toisena päivänä lokakuuta vuonna tuhatyhdeksänsataayhdeksänkymmentäseitsemän.

Upprättat i Amsterdam den andra oktober år nittonhundranittiosju.

Pour Sa Majesté le Roi des Belges
Voor Zijne Majesteit de Koning der Belgen
Für Seine Majestät den König der Belgier

Cette signature engage également la Communauté française, la Communauté flamande, la Communauté germanophone, la Région wallonne, la Région flamance et la Région de Bruxelles-Capitale.
Deze handtekening verbindt evneers de Viaamse Gemeenschap, de Franse Gemeenschap, de Duitstalige Gemeenschap, het Viaamse Gewest, het Waalse Gewest en het Brusselse Hoofdstedelijke Gewaes.
Diese Unterschrift bindet zugliech die Deutschsprachige Gemeinschaft, die Flàmische Gemeinschaft, die Französische gemeinschaft, die Wallonische Region, die Flàmische Region und die Region Brùssel-Hauptstadt.

For Hendes Majestæt Danmarks Dronning

Für den Präsidenten der Bundesrepublik Deutschland

Για τον Προεδρο της Ελληνικης Δημοκρατιας

Por Su Majestad el Rey de España

Pour le Président de la République française

168

Thar ceann an Choimisiúin arna údarú le hAirteagal 14 Bhunreacht na hÉireann chun cumhachtai agus feidhmeanna Uachtarán na hEireann a oibriú agus a chomhlíonadh
For the Commission authorised by Article 14 of the Constitution of Ireland to exercise and perform the powers and functions of the President of Ireland

Per il Presidente della Repubblica italiana

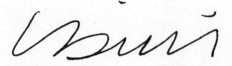

Pour Son Altesse Royale le Grand-Duc de Luxembourg

Voor Hare Majesteit de Koningin der Nederlanden

Für den Bundespräsidenten der Republik Österreich

Pelo Presidente da República Portuguesa

Suomen Tasavallan Presidentin Puolesta
För Republiken Finlands President

För Hans Majestät Konungen av Sverige

170

For Her Majesty the Queen of the United Kingdom of Great Britain and Northern Ireland

****

FINAL ACT

The CONFERENCE OF THE REPRESENTATIVES OF THE GOVERNMENTS OF THE MEMBER STATES convened in Turin on the twenty-ninth day of March in the year nineteen hundred and ninety-six to adopt by common accord the amendments to be made to the Treaty on European Union, the Treaties establishing respectively the European Community, the European Coal and Steel Community and the European Atomic Energy Community and certain related Acts has adopted the following texts:

I.

THE TREATY OF AMSTERDAM AMENDING THE TREATY ON EUROPEAN UNION, THE TREATIES ESTABLISHING THE EUROPEAN COMMUNITIES AND CERTAIN RELATED ACTS

II.

PROTOCOLS

A.   Protocol annexed to the Treaty on European Union:

1.   Protocol on Article **17** of the Treaty on European Union

B.   Protocols annexed to the Treaty on European Union and to the Treaty establishing the European Community:

2.   Protocol integrating the Schengen *acquis* into the framework of the European Union;

3.   Protocol on the application of certain aspects of Article **14** of the Treaty establishing the European Community to the United Kingdom and to Ireland;

4.   Protocol on the position of the United Kingdom and Ireland;

5.   Protocol on the position of Denmark.

C.   Protocols annexed to the Treaty establishing the European Community:

6.   Protocol on asylum for nationals of Member States of the European Union;

7.   Protocol on the application of the principles of subsidiarity and proportionality;

8.   Protocol on external relations of the Member States with regard to the crossing of external borders;

9.   Protocol on the system of public broadcasting in the Member States;

10. Protocol on protection and welfare of animals.

D. Protocols annexed to the Treaty on European Union and to the Treaties establishing the European Community, the European Coal and Steel Community and the European Atomic Energy Community;

11. Protocol on the institutions with the prospect of enlargement of the European Union;

12. Protocol on the location of the seats of the institutions and of certain bodies and departments of the European Communities and of Europol;

13. Protocol on the role of national parliaments in the European Union.

III.

DECLARATIONS

The Conference adopted the following declarations annexed to this Final Act:

1. Declaration on the abolition of the death penalty;

2. Declaration on enhanced co-operation between the European Union and the Western European Union;

3. Declaration relating to Western European Union;

4. Declaration on Articles **24** and **38** of the Treaty on European Union;

5. Declaration on Article **25** of the Treaty on European Union;

6. Declaration on the establishment of a policy planning and early warning unit;

7. Declaration on Article **30** of the Treaty on European Union;

8. Declaration on Article **31**(e) of the Treaty on European Union;

9. Declaration on Article **34**(2) of the Treaty on European Union;

10. Declaration on Article **35** of the Treaty on European Union;

11. Declaration on the status of churches and non-confessional organisations;

12. Declaration on environmental impact assessments;

13. Declaration on Article **16** of the Treaty establishing the European Community;

14. Declaration on the repeal of Article 44 of the Treaty establishing the European Community;

15. Declaration on the preservation of the level of protection and security provided by the Schengen *acquis*;

16. Declaration on Article **62**(2)(b) of the Treaty establishing the European Community;

17. Declaration on Article **63** of the Treaty establishing the European Community;

18. Declaration on Article **63**(3)(a) of the Treaty establishing the European Community;

19. Declaration on Article **64**(1) of the Treaty establishing the European Community;

20. Declaration on Article **65** of the Treaty establishing the European Community;

21. Declaration on Article **67** of the Treaty establishing the European Community;

22. Declaration regarding persons with a disability;

23. Declaration on incentive measures referred to in Article **129** of the Treaty establishing the European Community;

24. Declaration on Article **129** of the Treaty establishing the European Community;

25. Declaration on Article **137** of the Treaty establishing the European Community;

26. Declaration on Article **137**(2) of the Treaty establishing the European Community;

27. Declaration on Article **139**(2) of the Treaty establishing the European Community;

28. Declaration on Article **141**(4) of the Treaty establishing the European Community;

29. Declaration on sport;

30. Declaration on island regions;

31. Declaration relating to the Council Decision of 13 July 1987;

32. Declaration on the organisation and functioning of the Commission;

33. Declaration on Article **248**(3) of the Treaty establishing the European Community;

34. Declaration on respect for time limits under the co-decision procedure;

35. Declaration on Article **255**(1) of the Treaty establishing the European Community;

36. Declaration on the Overseas Countries and Territories;

37. Declaration on public credit institutions in Germany;

38. Declaration on voluntary service activities;

39. Declaration on the quality of the drafting of Community legislation;

40. Declaration concerning the procedure for concluding international agreements by the European Coal and Steel Community;

41. Declaration on the provisions relating to transparency, access to documents and the fight against fraud;

42. Declaration on the consolidation of the Treaties;

43. Declaration relating to the Protocol on the application of the principles of subsidiarity and proportionality;

44. Declaration on Article 2 of the Protocol integrating the Schengen *acquis* into the framework of the European Union;

45. Declaration on Article 4 of the Protocol integrating the Schengen *acquis* into the framework of the European Union;

46. Declaration on Article 5 of the Protocol integrating the Schengen *acquis* into the framework of the European Union;

47. Declaration on Article 6 of the Protocol integrating the Schengen *acquis* into the framework of the European Union;

48. Declaration relating to the Protocol on asylum for nationals of Member States of the European Union;

49. Declaration relating to sub-paragraph (d) of the Sole Article of the Protocol on asylum for nationals of Member States of the European Union;

50. Declaration relating to the Protocol on the institutions with the prospect of enlargement of the European Union;

51. Declaration on Article 10 of the Treaty of Amsterdam.

The Conference also took note of the following declarations annexed to this Final Act:

1. Declaration by Austria and Luxembourg on credit institutions;

2. Declaration by Denmark relating to Article **42** of the Treaty on European Union;

3. Declaration by Germany, Austria and Belgium on subsidiarity;

4. Declaration by Ireland on Article 3 of the Protocol on the position of the United Kingdom and Ireland;

5. Declaration by Belgium on the Protocol on asylum for nationals of Member States of the European Union;

6. Declaration by Belgium, France and Italy on the Protocol on the institutions with the prospect of enlargement of the European Union;

7. Declaration by France concerning the situation of the overseas departments in the light of the Protocol integrating the Schengen *acquis* into the framework of the European Union;

8. Declaration by Greece on the Declaration on the status of churches and non-confessional organisations.

Finally, the Conference agreed to attach, for illustrative purposes, to this Final Act the texts of the Treaty on European Union and the Treaty establishing the European Community, as they result from the amendments made by the Conference.

Done at Amsterdam on the second day of October in the year one thousand nine hundred and ninety-seven.

The signatures of the plenipotentiaries of the fifteen Member States now follow. Since the signatories are the same as those at the end of the main Act of the Treaty of Amsterdam, their signatures are not reproduced here.

DECLARATIONS

1.   DECLARATION ON THE ABOLITION OF THE DEATH PENALTY

With reference to Article **6**(2) of the Treaty on European Union, the Conference recalls that Protocol No. 6 to the European Convention for the Protection of Human Rights and Fundamental Freedoms signed in Rome on 4 November 1950, and which has been signed and ratified by a large majority of Member States, provides for the abolition of the death penalty.

In this context, the Conference notes the fact that since the signature of the above-mentioned Protocol on 28 April 1983, the death penalty has been abolished in most of the Member States of the Union and has not been applied in any of them.

2.   DECLARATION ON ENHANCED CO-OPERATION BETWEEN THE EUROPEAN UNION AND THE WESTERN EUROPEAN UNION

With a view to enhanced co-operation between the European Union and the Western European Union, the Conference invites the Council to seek the early adoption of appropriate arrangements for the security clearance of the personnel of the General Secretariat of the Council.

3.   DECLARATION RELATING TO WESTERN EUROPEAN UNION

The Conference notes the following Declaration, adopted by the Council of Ministers of the Western European Union on 22 July 1997

"DECLARATION OF WESTERN EUROPEAN UNION ON THE ROLE OF WESTERN EUROPEAN UNION AND ITS RELATIONS WITH THE EUROPEAN UNION AND WITH THE ATLANTIC ALLIANCE

INTRODUCI1ON

1.   The Western European Union (WEU) Member States agreed at Maastricht in 1991 on the need to develop a genuine European Security and Defence Identity (ESDI) and to assume a greater European responsibility for defence matters. In the light of the Treaty of Amsterdam, they reaffirm the importance of continuing and strengthening these efforts. WEU is an integral part of the development of the European Union (EU) providing the Union with access to an operational capability, notably in the context of the Petersberg tasks and is an essential element of the development of the ESDI within the Atlantic Alliance in accordance with the Paris Declaration and with the decisions taken by NATO ministers in Berlin.

2.   Today the WEU Council brings together all the Member States of the European Union and all the European Members of the Atlantic Alliance in accordance with their respective status. The Council also brings together those States with the Central and Eastern European States linked to the European Union by an Association Agreement and that are applicants for accession to both the European Union and the Atlantic Alliance. WEU is thus establishing itself as a genuine framework for dialogue and co-operation among Europeans on wider European security and defence issues.

3.   In this context, WEU takes note of Title V of the Treaty on European Union regarding the EU's common foreign and security policy, in particular Articles **13**(1), **17** and the Protocol to Article **17**, which read as follows:

Article **13**(1)
"1.   The European Council shall define the principles of and general guidelines for the common foreign and security policy, including for matters with defence implications."

Article **17**

"1.   *The common foreign and security policy shall include all questions relating to the security of the Union, including the progressive framing of a common defence policy, in accordance with the second sub-paragraph, which might lead to a common defence, should the European Council so decide. It shall in that case recommend to the Member States the adoption of such a decision in accordance with their respective constitutional requirements.*

The Western European Union (WEU) is an integral part of the development of the Union providing the Union with access to an operational capability notably in the context of paragraph 2. It supports the Union in framing the defence aspects of the common foreign and security policy as set out in this Article. The Union shall accordingly foster closer institutional relations with the WEU with a view to the possibility of the integration of the WEU into the Union, should the European Council so decide. It shall in that case recommend to the Member States the adoption of such a decision in accordance with their respective constitutional requirements.

The policy of the Union in accordance with this Article shall not prejudice the specific character of the security and defence policy of certain Member States and shall respect the obligations of certain Member States, which see their common defence realised in the North Atlantic Treaty Organisation (NATO), under the North Atlantic Treaty and be compatible with the common security and defence policy established within that framework.

The progressive framing of a common defence policy will be supported, as Member States consider appropriate, by co-operation between them in the field of armaments.

2.   *Questions referred to in this Article shall include humanitarian and rescue tasks, peacekeeping tasks and tasks of combat forces in crisis management, including peacemaking.*

3.   *The Union will avail itself of the WEU to elaborate and implement decisions and actions of the Union which have defence implications.*

*The competence of the European Council to establish guidelines in accordance with Article **13** shall also obtain in respect of the WEU for those matters for which the Union avails itself of the WEU.*

When the Union avails itself of the WEU to elaborate and implement decisions of the Union on the tasks referred to in paragraph 2, all Member States of the Union shall be entitled to participate fully in the tasks in question. The Council, in agreement with the institutions of the WEU, shall adopt the necessary practical arrangements to allow all Member States contributing to the tasks in question to participate fully and on an equal footing in planning and decision-taking in the WEU.

Decisions having defence implications dealt with under this paragraph shall be taken without prejudice to the policies and obligations referred to in paragraph 1, third sub-paragraph.

4.   *The provisions of this Article shad not prevent the development of closer co-operation between two or more Member States on a bilateral level, in the framework of the WEU and the Atlantic Alliance, provided such co-operation does not run counter to or impede that provided for in this Title.*

5.   *With a view to furthering the objectives of this Article, the provisions of this Article will be reviewed in accordance with Article **48** [**of the Treaty on European Union**]. "*

Protocol on Article **17**

'THE HIGH CONTRACTING PARTIES,

BEARING IN MIND the need to implement fully the provisions of Article 17(1), second sub-paragraph, and (3) of the Treaty on European Union,

*BEARING IN MIND that the policy of the Union in accordance with Article **17** shall not prejudice the specific character of the security and defence policy of certain Member States and shall respect the obligations of certain Member States, which see their common defence realised in NATO, under the North Atlantic Treaty and be compatible with the common security and defence policy established within that framework,*

HAVE AGREED UPON the following provision, which is annexed to the Treaty on European Union,

The European Union shall draw up, together with the Western European Union, arrangements for enhanced co-operation between them, within a year from the entry into force of the Treaty of Amsterdam.'

A. WEU's RELATIONS WITH THE EUROPEAN UNION: ACCOMPANYING THE IMPLE-
MENTATION OF THE TREATY OF AMSTERDAM

4.   In the "Declaration on the Role of the Western European Union and its Relations with the European Union and with the Atlantic Alliances" of 10 December 1991, WEU Member States set as their objective 'to build up WEU in stages as the defence component of the European Union'. They today reaffirm this aim as developed by the Treaty of Amsterdam.

5.   When the Union avails itself of WEU, WEU will elaborate and implement decisions and actions of the EU which have defence implications.
In elaborating and implementing decisions and actions of the EU for which the Union avails itself of WEU, WEU will act consistently with guidelines established by the European Council.
WEU supports the Union in framing the defence aspects of the European Union Common Foreign and Security Policy as set out in Article 17 of the Treaty on European Union.

6.   WEU confirms that when the European Union avails itself of WEU to elaborate and implement decisions of the Union on the tasks referred to in Article 17(2) of the Treaty on European Union, all Member States of the Union shall be entitled to participate fully in the tasks in question in accordance with Article 17(3) of the Treaty on European Union.
WEU will develop the role of the Observers in WEU in line with provisions contained in Article 17(3) and will adopt the necessary practical arrangements to allow all Member States of the EU contributing to the tasks undertaken by WEU at the request of the EU to participate fully and on an equal footing in planning and decision-taking in the WEU.

7.   Consistent with the Protocol on Article 17 of the Treaty on European Union, WEU shall draw up, together with the European Union, arrangements for enhanced co-operation between them. In this regard, a range of measures, on some of which work is already in hand in WEU, can be taken forward now, such as:
-    arrangements for improving the co-ordination of the consultation and decision-making processes of the respective Organisations, in particular in crisis situations;
-    holding of joint meetings of the relevant bodies of the two Organisations;
-    harmonisation as much as possible of the sequence of the Presidencies of WEU and the EU, as well as the administrative rules and practices of the two Organisations;
-    close co-ordination of the work of the staff of the Secretariat-General of the WEU and the General Secretariat of the Council of the EU, including through the exchange and secondment of personnel;
-    arrangements to allow the relevant bodies of the EU, including its Policy Planning and Early Warning Unit, to draw on the resources of WEU's Planning Cell, Situation Centre and Satellite Centre;
-    co-operation in the field of armaments, as appropriate, within the framework of the Western European Armaments Group (WEAG), as the European forum for armaments co-operation, the EU and WEU in the context of rationalisation of the European armaments market and the establishment of a European Armaments Agency;
-    practical arrangements for ensuring co-operation with the European Commission reflecting its role in the CFSP as defined in the revised Treaty on European Union;
-    improved security arrangements with the European Union.

B. RELATIONS BETWEEN WEU AND NATO IN THE FRAMEWORK OF THE DEVELOPMENT OF AN ESDI WITHIN THE ATLANTIC ALLIANCE

8.   The Atlantic Alliance continues to be the basis of collective defence under the North Atlantic Treaty. It remains the essential forum for consultation among Allies and the framework in which they agree on policies bearing on their security and defence commitments under the Washington Treaty. The Alliance has embarked on a process of adaptation and reform so that it can more effectively carry out the full range of its missions. This process is aimed at strengthening and renewing the transatlantic partnership, including building an ESDI within the Alliance.

9.   WEU is an essential element of the development of the European Security and Defence Identity within the Atlantic Alliance and will accordingly continue its efforts to strengthen institutional and practical co-operation with NATO.

10.   In addition to its support for the common defence enshrined in Article 5 of the Washington Treaty and Article V of the modified Brussels Treaty, WEU takes an active role in conflict prevention and crisis management as provided for in the Petersberg Declaration. In this context, WEU undertakes to perform its role to the full, respecting the full transparency and complementarity between the two Organisations.

11.   WEU affirms that this identity will be grounded on sound military principles and supported by appropriate military planning and will permit the creation of militarily coherent and effective forces capable of operating under the political control and strategic direction of WEU.

12.   To this end, WEU will develop its co-operation with NATO, in particular in the following fields:
-    mechanisms for consultation between WEU and NATO in the context of a crisis;
-    WEU's active involvement in the NATO defence planning process;
-    operational links between WEU and NATO for the planning, preparation and conduct of operations using NATO assets and capabilities under the political control and strategic direction of WEU, including:
    -    military planning, conducted by NATO in co-ordination with WEU, and exercises;
    -    a framework agreement on the transfer, monitoring and return of NATO assets and capabilities;
    -    liaison between WEU and NATO in the context of European command arrangements.
This co-operation will continue to evolve, also taking account of the adaptation of the Alliance.

C.   WEU's OPERATIONAL ROLE IN THE DEVELOPMENT OF THE ESDI

13.   WEU will develop its role as the European politico-military body for crisis management, by using the assets and capabilities made available by WEU nations on a national or multinational basis, and having recourse, when appropriate, to NATO's assets and capabilities under arrangements being worked out. In this context, WEU will also support the UN and OSCE in their crisis management tasks.
WEU will contribute, in the framework of Article 17 of the Treaty on European Union, to the progressive framing of a common defence policy and carry forward its concrete implementation through the further development of its own operational role.

14.   To this end, WEU will take forward work in the following fields:
-    WEU has developed crisis management mechanisms and procedures which will be updated as WEU gains experience through exercises and operations. The implementation of Petersberg missions calls for flexible modes of action geared to the diversity of crisis situations and making optimum use of the available capabilities including through recourse to a national headquarters, which might be one provided by a framework nation, or to a multinational headquarters answerable to WEU or to NATO assets and capabilities;
-    WEU has already worked out Preliminary Conclusions on the Formulation of a Common European Defence Policy which is an initial contribution on the objectives, scope and means of a common European defence policy.
    WEU will continue this work on the basis in particular of the Paris Declaration and taking account of the relevant elements of the decisions of WEU and NATO summits and ministerial meetings since Birmingham. It will focus on the following fields:
    -    definition of principles for the use of armed forces of the WEU States for WEU Petersberg operations in pursuit of common European security interests;
    -    organisation of operational means for Petersberg tasks, such as generic and contingency planning and exercising, preparation and interoperability of forces, including through participation in the NATO defence planning process, as appropriate;
    -    strategic mobility on the basis of its current work;
    -    defence intelligence, through its Planning Cell, Situation Centre and Satellite Centre;
-    WEU has adopted many measures to strengthen its operational role (Planning Cell, Situation Centre, Satellite Centre). The improvement of the functioning of the military components at WEU Headquarters and the establishment, under the Council's authority, of a military committee will represent a further enhancement of structures which are important for the successful preparation and conduct of WEU operations;
-    with the aim of opening participation in all its operations to Associate Members and Observer States, WEU will also examine the necessary modalities to allow Associate Members and Observer States to participate fully in accordance with their status in all operations undertaken by WEU;

- WEU recalls that Associate Members take part on the same basis as full members in operations to which they contribute, as well as in relevant exercises and planning. WEU will also examine the question of participation of the Observers as fully as possible in accordance with their status in planning and decision-taking within WEU in all operations to which they contribute;
- WEU will, in consultation where appropriate with the relevant bodies, examine the possibilities for maximum participation in its activities by Associate Members and Observer States in accordance with their sums. It will address in particular activities in the fields of armaments, space and military studies;
- WEU will examine how to strengthen the Associate Partners' participation in an increasing number of activities."

4. DECLARATION ON ARTICLES 24 AND 38 OF THE TREATY ON EUROPEAN UNION

The provisions of Articles **24** and **38** of the Treaty on European Union and any agreements resulting from them shall not imply any transfer of competence from the Member States to the European Union.

5. DECLARATION ON ARTICLE 25 OF THE TREATY ON EUROPEAN UNION

The Conference agrees that Member States shall ensure that the Political Committee referred to in Article **25** of the Treaty on European Union is able to meet at any time, in the event of international crises or other urgent matters, at very short notice at Political Director or deputy level.

6. DECLARATION ON THE ESTABLISHMENT OF A POLICY PLANNING AND EARLY WARNING UNIT

The Conference agrees that:

1. A policy planning and early warning unit shall be established in the General Secretariat of the Council under the responsibility of its Secretary-General, High Representative for the CFSP. Appropriate co-operation shall be established with the Commission order to ensure full coherence with the Union's external economic and development policies.

2. The tasks of the unit shall include the following:
(a) monitoring and analysing developments in areas relevant to the CFSP;
(b) providing assessments of the Union's foreign and security policy interests and identifying areas where the CFSP could focus in future;
(c) providing timely assessments and early warning of events or situations which may have significant repercussions for the Union's foreign and security policy, including potential political crises;
(d) producing, at the request of either the Council or the Presidency or on its own initiative, argued policy options papers to be presented under the responsibility of the Presidency as a contribution to policy formulation in the Council, and which may contain analyses, recommendations and strategies for the CFSP.

3. The unit shall consist of personnel drawn from the General Secretariat, the Member States, the Commission and the WEU.

4. Any Member State or the Commission may make suggestions to the unit for work to be undertaken.

5. Member States and the Commission shall assist the policy planning process by providing, to the fullest extent possible, relevant information, including confidential information.

7.   DECLARATION ON ARTICLE 30 OF THE TREATY ON EUROPEAN UNION

Action in the field of police co-operation under Article **30** of the Treaty on European Union, including activities of Europol, shall be subject to appropriate judicial review by the competent national authorities in accordance with rules applicable in each Member State.

8.   DECLARATION ON ARTICLE 31(e) OF THE TREATY ON EUROPEAN UNION

The Conference agrees that the provisions of Article **31**(e) of the Treaty on European Union shall not have the consequence of obliging a Member State whose legal system does not provide for minimum sentences to adopt them.

9.   DECLARATION ON ARTICLE 34(2) OF THE TREATY ON EUROPEAN UNION

The Conference agrees that initiatives for measures referred to in Article **34**(2) of the Treaty on European Union and acts adopted by the Council thereunder shall be published in the *Official Journal of the European Communities,* in accordance with the relevant Rules of Procedure of the Council and the Commission.

10.   DECLARATION ON ARTICLE 35 OF THE TREATY ON EUROPEAN UNION

The Conference notes that Member States may, when making a declaration pursuant to Article **35**(2) of the Treaty on European Union, reserve the right to make provisions in their national law to the effect that, where a question relating to the validity or interpretation of an act referred to in Article **35**(1) is raised in a case pending before a national court or tribunal against whose decision there is no judicial remedy under national law, that court or tribunal will be required to refer the matter to the Court of Justice.

11.   DECLARATION ON THE STATUS OF CHURCHES AND NON-CONFESSIONAL ORGANISATIONS

The European Union respects and does not prejudice the status under national law of churches and religious associations or communities in the Member States.

The European Union equally respects the status of philosophical and non-confessional organisations.

12.   DECLARATION ON ENVIRONMENTAL IMPACT ASSESSMENTS

The Conference notes that the Commission undertakes to prepare environmental impact assessment studies when making proposals which may have significant environmental implications.

13.   DECLARATION ON ARTICLE 16 OF THE TREATY ESTABLISHING THE EUROPEAN COMMUNITY

The provisions of Article **16** of the Treaty establishing the European Community on public services shall be implemented with full respect for the jurisprudence of the Court of Justice, *inter alia* as regards the principles of equality of treatment quality and continuity of such services.

14.   DECLARATION ON THE REPEAL OF ARTICLE 44 OF THE TREATY ESTABLISHING THE EUROPEAN COMMUNITY

The repeal of Article 44 of the Treaty establishing the European Community, which contains a reference to a natural preference between Member States in the context of fixing minimum prices during the transitional period, has no effect on the principle of Community preference as defined by the case law of the Court of Justice.

15.   DECLARATION ON THE PRESERVATION OF THE LEVEL OF PROTECTION AND SECURITY PROVIDED BY THE SCHENGEN *ACQUIS*

The Conference agrees that measures to be adopted by the Council, which will have the effect of replacing provisions on the abolition of checks at common borders contained in the 1990 Schengen Convention, should provide at least the same level of protection and security as under the aforementioned provisions of the Schengen Convention.

16.   DECLARATION ON ARTICLE 62(2)(b) OF THE TREATY ESTABLISHING THE EUROPEAN COMMUNITY

The Conference agrees that foreign policy considerations of the Union and the Member States shall be taken into account in the application of Article **62**(2)(b) of the Treaty establishing the European Community.

17.   DECLARATION ON ARTICLE 63 OF THE TREATY ESTABLISHING THE EUROPEAN COMMUNITY

Consultations shall be established with the United Nations High Commissioner for Refugees and other relevant international organisations on matters relating to asylum policy.

18.   DECLARATION ON ARTICLE 63(3)(a) OF THE TREATY ESTABLISHING THE EUROPEAN COMMUNITY

The Conference agrees that Member States may negotiate and conclude agreements with third countries in the domains covered by Article **63**(3)(a) of the Treaty establishing the European Community as long as such agreements respect Community law.

19.   DECLARATION ON ARTICLE 64 OF THE TREATY ESTABLISHING THE EUROPEAN COMMUNITY

The Conference agrees that Member States may take into account foreign policy considerations when exercising their responsibilities under Article **64**(1) of the Treaty establishing the European Community.

20.   DECLARATION ON ARTICLE 65 OF THE TREATY ESTABLISHING THE EUROPEAN COMMUNITY

Measures adopted pursuant to Article **65** of the Treaty establishing the European Community shall not prevent any Member State from applying its constitutional rules relating to freedom of the press and freedom of expression in other media.

21.   DECLARATION ON ARTICLE 67 OF THE TREATY ESTABLISHING THE EUROPEAN COMMUNITY

The Conference agrees that the Council will examine the elements of the decision referred to in Article **67**(2), second indent, of the Treaty establishing the European Community before the end of the five year period referred to in Article **67** with a view to taking and applying this decision immediately after the end of that period.

22.   DECLARATION REGARDING PERSONS WITH A DISABILITY

The Conference agrees that, in drawing up measures under Article **95** of the Treaty establishing the European Community, the institutions of the Community shall take account of the needs of persons with a disability.

23.   DECLARATION ON INCENTIVE MEASURES REFERRED TO IN ARTICLE 129 OF THE TREATY ESTABLISHING THE EUROPEAN COMMUNITY

The Conference agrees that the incentive measures referred to in Article **129** of the Treaty establishing the European Community should always specify the following:
-    the grounds for taking them based on an objective assessment of their need and the existence of an added value at Community level;
-    their duration, which should not exceed five years;
-    the maximum amount for their financing, which should reflect the incentive nature of such measures.

24.   DECLARATION ON ARTICLE 129 OF THE TREATY ESTABLISHING THE EUROPEAN COMMUNITY

It is understood that any expenditure under Article **129** of the Treaty establishing the European Community will fall within Heading 3 of the financial perspectives.

25.   DECLARATION ON ARTICLE 137 OF THE TREATY ESTABLISHING THE EUROPEAN COMMUNITY

It is understood that any expenditure under Article **137** of the Treaty establishing the European Community will fall within Heading 3 of the financial perspectives.

26.   DECLARATION ON ARTICLE 137(2) OF THE TREATY ESTABLISHING THE EUROPEAN COMMUNITY

The High Contracting Parties note that in the discussions on Article **137**(2) of the Treaty establishing the European Community it was agreed that the Community does not intend, in laying down minimum requirements for the protection of the safety and health of employees, to discriminate in a manner unjustified by the circumstances against employees in small and medium-sized undertakings.

27. DECLARATION ON ARTICLE 139(2) **OF THE TREATY ESTABLISHING THE EUROPEAN COMMUNITY**

The High Contracting Parties declare that the first of the arrangements for application of the agreements between management and labour at Community level - referred to in Article **139**(2) of the Treaty establishing the European Community - will consist in developing, by collective bargaining according to the rules of each Member State, the content of the agreements, and that consequently this arrangement implies no obligation on the Member States to apply the agreements directly or to work out rules for their transposition, nor any obligation to amend national legislation in force to facilitate their implementation.

28. DECLARATION ON ARTICLE 141(4) **OF THE TREATY ESTABLISHING THE EUROPEAN COMMUNITY**

When adopting measures referred to in Article **141**(4) of the Treaty establishing the European Community, Member States should, in the first instance, aim at improving the situation of women in working life.

29. DECLARATION ON SPORT

The Conference emphasises the social significance of sport, in particular its role in forging identity and bringing people together. The Conference therefore calls on the bodies of the European Union to listen to sports associations when important questions affecting sport are at issue. In this connection, special consideration should be given to the particular characteristics of amateur sport.

30. DECLARATION ON ISLAND REGIONS

The Conference recognises that island regions suffer from structural handicaps linked to their island status, the permanence of which impairs their economic and social development.

The Conference accordingly acknowledges that Community legislation must take account of these handicaps and that specific measures may be taken, where justified, in favour of these regions in order to integrate them better into the internal market on fair conditions.

31. DECLARATION RELATING TO THE COUNCIL DECISION OF 13 JULY 1987

The Conference calls on the Commission to submit to the Council by the end of 1998 at the latest a proposal to amend the Council decision of 13 July 1987 laying down the procedures for the exercise of implementing powers conferred on the Commission.

32. DECLARATION ON THE ORGANISATION AND FUNCTIONING OF THE COMMISSION

The Conference notes the Commission's intention to prepare a reorganisation of tasks within the college in good time for the Commission which will take up office in 2000, in order to ensure an optimum division between conventional portfolios and specific tasks.

In this context, it considers that the President of the Commission must enjoy broad discretion in the allocation of tasks within the College, as well as in any reshuffling of those tasks during a Commission's term of office.

The Conference also notes the Commission's intention to undertake in parallel a corresponding reorganisation of its departments. It notes in particular the desirability of bringing external relations under the responsibility of a Vice-President.

33.   DECLARATION ON ARTICLE 248(3) OF THE TREATY ESTABLISHING THE EUROPEAN COMMUNITY

The Conference invites the Court of Auditors, the European Investment Bank and the Commission to maintain in force the present Tripartite Agreement. If a succeeding or amending text is required by any party, they shall endeavour to reach agreement on such a text having regard to their respective interests.

34.   DECLARATION ON RESPECT FOR TIME LIMITS UNDER THE CO-DECISION PROCEDURE

The Conference calls on the European Parliament, the Council and the Commission to make every effort to ensure that the co-decision procedure operates as expeditiously as possible. It recalls the importance of strict respect for the deadlines sat out in Article **251** of the Treaty establishing the European Community and confirms that recourse, provided for in paragraph 7 of that Article, to extension of the periods in question should be considered only when strictly necessary. In no case should the actual period between the second reading by the European Parliament and the outcome of the Conciliation Committee exceed nine months.

35.   DECLARATION ON ARTICLE 255(1) OF THE TREATY ESTABLISHING THE EUROPEAN COMMUNITY

The Conference agrees that the principles and conditions referred to in Article **255**(1) of the Treaty establishing the European Community will allow a Member State to request the Commission or the Council not to communicate to third parties a document originating from that State without its prior agreement.

36.   DECLARATION ON THE OVERSEAS COUNTRIES AND TERRITORIES

The Conference recognises that the special arrangements for the association of the overseas countries and territories (OCTs) under Part Four of the Treaty establishing the European Community were designed for countries and territories that were numerous, covered vast areas and had large populations. The arrangements have changed little since 1957.

The Conference notes that there are today only 20 OCTs and that they are extremely scattered island territories with a total population of approximately 900,000. Moreover, most OCTs lag far behind in structural terms, a fact linked to their particularly severe geographical and economic handicaps. In these circumstances, the special arrangements for association as they were conceived in 1957 can no longer deal effectively with the challenges of OCT development.

The Conference solemnly restates that the purpose of association is to promote the economic and social development of the countries and territories, and to establish close economic relations between them and the Community as a whole.

The Conference invites the Council, acting in accordance with the provisions of Article **187** of the Treaty establishing the European Community, to review the association arrangements by February 2000, with the fourfold objective of:
- promoting the economic and social development of the OCTs more effectively;
- developing economic relations between the OCTs and the European Union;
- taking greater account of the diversity and specific characteristics of the individual OCTs, including aspects relating to freedom of establishment;
- ensuring that the effectiveness of the financial instrument is improved.

37.   DECLARATION ON PUBLIC CREDIT INSTITUTIONS IN GERMANY

The Conference notes the Commission's opinion to the effect that the Community's existing competition rules allow services of general economic interest provided by public credit institutions existing in Germany and the facilities granted to them to compensate for the costs connected with such services to be taken into account in full. In this context, the way in which Germany enables local authorities to carry out their task of making available in their regions a comprehensive and efficient financial infrastructure is a matter for the organisation of that Member State. Such facilities may not adversely affect the conditions of competition to an extent beyond that required in order to perform these particular tasks and which is contrary to the interests of the Community.

The Conference recalls that the European Council has invited the Commission to examine whether similar cases exist in the other Member States, to apply as appropriate the same standards on similar cases and to inform the Council in its ECOFIN formation.

38.   DECLARATION ON VOLUNTARY SERVICE ACTIVITIES

The Conference recognises the important contribution made by voluntary service activities to developing social solidarity.

The Community will encourage the European dimension of voluntary organisations with particular emphasis on the exchange of information and experiences as well as on the participation of the young and the elderly in voluntary work.

39.   DECLARATION ON THE QUALITY OF THE DRAFTING OF COMMUNITY LEGISLATION

The Conference notes that the quality of the drafting of Community legislation is crucial if it is to be properly implemented by the competent national authorities and better understood by the public and in business circles. It recalls the conclusions on this subject reached by the Presidency of the European Council in Edinburgh on 11 and 12 December 1992, as well as the Council Resolution on the quality of drafting of Community legislation adopted on 8 June 1993 (*Official Journal of the European Communities*, No C 166 of 17 June 1993, p. 1).

The Conference considers that the three institutions involved in the procedure for adopting Community legislation, the European Parliament, the Council and the Commission, should lay down guidelines on the quality of drafting of the said legislation. It also stresses that Community legislation should be made more accessible and welcomes in this regard the adoption and first implementation of an accelerated working method for official codification of legislative texts, established by the Inter-institutional Agreement of 20 December 1994 (*Official Journal of the European Communities*, No C 102 of 4 April 1996, p. 2).

Therefore, the Conference declares that the European Parliament, the Council and the Commission ought to:
-    establish by common accord guidelines for improving the quality of the drafting of Community legislation and follow those guidelines when considering proposals for Community legislation or draft legislation, taking the internal organisational measures they deem necessary to ensure that these guidelines are properly applied;
-    make their best efforts to accelerate the codification of legislative texts.

40.   DECLARATION CONCERNING THE PROCEDURE FOR CONCLUDING INTER-NATIONAL AGREEMENTS BY THE EUROPEAN COAL AND STEEL COMMUNITY

The repeal of Article 14 of the Convention on the Transitional Provisions annexed to the Treaty establishing the European Coal and Steel Community does not alter existing practice concerning the procedure for the conclusion of international agreements by the European Coal and Steel Community.

41. DECLARATION ON THE PROVISIONS RELATING TO TRANSPARENCY, ACCESS TO DOCUMENTS AND THE FIGHT AGAINST FRAUD

The Conference considers that the European Parliament, the Council and the Commission, when they act in pursuance of the Treaty establishing the European Coal and Steel Community and the Treaty establishing the European Atomic Energy Community, should draw guidance from the provisions relating to transparency, access to documents and the fight against fraud in force within the framework of the Treaty establishing the European Community.

42. DECLARATION ON THE CONSOLIDATION OF THE TREATIES

The High Contracting Parties agreed that the technical work begun during the course of this Inter-governmental Conference shall continue as speedily as possible with the aim of drafting a consolidation of all the relevant Treaties, including the Treaty on European Union.

They agreed that the final results of this technical work, which shall be made public for illustrative purposes under the responsibility of the Secretary-General of the Council, shall have no legal value.

43. DECLARATION RELATING TO THE PROTOCOL ON THE APPLICATION OF THE PRINCIPLES OF SUBSIDIARITY AND PROPORTIONALITY

The High Contracting Parties confirm, on the one hand, the Declaration on the implementation of Community law annexed to the Final Act of the Treaty on European Union and, on the other, the conclusions of the Essen European Council stating that the administrative implementation of Community law shall in principle be the responsibility of the Member States in accordance with their constitutional arrangements. This shall not affect the supervisory, monitoring and implementing powers of the Community Institutions as provided under Articles **202** and **211** of the Treaty establishing the European Community.

[*Note:* *the Declaration on the implementation of Community law, from the Maastricht Treaty, is shown below:*

'1. *The Conference stresses that it is central to the coherence and unity of the process of European construction that each Member State should fully and accurately transpose into national law the Community Directives addressed to it within the deadlines laid down therein.*

Moreover, the Conference, while recognizing that it must be for each Member State to determine how the provisions of Community law can best be enforced in the light of its own particular institutions, legal system and other circumstances, but in any event in compliance with Article 189 of the Treaty establishing the European Community, considers it essential for the proper functioning of the Community that the measures taken by the different Member States should result in Community law being applied with the same effectiveness and rigour as in the application of their national law.

2. *The Conference calls on the Commission to ensure, in exercising its powers under Article 155 of this Treaty, that Member States fulfil their obligations. It asks the Commission to publish periodically a full report for the Member States and the European Parliament.'*]

44. DECLARATION ON ARTICLE 2 OF THE PROTOCOL INTEGRATING THE SCHENGEN *ACQUIS* INTO THE FRAMEWORK OF THE EUROPEAN UNION

The High Contracting Parties agree that the Council shall adopt all the necessary measures referred to in Article 2 of the Protocol integrating the Schengen *acquis* into the framework of the European Union upon the date of entry into force of the Treaty of Amsterdam. To that end, the necessary preparatory work shall be undertaken in due time in order to be completed prior to that date.

45.   DECLARATION ON ARTICLE 4 OF THE PROTOCOL INTEGRATING THE SCHENGEN *ACQUIS* INTO THE FRAMEWORK OF THE EUROPEAN UNION

The High Contracting Parties invite the Council to seek the opinion of the Commission before it decides on a request under Article 4 of the Protocol integrating the Schengen *acquis* into the framework of the European Union by Ireland or the United Kingdom of Great Britain and Northern Ireland to take part in some or all of the provisions of the Schengen *acquis*. They also undertake to make their best efforts with a view to allowing Ireland or the United Kingdom of Great Britain and Northern Ireland, if they so wish, to use the provisions of Article 4 of the said Protocol so that the Council may be in a position to take the decisions referred to in that Article upon the date of entry into force of that Protocol or at any time thereafter.

46.   DECLARATION ON ARTICLE 5 OF THE PROTOCOL INTEGRATING THE SCHENGEN *ACQUIS* INTO THE FRAMEWORK OF THE EUROPEAN UNION

The High Contracting Parties undertake to make all efforts in order to make action among all Member States possible in the domains of the Schengen *acquis*, in particular whenever Ireland and the United Kingdom of Great Britain and Northern Ireland have accepted some or all of the provisions of that *acquis* in accordance with Article 4 of the Protocol integrating the Schengen *acquis* into the framework of the European Union.

47.   DECLARATION ON ARTICLE 6 OF THE PROTOCOL INTEGRATING THE SCHENGEN *ACQUIS* INTO THE FRAMEWORK OF THE EUROPEAN UNION

The High Contracting Parties agree to take all necessary steps so that the Agreements referred to in Article 6 of the Protocol integrating the Schengen *acquis* into the framework of the European Union may enter into force on the same date as the date of entry into force of the Treaty of Amsterdam.

48.   DECLARATION RELATING TO THE PROTOCOL ON ASYLUM FOR NATIONALS OF MEMBER STATES OF THE EUROPEAN UNION

The Protocol on asylum for nationals of Member States of the European Union does not prejudice the right of each Member State to take the organisational measures it deems necessary to fulfil its obligations under the Geneva Convention of 28 July 1951 relating to the status of refugees.

49.   DECLARATION RELATING TO SUB-PARAGRAPH (d) OF THE SOLE ARTICLE OF THE PROTOCOL ON ASYLUM FOR NATIONALS OF MEMBER STATES OF THE EUROPEAN UNION

The Conference declares that, while recognising the importance of the Resolution of the Ministers of the Member States of the European Communities responsible for immigration of 30 November/1 December 1992 on manifestly unfounded applications for asylum and of the Resolution of the Council of 20 June 1995 on minimum guarantees for asylum procedures, the question of abuse of asylum procedures and appropriate rapid procedures to dispense with manifestly unfounded applications for asylum should be further examined with a view to introducing new improvements in order to accelerate these procedures.

50.   DECLARATION RELATING TO THE PROTOCOL ON THE INSTITUTIONS WITH THE PROSPECT OF ENLARGEMENT OF THE EUROPEAN UNION

Until the entry into force of the first enlargement it is agreed that the decision of the Council of 29 March 1994 ('the Ioannina Compromise') will be extended and, by that date, a solution for the special case of Spain will be found.

51.   DECLARATION ON ARTICLE 10 OF THE TREATY OF AMSTERDAM

The Treaty of Amsterdam repeals and deletes lapsed provisions of the Treaty establishing the European Community, the Treaty establishing the European Coal and Steel Community and the Treaty establishing the European Atomic Energy Community as they were in force before the entry into force of the Treaty of Amsterdam and adapts certain of their provisions, including the insertion of certain provisions of the Treaty establishing a single Council and a single Commission of the European Communities and the Act concerning the election of the representatives of the European Parliament by direct universal suffrage. Those operations do not affect the "*acquis communautaire*".

DECLARATIONS
OF WHICH THE CONFERENCE TOOK NOTE

1.   DECLARATION BY AUSTRIA AND LUXEMBOURG ON CREDIT INSTITUTIONS

Austria and Luxembourg consider that the Declaration on public credit institutions in Germany also applies to credit institutions in Austria and Luxembourg with a comparable organisational structure.

2.   DECLARATION BY DENMARK ON ARTICLE 42 OF THE TREATY ON EUROPEAN UNION

Article **42** of the Treaty on European Union requires the unanimity of all members of the Council of the European Union, i.e. all Member States, for the adoption of any decision to apply the provisions of Title **IV** of the Treaty establishing the European Community on visas, asylum, immigration and other policies related to free movement of persons to action in areas referred to in Article **29**. Moreover, any unanimous decision of the Council, before coming into force, will have to be adopted in each Member State, in accordance with its constitutional requirements. In Denmark, such adoption will, in the case of a transfer of sovereignty, as defined in the Danish constitution, require either a majority of five-sixths of members of the Folketing or both a majority of the members of the Folketing and a majority of voters in a referendum.

3.   DECLARATION BY GERMANY, AUSTRIA AND BELGIUM ON SUBSIDIARITY

It is taken for granted by the German, Austrian and Belgian governments that action by the European Community in accordance with the principle of subsidiarity not only concerns the Member States but also their entities to the extent that they have their own law-making powers conferred on them under national constitutional law.

4.   DECLARATION BY IRELAND ON ARTICLE 3 OF THE PROTOCOL ON THE POSITION OF THE UNITED KINGDOM AND IRELAND

Ireland declares that it intends to exercise its right under Article 3 of the Protocol on the position of the United Kingdom and Ireland to take part in the adoption of measures pursuant to Title **IV** of the Treaty establishing the European Community to the maximum extent compatible with the maintenance of its Common Travel Area with the United Kingdom. Ireland recalls that its participation in the Protocol on the application of certain aspects of Article **14** of the Treaty establishing the European Community reflects its wish to maintain its Common Travel Area with the United Kingdom in order to maximise freedom of movement into and out of Ireland.

5. **DECLARATION BY BELGIUM ON THE PROTOCOL ON ASYLUM FOR NATIONALS OF MEMBER STATES OF THE EUROPEAN UNION**

In approving the Protocol on asylum for nationals of Member States of the European Union, Belgium declares that, in accordance with its obligations under the 1951 Geneva Convention and the 1967 New York Protocol, it shall, in accordance with the provision set out in point (d) of the sole Article of that Protocol, carry out an individual examination of any asylum request made by a national of another Member State.

6. **DECLARATION BY BELGIUM, FRANCE AND ITALY ON THE PROTOCOL ON THE INSTITUTIONS WITH THE PROSPECT OF ENLARGEMENT OF THE EUROPEAN UNION**

Belgium, France and Italy observe that, on the basis of the results of the Intergovernmental Conference, the Treaty of Amsterdam does not meet the need, reaffirmed at the Madrid European Council, for substantial progress towards reinforcing the institutions.

Those countries consider that such reinforcement is an indispensable condition for the conclusion of the first accession negotiations. They are determined to give the fullest effect appropriate to the Protocol as regards the composition of the Commission and the weighting of votes and consider that a significant extension of recourse to qualified majority voting forms part of the relevant factors which should be taken into account.

7. **DECLARATION BY FRANCE CONCERNING THE SITUATION OF THE OVERSEAS DEPARTMENTS IN THE LIGHT OF THE PROTOCOL INTEGRATING THE SCHENGEN *ACQUIS* INTO THE FRAMEWORK OF THE EUROPEAN UNION**

France considers that the implementation of the Protocol integrating the Schengen *acquis* into the framework of the European Union does not affect the geographical scope of the Convention implementing the Schengen Agreement of 14 June 1985 signed in Schengen on 19 June 1990, as it is defined by Article 138, first paragraph, of that Convention.

8. **DECLARATION BY GREECE CONCERNING THE DECLARATION ON THE STATUS OF CHURCHES AND NON-CONFESSIONAL ORGANISATIONS**

With reference to the Declaration on the status of churches and non-confessional organisations, Greece recalls the Joint Declaration on Mount Athos annexed to the Final Act of the Treaty of Accession of Greece to the European Communities.

* * * * * * *

190

191

APPENDICES

* * * * * * *

ACT CONCERNING THE ELECTION OF THE REPRESENTATIVES OF THE EUROPEAN PARLIAMENT BY DIRECT UNIVERSAL SUFFRAGE

ARTICLE 1

The representatives in the European Parliament of the peoples of the states brought together in the Community shall be elected by direct universal suffrage.

ARTICLE 2

The number of representatives elected in each Member State shall be as follows: Belgium: 25; Denmark: 16; Germany: 99; Greece: 25; Spain: 64; France: 87; Ireland: 15; Italy: 87; Luxembourg: 6; Netherlands: 31; Austria: 21; Portugal: 25; Finland: 16; Sweden: 22; United Kingdom: 87.

In the event of amendments to this Article, the number of representatives elected in each Member State must ensure appropriate representation of the peoples of the States brought together in the Community.

ARTICLE 3

1.   Representatives shall be elected for a term of five years.

2.   This five-year period shall begin at the opening of the first session following each election. It may be extended or curtailed pursuant to the second subparagraph of Article 10 (2).

3.   The term of office of each representative shall begin and end at the same time as the period referred to in paragraph 2.

ARTICLE 4

1.   Representatives shall vote on an individual and personal basis. They shall not be bound by any instructions and shall not receive a binding mandate.

2.   Representatives shall enjoy the privileges and immunities applicable to Members of the European Parliament by virtue of the Protocol on the privileges and immunities of the European Communities annexed to the Treaty establishing a single Council and a single Commission of the European Communities.

ARTICLE 5

The office of representative in the European Parliament shall be compatible with Membership of the Parliament of a Member State.

ARTICLE 6

1.   The office of representative in the European Parliament shall be incompatible with that of:
-    Member of the government of a Member State,
-    Member of the Commission of the European Communities,
-    Judge, Advocate-General or Registrar of the Court of Justice of the European Communities,
-    Member of the Court of Auditors of the European Communities,
-    Member of the consultative committee of the European Coal and Steel Community or Member of the Economic and Social Committee of the European Economic Community and of the European Atomic Energy Community,
-    **Member of the Committee of the Regions,**
-    Member of committees or other bodies set up pursuant to the Treaties establishing the European Coal and Steel Community, the European Economic Community and the European Atomic Energy Community for the purpose of managing the Communities' funds or carrying out a permanent direct administrative task,
-    Member of the board of directors, management committee or staff of the European Investment Bank,

-    active official or servant of the institutions of the European Communities or of the specialised bodies attached to them.

2.   In addition, each Member State may, in the circumstances provided for in Article 7 (2), lay down rules at national level relating to incompatibility.

3.   Representatives in the European Parliament to whom paragraphs 1 and 2 become applicable in the course of the five-year period referred to in Article 3 shall be replaced in accordance with Article 12.

ARTICLE 7
1.   Pursuant to Article 21(3) of the Treaty establishing the European Coal and Steel Community, Article 138(3) of the Treaty establishing the European Economic Community and 108(3) of the Treaty establishing the European Atomic Energy Community, the European Parliament shall draw up a proposal for a uniform electoral procedure.

2.   Pending the entry into force of a uniform electoral procedure **or a procedure based on common principles** and subject to the other provisions of this Act, the electoral procedure shall be governed in each Member State by its national provisions.

ARTICLE 8
No-one may vote more than once in any election of representatives to the European Parliament.

ARTICLE 9
1.   Elections to the European Parliament shall be held on the date fixed by each Member State.
For all Member States this date shall fall within the same period starting on a Thursday morning and ending on the following Sunday.

2.   The counting of votes may not begin until after the close of polling in the Member State whose electors are the last to vote within the period referred to in paragraph 1.

3.   If a Member State adopts a double ballot system for elections to the European Parliament, the first ballot must take place during the period referred to in paragraph 1.

ARTICLE 10
1.   The Council, acting unanimously after consulting the European Parliament, shall determine the period referred to in Article 9(1) for the first elections.

2.   Subsequent elections shall take place in the corresponding period in the last year of the five-year period referred to in Article 3.
Should it prove impossible to hold the elections in the Community during that period, the Council acting unanimously shall, after consulting the European Parliament, determine another period which shall be not more than one month before or one month after the period fixed pursuant to the preceding subparagraph.

3.   Without prejudice to Article 22 of the Treaty establishing the European Coal and Steel Community Article 139 of the Treaty establishing the European Economic Community and Article 109 of the Treaty establishing the European Atomic Energy Community, the European Parliament shall meet, without requiring to be convened, on the first Tuesday after expiry of an interval of one month from the end of the period referred to in Article 9(1).

4.   The powers of the outgoing European Parliament shall cease upon the opening of the first sitting of the new European Parliament.

ARTICLE 11
Pending the entry into force of the uniform electoral procedure **or the procedure based on common principles** referred to in Article **7**, the European Parliament shall verify the credentials of representatives. For this purpose it shall take note of the results declared officially by the Member States and shall rule on any disputes which may arise out of the provisions of this Act other than those arising out of the national provisions to which the Act refers.

ARTICLE 12

1.   Pending the entry into force of the uniform electoral procedure **or the procedure based on common principles** referred to in Article **7** and subject to the other provisions of this Act, each Member State shall lay down appropriate procedures for filling any seat which falls vacant during the five-year term of office referred to in Article 3 for the remainder of that period.

2.   Where a seat falls vacant pursuant to national provisions in force in a Member State, the latter shall inform the European Parliament, which shall take note of that fact.
In all other cases, the European Parliament shall establish that there is a vacancy and inform the Member State thereof.

ARTICLE 13

Should it appear necessary to adopt measures to implement this Act, the Council, acting unanimously on a proposal from the European Parliament after consulting the Commission, shall adopt such measures after endeavouring to reach agreement with the European Parliament in a conciliation committee consisting of the Council and representatives of the European Parliament.

ARTICLE 14

Article 21(1) and (2) of the Treaty establishing the European Coal and Steel Community, Article 138(1) and (2) of the Treaty establishing the European Economic Community and Article 108(1) and (2) of the Treaty establishing the European Atomic Energy Community shall lapse on the date of the sitting held in accordance with Article 10(3) by the first European Parliament elected pursuant to this Act.

ARTICLE 15

This Act is drawn up in the Danish, Dutch, English, French, German, Irish and Italian languages, all the texts being equally authentic.
Annexes I to III shall form an integral part of this Act.
A Declaration by the government of the Federal Republic of Germany is attached hereto.

ARTICLE 16

The provisions of this Act shall enter into force on the first day of the month following that during which the last of the notifications referred to in the Decision is received.

Done at Brussels on the twentieth day of September in the year one thousand nine hundred and seventy-six.

ANNEXES

ANNEX I

The Danish authorities may decide on the dates on which the election of Members to the European Parliament shall take place in Greenland.

ANNEX II

The United Kingdom will apply the provisions of this Act only in respect of the United Kingdom.

ANNEX III
DECLARATION ON ARTICLE 13:

As regards the procedure to be followed by the conciliation committee, it is agreed to have recourse to the provisions of paragraphs 5, 6 and 7 of the procedure laid down in the joint Declaration of the European Parliament, the Council and the Commission of 4 March 1975.

196

DECLARATION BY THE GOVERNMENT OF THE FEDERAL REPUBLIC OF GERMANY:

The government of the Federal Republic of Germany declares that the Act concerning the election of the Members of the European Parliament by direct universal suffrage shall equally apply to *Land* Berlin.
In consideration of the rights and responsibilities of France, the United Kingdom of Great Britain and Northern Ireland, and the United States of America, the Berlin House of Deputies will elect representatives to those seats within the quota of the Federal Republic of Germany that fall to *Land* Berlin.

* * * * * * *

COUNCIL DECISION OF 31 OCTOBER 1994
ON THE SYSTEM OF
THE COMMUNITIES' OWN RESOURCES

THE COUNCIL OF THE EUROPEAN COMMUNITIES,

HAVING REGARD to the Treaty establishing the European Community, and in particular Article **269** thereof,

HAVING REGARD to the Treaty establishing the European Atomic Energy Community, and in particular Article 173 thereof,

HAVING REGARD to the proposal from the Commission,

HAVING REGARD to the opinion of the European Parliament,

HAVING REGARD to the opinion of the Economic and Social Committee,

WHEREAS Council Decision 88/376/EEC, Euratom of 24 June 1988 on the system of the Communities' own resources expanded and amended the composition of own resources by capping the VAT resources base at 55% of gross national product ('GNP') for the year at market prices, with the maximum call-in rate being maintained at 1.4%, and by introducing an additional resource based on the total GNP of the Member States;

WHEREAS the European Council meeting in Edinburgh on 11 and 12 December 1992 reached certain conclusions;

WHEREAS the Communities must have adequate resources to finance their policies;

WHEREAS, in accordance with these conclusions, the Communities will, by 1999, be assigned a maximum amount of own resources corresponding to 1.27% of the total of the Member States' GNPs for the year at marled prices;

WHEREAS observance of this ceiling requires that the total amount of own resources at the Community's disposal for the period 1995 to 1999 does not in any one year exceed a specified percentage of the sum of the Member States' GNPs for the year in question;

WHEREAS on overall ceiling of 1.335% of the Member States' GNPs is set for commitment appropriations; whereas an orderly progression of commitment appropriations and payment appropriations should be ensured;

WHEREAS these ceilings should remain applicable until this Decision is amended;

WHEREAS, in order to make allowance for each Member State's ability to contribute to the system of own resources and to correct the regressive aspects of the current system for the least prosperous Member States, in accordance with the Protocol on Economic and Social Cohesion annexed to the Treaty on European Union, the Communities' financing rules should be further amended:
-   by lowering the ceiling for the uniform rate to be allied to the uniform value-added tax base of each Member State from 1.4 to 1.0% in equal steps between 1995 and 1999,
-   by limiting at 50% of GNP from 1995 onwards the value-added tax base of the Member States whose per capita GNP in 1991 was less than 90% of the Community average, i.e. Greece, Spain, Ireland and Portugal, and by reducing the base from 55 to 50% in equal steps over the period 1995 to 1999 for the other Member States;

WHEREAS the European Council has examined the correction of budgetary imbalances on numerous occasions, particularly at its meeting on 25 and 26 June 1984;

WHEREAS the European Council of 11 and 12 December 1992 confirmed the formula for calculating the connection of budgetary imbalances defined in Decision 88/376/EEC, Euratom;

WHEREAS the budgetary imbalances should be corrected in such a way as not to affect the own resources available for Community policies;

WHEREAS the monetary reserve, hereinafter referred to as 'the EAGGF monetary reserve', is covered by specific provisions;

WHEREAS the conclusions of the European Council provided for the creation in the budge of two reserve, one for the financing of the Loan Guarantee Fund, and the other for emergency aid in non-member countries, whereas these reserves should be covered by specific provisions;

WHEREAS the Commission will by the end of 1999 submit a report on the operation of the system, which will contain a review of the mechanism for correcting budgetary imbalances granted to the United Kingdom, whereas it will also by the end of 1999 present a report containing the result of a study on the feasibility of creating a new own resource, as well as on arrangements for the possible introduction of a fixed uniform rate applicable to the VAT base;

WHEREAS provisions must be laid down to cover the changeover from the system introduced by Decision 88/376/EEC, Euratom to that arising from this Decision;

WHEREAS the European Council provided that this Decision should take effect on 1 January 1995,

HAS LAID DOWN these provisions, which it recommends to the member states for adoption:

ARTICLE 1

The Communities shall be allocated resources of their own in accordance with the detailed rules laid down in the following Articles in order to ensure the financing of their budget.

The budget of the Communities shall, without prejudice to other revenue, be financed wholly from the Communities' own resources.

ARTICLE 2

1.   Revenue from the following shall constitute own resources entered in the budget of the Communities:

(a)   levies, premiums, additional or compensatory amounts, additional surmounts or factors and other duties established or to be established by the institutions of the Communities in respect of trade with non-member countries within the framework of the common agricultural policy, and also contributions and other duties provided for within the framework of the common organisation of the markets in sugar;

(b)   Common Customs Tariff duties end other duties established or to be established by the institutions of the Communities in respect of trade with non-member countries and customs duties on products coming under the Treaty establishing the European Coal and Steel Community;

(c)   the application of a uniform rate valid for all Member States to the VAT assessment base which is determined in a uniform manner for Member States according to Community rules. However, the assessment base to be taken into account for the purposes of this Decision shall, from 1995, not exceed 50% of GNP in the case of Member States whose per capita GNP, in 1991 was less than 90% of the Community average; for the other Member States the assessment base to be taken into account shall not exceed:

-    54% of their GNP in 1995,
-    53% of their GNP in 1996,
-    52% of their GNP in 1997,
-    51% of their GNP in 1998,
-    50% of their GNP in 1999,

The cap of 50% of their GNP to be introduced for all Member States in 1999 shall remain applicable until such time as this Decision is amended;

(d)   the application of a rate - to be determined pursuant to the budgetary procedure in the light of the total of all other revenue - to the sum of all the Member States' GNP established in accordance with the Community rules laid down in Directive 89/130/EEC, Euratom.

2.   Revenue deriving from any now charges introduced within the frame-work of a common policy, in accordance with the Treaty establishing the European Community or the Treaty establishing the European Atomic Energy Community, provided the procedure laid down in Article **269** of the Treaty establishing the European Community or in Article 173 of the Treaty establishing the European Atomic Energy Community has been followed, shall also constitute own resources entered in the budget of the Communities.

3.   Member States shall retain, by way of collection costs, 10% of the amounts paid under l(a) and (b).

4.   The uniform rate referred to in paragraph 1(c) shall correspond to the rate resulting from:
(a)   the application to the VAT assessment base for the Member States of:
   -   1.32% in 1995,
   -   1.24% in 1996,
   -   1.16% in 1997,
   -   1.08% in 1998,
   -   1.00% in 1999.
   The 1.00% rate in 1999 shall remain applicable until such time as this Decision is amended;
(b)   the deduction of the gross amount of the reference compensation referred to in Article 4(2). The gross amount shall be the compensation amount adjusted for the fact that the United Kingdom is not participating in the financing of its own compensation and the Federal Republic of Germany's share is reduced by one-third. It shall be calculated as if the reference compensation amount were financed by Member States according to their VAT assessment bases established in accordance with Article 2(1)(c).

5.   The rate fixed under paragraph l(d) shall apply to the GNP of each Member State.

6.   If, at the beginning of the financial year, the budget has not been adopted, the previous uniform VAT rate and rate applicable to Member States' GNPs, without prejudice to the provisions adopted in accordance with Article 8(2) as regards the EAGGF monetary reserve, the reserve for financing the Loan Guarantee Fund and the reserve for emergency aid in third countries, shall remain applicable until the entry into force of the new rates.

7.   For the purposes of applying this Decision, GNP shall mean gross national product for the year at market prices.

ARTICLE 3
1.   The total amount of own resources assigned to the Communities may not exceed 1.27% of the total GNPs of the Member States for payment appropriations.
The total amount of own resources assigned to the Communities may not, for any of the years during the period 1995 to 1999, exceed the following percentages of the total GNPs of the Member States for the year in question:
-   1995:   1.21,
-   1996:   1.22,
-   1997:   1.24,
-   1998:   1.26,
-   1999:   1.27.

2.   The commitment appropriations entered in the general budget of the Communities over the period 1995 to 1999 must follow an orderly progression resulting in a total amount which does not exceed 1.335% of the total GNPs of the Member States in 1999. An orderly ratio between commitment appropriations and payment appropriations shall be maintained to guarantee their compatibility and to enable the ceilings mentioned in paragraph 1 to be observed in subsequent years.

3.   The overall ceilings referred to in paragraphs 1 and 2 shall remain applicable until such time as this Decision is amended.

ARTICLE 4
The United Kingdom shall be granted a correction in respect of budgetary imbalances. This correction shall consist of a basic amount and an adjustment. The adjustment shall correct the basic amount to a reference compensation amount.
1.   The basic amount shall be established by:
(a)   calculating the difference, in the financial year, between:
   -   the percentage share of the United Kingdom in the sum total of the payments referred to in Article 2(1)(c) and (d) made during the financial year, including adjustments at the uniform rate in respect of earlier financial years, and

- the percentage share of the United Kingdom in total allocated expenditure;
(b) applying the difference thus obtained to total allocated expenditure;
(c) multiplying the result by 0.66.

2. The reference compensation shall be the correction resulting from application of (a), (b) and (c) of this paragraph, corrected by the effects arising for the United Kingdom from the changeover to capped VAT and the payments referred to in Article 2(1)(d).
It shall be established by:
(a) calculating the difference, in the preceding financial year, between:
- the percentage share of the United Kingdom in the sum total of VAT payments which would have been made during that financial year, including adjustments in respect of earlier financial years, for the amounts financed by the resources referred to in Article 2(1)(c) and (d) if the uniform VAT rate had been applied to non-capped bases, and
- the percentage share of the United Kingdom in total allocated expenditure;
(b) applying the difference thus obtained to total allocated expenditure;
(c) multiplying the result by 0.66;
(d) subtracting the payments by the United Kingdom taken into account in the first indent of point 1(a) from those taken into account in point(a), first indent of this sub-paragraph;
(e) subtracting the amount calculated at (d) from the amount calculated at (c).

3. The basic amount shall be adjusted in such a way as to correspond to the reference compensation amount.

ARTICLE 5
1. The cost of the correction shall be borne by the other Member States in accordance with the following arrangements:
The distribution of the cost shall first be calculated by reference to each Member State's share of the payments referred to in Article 2(1)(d), the United Kingdom being excluded; it shall then be adjusted in such a way as to restrict the share of the Federal Republic of Germany to two-thirds of the share resulting from this calculation.

2. The correction shall be granted to the United Kingdom by a reduction in its payments resulting from the application of Article 2(1)(c) and (d). The Costs borne by the other Member States shall be added to their payments resulting from the application for each Member State of Article 2(1)(c) and (d).

3. The Commission shall perform the calculations required for the application of Article 4 and this Article.

4. If, at the beginning of the financial year, the budget has not been adopted, the correction granted to the United Kingdom and the costs borne by the other Member States as entered in the last budget finally adopted shall remain applicable.

ARTICLE 6
The revenue referred to in Article 2 shall be used without distinction to finance all expenditure entered in the budget. However, the revenue needed to cover in full or in part the EAGGF monetary reserve the reserve for the financing of the Loan Guarantee Fund and the reserve for emergency aid in third countries, entered in the budget shall not be called up from the Member States until the reserves are implemented. Provisions for the operation of those reserves shall be adopted as necessary in accordance with Article 8(2).
The first paragraph shall be without prejudice to the treatment of contributions by certain Member States to supplementary programmes provided for in Article **169** of the Treaty establishing the European Community.

ARTICLE 7
Any surplus of the Communities' revenue over total actual expenditure during a financial year shall be carried over to the following financial year.
Any surpluses generated by a transfer from EAGGF Guarantee Section chapters, or surplus from the Guarantee Fund arising from external measures, transferred to the revenue account in the budget, shall be regarded as constituting own resources.

ARTICLE 8
1. The Community own resources refared to in Article 2(1)(a) and (b) shall be collected by the Member States in accordance with the national provisions imposed by law, regulation or administrative action, which shall, where appropriate, be adapted to meet the requirements of Community rules. The

Commission shall examine at regular intervals the national provisions communicated to it by the Member States, transmit to the Member States the adjustments it deems necessary in order to ensure that they comply with Community rules and report to the budget authority. Member States shall make the resources provided for in Article 2(1)(a) to (d) available to the Commission.

2.   Without prejudice to the auditing of the accounts and to checks that they are lawful and regular and as laid down in Article **248** of the Treaty establishing the European Community, such auditing and checks being mainly concerned with the reliability and effectiveness of national systems and procedures for determining the base for own resources accruing from VAT and GNP and without prejudice to the inspection arrangements made pursuant to Article **279**(c) of that Treaty, the Council shall, acting unanimously on a proposal from the Commission and after consulting the European Parliament, adopt the provisions necessary to apply this Decision and to make possible the inspection of the collection, the making available to the Commission and part of the revenue referred to in Articles 2 and 5.

ARTICLE 9
The mechanism for the graduated refund of own resources accruing from VAT or GNP-based financial contributions introduced for Greece up to 1985 by Article 127 of the 1979 Act of Accession and for Spain and Portugal up to 1991 by Articles 187 and 374 of the 1985 Act of Accession shall apply to the own resources accruing from VAT and the GNP-based resources referred to in Article 2(1)(c) and (d) of this Decision. It shall also apply to payments by the two last-named Member States in accordance with Article 5(2) of this Decision. In the latter case the rate of refund shall be that applicable for the year in respect of which the correction is granted.

ARTICLE 10
The Commission shall submit, by the end of 1999, a report on the operation of system, including a re-examination of the correction of budgetary imbalances granted to the United Kingdom, established by this Decision. It shall also by the end of 1999 submit a report on the findings of a study on the feasibility of creating a new own resource, as well as on arrangements for the possible introduction of a fixed uniform rate applicable to the VAT base.

ARTICLE 11
1.   Member States shall be notified of this Decision by the Secretary-General of the Council and the Decision shall be published in the *Official Journal of the European Communities.*
Member States shall notify the Secretary-General of the Council without delay of the completion of the procedures for the adoption of this Decision in accordance with their respective constitutional requirements.
This Decision shall enter into force on the first day on the month following receipt of the last of the notifications referred to in the second sub-paragraph. It shall take effect on 1 January 1995.

2.   (a)   Subject to (b), Decision 88/376/EEC, Euratom shall be repealed as of 1 January 1995. Any references to the Council Decision of 21 April 1970 on the replacement of financial contributions from Member States by the Communities own resources, to Council Decision 85/257/EEC, Euratom of 7 May 1985 on the Communities' system of own resources or to Decision 88/376/EEC, Euratom shall be construed as references to this Decision.
      (b)   Article 3 of Decision 85/257/EEC, Euratom shall continue to apply to the calculation and adjustment of revenue from the application of rates to the uncapped uniform VAT base for 1987 and earlier years.
Articles 2, 4 and 5 of Decision 88/376/EEC, Euratom shall continue to apply to the calculation and adjustment of revenue accruing from the application of a uniform rate valid for all Member States to the VAT base determined in a uniform manner and limited to 55% of the GNP of each Member State and to the calculation of the correction of budgetary imbalances granted to the United Kingdom for the years 1988 to 1994. When Article 2(7) of that Decision has to be applied, the value-added tax payments shall be replaced by financial contributions in the calculations referred to in this paragraph for any Member State concerned; this system shall also apply to the payment of adjustments of corrections for earlier years.

Done at Luxembourg, 31 October 1994.
For the Council
The President, K. KINKEL

202

INTER-INSTITUTIONAL AGREEMENT
BETWEEN
THE EUROPEAN PARLIAMENT,
THE COUNCIL AND THE EUROPEAN COMMISSION
ON PROVISIONS REGARDING FINANCING OF
THE COMMON FOREIGN AND SECURITY POLICY

This agreement is attached to the Treaty of Amsterdam, but does not form part of the formal Treaty on European Union. The Agreement was finalised in July 1997 and the provisions are now in force. At the time of writing, the European Parliament considers that the 'information and consultation' aspects have not yet been adequately interpreted by the other institutions.

GENERAL PROVISIONS

A.   CFSP operational expenditure shall be charged to the budget of the European Communities, unless the Council decides otherwise, in accordance with Article **27** of the Treaty [*on European Union*].

B.   CFSP expenditure shall be treated as expenditure not necessarily resulting from the Treaty. However, the following specific modalities of implementation of the expenditure in question are hereby laid down by common agreement between the European Parliament, the Council and the Commission.

FINANCIAL ARRANGEMENTS

C.   On the basis of the preliminary draft budget established by the Commission, the European Parliament and the Council shall annually secure agreement on the amount of the operational CFSP expenditure to be charged to the Communities' budget and on the allocation of this amount among the Articles of the CFSP budget chapter (for Articles: see suggestions under G).
In the absence of agreement, it is understood that the European Parliament and the Council shall at least agree to enter in the CFSP budget the amount contained in the previous budget, unless the Commission proposes to lower that amount.

D.   The total amount of operational CFSP expenditure shall be entirely entered in one (CFSP) budget chapter, under the Articles of this chapter (as suggested in G.). This amount shall cover the real predictable needs and a reasonable margin for unforeseen actions. No funds will be entered into a reserve. Each Article shall cover common strategies or joint actions already adopted, measures which are foreseen but not yet adopted and all future - i.e. unforeseen - actions to be adopted by the Council during the financial year concerned.

E.   In conformity with the Financial Regulation, the Commission, on the basis of a Council decision, will have the authority to, autonomously, make credit-transfers between Articles within one budget chapter, i.e. the CFSP envelope, the flexibility deemed necessary for a speedy implementation of CFSP actions will be assured.

F.   In the event of the amount of the CFSP budget during the financial year being insufficient to cover the necessary expenses, the European Parliament and the Council shall agree to find a solution as a matter of urgency, on a proposal by the Commission.

G.   Within the CFSP budget chapter, the Articles into which the CFSP actions are to be entered, could read along the following lines:
-   observation and organisation of elections/participation in democratic transition processes;
-   EU-envoys;
-   Prevention of conflicts/peace and security processes;
-   Financial assistance to disarmament processes;
-   Contributions to international conferences;
-   Urgent actions.
The European Parliament, the Council and the Commission agree that the amount for actions entered under the Article mentioned in the sixth indent cannot exceed 20 per cent of the global amount of the CFSP budget chapter.

AD HOC CONCERTATION PROCEDURE

H.   An *ad hoc* concertation procedure shall be set up, with a view to reaching an agreement between the two arms of the budgetary authority as far as the aforementioned amount of CFSP expenditure and the distribution of this amount over the Articles of CFSP budget chapter are concerned.

I.   This procedure will be applied at the request of the European Parliament or the Council, notably if either of these institutions intends to depart from the preliminary draft budget of the Commission.

J.   The *ad hoc* concertation procedure has to be concluded before the date set by the Council for establishing its draft budget.

K.   Each arm of the budgetary authority shall take whatever steps are required to ensure that the results which will be secured in the ad hoc concertation procedure, are respected throughout the budgetary procedure.

CONSULTATION AND INFORMATION OF THE EUROPEAN PARLIAMENT

L.   On a yearly basis the Presidency of the Council shall consult the European Parliament on a document established by the Council on the main aspects and basic choices of the CFSP, including the financial implications for the Communities budget. Furthermore, the Presidency shall on a regular basis inform the European Parliament on the development and implementation of CFSP actions.

M.   The Council shall, each time it adopts a decision in the field of CFSP entailing expenses, immediately and in each case communicate to the European Parliament an estimate of the costs envisaged (*"fiche financière"*), in particular those regarding time-frame, staff employed, use of premises and other infrastructure, transport facilities, training requirements and security arrangements.

N.   The Commission shall inform the budgetary authority on the execution of CFSP actions and the financial forecasts for the remaining period of the year on a quarterly basis.

* * * * * *

RESOLUTION OF THE EUROPEAN COUNCIL ON THE STABILITY AND GROWTH PACT

I.   Meeting in Madrid in December 1995, the European Council confirmed the crucial importance of securing budgetary discipline in stage three of Economic and Monetary Union (EMU). In Florence, six months later, the European Council reiterated this view and in Dublin, in December 1996, it reached an agreement on the main elements of the Stability and Growth pact. In stage three of EMU, Member States shall avoid excessive general government deficits: this is a clear Treaty obligation.[†]

The European Council underlines the importance of safeguarding sound government finances as a means to strengthening the conditions for price stability and for strong sustainable growth conducive to employment creation. It is also necessary to ensure that national budgetary policies support stability oriented monetary policies. Adherence to the objective of sound budgetary positions close to balance or in surplus will allow all Member States to deal with normal cyclical fluctuations while keeping the government deficit within the 3 percent of GDP reference value.

II.   Meeting in Dublin in December 1996, the European Council requested the preparation of a Stability and Growth pact to be achieved in accordance with the principles and procedures of the Treaty. This Stability and Growth pact in no way changes the requirements for participation in stage three of EMU, either in the first group or at a later date. Member States remain responsible for their national budgetary policies, subject to the provisions of the Treaty; they will take the necessary measures in order to meet their responsibilities in accordance with those provisions.

III.   The Stability and Growth pact, which provides both for prevention and deterrence, consists of this resolution and two Council Regulations, one on the strengthening of the surveillance of budgetary positions and the surveillance and co-ordination of economic policies and another on speeding up and clarifying the implementation of the excessive deficit procedure.

IV.   The European Council solemnly invites all parties, namely the Member States, the Council and the Commission, to implement the Treaty and the Stability and Growth pact in a strict and timely manner. This resolution provides firm political guidance to the parties who will implement the Stability and Growth Pact. To this end, the European Council has agreed upon the following guidelines:

The Member States

1.   commit themselves to respect the medium-term budgetary objective of close to balance or in surplus set out in their stability or convergence programmes and to take the corrective budgetary action they deem necessary to meet the objectives of their stability or convergence programmes, whenever they have information indicating actual or expected significant divergence from those objectives;

2.   are invited to make public, on their own initiative, the Council recommendations made to them in accordance with Article **99**(4);

3.   commit themselves to take the corrective budgetary action they deem necessary to meet the objectives of their stability or convergence programmes once they receive an early warning in the form of a Council recommendation issued under Article **99**(4);

4.   will launch the corrective budgetary adjustments they deem necessary without delay on receiving information indicating the risk of an excessive deficit;

[†]   Under Article 5 of Protocol **25**, the obligation does not apply to the United Kingdom unless it moves to the third stage; the obligation under Article **116**(4) to endeavour to avoid excessive deficits shall continue to apply to the United Kingdom.

5.   will correct excessive deficits as quickly as possible after their emergence; this correction should be completed no later than the year following the identification of the excessive deficit, unless there are special circumstances;

6.   are invited to make public, on their own initiative, recommendations made in accordance with Article **104**(7);

7.   commit themselves not to invoke the benefit of Article 2 paragraph 3 of the Council Regulation on speeding up and clarifying the excessive deficit procedure unless they are in severe recession; in evaluating whether the economic downturn is severe, the Member States will, as a rule, take as a reference point an annual fall in real GDP of at least 0.75%.

The Commission

1.   will exercise its right of initiative under the Treaty in a manner that facilitates the strict, timely and effective functioning of the Stability and Growth pact;

2.   will present, without delay, the necessary reports, opinions and recommendations to enable the adoption of Council decisions under Article **99** and Article **104**; this will facilitate the effective functioning of the early warning system and the rapid launch and strict application of the excessive deficit procedure;

3.   commits itself to prepare a report under Article **104**(3) whenever there is the risk of an excessive deficit or whenever the planned or actual government deficit exceeds the 3 per cent of GDP reference value, thereby triggering the procedure under Article **104**(3);

4.   commits itself, in the event that the Commission considers that a deficit exceeding 3% of GDP is not excessive and this opinion differs from that of the Economic and Financial Committee, to present in writing to the Council the reasons for its position;

5.   commits itself, following a request from the Council under Article **115**, to make, as a rule, a recommendation for a Council decision on whether an excessive deficit exists under Article **104**(6).

The Council

1.   is committed to a rigorous and timely implementation of all elements of the stability and growth pact in its competence; it will take the necessary decisions under Article **99** and Article **104** as quickly as is practicable;

2.   is urged to regard the deadlines for the application of the excessive deficit procedure as upper limits; in particular, the Council, acting under Article **104**(7), shall recommend that excessive deficits will be corrected as quickly as possible after their emergence, no later than the year following their identification, unless there are special circumstances;

3.   is invited always to impose sanctions if a participating Member State fails to take the necessary steps to bring the excessive deficit situation to an end as recommended by the Council;

4.   is urged always to require a non-interest bearing deposit, whenever the Council decides to impose sanctions on a participating Member State in accordance with Article **104**(11);

5.   is urged always to convert a deposit into a fine after two years of the decision to impose sanctions in accordance with Article **104**(11), unless the excessive deficit has in the view of the Council been corrected;

6.   is invited to always state in writing the reasons which justify a decision not to act, if at any stage of the excessive deficit or surveillance of budgetary positions procedures the Council did not act on a Commission recommendation, and, in such a case, to make public the votes cast by each Member State.

* * * * * * *

RESOLUTION OF THE EUROPEAN COUNCIL ON GROWTH AND EMPLOYMENT

The European Council, meeting in Amsterdam on 16 June 1997,

RECALLING the conclusions of the Essen European Council, the Commission's initiative for 'Action on Employment: a Confidence Pact', the Dublin declaration on employment,

has adopted the following guidelines.

Introduction

1.   It is imperative to give a new impulse for keeping employment firmly at the top of the political agenda of the Union. EMU and the Stability and Growth Pact will enhance the Internal Market and will foster a non-inflationary macro-economic environment with low interest rates, thereby strengthening conditions for economic growth and employment opportunities. In addition, we will need to strengthen the links between a successful and sustainable Economic and Monetary Union, a well-functioning Internal Market and employment. To that end, it should be a priority aim to develop a skilled, trained and adaptable workforce and to make labour markets responsive to economic change. Structural reforms need to be comprehensive in scope, as opposed to limited or occasional measures, so as to address in a coherent manner the complex issue of incentives in creating and taking up a job.

Economic and social policies are mutually reinforcing. Social protection systems should be modernised so as to strengthen their functioning in order to contribute to competitiveness, employment and growth, establishing a durable basis for social Cohesion.

This approach, coupled with stability-based policies, provides the basis for an economy founded on principles of inclusion, solidarity, justice and a sustainable environment, and capable of benefiting all its citizens. Economic efficiency and social inclusion are complementary aspects of the more cohesive European society that we all seek.

Taking account of this statement of principles, the European Council calls upon all the social and economic agents, including the national, regional and local authorities and the social partners, to face fully their responsibilities within their respective sphere of activity.

Developing the Economic Pillar

2.   The Treaty, in particular Articles **98** and **99**, provides for close co-ordination of the Member States' economic policies, referred to in Article **4** of the Treaty. While primarily responsibility in the fight against unemployment rests with the Member States, we should recognise the need both to enhance the effectiveness and to broaden the content of this co-ordination, focusing in particular on policies for employment. To this end, several steps are necessary.

3.   The broad guidelines of the economic policies will be enhanced and developed into an effective instrument for ensuring sustained convergence of the economic performances of the Member States. Within the framework of sound and sustainable macro-economic policies and on the basis an evaluation of the economic situation in the European Union and in each Member State, more attention will be given to improving European competitiveness as a prerequisite for growth and employment, so as to, among other objectives, bring more jobs within the reach of the citizens of Europe. In this context, special attention should be given to labour and product market efficiency, technological innovation and the potential for small and medium-sized enterprises to create jobs. Full attention should also be given to training and education systems including life-long learning, work incentives in the tax and benefit systems and reducing non-wage labour costs, in order to increase employability.

4.   Taxation and social protection systems should be made more employment friendly and by that improving the functioning of labour markets. The European Council stresses the importance for the Member States of creating a tax environment that stimulates enterprise and the creation of jobs. These and other policies for employment will become an essential part of the broad guidelines, taking into account national employment policies and good practices arising from these policies.

208

5.   The Council is therefore called upon to take the multi-annual employment programmes, as envisaged in the Essen procedure, into account when formulating the broad guidelines, in order to strengthen their employment focus. The Council may make the necessary recommendations to the Member States, in accordance with Article **99**(4) of the Treaty.

6.   This enhanced co-ordination of economic policies will complement the procedure as envisaged in the new Title on Employment in the Treaty, which provides for the creation of an Employment Committee, which is asked to work together closely with the Economic Policy Committee. The Council should seek to make those provisions immediately effective. In both procedures the European Council will play its integrating and guiding role in accordance with the Treaty.

7.   The European Union should complement national measures by systematically examining all relevant exiting Community policies, including Trans-European Networks ant Research and Development programmes, to ensure that they are geared towards job creation and economic growth, while respecting the Financial Perspectives and the Inter-Institutional Agreement.

8.   The European Council has agreed concrete action on making maximum progress with the final completion of the Internal Market: making the rules more effective, dealing with the key remaining market distortions, avoiding harmful tax competition, removing the sectoral obstacles to market integration and delivering an Internal Market for the benefit of all citizens.

9.   Whereas the task of the European Investment Bank, as stated in Article **267** of the Treaty, is to contribute, by having recourse to the capital market and utilising its own resources, to the balanced and steady development of the common market in the interest of the Community, we recognise the important role of the European Investment Bank and the European Investment Fund in creating employment through investment opportunities in Europe. We urge the EIB to step up its activities in this respect, promoting investment projects consistent with sound banking principles and practices, and more in particular:
-    to examine the establishment of a facility for the financing of high-technology projects of small and medium-sized enterprises in co-operation with the European Investment Fund, possibly making use of venture capital with involvement of the private banking sector;
-    to examine its scope of intervention in the areas of education, health, urban environment and environmental protection;
-    to step up its interventions in the area of large infrastructure networks by examining the possibility of granting very long-term loans, primarily for the large priority projects adopted in Essen.

10.   The Commission is invited to make the appropriate proposals in order to ensure that, upon expiration of the ECSC Treaty in 2002, to use the revenues of outstanding reserves for a research fund for sectors related to the coal and steel industry.

11.   This overall strategy will maximise our efforts to promote employment and social inclusion and to combat unemployment. In doing so, job promotion, worker protection and security will be combined with the need for improving the functioning of labour markets. This also contributes to the good functioning of EMU.

Renewed Commitment

12.   The European Council invites all parties, namely the Member States, the Council and the Commission, to implement these provisions with vigour and commitment.
The possibilities offered to social partners by the Social Chapter, which has been integrated into the new Treaty, should serve to underpin the Council's work on employment. The Europe Council recommends social dialogue and the full use of present Community law concerning the consultation of social partners, including, where relevant, in processes of restructuring, and taking into account national practices.

13.   Together, these policies allow the Member States to build on the strengths of the European construction to co-ordinate their economic policies effectively within the Council so as to create more jobs and pave the way for a successful and sustainable stage three of Economic and Monctay Union in accordance with the Treaty. The European Council asks social partners to fully face their responsibilities within their respective sphere of activity.

* * * * * * *

RESOLUTION OF THE EUROPEAN COUNCIL

ON THE ESTABLISHMENT OF AN EXCHANGE-RATE MECHANISM IN THE THIRD STAGE OF ECONOMIC AND MONETARY UNION

This Resolution sets out the basic principles of the new ERM. The States not entering EMU are required to follow particular disciplines, in particular, fluctuation margins, and to prepare for entry to EMU. The governors of the central banks agreed to the Resolution, including the fluctuation margins allowed.

Building on the agreements reached at its meetings in Florence and Dublin, the European Council has today agreed as follows:

AN EXCHANGE RATE MECHANISM WILL BE SET UP WHEN THE THIRD STAGE OF ECONOMIC AND MONETARY UNION BEGINS ON 1 JANUARY 1999

With the start of the third stage of Economic and Monetary Union, the European Monetary System will be replaced by the exchange-rate mechanism as defined in this Resolution. The operating procedures will be laid down in an agreement between the European Central Bank and the national central banks of the Member States outside the Euro area. The exchange-rate mechanism will link currencies of Member States outside the Euro area to the Euro. The Euro will be the centre of the new mechanism. The mechanism will function within the requisite framework of stability-oriented policies in accordance with the Treaty establishing the European Community which are at the core of economic and monetary union.

1.   PRINCIPLES AND OBJECTIVES

1.1.   Lasting convergence of economic fundamentals is a prerequisite for sustainable exchange-rate stability. To this end, in the third stage of Economic and Monetary Union, all Member States must pursue disciplined and responsible monetary policies directed towards price stability. Sound fiscal and structural policies in all Member States are, at least, equally essential for sustainable exchange-rate stability.

1.2.   A stable economic environment is necessary for the good functioning of the single market and for higher investment, growth and employment and is therefore in the interest of all Member States. The single market must not be endangered by real exchange-rate misalignments, or by excessive nominal exchange-rate fluctuations between the Euro and the other EU currencies, which would disrupt trade flows between Member States. Moreover, under Article **124** of the Treaty establishing the European Community, each Member State has an obligation to treat its exchange-rate policy as a matter of common interest. The surveillance of Member States' macro-economic policies in the Council under Article **99** of the Treaty establishing the European Community will be organised, *inter alia*, with a view to avoiding such misalignments or fluctuations.

1.3.   The exchange-rate mechanism will help to ensure that Member States outside the Euro-area participating in the mechanism orient their policies to stability, foster convergence and thereby help them in their efforts to adopt the Euro. It will provide those Member States with a reference for their conduct of sound economic policies in general and monetary policy in particular. At the same time, the mechanism will also help to protect them and the Member States adopting the Euro from unwarranted pressures in the foreign-exchange markets. In such cases, it may assist Member States outside the Euro area participating in it, when their currencies come under pressure, to combine appropriate policy responses, including interest-rate measures, with co-ordinated intervention.

1.4.   It will also help to ensure that Member States seeking to adopt the Euro after 1 January 1999 receive treatment equal to that of those initially adopting the Euro with respect to the fulfilment of the convergence criteria.

1.5.   The exchange-rate mechanism will function without prejudice to the primary objective of the European Central Bank and the national central banks to maintain price stability. It should be ensured that any adjustment of central rates is conducted in a timely fashion so as to avoid significant misalignments.

1.6.   Participation in the exchange-rate mechanism will be voluntary for the Member States outside the Euro area. Nevertheless, Member States with a derogation can be expected to join the mechanism. A Member State which does not participate from the outset in the exchange-rate mechanism may participate at a later date.

1.7.   The exchange-rate mechanism will be based on central rates against the Euro. The standard fluctuation band will be relatively wide. Through the implementation of stability-oriented economic and monetary policies, the central rates will remain the focus for the Member States outside the Euro area participating in the mechanism.

1.8.   Furthermore, sufficient flexibility is allowed, in particular to accommodate the varying degrees, paces and strategies of economic convergence of Member States outside the Euro area joining the mechanism. Exchange-rate policy co-operation may be further strengthened, for example by allowing closer exchange-rate links between the Euro and other currencies in the exchange-rate mechanism, where, and to the extent that, these are appropriate in the light of progress towards convergence. The existence of such closer links, particularly if it implied narrower fluctuation bands, would be without prejudice to the interpretation of the exchange-rate criterion of Article **121** of the Treaty establishing the European Community.

2.   MAIN FEATURES

2.1.   A central rate against the Euro will be defined for the currency of each Member State outside the Euro area participating in the exchange-rate mechanism. There will be one standard fluctuation band of plus or minus 15% around the central rates. Intervention at the margins will in principle be automatic and unlimited, with very short-term financing available. However, the ECB and the central banks of the other participants could suspend intervention if this were to conflict with their primary objective. In their decision they would take due account of all relevant factors and in particular of the need to maintain price stability and the credible functioning of the exchange-rate mechanism.

2.2.   As is made clear in the agreement laying down the operating procedures of the exchange-rate mechanism which is expected to be concluded between the European Central Bank and the national central banks, the flexible use of interest rates will be an important feature of the mechanism and there will be the possibility of co-ordinated intra-marginal intervention.

2.3.   Decisions on central rates and the standard fluctuation band shall be taken by mutual agreement of the ministers of the Euro-area Member States, the ECB and the ministers and central bank governors of the non-Euro area Member States participating in the new mechanism, following a common procedure involving the European Commission, and after consultation of the Economic and Financial Committee. The ministers and governors of the central banks of the Member States not participating in the exchange-rate mechanism will take part but will not have the right to vote in the procedure. All parties to the mutual agreement, including the ECB, will have the right to initiate a confidential procedure aimed at reconsidering central rates.

2.4.   On a case-by-case basis, formally agreed fluctuation bands narrower than the standard one and backed up in principle by automatic intervention and financing may be set at the request of the non-Euro area Member State concerned. Such a decision to narrow the band would be taken by the ministers of the Euro-area Member States, the ECB and the minister and governor of the central bank of the non-Euro area Member State concerned, following a common procedure involving the European Commission, and after consultation of the Economic and Financial Committee. The ministers and central bank governors of the other Member States will take part in the procedure, but will not have the right to vote.

2.5.   The standard and narrower bands shall not prejudice the interpretation of the third indent of Article **121**(1) of the Treaty establishing the European Community.

2.6.   The details of the very short-term financing mechanism will be determined in the agreement between the ECB and the national central banks, broadly on the basis of the present arrangements. The European Monetary Institute has drafted such an agreement incorporating the operating procedures required by this Resolution. The EMI will submit it to the ECB and to the central banks of the non-Euro area Member States on the date of the establishment of the ECB.

Agreed at Amsterdam,
16 June 1997.

* * * * * * *

RESOLUTION OF THE EUROPEAN PARLIAMENT ON THE AMSTERDAM TREATY

The European Parliament,

- HAVING REGARD to the Amsterdam Treaty signed on 2 October 1997 and the Protocol on the institutions with the prospect of enlargement of the European Union,

- HAVING REGARD to its resolutions of 17 May 1995, 13 March 1996, 16 January 1997, 13 March 1997 and 11 June 1997 on the Intergovernmental Conference and of 26 June 1997 on the Amsterdam European Council,

- HAVING REGARD to its resolutions of 14 February 1984 on the draft Treaty establishing the European Union and of 7 April 1992 on the results of the Intergovernmental Conferences,

- HAVING REGARD to the opinions of the non-governmental Organisations which responded to the invitation from the Committee on Institutional Affairs and took part in the joint session of 7 October 1997,

- HAVING REGARD to the report of the Committee on Institutional Affairs and the Opinions of The Committee on Foreign Affairs, Security and Defence Policy, Committee on Agriculture and Rural Development, Committee on Budgets, Committee on Economic and Monetary Affairs and Industrial Policy, Committee on Research, Technological Development and Energy Committee on External Economic Relations, Committee on Legal Affairs and Citizens' Rights, Committee on Employment and Social Affairs, Committee on Regional Policy, Committee on the Environment, Public Health and Consumer protection, Committee on Culture, Youth, Education ant the Media, Committee on Development and Co-operation, Committee on Civil Liberties and Internal Affairs, Committee on Budgetary Control, Committee on Fisheries, Committee on the Rules of Procedure, the Verification of Credentials and Immunities, Committee on Women's Rights and the Committee on Petitions,

A.   WHEREAS the peoples and the parliaments of the Member States and the bodies of the Union expect an opinion from the European Parliament on the Amsterdam Treaty,

B.   WHEREAS in view of the dual legitimation of the European Union as a union of the states and a union of the peoples of Europe, the task of the European Parliament must be to give voice, in complete independence, to the will of the peoples of the Union for integration,

C.   WHEREAS the recent inter-governmental Conference has shown the limits of the method of diplomatic negotiation; whereas Parliament must claim a much greater role in respect of future Treaty amendments, in view of the constructive role it played in the Revision of the treaties and because of its function as the legitimate representative of European citizens,

D.   WHEREAS the future will demand a clearer Union identity to pursue the international interests of the European Union,

E.   WHEREAS the additional political powers conferred on the Union by the Amsterdam Treaty are too limited to be a valid accompaniment to monetary union; whereas, consequently, there is a need to focus as quickly as possible on the institutional *modus operandi* of monetary union, in particular democratic accountability;

F.   WHEREAS the following six criteria in particular should be used to evaluate the new Treaty:

(a)   any new step towards integration most enhance the democratic quality of the Union and must itself enjoy democratic legitimation,

(b)   the dual nature of the Union as a union of the peoples and a union of states requires any step towards integration to strengthen the identity of the Union and to increase its ability to take action, while also respecting and protecting the identity of the Member States, the core features of the constitutional cultures of the individual states, and retaining the equal status of the Member States and the cultural diversity of their peoples,

(c)   the yardstick of any step towards integration is whether, and to what extent, it presents and develops the Union not only as a common market but also as a system of values, and what improvements it facilitates in the quality of life of its citizens, their job prospects and the quality of society, in particular the exercise in practice of European citizenship,

(d)   any new step towards integration must involve progress, a constructive move beyond the present *acquis*,

(e)   the present move towards integration will have to be measured against the requests and expectations expressed by the European Parliament before and during the intergovernmental Conference,

(f)   the new move towards integration must be measured against the yardstick of whether it creates the institutional basis for forthcoming enlargements,

G.   WHEREAS further improvements in the interest of Union citizens are possible only if the criticism arising from application of the above-mentioned criteria is translated, by all the political and social forces in the Union acting in a spirit of solidarity, into a constructive struggle with tangible pointers for the immediate future,

H.   CONSCIOUS THAT the values of peace, democracy, freedom, human rights, the rule of law, social justice, solidarity and cohesion underpinning the European Union can never be deemed to have been achieved but must always be fought for anew,

Overall Evaluation

1.   Recommends that the Member States ratify the Amsterdam Treaty;

2.   Considers that the Amsterdam Treaty marks a further step on the unfinished path towards the construction of a European political union; considers that it represents some not inconsiderable advances for certain institutions but leaves other issues unresolved;

3.   Regrets the absence from the Amsterdam Treaty of the institutional reforms needed for the effective and democratic functioning of an enlarged Union and affirms that these reforms should be completed before enlargement and as soon as possible so as not to delay the accessions;

4.   Calls on the European Council to affirm that no accession will enter into force before the completion of the institutional reforms necessary for the proper functioning of an enlarged Union, to begin its work in this connection on the basis of this resolution, and to engage, in this context, in a political dialogue with Parliament on this subject;

Principles

5.   Stresses that on the one hand the Amsterdam Treaty essentially gives precedence to the Community method, and on the other hand it reduces to an acceptable level the risks of differentiated integration (which is unavoidable in some areas) through precise criteria and its exceptional nature; emphasises, however, that more courageous ant more consistent steps in the transition to the Community method would have been appropriate;

6.   Regards the confirmation in the Amsterdam Treaty of the objectives of the Union and the principles of the Community as a sign of the requisite will for integration on the part of the people and the states; regrets, however, the absence of a preamble such as those used in previous treaties to express clearly a common political will amongst the contracting parties which should be directed towards belonging to a Community which is more than the sum of its parts and more than a mere interest group whose members have no other aim than striking a balance between what they put in and the advantages they derive from it;

7.   Stresses that the new opportunities afforded by the Amsterdam Treaty will only lead to tangible results if a sufficient political will, lacking at present, is generated for common action in all areas of the Treaties, and a new relationship of mutual trust develops between the Member States themselves and between them and the Community institutions;

Basis of Union policies

8.   Notes, with reference to the details set out in the session dock A4-0347/97, that the Amsterdam Treaty has, in Part, significantly improved the Union's instruments for shaping policy in the interests of its citizens, in the area of Community policies, such as employment and social Policy, environmental and heath policies and internal security; there is a need for farther improvements; calls in particular on:
-      the Council to take speedy decisions to ensure that the general rules of the Community method will be applied, as soon as possible, to the communitarised area of freedom, security and justice and to enable further development on Community lines of the Schengen *acquis*; calls on the governments of Denmark, Ireland and the United Kingdom to take part from the earliest stages in the Community measures in this field;
-      the Commission, the Council and the Member States to show the political will to use the new opportunities resolutely in the interests of all European citizens and, in particular, to use the new Community political instruments to achieve clear and lasting improvements in the employment situation throughout the Union;
-      its committees to examine, prior to entry into force of the Amsterdam Treaty, what initiatives can be used, in those areas for which they are responsible, to use the new opportunities as effectively as possible;

9.   Considers that although the Amsterdam Treaty contains a number of institutional, budgetary and practical improvements in the area of the Common Foreign and Security Policy, it clearly fails to satisfy expectations, and not merely in respect of the decision-making mechanisms; stresses, in particular, that:
-      the prospect of developing a common defence Policy, in particular solidarity between the Member States in the face of threats on and violations of, external frontiers must be strengthened; welcomes the inclusion of the so-called Petersberg Tasks into the Treaty as an important step in the direction of a common European security policy equipped with operational capabilities provided by the Western European Union (WEU);
-      all the members of the new troika, including the Commission, must co-operate closely, in a spirit of trust and as equal partners, in order to achieve the goals of greater visibility, efficiency and coherence;
-      the policy planning and early warning unit must adopt a common Union perspective in the course of its work;
-      in the area of external economic relations the Community must become competent for all questions considered in the context of the World Trade Organisation; until the Treaty is amended, the Commission should point out to the Member States, promptly and clearly, the risks for the Community stemming from the fragmentation of responsibilities in future negotiations, and should propose to the Council that it take a speedy decision on the requisite transfer of responsibilities; this transfer of responsibilities should not, however, weaken democratic control over the actions of the executive in external economic relations;

10.   Recognises that there has been some progress in those areas of justice ant home affairs remaining subject to intergovernmental co-operation, ant calls on the Council and/or the Member States:
-      to take decisions as soon as possible on more effective common approaches toward fighting organised and international crime;
-      to establish working relations with Parliament that will allow consultations to run smoothly in this field;
-      to improve the legal protection of Union citizens and, in particular, to deliver the requisite declarations so that appeals can be made to the European Court of Justice under the preliminary ruling procedure;
-      to prevent loopholes in legal protection arising in the national implementation of Council acts;

Institutional matters

11.   Acknowledges that the Amsterdam Treaty confirms, and in some areas further develops, the European Union as a system of values of a free, democratic, social Community based on the rule of law and solidarity and on shared fundamental freedoms and civil rights;

12.   Welcomes the extension of the co-decision procedure to numerous new areas and the right to approve the appointment of the Commission president; calls in addition, however, for:
-      any amendment of the constituent Treaties to be subject to parliament's assent, and a new method to be introduced for preparing and adopting Treaty amendments;

- the co-decision procedure to be extended to the remaining areas of legislation (in particular in the new Title IV (former IIIa) of the EC Treaty, in agricultural, fisheries, fiscal and competition policy, structural policies, tourism and water resources, the approximation of laws pursuant to Article 94 (former Article 100) EC Treaty and legislative acts under the third pillar); regrets the fact that, in four areas of particular importance for European citizenship (Article 18(2) (former 8a), Article 42 (former 57) and Article 151 (former 128) EC Treaty), the co-decision procedure exists alongside unanimous voting in the Council, which in practice constitutes a significant reduction in the democratic legitimacy of this procedure;
- the Commission, pursuant to the declaration on commitology, to submit in June 1998 a proposal to amend the Council decision of 13 July 1987 on the understanding that the European Parliament must be involved in drafting and finalising the definitive text, which must receive Parliament's agreement;
- the Union and the Communities to be merged into a single legal personality;
- significant international agreements to be subject to Parliament's assent;
- an equal, functional and democratic relationship to be established between the two arms of the budgetary authority in respect of budgetary matters, including the European Development Fund, and for the system of own resources to be reformed and made subject to Parliament's assent; calls further for substance to be given to be the principles of subsidiarity, proportionality and solidarity when operational policies or measures are financed at Community level;
- the democratic accountability of the future European Central Bank to be defined;
- a specific charter of fundamental rights of the Union to be drawn up;
- any "suspension of certain rights of a Member State" (Article 7 (former F.1) Treaty on European Union) on the grounds of a serious and persistent breach by a Member State of general principles mentioned in Article 6 (former F) to be subject to control by the Court of Justice and under no circumstances affect Union citizens' rights;
- in the area of social policy, Parliament to be kept informed of negotiations between management and labour, and where agreements between the latter are implemented by a Council decision they should also be subject to Parliament's assent;
- progress in the field of equality between men and women at all levels to be implemented resolutely, and evolved further, and active promotion of women's interests to be pursued until full equality of opportunities is achieved;
- in view of the Amsterdam Treaty's new emphasis on the role of culture, qualified majority voting to be extended to this sphere; recalls the need to respect and promote the diversity of the Union's cultures;
- the mechanisms for solidarity and economic, social and territorial cohesion to be perfected with a view to an enlarged Europe;
- the Treaty provisions for the further development of European political parties to be improved;
- the Euratom Treaty to be revised as a matter of urgency, in particular with a view to making up the democratic deficit in its functioning;
- regrets that the Amsterdam Treaty has determined the seat of the European Parliament without the latter's involvement;

13.   Recognises that there has been progress in the area of transparency and publicity as a result of a simplification, and reduction in the number, of decision-making procedures, through rules in the Treaty on access to documents and through a simplification of the text of the Treaty; stresses, however, that the principle of public access requires the completion of these efforts with:
- implementing measures to ensure that the public really have efficient access to information;
- documents which are comprehensible to Union citizens and which show who bears political responsibility;
- consolidation and simplification of the founding Treaties;

14.   Regrets that the Amsterdam Treaty has failed adequately to improve the efficiency of decision-making procedures by extending qualified majority voting;

15.   Stresses that in the Protocol on the institutions the Amsterdam Treaty recognises to need for further institutional reforms before enlargement of the Union to more than twenty members; in this context unreservedly approves of the joint declaration by Belgium, France and Italy advocating such reforms as the precondition for any enlargement;

16. Calls therefore for the following steps to be taken before any enlargement:
-    adjustments to be made to the weighing of votes in the Council and to the number of Commission members, with the Member States retaining equal status with each other,
-    qualified majority voting to become the general rule in the Council;
-    the requirement of unanimity to be restricted to decisions of a constitution nature (amendments to the Treaty, accessions, decisions on own resources, electoral procedure, application of Article 308 (former 235) of the Treaty establishing the European Community);
-    all other reforms required for enlargement to be adopted;

17. Calls on the Member States to ensure that the possibility provided for in the Amsterdam Treaty in the context of foreign policy and of 'closer co-operation' - of preventing a decision by a majority vote on the grounds of important national interests - be used as a brake only in dire emergencies;

Future strategy

18. Considers that the Amsterdam Treaty marks the end of an historical era when the work of European unification could be undertaken, stage by stage, using die methods of classic diplomacy;

19. Is convinced, instead, that politics should become the driving force behind shaping the new European Union and that the European Parliament and the parliaments of the Member States should play a full role in this respect;

20. Calls on the Commission to submit to Parliament, in good time before the European Council of December 1998, a report with proposals for a comprehensive reform of the Treaties, which is particularly needed in institutional terms and in connection with enlargement; requests that this report in accordance with the new protocol on the role of the national parliaments in the European Union be forwarded to the parliaments of the Member States; intends in due course as part of this process to define its own portion in the light of these proposals in order to launch a dialogue between the Commission and the European Parliament; requests that, even before Article 48 (former N) is amended, Parliament should be fully involved in the next Intergovernmental Conference and that a common binding arrangement (and modelled on inter-institutional agreements) will be achieved to the effect that the Treaty may cater into force only with Parliament's approval;

21. Awaits with interest the views of the parliaments of the Member States on this report; declares its intention to increase, on a systematic basis, its contacts with the parliaments of the Member States in order to conduct a political dialogue and to discuss jointly the future shape of the European Union;

22. Calls on the Commission to then take over the position of the European Parliament and to submit formal proposals for a revision of the treaties pursuant to Article 48 (former N) of the Treaty on European Union; calls for the European Parliament to be associated on an equal footing in the follow-up;

* * * * * *

23. Instructs its President to forward this resolution to the Commission, the Council and do parliaments and governments of the Member States and to ensure that, together with the session document on which it is based, it is made available to the public in Europe.

* * * * * * *

OTHER DOCUMENTS FROM THE TREATY OF AMSTERDAM

Minutes of the Signing

of the Treaty of Amsterdam amending the Treaty on European Union, the Treaties establishing the European Communities and certain related acts

(97/C 340/04)

On 2 October 1997 in Amsterdam the Plenipotentiaries of the Kingdom of Belgium, the Kingdom of Denmark, the Federal Republic of Germany, the Hellenic Republic, the Kingdom of Spain, the French Republic, Ireland, the Italian Republic, the Grand Duchy of Luxembourg, the Kingdom of the Netherlands, the Republic of Austria, the Portuguese Republic, the Republic of Finland, the Kingdom of Sweden and the United Kingdom of Great Britain and Northern Ireland signed the Treaty of Amsterdam amending the Treaty on European Union, the Treaties establishing the European Communities and certain related acts.

On that occasion the Plenipotentiary of the Kingdom of Belgium added the following statement to his signature:

'This signature also binds the French Community, the Flemish Community, the German-speaking Community, the Walloon Region. the Flemish Region and the Brussels Capital Region'

The Plenipotentiary of the Kingdom of Belgium stated that it was in all cases the Kingdom of Belgium as such that was bound in respect of its entire territory by the Treaty of Amsterdam and that the Kingdom alone, as such, would bear full responsibility for compliance with the obligations entered into in the Treaty.

The Plenipotentiaries of the other Signatory States took note thereof.

Done in Luxembourg, 22 October 1997

The President of the Intergovernmental Conference
Jacques POOS

The Secretary-General of the Council of the European Union,
Secretary to the Intergovernmental Conference
Jürgen TRUMPF

* * * * * *

Declarations
on Article 35 of the Treaty on European Union as amended by the Treaty of Amsterdam

(97/C 340/05)

On the occasion of the signing of the Treaty of Amsterdam on 2 October 1997 the Italian Republic, the depository of the Treaty, received, pursuant to Article **35** of the Treaty on European Union as amended by the Treaty of Amsterdam, the following declarations:

'On the signing of the Treaty of Amsterdam the following Member States stated that they accepted the jurisdiction of the Court of justice of the European Communities in accordance with the procedure laid down in Article **35**(2) and (3):

the Kingdom of Belgium, the Federal Republic of Germany, the Hellenic Republic, the Grand Duchy of Luxembourg and the Republic of Austria, in accordance with the procedure laid down in paragraph 3(b).

When making the above declaration, the Kingdom of Belgium, the Federal Republic of Germany, the Grand Duchy of Luxembourg and the Republic of Austria reserved the right to make provisions in their national law to the effect that, where a question relating to the validity or interpretation of an act referred to in Article **35**(1) is raised in a case pending before a national court or tribunal against whose decision there is no judicial remedy under national law, that court or tribunal will be required to refer the matter to the Court of Justice'.

In addition, the Kingdom of the Netherlands declared that the Netherlands would accept the jurisdiction of the Court of justice of the European Communities as laid down in the afore-mentioned Article **35**; its government was still considering whether, under Article **35**(3), the option of bringing a matter before the Court could be granted to courts or tribunals other than those against whose decisions there is no remedy.

* * * * * *

INDEX

INDEX

The Index covers **the Treaty on European Union**, consisting of Titles V, VI, VII and VIII, and **the Treaty establishing the European Community** (Title II) and is intended to be a guide to the more important areas.

Protocols and Declarations are referred to where relevant under the appropriate heading. A full listing of the Protocols is shown on pages 97 – 98, and a full listing of the Declarations is shown on pages 172 – 174.

The references refer to the Title number, Article number and page number. Protocols and Declarations have page references.

The **new numbering system** for the Articles, introduced by the Treaty of Amsterdam, has been used. The Table of Equivalencies, from the Treaty, is shown on pages 227-231.

	Title	Article	Page
Economic and Monetary Union:			
- Criteria for Third Stage	II	104	48
- Economic Policy	II	98	46
- Institutional Provisions	II	112	51
- Monetary Policy	II	105	49
- 'No Bail Out' Clause	II	103	47
- Selection of members for EMU	II	122	55
- Stability Pact			XXIV
- Transitional Provisions	II	116	52
- Protocol No 20 (Excessive Deficits Procedure)			146
- Protocol No 21 (Convergence Criteria)			146
- Protocols No 24 (Transition to 3rd Stage)			148
- Protocols No 25-26 (Re UK and Denmark)			150
- Resolutions by European Council			205
Economic and Social Committee:			
- Organisation and composition	II	257	84
Employment:			
- Employment Committee	II	130	58
- General	II	125	57
- Guidelines for policies	II	128	57
- Voting	II	129	57
Enlargement of the European Union:			
- General	VIII	49	23
- Protocol No 7			108
Environment:			
- General	II	2, 6	25, 27
- Harmonisation considerations	II	94	45
Equality of men and women	II	2, 141	25, 61
European Central Bank:			
- General	II	105	49
- Protocol No 18 (on ESCB and ECB)			128
European Council:			
- Breach of EU Principles	I	7	8
- Closer co-operation	II	11	27
- Economic Policy	II	99	46
- Economic & Monetary Union	II	121	54
- Employment	II	128	57
- Foreign and Security Policy	V	13	11
- General	I	4	7
- Member States' national security	V	23	14
- Police and Judicial Co-operation	VI	40	20
European Investment Bank:			
- General	II	266	85
- Protocol No 10			110
European Parliament:			
- Breach of EU principles	I	7	8
- Act on election of members			193
- Foreign Policy	V	21	14
- Legislative Procedures – summary			XIII
- Organisation and composition	II	189	71
- Police & Judicial co-operation	VI	39	19
- Resolution on Amsterdam			211
Europol – *see Police Co-operation*			
Exchange rate Mechanism			209
External Border Controls:			
- Protocol No 31 (External Relations)			155
External economic relations	II	133, 300	58, 92

* * * * * * *

TABLES OF EQUIVALENCIES
Referred to in Article 12 of the Treaty of Amsterdam

These Tables of Equivalencies are included to aid the reader in tracing particular Articles from previous Treaties to the newly numbered and consolidated Treaties shown in this book.

These Tables show the old and new numbers of the Articles of the Treaty, as adjusted by the Treaty of Amsterdam. The new numbering system has been used throughout this book for simplicity and consistency, although the new numbering only comes into effect once all the Member States have ratified Amsterdam.

(*)   Represents a new Article or Title introduced by the Treaty of Amsterdam

Old Number	New Number	Old Number	New Number
A: Treaty on European Union		Article K.11	Article 39
Title I	*Title I*	Article K.12	Article 40
Article A	Article 1	Article K.13	Article 41
Article B	Article 2	Article K.14	Article 42
Article C	Article 3	*Title VIa (*)*	*Title VII*
Article D	Article 4	Article K.15	Article 43
Article E	Article 5	Article K.16	Article 44
Article F	Article 6	Article K.17	Article 45
Article F.1 (*)	Article 7	*Title VII*	*Title VIII*
Title II	*Title II*	Article L	Article 46
Article G	Article 8	Article M	Article 47
Title III	*Title III*	Article N	Article 48
Article H	Article 9	Article O	Article 49
Title IV	*Title IV*	Article P	Article 50
Article I	Article 10	Article Q	Article 51
Title V	*Title V*	Article R	Article 52
Article J.1	Article 11	Article S	Article 53
Article J.2	Article 12		
Article J.3	Article 13		
Article J.4	Article 14	*B: Treaty establishing the European Community*	
Article J.5	Article 15	*Part One*	*Part One*
Article J.6	Article 16	Article 1	Article 1
Article J.7	Article 17	Article 2	Article 2
Article J.8	Article 18	Article 3	Article 3
Article J.9	Article 19	Article 3a	Article 4
Article J.10	Article 20	Article 3b	Article 5
Article J.11	Article 21	Article 3c (*)	Article 6
Article J.12	Article 22	Article 4	Article 7
Article J.13	Article 23	Article 4a	Article 8
Article J.14	Article 24	Article 4b	Article 9
Article J.15	Article 25	Article 5	Article 10
Article J.16	Article 26	Article 5a (*)	Article 11
Article J.17	Article 27	Article 6	Article 12
Article J.18	Article 28	Article 6a (*)	Article 13
Title VI	*Title VI*	Article 7 (repealed)	-
Article K.1	Article 29	Article 7a	Article 14
Article K.2	Article 30	Article 7b (repealed)	-
Article K.3	Article 31	Article 7c	Article 15
Article K.4	Article 32	Article 7d (*)	Article 16
Article K.5	Article 33	*Part Two*	*Part Two*
Article K.6	Article 34	Article 8	Article 17
Article K.7	Article 35	Article 8a	Article 18
Article K.8	Article 36	Article 8b	Article 19
Article K.9	Article 37	Article 8c	Article 20
Article K.10	Article 38	Article 8d	Article 21

Old Number	New Number	Old Number	New Number
Article 8e	Article 22	Article 73f	Article 59
Part Three	*Part Three*	Article 73g	Article 60
Title I	*Title I*	Article 73h (repealed)	-
Article 9	Article 23	*Title IIIa* (*)	*Title IV*
Article 10	Article 24	Article 73I (*)	Article 61
Article 11 (repealed)	-	Article 73j (*)	Article 62
Chapter 1	*Chapter 1*	Article 73k (*)	Article 63
Section 1 (deleted)	-	Article 73*l* (*)	Article 64
Article 12	Article 25	Article 73m (*)	Article 65
Articles 13 – 17 (repealed)	-	Article 73n (*)	Article 66
Section 2 (deleted)	-	Article 73o (*)	Article 67
Articles 18 – 27 (repealed)	-	Article 73p (*)	Article 68
Article 28	Article 26	Article 73q (*)	Article 69
Article 29	Article 27	*Title IV*	*Title V*
Chapter 2	*Chapter 2*	Article 74	Article 70
Article 30	Article 28	Article 75	Article 71
Articles 31 – 33 (repealed)	-	Article 76	Article 72
Article 34	Article 29	Article 77	Article 73
Article 35 (repealed)	-	Article 78	Article 74
Article 36	Article 30	Article 79	Article 75
Article 37	Article 31	Article 80	Article 76
Title II	*Title II*	Article 81	Article 77
Article 38	Article 32	Article 82	Article 78
Article 39	Article 33	Article 83	Article 79
Article 40	Article 34	Article 84	Article 80
Article 41	Article 35	*Title V*	*Title VI*
Article 42	Article 36	*Chapter 1*	*Chapter 1*
Article 43	Article 37	*Section 1*	*Section 1*
Articles 44 – 45 (repealed)	-	Article 85	Article 81
Article 46	Article 38	Article 86	Article 82
Article 47 (repealed)	-	Article 87	Article 83
Title III	*Title III*	Article 88	Article 84
Chapter 1	*Chapter 1*	Article 89	Article 85
Article 48	Article 39	Article 90	Article 86
Article 49	Article 40	*Section 2* (deleted)	-
Article 50	Article 41	Article 91 (repealed)	-
Article 51	Article 42	*Section 3*	*Section 2*
Chapter 2	*Chapter 2*	Article 92	Article 87
Article 52	Article 43	Article 93	Article 88
Article 53 (repealed)	-	Article 94	Article 89
Article 54	Article 44	*Chapter 2*	*Chapter 2*
Article 55	Article 45	Article 95	Article 90
Article 56	Article 46	Article 96	Article 91
Article 57	Article 47	Article 97 (repealed)	-
Article 58	Article 48	Article 98	Article 92
Chapter 3	*Chapter 3*	Article 99	Article 93
Article 59	Article 49	*Chapter 3*	*Chapter 3*
Article 60	Article 50	Article 100	Article 94
Article 61	Article 51	Article 100a	Article 95
Article 62 (repealed)	-	Articles 100b-100d (repealed)	-
Article 63	Article 52	Article 101	Article 96
Article 64	Article 53	Article 102	Article 97
Article 65	Article 54	*Title VI*	*Title VII*
Article 66	Article 55	*Chapter 1*	*Chapter 1*
Chapter 4	*Chapter 4*	Article 102a	Article 98
Articles 67 – 73a (repealed)	-	Article 103	Article 99
Article 73b	Article 56	Article 103a	Article 100
Article 73c	Article 57	Article 104	Article 101
Article 73d	Article 58	Article 104a	Article 102
Article 73e (repealed)	-	Article 104b	Article 103

Old Number	New Number	Old Number	New Number
Article 104c	Article 104	*Title IX*	*Title XII*
Chapter 2	*Chapter 2*	Article 128	Article 151
Article 105	Article 105	*Title X*	*Title XIII*
Article 105a	Article 106	Article 129	Article 152
Article 106	Article 107	*Title XI*	*Title XIV*
Article 107	Article 108	Article 129a	Article 153
Article 108	Article 109	*Title XII*	*Title XV*
Article 108a	Article 110	Article 129b	Article 154
Article 109	Article 111	Article 129c	Article 155
Chapter 3	*Chapter 3*	Article 129d	Article 156
Article 109a	Article 112	*Title XIII*	*Title XVI*
Article 109b	Article 113	Article 130	Article 157
Article 109c	Article 114	*Title XIV*	*Title XVII*
Article 109d	Article 115	Article 130a	Article 158
Chapter 4	*Chapter 4*	Article 130b	Article 159
Article 109e	Article 116	Article 130c	Article 160
Article 109f	Article 117	Article 130d	Article 161
Article 109g	Article 118	Article 130e	Article 162
Article 109h	Article 119	*Title XV*	*Title XVIII*
Article 109I	Article 120	Article 130f	Article 163
Article 109j	Article 121	Article 130g	Article 164
Article 109k	Article 122	Article 130h	Article 165
Article 109*l*	Article 123	Article 130i	Article 166
Article 109m	Article 124	Article 130j	Article 167
Title VIa (*)	*Title VIII*	Article 130k	Article 168
Article 109n (*)	Article 125	Article 130*l*	Article 169
Article 109o (*)	Article 126	Article 130m	Article 170
Article 109p (*)	Article 127	Article 130n	Article 171
Article 109q (*)	Article 128	Article 130o	Article 171
Article 109r (*)	Article 129	Article 130p	Article 173
Article 109s (*)	Article 130	Article 130q (repealed)	-
Title VII	*Title IX*	*Title XVI*	*Title XIX*
Article 110	Article 131	Article 130r	Article 174
Article 111 (repealed)	-	Article 130s	Article 175
Article 112	Article 132	Article 130t	Article 176
Article 113	Article 133	*Title XVII*	*Title XX*
Article 114 (repealed)	-	Article 130u	Article 177
Article 115	Article 134	Article 130v	Article 178
Article 116 (repealed)	-	Article 130w	Article 179
Title VIIa (*)	*Title X*	Article 130x	Article 180
Article 116 (*)	Article 135	Article 130y	Article 181
Title VIII	*Title XI*	*Part Four*	*Part Four*
Chapter 1	*Chapter 1*	Article 131	Article 182
Article 117	Article 136	Article 132	Article 183
Article 118	Article 137	Article 133	Article 184
Article 118a	Article 138	Article 134	Article 185
Article 118b	Article 139	Article 135	Article 186
Article 118c	Article 140	Article 136	Article 187
Article 119	Article 141	Article 136a	Article 188
Article 119a	Article 142	*Part Five*	*Part Five*
Article 120	Article 143	*Title I*	*Title I*
Article 121	Article 144	*Chapter 1*	*Chapter 1*
Article 122	Article 145	*Section 1*	*Section 1*
Chapter 2	*Chapter 2*	Article 137	Article 189
Article 123	Article 146	Article 138	Article 190
Article 124	Article 147	Article 138a	Article 191
Article 125	Article 148	Article 138b	Article 192
Chapter 3	*Chapter 3*	Article 138c	Article 193
Article 126	Article 149	Article 138d	Article 194
Article 127	Article 150	Article 138e	Article 195

230

Old Number	New Number	Old Number	New Number
Article 139	Article 196	Article 189a	Article 250
Article 140	Article 197	Article 189b	Article 251
Article 141	Article 198	Article 189c	Article 252
Article 142	Article 199	Article 190	Article 253
Article 143	Article 200	Article 191	Article 254
Article 144	Article 201	Article 191a (*)	Article 255
Section 2	*Section 2*	Article 192	Article 256
Article 145	Article 202	*Chapter 3*	*Chapter 3*
Article 146	Article 203	Article 193	Article 257
Article 147	Article 204	Article 194	Article 258
Article 148	Article 205	Article 195	Article 259
Article 149 (repealed)	-	Article 196	Article 260
Article 150	Article 206	Article 197	Article 261
Article 151	Article 207	Article 198	Article 262
Article 152	Article 208	*Chapter 4*	*Chapter 4*
Article 153	Article 209	Article 198a	Article 263
Article 154	Article 210	Article 198b	Article 264
Section 3	*Section 3*	Article 198c	Article 265
Article 155	Article 211	*Chapter 5*	*Chapter 5*
Article 156	Article 212	Article 198d	Article 266
Article 157	Article 213	Article 198e	Article 267
Article 158	Article 214	*Title II*	*Title II*
Article 159	Article 215	Article 199	Article 268
Article 160	Article 216	Article 200 (repealed)	-
Article 161	Article 217	Article 201	Article 269
Article 162	Article 218	Article 201a	Article 270
Article 163	Article 219	Article 202	Article 271
Section 4	*Section 4*	Article 203	Article 272
Article 164	Article 220	Article 204	Article 273
Article 165	Article 221	Article 205	Article 274
Article 166	Article 222	Article 205a	Article 275
Article 167	Article 223	Article 206	Article 276
Article 168	Article 224	Article 206a (repealed)	-
Article 168a	Article 225	Article 207	Article 277
Article 169	Article 226	Article 208	Article 278
Article 170	Article 227	Article 209	Article 279
Article 171	Article 228	Article 209a	Article 280
Article 172	Article 229	*Part Six*	*Part Six*
Article 173	Article 230	Article 210	Article 281
Article 174	Article 231	Article 211	Article 282
Article 175	Article 232	Article 212 (*)	Article 283
Article 176	Article 233	Article 213	Article 284
Article 177	Article 234	Article 213a (*)	Article 285
Article 178	Article 235	Article 213b	Article 286
Article 179	Article 236	Article 214	Article 287
Article 180	Article 237	Article 215	Article 288
Article 181	Article 238	Article 216	Article 289
Article 182	Article 239	Article 217	Article 290
Article 183	Article 240	Article 218 (*)	Article 291
Article 184	Article 241	Article 219	Article 292
Article 185	Article 242	Article 220	Article 293
Article 186	Article 243	Article 221	Article 294
Article 187	Article 244	Article 222	Article 295
Article 188	Article 245	Article 223	Article 296
Section 5	*Section 5*	Article 224	Article 297
Article 188a	Article 246	Article 225	Article 298
Article 188b	Article 247	Article 226 (repealed)	-
Article 188c	Article 248	Article 227	Article 299
Chapter 2	*Chapter 2*	Article 228	Article 300
Article 189	Article 249	Article 228a	Article 301

Old Number	New Number
Old Number	**New Number**
Article 229	Article 302
Article 230	Article 303
Article 231	Article 304
Article 232	Article 305
Article 233	Article 306
Article 234	Article 307
Article 235	Article 308
Article 236 (*)	Article 309
Article 237 (repealed)	-
Article 238	Article 310
Article 239	Article 311
Article 240	Article 312
Articles 241 - 246 (repealed)	-
Final Provisions	*Final Provisions*
Article 247	Article 313
Article 248	Article 314

* * * * * * *